Writing Windows™
Virtual Device Drivers

David Thielen and Bryan Woodruff

Addison-Wesley Publishing Company

Reading, Massachusetts Menlo Park, California New York

Don Mills, Ontario Wokingham, England Amsterdam Bonn

Sydney Singapore Tokyo Madrid San Juan

Paris Seoul Milan Mexico City Taipei

The Library of Congress has cataloged the first edition as follows:

Thielen, David.
    Writing Windows : virtual device drivers / by David Thielen and
Bryan Woodruff.
       p.   cm.
    Includes index.
    ISBN 0-201-62706-X
    1. Windows (Computer programs) 2. Virtual computer systems.
I. Woodruff, Bryan. II. Title.
QA76.76.W56T48 1993
005.4'3--dc20

ISBN 0-201-48921-X

Set in 10.5 point Times Roman by Benchmark Productions, Inc.

3 4 5 6 7 8 9 10–MA–9998979695
Third printing, October 1995

Addison-Wesley books are available for bulk purchases by corporations, institutions, and other organizations. For more information please contact the Corporate, Government and Special Sales Department at (617) 944-3700 x2915.

To my wife, Shirley Clawson Thielen

I never knew I could be so happy.

— Dave Thielen

For my wife, Lisa, who puts up with me through it all.

— Bryan A. Woodruff

Table of Contents

SECTION I
An Introduction to Virtual Device Drivers

SECTION II
Advanced Topics

SECTION III
Putting it All Together

SECTION IV
VMM and VxD Service Reference

Appendix A—API Reference 171

Acknowledgments

Several key people were helpful in making this book become a reality and must be acknowledged for their efforts — without them, this book would not exist. I would like to thank the publisher, Addison-Wesley and David Thielen, my co-author. Also a thank-you to Keith Jin, Brian Lieuellen, and Glen Slick at Microsoft Developer Support for their informative answers and technical accuracy. A special thank you to Neil Sandlin who provided assistance when I was first floundering around with VxDs.

Thank you to Thomas Pyzdek at Quality Publishing for encouraging me to put my knowledge down in words. Thanks also to my friends Charles E. Kindel Jr., Curtis Palmer, Kyle Sparks and Garrett McAuliffe for their suupport. I would like to thank my parents for nurturing my aspiration to be become a software design engineer. And to my wife, Lisa, who endured the late nights, clicking keyboard, and noisy printer, *"I Love You"* and thank you for putting up with yet another project.

Bryan A. Woodruff

This book came in to being for one simple reason: Bryan Woodruff. He was the one who pulled the pieces together. The parts he wrote are better than I could have done myself. Major thanks are also due to the people at Addison-Wesley who were farsighted enough to believe this was a subject worth writing about. Thanks to Amy Pedersen and Chris Williams at Benchmark Productions for their assistance.

I first learned about VxDs from the three developers who wrote WIN386 for Windows 3.1; Aaron Reynolds, Ralph Lipe, and Rich Pletcher — brilliant programmers all. I owe them all a debt of graditude for helping me as I first learned this challenging subject.

I also owe a debt of thanks to my co-workers in the Chicago group, especially Mike McLaughlin, as we all learned the ins and outs of VxD-land. It is a joy to work with people who are as brilliant and nice as that group was — even if they didn't always fully appreciate all of my humor.

In August of 92 I left Redmond to go work in the Far East for six months on Windows 3.1. I spent that time living in and working with the Microsoft developers in Tokyo,

Taipei, and Seoul. It was one of the most interesting and enjoyable periods of my life. The developers and management in Taiwan and Korea and the developers in Japan are as competent and talented as any I have seen anywhere in the world. And I owe a debt I can never repay to them for making me feel a part of their group. While too numerous to list here, I thank all of you who became good friends.

Finally, I would like to thank my daughters; Winter Maile, Tanya Nicole, and Brianna Leilani, who sometimes wonder if the keyboard is surgically attached to my fingers. I promise I'll come play with you as soon as I finish this one last compile...

David Thielen
Redmond, WA

Preface

David Thielen. . .

About a year ago, I was talking to J. D. Hidlebrand about a new magazine he was starting, *Windows Tech Journal*. I told him that he should include a column on VxDs (Virtual Device Drivers) in the magazine. His reply, typical of Windows developers at the time, was "what's a VxD?" Since then, articles have run in *Win Tech,* and VxDs have become an important part of Windows programming for a substantial number of Windows developers.

Unfortunately, to date noone has published a book devoted to explaining VxDs. On CompuServe I constantly found myself referring people to the articles I wrote in *Win Tech,* requiring them to go order the back issues. Equally important, there have been a lot of questions about subjects that my two articles did not cover. Most of these questions are answered in a combination VxD and Windows program I wrote to support InterProcess Communication between Windows and DOS applications.

This book does not attempt to answer every question you have about VxDs, but it should give you a good grounding in how to write a VxD. It also provides complete working source code to two very different VxDs. With this information, and with the Windows DDK (Device Development Kit), you should be able to write a VxD.

My main hope is that this book will give enough help so that developers will no longer be afraid to write VxDs. I have talked to too many developers who avoid VxDs because of the perceived difficulty. VxDs are not that hard to write — they're just something new.

More importantly, and this can't be stressed enough, *all* interaction with hardware should be done with a VxD. Yes, a DLL or a Windows application can handle IRQs, perform DMA, and talk to ports, but even if you handle everything perfectly, they will still be slow. VxDs were designed to give you a fast and safe method to communicate with your hardware. A system that uses VxDs exclusively to talk to hardware is not only more solid but is more responsive to the user. And once you learn how to write a VxD, you will find that using a VxD is a lot easier than the alternatives. VxDs are the way Windows works best with hardware.

VxDs also let you do the things Windows itself won't let you do. While Windows has a number of strict rules and enforces those rules pretty well, VxDs are not as rigid. With a VxD you can see all the memory in the entire system, intercept or create any interrupts you wish, make hardware disappear, or have hardware that doesn't exist on the system appear.

This book demonstrates how you can perform some of these tricks. It has a fully commented VCD that should provide a good example of how to talk to virtually any hardware device. It also has the source to Win-Link, which can show you a lot of tricks you can perform with VxDs.

There is no way to document all the things you can do with VxDs. Many of the uses VxDs will be put to next year probably haven't even been thought of yet. That's for you to do. Have fun.

Bryan Woodruff. . .

When Dave first approached me about completing this book, I thought about developing a method to help other software developers understand the complexities of the Microsoft Windows 386 Enhanced Mode operating system. I had also fielded questions on CompuServe regarding the interactions of VxDs with the Windows 386 system and felt that we could provide some of the knowledge we gained while working with VxDs.

There are so many areas of this complex system to cover that a single book cannot handle every aspect. Just the basics can give the developer enough weapons to bring the system down to its knees, intentionally or not. So the challenge was to provide the developer with enough fire power to take on any Windows programming problem while allowing them to operate this advanced weaponry without shooting off their own foot. Of course, this book isn't 42 (the answer to life, the universe, and everything), but I think it will help the novice as well as the advanced Windows 386 developer.

I hope that this book will assist you in your programming endeavors. Enjoy programming in 32-bit flat model — once you have you many never want to go back.

SECTION I

An Introduction to Virtual Device Drivers

Chapter 1

The Anatomy of a VxD

Virtual device drivers (VxDs) are not just for people writing drivers for hardware devices anymore than DOS device drivers are used for the same. A VxD is Windows' way of letting you do almost anything you want. If you miss the DOS world — where you have direct access to the hardware, can interface to vital CPU functions, or can take over parts of the operating system — then welcome to VxDs, where you can do the a lot of same under Windows.

A VxD is code and data that runs at ring 0 in 32-bit flat model as part of the Windows 386 virtual machine manager (VMM). In fact, the VMM (WIN386.EXE) is primarily a number of standard VxDs compounded in a single file. VxDs only operate when Windows runs in 386 Enhanced mode.

VMM is not really a part of Windows; instead, it is a preemptive, multitasking kernel that controls multiple virtual machines. Once VMM has initialized, the Windows Graphical User Interface composed of KRNL386.EXE, GDI.EXE, USER.EXE, and all of the supporting drivers are loaded into the System VM (the initial virtual machine created when VMM is started). However, VMM could easily load COMMAND.COM into the System VM and with the assistance of a VxD and some helper hot-keys, so that you have a multitasking DOS instead of the fancy Windows GUI.

Because VxDs operate at ring 0, the operating-system level of protection, the CPU allows the code to execute any 386 instruction. At higher ring levels, access to memory addresses or I/O ports can be restricted from the VM, allowing the VMM or a VxD to process the exception as it wishes. Of course, certain instructions executed by the VM always cause processor exceptions, but a VxD can simulate the functionality of that instruction for the VM, allowing it to operate as if it has sufficient privilege.

With this power comes responsibility. Although a VxD can play with the Interrupt Descriptor Table (IDT) entries directly, this is something that should probably be avoided.

Besides, the VMM provides enough functionality to get as close the IDT as needed, so why reinvent the wheel?

A VxD is always active, unlike any other part of Windows. When a DOS box is running exclusive mode, the primary code executing apart from the DOS box itself includes any VxDs responding to IRQs, code causing faulting instructions, and trapped I/O or page faults in the DOS box.

A VxD is the only program with unobstructed access to the hardware. If a VxD performs I/O to a port, it communicates directly to the physical port, without restrictions. If a VxD owns a hardware interrupt, the VxD receives the IRQ directly from the Virtual Programmable Interrupt Controller Driver (VPICD), without ring transitions. For example, an interrupt service routine for an non-owned interrupt in a VM sees a virtualized interrupt through events scheduled by the VPICD, whereas a VxD has a more direct path for interrupt servicing. Where code communicating to hardware in a VM may be restricted or slowed by ring transitions and access permission lookups, a VxD is unrestricted and extremely fast.

VxDs operate in 32-bit flat model, the 386 equivalent of small model. All of the segment registers are fixed to the same base address. The CS and DS selector values differ, due to access and execution restrictions (code versus data), but point to the same memory. Because a VxD is in 32-bit flat model, all offsets to code and data are 32-bit; therefore, you can access any part of the address space (4 gigabytes) with just an offset.

A VxD is also given priority on all actions in a VM. A VxD can intercept and/or generate interrupts (hardware or software), trap port I/O, and even restrict access to specific regions of memory. VxDs can determine whether to allow such access to occur, provide simulation, terminate (or nuke) the VM, or simply ignore the request.

Because VxDs utilize the base components of the 80386 chipset, it is important that you have a working knowledge of 386 architecture[1].

A misbehaving MS-DOS application will usually crash the DOS virtual machine. A misbehaving Windows application may affect the operation of other Windows applications. However, a misbehaving VxD will crash the entire Windows operating system. Because a VxD is part of the WIN386 kernel, the VxD is active during critical processing of the Windows operating system. The smallest, most subtle bug can have devastating effects on the operating system. Thorough testing of virtual device drivers is absolutely necessary. Do not simply test how the VxD operates under stringent

---

[1]   For a good description of 80386/80486 system architecture, see Hummel, Robert L. (1992), *PC Magazine Programmer's Technical Reference: The Processor and Coprocessor*, Emeryville, CA: Ziff-Davis Press.

configurations; instead, expand your testing to include all possible permutations of end-user system configurations you can design (limited only by a testing hardware budget of course!).

VxDs were originally designed to handle hardware device contention between multiple processes and to translate or buffer data transfers from a VM to hardware devices. When two or more programs attempt to access the same device, some method of contention management must be used. You can use a VxD to allow each process to act as though it has exclusive access to the device. For example, a Virtual Printer Device (VPD) would provide the process with a virtual printer port, and characters written to the port would be written to a print spooler. The VxD would then send the job to the printer when it becomes available. Windows 3.X does not operate in this fashion, but the Win-Link VxD provides this functionality (see Chapter 14 for more information). Another method would be to assign the physical device to only one process at a time, so that when a process attempts to access the device while it is in use, the VxD does not pass the request to the actual hardware, and the process operates as though the hardware did not exist. The Virtual COMM Device (VCD) uses this method.

Recently, the use of VxDs has been expanded to include interprocess communication (demonstrated in the Win-Link example). Some VxDs now also implement a truly virtual device, providing the necessary mechanisms to allow a virtual machine to see a device that may not actually exist in hardware. VxDs can also implement client-server hardware management, providing an interface to a VM that virtualizes I/O to the device and translates this information to commands to be sent across a network to a hardware server.

The VxD Structure

A VxD has a rather simple structure. It includes a 16-bit real-mode initialization code and data segment, 32-bit initialization code and data segments, 32-bit locked or "non-locked" code and data segments, and a virtual device driver declaration block (exported in the linear executable file as the VxD's DDB). Similar to the "suicide" fence of a DOS terminate-and-stay resident program, the initialization fragments of the VxD are discarded after initialization has been completed. Under Windows 3.x, all 32-bit code and data segments are locked, because the macros provided in the VMM.INC included with the Windows 3.X Device Driver Kit resolve to the same segment definition. However, you should not assume that non-locked segments are the same as locked segments, as these definitions most likely will change in the future. Note the distinction between the two now and save yourself the bug-tracking hassle later.

Real-Mode Initialization Segment

The real-mode initialization segment is a 16-bit code and data segment of the VxD defined by the `VxD_REAL_MODE_INIT_SEG` macro and is called during VMM's startup. This allows a VxD to communicate with TSRs or other real-mode procedures to gather and then pass vital information to the VxD's protected mode initialization routines or to fail the load of the VxD or VMM prior to entering protected mode. The term "real-mode initialization" is relative. If you have installed an EMM emulator (EMM386, 386Max, or QEMM), it is likely that the real-mode initialization procedures are invoked in V86 mode and are subject to trapped I/O or other virtualization occurring under these systems. In other words, during real-mode initialization, VMM does not switch the processor to real mode and then call these procedures. Instead, it executes the 16-bit code in the mode configured prior to the startup of VMM (such as invoking WIN.COM).

Note: Due to problems in Windows 3.x, you will need to make sure that your real-mode initialization segment is not exactly 4k, 8k, 12k, or 16k in size. Additionally, real-mode initialization segments greater than 8k (or 12k in Windows 3.1) must be a multiple of 4. Real-mode initialization segments cannot be greater than 12k under WIndows 3.0 or greater than 16k under Windows 3.1. Using code segments greater than these restrictions will cause problems and will eventually hang VMM. These problems were reported on the CompuServe WinSDK forum and confirmed by Developer Support Engineers. Avoid these problems with real-mode initialization by adding the necessary boundary checks in your code.

Protected-Mode Initialization Segment

The 32-bit initialization code and data segments defined by the `VxD_ICODE_SEG` and `VxD_IDATA_SEG` macros are present until VMM has completed initialization, at which time they are discarded, freeing the memory used by these sometimes cumbersome pieces of code. These initialization procedures can determine whether it is safe to load the VxD or to bail out prior to further initialization. Thus, the VxD load can fail, the user can be notified, and there will be no memory wasted for the VxD when the VMM completes initialization.

Pageable Data Segments

Because VxD segments are locked by default under Windows 3.x, using data segments to store large amounts of constant data can be a waste of physical memory. One method to resolve this issue is to store the data in the initialization data segment and allocate pageable memory using `_HeapAllocate` during the `Device_Init` call. You can copy the data from the initialization segment to this block, and when system initialization has completed, the original data will be discarded.

Device Declaration Block (DDB)

The device declaration block describes the virtual device to the VMM. It provides a VxD mnemonic, usually a somewhat descriptive title using V as the prefix and D as the suffix, such as VXFERD, suggesting a virtual transfer driver. It also provides a major and minor version, the main control procedure, the device ID number, the initialization order, and control procedures for the V86 or Protected-Mode (PM) API:

```
Declare_Virtual_Device     VSIMPLED, VSIMPLED_Major_Ver,\
                           VSIMPLED_Minor_Ver,\
                           VSIMPLED_Control_Proc,\
                           VSIMPLED_Device_ID,\
                           Undefined_Init_Order,\
                           VSIMPLED_V86_API_Proc,\
                           VSIMPLED_PM_API_Proc
```

This declaration dispatches the system control events to the `VSIMPLED_Control_Proc`. This procedure must be declared in a `VxD_LOCKED_CODE` segment, which handles system event control such as the initialization dispatch, VM control events (creation or suspension of VMs), device focus changes, and system shutdown notifications. Defining it in any other segment will cause problems.

VxD Control Procedure

The control procedure is the main dispatch entry point for the VxD. The initialization messages from VMM are sent to this procedure and then dispatched to the appropriate handlers:

```
VXD_LOCKED_CODE_SEG

;----------------------------------------------------------------
;
; VSIMPLED_Control_Proc
;
; Description:
;     This is the entry point for system control calls from VMM.
;     Control for system messages are dispatched through the
;     Control_Dispatch macro in VMM.INC.
;
;----------------------------------------------------------------
BeginProc VSIMPLED_Control_Proc

   Control_Dispatch Sys_Critical_Init, VSIMPLED_Sys_Critical_Init
   Control_Dispatch Device_Init, VSIMPLED_Device_Init

EndProc VSIMPLED_Control_Proc

VXD_LOCKED_CODE_ENDS
```

`VXD_LOCKED_CODE_SEG` and `VXD_LOCKED_CODE_ENDS` are macros that define a segment of 32-bit code in a page-locked segment. Defining this segment as "page-locked" is necessary because the calls are dispatched during critical processing of the VMM. This procedure cannot be included in the initialization code segments, because it would be discarded after VMM completed its startup procedures and system failure would occur when the VMM attempted to dispatch a control message to the VxD during later processing.

The `BeginProc` and `EndProc` macros define the beginning and end of a specific VxD entry point. These macros define the procedure name of a VxD, declare it callable by other VxD, align the procedure for "fast-calling", declare the procedure as public for access outside of this module, or additionally define the procedure as an asynchronous service callable from another VxD at interrupt time. The valid parameters to BeginProc macro are `PUBLIC`, `HIGH_FREQ`, `SERVICE`, and `ASYNC_SERVICE`, and their functionality corresponds to the following table:

```
PUBLIC
            Procedure is callable from an external module
HIGH_FREQ
            Aligns this procedure on a DWORD boundary. Useful
            for procedures called frequently such as hardware
            interrupt procedures or I/O trapping routines.
SERVICE
            Procedure can be called from another VxD.
            Requires an exported service table.
ASYNC_SERVICE
            Same as SERVICE, but the VxD routine can be called
            during interrupt procedures. VxD services that do
            not specify this option and are called at
            interrupt time will cause debug traces when using
            the debug version of VMM (WIN386.EXE). If you
            declare a service to be asychronous be sure that
            it is atomic or can be interrupted while
            processing the request.
```

Virtual Device ID

A specialized VxD ID may be required if your VxD provides an external V86 or PM API or if your VxD exports services callable by other VxDs. In these cases, you need to request a VxD ID from Microsoft (Internet address vxdid@microsoft.com; CompuServe email, >INTERNET:vxdid@microsoft.com). Microsoft will send you a registration form, which you will need to fill out and return for processing.

If you are replacing an existing VxD, such as the Virtual Comm Device (VCD), you should use the value specified in VMM.INC. The replacement VCD would then have a device ID of VCD_Device_ID. Otherwise, assuming that your VxD does not provide an external API or services, you can use the predefined value of Undefined_Device_ID.

Initialization Order

The initialization order of the DDB defines the load order of the virtual device drivers. VMM will load and initialize the VxDs in the order specified by the load-order values. For most secondary virtual device drivers, the Undefined_Init_Order equate is sufficient. If your VxD requires other VxDs to be present and initialized prior to calling your initialization procedures, you need to specify a load order constant here.

API Entry Procedures

API entry procedures are invoked when a VM running in either protected mode or V86 mode calls the VxD's entry point. A VxD entry point is available to VMs only when the VxD defines the necessary entry procedures in the DDB. These procedures are discussed in depth in Chapter 4.

Virtual Device Initialization

System Critical Initialization (Sys_Critical_Init)

VMM dispatches a Sys_Critical_Init message to all VxDs in the order defined by the Initialization Order values of the VxDs. During Sys_Critical_Init, interrupts are disabled, and VxDs perform system-critical initialization such as memory mapping and hooking V86 interrupts or faults. Because interrupts are disabled, you should keep the initialization during this message to a minimum.

Sys_Critical_Init may also be used to hook your VxD in front of certain handlers, such as GP fault or NMI processing. Sys_Critical_Init is an optional procedure, and you should only define this procedure if you have specific initialization to perform. Below is a sample Sys_Critical_Init handler as used in the VSIMPLED Sample:

```
;----------------------------------------------------------------
;
; VSIMPLED_Sys_Critical_Init
;
; Description:
;     On entry, interrupts are disabled. Critical initialization
;     for this VxD should occur here. For example, we can read
;     settings from VMM's cached copy of the SYSTEM.INI and set up
;     our VxD as appropriate.
;
;     This procedure is called when the VSIMPLED_Control_Proc
;     dispatches the Sys_Critical_Init notification from VMM.
;
```

```
;      We can notify VMM of failure by returning with carry set
;      or carry clear will suggest success.
;
;------------------------------------------------------------------
BeginProc VSIMPLED_Sys_Critical_Init

        clc
        ret

EndProc VSIMPLED_Sys_Critical_Init
```

Device Initialization (Device_Init)

Device initialization is where non-system critical initialization of your VxD is performed. For example, you may want to install I/O trap handlers, virtualize an interrupt using VPICD services, or allocate a VM control block. Returning from this procedure with carry set will fail the loading procedure of the VxD. If everything has passed initialzation, clear the carry flag and return.

The VSIMPLED Sources

Using the information provided in this chapter, we are ready to create our first VxD. This skeleton VxD declares a DDB, and defines a control procedure supporting the two system initialization messages (Sys_Critical_Init and Device_Init):

MAKEFILE

```
!IFDEF DEBUG
DEFS=-DDEBUG
!ENDIF

.asm.obj:
        masm5 -p -w2 -Mx $(DEFS) $*;

.asm.lst:
        masm5 -l -p -w2 -Mx $(DEFS) $*;

OBJS =          vsimpled.obj

all:            vsimpled.386

vsimpled.obj:   vsimpled.asm

vsimpled.386:   vsimpled.def $(OBJS)
                link386 /NOI /NOD /NOP /MAP @<<
$(OBJS)
vsimpled.386
vsimpled.map

vsimpled.def
```

```
<<
            addhdr vsimpled.386
            mapsym32 vsimpled

clean:
            del *.386
            del *.obj
            del *.map
            del *.sym
```

VSIMPLED.ASM

```
        page    60, 132

;******************************************************************
        title VSIMPLED - A simple virtual device driver example
;******************************************************************
;
;   (C) Copyright Woodruff Software Systems, 1993
;
;   Title:    VSIMPLED.386 - Sample virtual device driver
;
;   Module:   VSIMPLED.ASM - Core code
;
;   Version:  1.00
;
;   Date:     November 24, 1992
;
;   Author:   Bryan A. Woodruff
;
;******************************************************************
;
;   Change log:
;
;   DATE      REVISION  DESCRIPTION                    AUTHOR
;   --------  --------  ----------------------------   ----------
;   11/24/92  1.00      Wrote it.                      BryanW
;
;******************************************************************
;
;   Functional Description:
;
;     Provides a minimal virtual device driver interface.
;
;******************************************************************

        .386p


;==================================================================
;               I N C L U D E S   &   E Q U A T E S
;==================================================================

        .XLIST
        INCLUDE VMM.Inc
```

```
        INCLUDE Debug.Inc
        .LIST

VSIMPLED_Major_Ver        equ      01h
VSIMPLED_Minor_Ver        equ      00h
VSIMPLED_Device_ID        equ      Undefined_Device_ID

;==================================================================
;        V I R T U A L   D E V I C E   D E C L A R A T I O N
;==================================================================

Declare_Virtual_Device  VSIMPLED, VSIMPLED_Major_Ver,\
                        VSIMPLED_Minor_Ver, VSIMPLED_Control_Proc,\
                        VSIMPLED_Device_ID, Undefined_Init_Order,,,

;==================================================================
;                           I C O D E
;==================================================================

VxD_ICODE_SEG

;------------------------------------------------------------------
;
;    VSIMPLED_Sys_Critical_Init
;
;    Description:
;        On entry, interrupts are disabled. Critical initialization
;        for this VxD should occur here. For example, we can read
;        settings from VMM's cached copy of the SYSTEM.INI and act
;        set up our VxD as appropriate.
;
;        This procedure is called when the VSIMPLED_Control_Proc
;        dispatches the Sys_Critical_Init notification from VMM.
;
;        We can notify VMM of failure by returning with carry set
;        or carry clear will suggest success.
;
;------------------------------------------------------------------

BeginProc VSIMPLED_Sys_Critical_Init

        Trace_Out "VSIMPLED: Sys_Critical_Init"

        clc
        ret

EndProc VSIMPLED_Sys_Critical_Init

;------------------------------------------------------------------
;
;    VSIMPLED_Device_Init
;
;    Description:
;        This is a non-system critical initialization procedure.
;        IRQ virtualization, I/O port trapping and VM control
;        block allocation can occur here.
```

```
;
;       Again, the same return value applies...
;       CLC for success, STC for error notification.
;
;-----------------------------------------------------------------

BeginProc VSIMPLED_Device_Init

        Trace_Out "VSIMPLED: Device_Init"

        clc
        ret

EndProc VSIMPLED_Device_Init


VxD_ICODE_ENDS

VxD_LOCKED_CODE_SEG

;=================================================================
;                 N O N P A G E A B L E   C O D E
;=================================================================

;-----------------------------------------------------------------
;
;   VSIMPLED_Control_Proc
;
;   DESCRIPTION:
;       Dispatches VMM control messages to the appropriate handlers.
;
;   ENTRY:
;       EAX = Message
;       EBX = VM associated with message
;
;   EXIT:
;       Carry clear if no error (or if not handled by the VxD)
;       or set to indicate failure if the message can be failed.
;
;   USES:
;       All registers.
;
;-----------------------------------------------------------------

BeginProc VSIMPLED_Control_Proc

    Control_Dispatch Sys_Critical_Init, VSIMPLED_Sys_Critical_Init
    Control_Dispatch Device_Init, VSIMPLED_Device_Init

    clc
    ret

EndProc VSIMPLED_Control_Proc

VxD_LOCKED_CODE_ENDS
```

```
END

;----------------------------------------------------------------
;   End of File: vsimpled.asm
;----------------------------------------------------------------
```

VSIMPLED.DEF

```
LIBRARY   VSIMPLED

DESCRIPTION 'Win386 VSIMPLED Sample Device (Version 3.10)'

EXETYPE   DEV386

SEGMENTS
        _LTEXT PRELOAD NONDISCARDABLE
        _LDATA PRELOAD NONDISCARDABLE
        _ITEXT CLASS 'ICODE' DISCARDABLE
        _IDATA CLASS 'ICODE' DISCARDABLE
        _TEXT  CLASS 'PCODE' NONDISCARDABLE
        _DATA  CLASS 'PCODE' NONDISCARDABLE

EXPORTS
        VSIMPLED_DDB @1
```

Debugging the VSIMPLED VxD

Before entering the Windows environment, you need to copy the debug version of the VMM into your system directory. The Windows 3.1 Device Development Kit contains this special version. There are many reasons to use this version of the VMM when developing your VxDs:

- VMM displays debug traces when unexpected events occur. These messages help you track down problems with your VxD. You will know that you have a "clean" VxD, When the system does not display these messages while running with your VxD installed.

- VMM includes a special debugging trace log that logs faults, device calls, and interrupt counts. These logs help to pinpoint the exact cause of a failure in your VxD.

- Special services are enabled for debuggers to display VMM's execution state, VM information such as event lists, interrupt vector tables, the VM execution state, and other critical information not available in the retail release of VMM.

Using the debug version of WIN386.EXE requires either a serial terminal on COM1 or COM2 and WDEB386, the 386 debugger included with the Windows Software Development Kit and Device Driver Development Kit, or a Windows Enhanced Mode Debugger such as Soft-ICE/W™ available from NuMega.

The VSIMPLED device displays trace information at each initialization phase. Before the GUI starts, break into the debugger by using the appropriate hot-key (Control-D for Soft-ICE/W or a Control-C from the terminal keyboard for WDEB386) and unassemble the `VSIMPLED_Sys_Critical_Init` procedure:

```
Registration # SIW012345
:ALTSCR OFF
:LINES 50
:i1here on
:wc
:X
VSIMPLED: Sys_Critical_Init
Break Due to Hot Key
D800:00001A20    MOV     CX,0040
:u VSIMPLED_Sys_Critical_Init
VSIMPLED_Sys_Critical_Init
0028:8029478C    CALL    [Log_Proc_Call]
0028:80294792    PUSHFD
0028:80294793    PUSHAD
0028:80294794    MOV     ESI,VSIMPLED_DDB+38(800FEA2C)
0028:80294799    CALL    [Out_Debug_String]
0028:8029479F    POPAD
0028:802947A0    POPFD
:g
VSIMPLED: Device_Init
VMM Version 03.10 - Build Rev 00000103
Break Due to Hot Key
0028:800110A6    CMP     AX,0030
:u VSIMPLED_Sys_Critical_Init
VSIMPLED_Sys_Critical_Init
0028:8029478C    INVALID
0028:8029478E    INVALID
0028:80294790    INVALID
0028:80294796    INVALID
0028:80294798    INVALID
:g
```

Re-enter the debugger when the Windows GUI has completed initialization and unassemble the same procedure. You will find that the address is invalid because the initialization code and data segments were discarded after the device initialization was completed.

For more information on VMM's debugging services and debugging techniques, see Chapter 11, "Using the Debugging Services."

Chapter 2

The Virtual Machine Manager

The Virtual Machine Manager is a single-threaded, non-reentrant, preemptive multi-tasking, event-driven operating system. This operating system is often referred to as "WIN386" or "VMM." VMM provides an interface layer to VxDs for event scheduling, memory management, descriptor table management, and other vital system services.

The VMM creates, runs, and destroys virtual machines (VMs). On startup, the VMM creates the System VM for the Windows GUI. The System VM interfaces to the SHELL VxD in VMM to create new virtual machines or DOS boxes — each new VM starts operation in Virtual 8086 (V86) mode. Because a VxD is a part of the VMM, it runs within whatever VM is active when it is called. Consequently, when a DOS VM calls a VxD, the VxD runs in protected mode in the context of the calling VM.

To write a VxD, you must have a clear understanding of how the VMM works.

Event Processing

The execution path of VMM is driven by event lists. *Event lists* are linked lists of scheduled event procedure calls. These scheduled calls are created by the WIN386 system as the result of faults, interrupts, or specific VxD requests.

There are two types of event lists: the global event list and VM-specific event lists. The global event list is the event list for the VMM. As each VM is created, VMM creates an event list for specific events of that VM. Prior to returning control to a VM, VMM processes any events in the global event list, any pending NMI events (a special form of a global event), and then the VM event list as shown in Figure 2.1. Note that VM-specific events are only processed for the active VM.

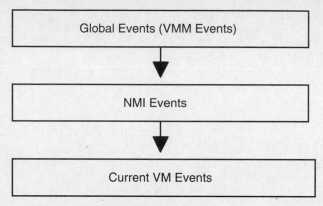

Figure 2.1
VMM Event Processing Order

When a VxD processes an event, it has complete control of the system. Because extended event processing reduces the system performance, the event procedure must be fast and avoid lengthy processing. Returning from the event allows VMM to continue the processing of the event list.

When VM events are created, the execution priority of the VM can be adjusted. This is also known as a "boost." The boost can be temporary (automatically removed by VMM) or can be specifically removed by the VxD when all of the necessary event processing for that VM is completed. The execution priority of a VM is used by the primary scheduler (execution priority scheduling) to determine the active VM. (See the section on *Scheduling* for more detail.)

When all events from the global event list and active VM event list have been processed, the primary scheduler walks the VM list searching for the VM with the highest execution priority. The VM with the highest execution priority becomes the active VM. VMM returns to the active VM until it is reactivated by interrupt or fault processing.

When a VxD is processing an event, asynchronous VMM services may be called and new events generated as the result of IRQ handling. When an IRQ is generated by the PIC, the handlers installed into the IDT by VPICD (Virtual PIC Device) call the Hw_Int_Proc for the IRQ. During non-virtualized IRQ processing, the default VPICD handlers then schedule VM events for interrupt simulation. VxDs must be aware that VPICD handles interrupts while events are processed, and disabling interrupts during event processing may be necessary for VxDs performing critical hardware processing. IRQ handling is detailed in Chapter 7.

Because a VM does not continue executing until all events in the global event list and VM event list have been dispatched, the results of event processing in a VxD can become stacked in the VM. For example, a VxD processing a global timeout event may schedule an asynchronous call to a procedure in a VM. During this processing, the VxD may request that the VM resume execution. Before resuming execution of the VM, VMM processes any remaining events on the event list. If this includes an interrupt event scheduled by VPICD, the VxD may request a simulated interrupt in the VM. Finally, when VMM returns to the VM, the actual results of the event processing are executed in reverse order as pushed onto the VM's stack: The interrupt service is be processed first, before the callback scheduled by the timeout event.

Scheduling

There are two schedulers used in the WIN386 system: the primary scheduler and the secondary, or time-slice scheduler. The *primary scheduler* (execution priority scheduler) selects the active VM based on highest execution priority of the non-suspended VMs. A VM will remain active until a higher priority VM is found in the queue.

When a VM is boosted, its order is changed in the queue. Normally, the active VM has a boost of Cur_Run_VM_Boost in as its execution priority. Devices that require a VM to become active as the result of I/O or interrupt processing may use a device boost of High_Pri_Device_Boost to force the VM to become active. This is typically implemented using the Call_Priority_VM_Event service. Using this service, VMM adjusts execution priority of the specified VM, and a callback is notified when the VM has activated. The VxD can then continue its processing for the VM. Figures 2.2 and 2.3 demonstrate the effect in the scheduling queue of changing the execution priority. The following code example demonstrates the technique of boosting a VM's execution priority:

```
// Example of calling priority VM event in 'C'

DWORD              dwEventHandle ;
static PEVENTPROC  pEventProc = NULL ;

if (!pEventProc)
   pEventProc =
      vmmwrapThunkEventProc( BoostEventProc ) ;
dwEventHandle =
   vmmCallPriorityVMEvent( hVM, High_Pri_Device_Boost,
                           PEF_Wait_Not_Crit, dwRefData,
                           pEventProc, 0 ) ;

// BoostEventProc - handler for VM event callback

VOID BoostEventProc( DWORD hVM, DWORD dwRefData, PCRS_32 pCRS )
{
   TRACEMSGPARAM( "VM #EAX is now active\r\n", hVM ) ;
} // end of BoostEventProc()
```

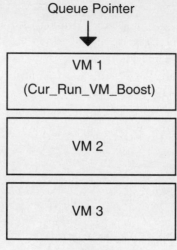

Figure 2.2
Scheduler queue prior to device boost

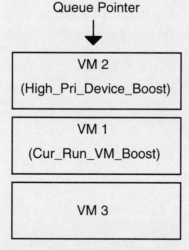

Figure 2.3
Scheduler queue after device boost.

The *secondary scheduler* (or time-slice scheduler) adjusts the execution priority for VMs for a period of time based on the background and foreground priorities set for each VM. The secondary scheduler determines which VM to boost based on the time-slice priorities specified in the .PIF file of a DOS application.

The time-slice priorities are also used to determine how long the execution priority of a VM will be boosted. The boost value is constant — that is, changing the time-slice priorities does not affect the amount of execution priority boost that a VM receives. When the next time-slice occurs and the VM's time-slice period has been exhausted, the VM is unboosted and the next VM in the time-slice scheduler's queue receives the execution priority boost.

The time-slice scheduler's execution priority boost for a VM is low compared to other high-priority event processing. Thus, the high-priority VM remains active until it is unboosted or until another VM of higher priority is found in the primary scheduler's queue.

Services and Dynalinking

VMM, its component VxDs, and third-party VxDs can provide services callable by other VxDs. The calls to these services are resolved at runtime by the dynalink mechanism. The **VxDCall** and **VMMCall** macros provided by VMM.INC are expanded in code as follows:

```
        <Push any C parameters>

        int     Dyna_Link_Int
        dd      VxD_ID SHL 16 + VxD_Service

        <Clean up C parameters>
```

When the IDT dispatches the software interrupt to VMM, the dynalink routine patches the int 20h and the following dword with a direct call to the VxD service handler. Stack parameters to the service are passed with the 'C' calling convention. **VxDJmp** is similar to **VxDCall**, with the exception that stack parameters cannot be used and the resulting code jumps to the VxD service handler, avoiding the extra cycles involved when the service call is followed by a return instruction.

Under some 386 'C' compilers, you cannot generate the appropriate in-line assembly instructions to duplicate this interface and/or load the registers required by the service. Consequently, you need to use .ASM thunks to provide a 'C' callable interface. Similarly, replacement VxDs (for example, a replacement VCD) may require register-parameter passing, and an assembly language front-end is necessary. The VDDVGA sample was written in 'C' and demonstrates the techniques required to interface to some of these services.

Critical Sections

The primary scheduler implements a single critical section using the `Begin_Critical_ Section` and `End_Critical_Section` services in VMM. The critical section can be claimed on behalf of a VM by a VxD. The critical section is most commonly used when calling MS-DOS or BIOS interrupt handlers because these real-mode code pieces are not reentrant. However, the critical section can also be used for other drivers or TSRs loaded prior to starting WIN386.

Note that the critical section does not halt scheduling of VMs; that is, other VMs may be scheduled while the critical section is claimed. If a second VM attempts to claim the critical section, the VM is suspended until the current critical section owner has released the critical claim. When a VM claims a critical section, the execution priority of the VM is adjusted by the predefined value of `Critical_Section_Boost`; the execution priority is restored when the critical section is released.

The critical section allows a VxD to prevent multiple VMs from entering the same piece of code. If two VMs are executing and interfacing to the same TSR and the TSR can not handle multiple VMs calling simultaneously because it maintains global non-instanced data for the specific procedure, a VxD may wrap the V86 interrupt chain and claim a critical section prior to reflecting the interrupt to the VM. It releases the critical section when the interrupt has returned. This prevents two VMs from simultaneously entering the same interrupt routine in the TSR. The following example demonstrates hooking the V86 interrupt, watching for a specific signature, and claiming a critical section around the API call:

```
;
;   Hook the V86 interrupt (Int 60h)
;

BeginProc VSIMPLED_Sys_Critical_Init

        pushad
        mov     eax, 60h
        mov     esi, OFFSET32 VSIMPLED_Int60_Hook
        VMMCall Hook_V86_Int_Chain
        popad
        clc

        ret

EndProc VSIMPLED_Sys_Critical_Init


;
;   Watches for the API signature. If found, claims
;   a critical section and hooks the "back-end".
;

BeginProc VSIMPLED_Int60_Hook, High_Freq
```

```
        cmp     [ebp.Client_AX], 4257h
        jne     SHORT VIH_Exit

        pushad


        ;
        ; Claim the critical section but allow interrupts
        ; to be serviced if we block.
        ;

        mov     ecx, Block_Svc_Ints or Block_Enable_Ints
        VMMCall Begin_Critical_Section


        ;
        ; Hook the back end of the Int60 call.
        ;

        xor     eax, eax
        xor     edx, edx
        mov     esi, OFFSET32 VSIMPLED_Int60_Complete
        VMMCall Call_When_VM_Returns

        popad

VIH_Exit:
        stc                                     ; always chain
        ret

EndProc VSIMPLED_Int60_Hook

;
;   Completes the Int 60h handling by releasing the
;   critical section and returning.
;

BeginProc VSIMPLED_Int60_Complete, High_Freq

        VMMCall End_Critical_Section
        ret

EndProc VSIMPLED_Int60_Complete
```

Suspending VMs, Resuming VMs, and Semaphores

VMM provides services to suspend and resume the execution of a VMs (Suspend_VM and Resume_VM). It is not possible for a VxD to suspend the execution of the System VM because VMM prevents this, but all other VMs can be suspended. Also, if a VM is the critical section owner, suspending the VM is not valid, and consequently the suspend call will fail.

When it suspends a VM, a VxD causes the VM to be removed from the active queue and added to the inactive queue. The primary scheduler does not activate this VM until it is resumed. If a VxD suspends a VM that is currently active, an immediate task switch occurs and the execution path in the VxD halts at the Suspend_VM call. To see this, try using debug traces to "wrap" the call to the `Suspend_VM` service. The debug trace in front of this call displays and a task switch occurs as when the active VM is placed in the inactive queue (the VM with the highest priority becomes the active VM), after which global events and VM events are processed. When the suspended VM has been resumed, the debug trace after the `Suspend_VM` call in the VxD is displayed, as the execution path of the VM continues.

VMM provides services (`Wait_Semaphore` and `Signal_Semaphore`) that allow VxDs to block and unblock VMs, based on events occurring in the VxD that decrement a token count by signaling the semaphore. A VM waiting on a semaphore resumes when the token count is less than or equal to zero. Additionally, it is possible to specify that certain events can be processed in a blocked VM. The following list describes the flags associated with the `Wait_Semaphore` service:

`Block_Enable_Ints`	Forces interrupts to be enabled and serviced even if interrupts are disabled in the blocked VM. (Only relevant if Block_Svc_Ints or Block_Svc_If_Int_Locked specified.)
`Block_Poll`	Causes the primary scheduler to not switch away from the blocked VM unless another VM has higher priority.
`Block_Svc_Ints`	Service interrupts in the VM even if the virtual machine is blocked.
`Block_Svc_If_Ints_Locked`	Same as Block_Svc_Ints with the additional requirement that the VMStat_V86IntsLocked flag is set.

Figure 2.4 shows the flow control possible using the semaphore services. For example, a VxD can signal or wait on semaphores in response to API calls from both the V86 VM (DOS application) and from the PM VM (Windows Application), allowing the VxD to control a data transfer channel through the VxD.

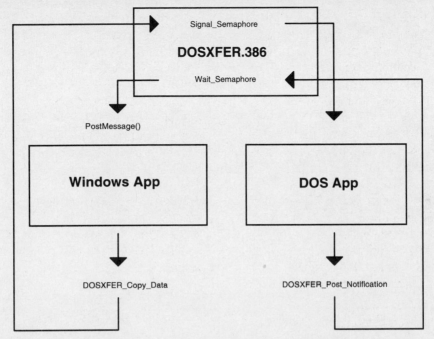

Figure 2.4
Possible design of semaphore implementation.

Asynchronous Services

Because VMM is non-reentrant, only a subset of VMM's API is available when a VxD is entered through an asynchronous interrupt. Services in a VxD can be declared **ASYNC** and are available at interrupt time. If your VxD declares such a service, it may call *only* asynchronous services. The following tables list all the asynchronous services that may be called in interrupt handlers:

Asynchronous VMM Services

Begin_Reentrant_Execution	Get_Time_Slice_Info
Call_Global_Event	Get_VM_Exec_Time
Call_Priority_VM_Event	Get_VMM_Reenter_Count
Call_VM_Event	Get_VMM_Version
Cancel_Global_Event	List_Allocate
Cancel_VM_Event	List_Attach
Close_VM	List_Attach_Tail

Crash_Cur_VM

End_Reentrant_Execution

Fatal_Error_Handler

Fatal_Memory_Error

Get_Crit_Section_Status

Get_Crit_Status_No_Block

Get_Cur_VM_Handle

Get_Execution_Focus

Get_Last_Updated_System_Time

Get_Last_Updated_VM_Exec_Time

Get_Next_VM_Handle

GetSetDetailedVMError

Get_System_Time

Get_Sys_VM_Handle

List_Deallocate

List_Get_First

List_Get_Next

List_Insert

List_Remove

List_Remove_First

Schedule_Global_Event

Schedule_VM_Event

Signal_Semaphore

Test_Cur_VM_Handle

Test_Debug_Installed

Test_Sys_VM_Handle

Update_System_Clock

Validate_VM_Handle

Asynchronous Debugging Services

Clear_Mono_Screen

Debug_Convert_Hex_Binary

Debug_Convert_Hex_Decimal

Debug_Test_Cur_VM

Debug_Test_Valid_Handle

Disable_Touch_1st_Meg

Enable_Touch_1st_Meg

Get_Mono_Chr

Get_Mono_Cur_Pos

In_Debug_Chr

Is_Debug_Chr

Log_Proc_Call

Out_Debug_Chr

Out_Debug_String

Out_Mono_Chr

Out_Mono_String

Queue_Debug_String

Set_Mono_Cur_Pos

Test_Reenter

Validate_Client_Ptr

Asychronous VxD Services

BlockDev_Command_Complete

BlockDev_Send_Command

DOSMGR_Get_DOS_Crit_Status

PageFile_Read_Or_Write

VPICD_Call_When_Hw_Int

VPICD_Get_Complete_Status

VPICD_Get_IRQ_Complete_Status

VPICD_Get_Status

VPICD_Phys_EOI

VPICD_Physically_Mask

VPICD_Clear_Int_Request

VPICD_Convert_Handle_To_IRQ

VPICD_Convert_Int_To_IRQ

VPICD_Convert_IRQ_To_Int

VPICD_Force_Default_Behavior

VPICD_Force_Default_Owner

VPICD_Physically_Unmask

VPICD_Set_Auto_Masking

VPICD_Set_Int_Request

VPICD_Test_Phys_Request

VTD_Update_System_Clock

Chapter 3

Memory Management

The VMM implements two memory managers. The V86MMGR VxD manages memory for V86-mode applications, including Expanded Memory Specification (EMS) and Extended Memory Specification (XMS), and the Memory Manager (MMGR) provides services such as GDT/LDT management, global heap management, physical memory management, protected mode address translation, and V86 page management, including V86 address mapping and allocation.

If you are writing a virtual display device or writing a VxD for a device requiring contiguous physical memory (such as devices using DMA transfers), you need to implement some form of memory management. Additionally, certain memory management implementations in your VxD such as memory mapped devices may require knowledge of the way the 80386 implements memory management using page tables.

VMM Memory Mangement Services

All memory in the system is allocated by the memory manager. This includes large allocations for VMs as well as a small heap available to VxDs requiring dynamic memory allocation.

While each VM has its own memory and linear address space, any VM that is presently executing is *also* mapped into the first megabyte of the linear address space. The MMGR performs this mapping on each task switch by updating the page tables to reflect the new mapping of the lower linear address space. Figure 3.1 shows a possible memory configuration with multiple VMs.

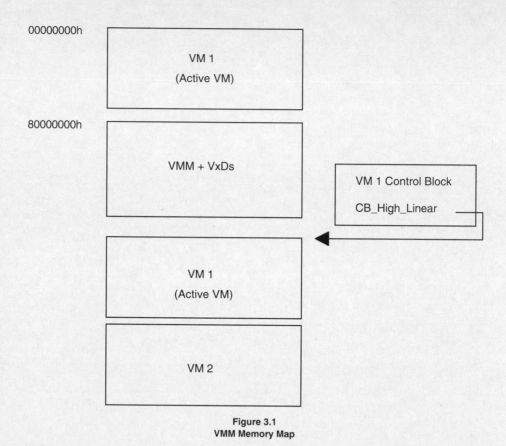

Figure 3.1
VMM Memory Map

The MMGR can provide per-VM data to a VxD. When a VxD initializes, it can request a number of bytes of control block data. The MMGR returns an offset from the VM handle, which is reserved for your VxD's control block area at the same offset in each VM control block. The following 'C' code sample shows how a VxD control block is allocated and assigned a pointer.

```
// Allocate part of VM control block for VDD usage

if (NULL == (dwVidCBOff =
                vmmAllocateDeviceCBArea( sizeof( VDDCB ), 0 )))
{
   vmmDebugOut( "VDD ERROR: Could not allocate control\
block area!\r\n" ) ;

   vddFatalMemoryError() ;
   return ( FALSE ) ;
}

pSysVMCB = (PVDDCB) (hVM + dwVidCBOff) ;
```

VMM allocates a control block containing vital information for each VM and is located at the zero offset from the VM handle. VMM's control block has the following structure:

```
//------------------------------------------------------------
//              VM control block structure (VMM)
//------------------------------------------------------------

typedef struct tagVMMCB
{
   DWORD   CB_VM_Status ;
   DWORD   CB_High_Linear ;
   DWORD   CB_Client_Pointer ;
   DWORD   CB_VMID ;

} VMMCB, *PVMMCB ;
```

Thus, given a VM handle, a VxD can obtain the VM's ID using the following method:

```
DWORD dwVMID ;

dwVMID = ((PVMMCB) hVM) -> CB_VMID ;
```

The low memory (interrupt vector table, BIOS & DOS data, and so forth) for each VM is located in high linear address space along with the rest of the memory for that VM. It is preferable to access VM memory using the high linear addresses, as these will not change. If a task switch occurs during memory reads or writes to a low linear address, your VxD may access an invalid address.

Translation Services

The MMGR provides an address translation API. While registers are preserved when making a ring transition between V86 mode and flat 32-bit mode, a pointer using a real-mode segment and offset is meaningless in protected mode. A number of macros in VMM.INC use MMGR services to convert the parameters in the client VM's registers automatically.

`Client_Ptr_Flat` is a macro that sets up a call to the `Map_Flat` service:

```
   Client_Ptr_Flat esi, DS, DX
```

which expands to:

```
   push     eax
   mov      ax, Client_DS * 100h + Client_DX
   VMMCall  Map_Flat
   mov      esi, eax
   pop      eax
```

The actual address mapping magic is performed in VMM's `Map_Flat` service. The following algorithm is used by `Map_Flat` to map the pointer to a 32-bit flat offset:

```
mov    esi, [ebp.Client_EDX]
mov    eax, [ebp.Client-DS]
if (VM is V86 mode)
   shl    eax, 4
   movzx esi, si               ; zero high order offset
   add    eax, esi
   add    eax, [ebx.CB_High_Linear]
else (VM is prot. mode)
   if (!32-bit)
      movzx  esi, si
   eax = _Selector_Map_Flat( hVM, [ebp.Client_DS], 0 )
   if (eax != -1)
      add   eax, esi
   if (eax < 1 MB + 64KB)
      add   eax, [ebx.CB_High_Linear]
endif
```

The translation APIs are often used when accessing memory specified through V86 or PM APIs. Dual-mode (combination V86 and PM) APIs accessing application-provided buffers can be easily implemented using the **Map_Flat** service as demonstrated here:

```
;-----------------------------------------------------------------
;
;    VSIMPLED_Get_Info, PMAPI, RMAPI
;
;    DESCRIPTION:
;        This function is used to get information about the
;        VSIMPLED configuration.
;    ENTRY:
;        Client_ES = selector/segment of VSIMPLEDINFO structure
;        Client_BX = offset of VSIMPLEDINFO structure
;
;    EXIT:
;        IF carry clear
;            success
;            Client_AX = non-zero
;            Client_ES:BX ->filled in VSIMPLEDINFO structure
;        ELSE carry set
;            Client_AX = 0
;
;    USES:
;        Flags, EAX, EBX, ECX, ESI, EDI
;
;-----------------------------------------------------------------
BeginProc VSIMPLED_API_Get_Info

        Assert_Client_Ptr ebp

        Trace_Out "VSIMPLED_API_Get_Info: called"

        Client_Ptr_Flat edi, ES, BX
        cmp     edi, -1
        je      SHORT GI_Fail

        lea     esi, [gVxDInfo]
```

```
        mov       ecx, size VSIMPLEDINFO
        cld
        shr       ecx, 1
        rep       movsw
        adc       cl, cl
        rep       movsb

        mov       [ebp.Client_AX], 1           ; success
        clc
        ret


GI_Fail:
        Debug_Out "VSIMPLED_API_Get_Info: FAILED!!"
        mov       [ebp.Client_AX], 0           ; failed
        stc
        ret

EndProc VSIMPLED_API_Get_Info
```

Page Allocation

Allocation of memory can be accomplished using either the `_HeapAllocate` or `_PageAllocate` VMM services. In most cases, using the heap allocation services is sufficient for your VxD and may make implementation easier than using the page allocation services. To allocate memory using the heap services use the following code:

```
    VMMCall    _HeapAllocate, <cbSize, dwFlags>
    or         eax, eax
    jz         SHORT Alloc_Failed
    mov        pDataBlock, eax
```

VMM allocates the memory on a doubleword boundary, but the cbSize parameter does not have to be dword aligned. The VxD is responsible for making sure that it stays within the bounds of the memory block, because VMM does not provide protection against accessing memory beyond the allocated range. The memory allocated by this service is fixed, and frequent allocating and freeing of memory may fragment the heap. Also, the memory block is not page-locked and may not be present when accessed. PageSwap VxD resolves the not-present fault so your VxD can continue with memory accesses.

If you require page-locked memory and are using the heap management services, the service `_LinPageLock` can be implemented. This avoids the possibility of VMM discarding the physical memory between accesses by a VxD. However, because physical memory is a limited resource, you should only use this service in cases where page-locked memory is vital to your implementation.

`_HeapGetSize`, `_HeapReAllocate`, and `_HeapFree` are used to determine the block size and to, reallocate and free the memory block, respectively. Using `_HeapReAllocate` may cause the address of the block to change, and VxDs must not rely on the possibility of the address remaining constant. _HeapReAllocate can preserve the contents of the old block by copying the contents to the new block. The following flags are defined for use with this service:

HeapNoCopy	Do not copy the contents of the existing block.
HeapZeroInit	Initialize the new bytes in the heap to zero.
HeapZeroReInit	Fill all bytes in the block with zero.

MMGR also provides low-level memory management services, allowing a VxD to allocate memory within a physical address range, to perform allocations within physical boundary constraints (not crossing 64k or 128k boundaries), and to allocate memory visible to all VMs or to only a single VM. Additionally, the page-fault handler for the allocated pages can be redirected to a specific handler in your VxD. (See the next section for more information on hooked pages.)

Allocation of pages with physical boundary restrictions and/or physical address limitations can only be performed during initialization. The following example demonstrates allocating a buffer for use with a DMA device:

```
;-----------------------------------------------------------------
;
;    VSIMPLED_Allocate_DMA_Buffer
;
;    DESCRIPTION:
;
;    This function allocates a buffer suitable for DMA transfers.
;    It attempts to allocate enough contiguous pages to hold the
;    requested size. If the request fails, the size is halved
;    until all allocation attempts have failed.
;
;    ENTRY:
;
;    EAX = Desired size (in KB) of the  DMA buffer to allocate.
;          This size cannot be exceed 64.
;
;    EXIT:
;
;    IF carry clear
;       EAX = memory handle of the memory block allocated
;       EBX = _physical address_ of memory block
;       ECX = actual size in _bytes_ of memory block allocated
;       EDX = _ring 0 linear address_ of memory block
;    ELSE carry set
;       EAX = EBX = ECX = EDX = 0
;
;    USES:
;
;    Flags, EAX, EBX, ECX, EDX
;
;-----------------------------------------------------------------;
```

```
BeginProc VSIMPLED_Allocate_DMA_Buffer

        cmp     eax, 64
        jle     SHORT ADB_Start

        Debug_Out "Requested size #EAX too big!"
        mov     eax, 64

ADB_Start:

        add     eax, 3          ; round up to get
        shr     eax, 2          ; # of pages

ADB_Allocate_DMA_Buffer_Loop:

        mov     ebx, eax        ; EBX = # of pages to allocate
                                ; (examples:        3       7      11
                                ;                  12K     28K     44K
        dec     eax             ; # pages - 1      10b    111b   1011b
        bsr     cx, ax          ; max power of 2    1       2       3
        inc     cl              ; shift cnt         2       3       4
        mov     eax, 1
        shl     eax, cl         ; mask + 1        100b   1000b  10000b
        dec     eax             ; mask             11b    111b   1111b
                                ; alignment        16K     32K     64K


        mov     ecx, ebx

        Trace_Out "pages=#ECX alignment=#EAX"


        ;
        ; EAX = alignment mask for allocation
        ; ECX = number of pages to allocate
        ;

        push    ecx
        VMMcall _PageAllocate <ecx, PG_SYS, 0, eax,\
                              0, 0FFFh, ebx,\
                              <PageUseAlign + PageContig +\
                              PageFixed>>
        pop     ecx
        or      eax, eax
        jnz     short ADB_Success

        Trace_Out "Allocation failed! pages=#ECX"

        mov     eax, ecx
        shr     eax, 1
        jnz     short  ADB_Loop

        xor     ebx, ebx
        xor     ecx, ecx
        stc
        ret

ADB_Success:
```

```
        shl     ecx, 12                      ; pages-->bytes

        ;
        ; Returns:
        ;
        ; EAX = memory handle of the memory block allocated
        ; EBX = _physical address_ of memory block
        ; ECX = size in _bytes_ of memory block allocated
        ; EDX = _ring 0 linear address_ of memory block
        ;

        clc                                  ; success
        ret

EndProc VSIMPLED_Allocate_DMA_Buffer
```

Hooked Pages and Page Faults

Hooked pages are allocated with _PageAllocate, using the PG_HOOKED attribute. This form of memory management is most commonly used in virtual display drivers to manage multiple VMs that access video display memory. A range of V86 pages is assigned to the VxD and then hooked using the _Assign_Device_V86_Pages and Hook_V86_Page services, respectively. V86 pages can be assigned globally (global to all VMs) to a device at any time, provided that the page is not already assigned. V86 page assignment to a specific VM can only be performed after device initialization, again with the restriction that the page is not already assigned to a device.

To hook V86 pages, a range of pages is first assigned to the VxD:

```
// Buffer used for reserving pages
DWORD aVMPagesBuf[ 9 ] ;

vmmGetDeviceV86PagesArray( NULL, &aVMPagesBuf, NULL ) ;
if (aVMPagesBuf[ 0xA0/32 ] & 0xFF00FFFF)
{
   vmmDebugOut( "VDD ERROR: Pages already allocated\r\n" ) ;
   vmmFatalError( szVDD_Str_CheckVidPgs ) ;
   return ( FALSE ) ;
}
if (!vmmAssignDeviceV86Pages( 0xA0, 16, NULL, NULL ))
{
   vmmDebugOut( "VDD ERROR: Could not allocate pages\r\n" ) ;
   vmmFatalError( szVDD_Str_CheckVidPgs ) ;
   return ( FALSE ) ;
}
if (!vmmAssignDeviceV86Pages( 0xB8, 8, NULL, NULL ))
{
   vmmDebugOut( "VDD ERROR: Could not allocate pages\r\n" ) ;
   vmmFatalError( szVDD_Str_CheckVidPgs ) ;
```

```
        return ( FALSE ) ;
}
```

The V86 pages are then directed to a page fault handler:

```
// Put an .ASM front end on the page-fault procedure.

if (NULL == (pVDD_PFault = VMMWRAP_ThunkV86PHProc( VDD_PFault )))
{
    vmmDebugOut( "VDD ERROR: Could not thunk VDD_PFault!\r\n" ) ;
    vmmFatalError( ) ;
    return ( FALSE ) ;
}

// Hook graphics pages

for (i = 0; i < 16; i++)
    vmmHookV86Page( 0xA0 + i, pVDD_PFault ) ;

// Hook text pages

for (i = 0; i < 8; i++)
    vmmHookV86Page( 0xB8 + i, pVDD_PFault ) ;
```

During the `Create_VM` message processing, the V86 pages are marked as not available
(not present and not writeable), using the `_ModifyPageBits` service:

```
vmmModifyPageBits( hVM, 0xA0, 16, ~P_AVAIL, NULL,
                        PG_HOOKED, NULL ) ;
vmmModifyPageBits( hVM, 0xB8, 8, ~P_AVAIL, NULL,
                        PG_HOOKED, NULL ) ;
```

Note that it is necessary to specify the `PG_HOOKED` in the type parameter of the
`_ModifyPageBits` service when clearing any of the `PG_PRES`, `PG_USER`, or `PG_WRITE`
bits.

After the initialization is complete, any read or write access of the hooked pages causes a
page fault. The page fault handler is called with the faulting page number and the handle
of the VM, causing the fault. It is the responsibility of the page fault handler to map
memory into the page to resolve the fault or terminate the virtual machine. To map
physical memory into the faulting page, use the following code:

```
// dwPhysPage is the physical page allocated using
// _PageAllocate with PG_HOOKED

vmmPhysIntoV86( dwPhysPage, hVM, uFaultPage, nPages, 0 ) ;
```

Under some circumstances (such as low memory or other memory mapping error), it may
be more desirable to allow the VM to continue without crashing the VM. In these cases,
the system null page is assigned to this linear page:

```
vmmMapIntoV86( VMM_GetNulPageHandle(),
                hVM, uFaultPage, 1, 0, 0 ) ;
```

The system null page is guaranteed to contain invalid information for any given VM. Do not rely on its contents for further processing in your VxD.

The VDD uses these techniques to allow multiple VMs to access the video display hardware and maintain separate virtual displays for virtual machines. It is also possible to simulate ROM in a virtual machine using hooked pages. When the page fault occurs, map the pages using `_PhysIntoV86` and clear the `P_WRITE` bit using `_ModifyPageBits`. Note, however, that when the VM restarts, the instruction causing the fault also restarts. If the VM was performing a write operation, a page fault would occur immediately. To resolve this loop, you would need to modify the VM client registers to point the IP to the instruction following the faulting instruction.

Examining Page Table Entries

A VM can determine whether pages in the linear address space have been accessed and whether data has been written on these pages by examining the page table entries (PTEs) using VMM's `_CopyPageTable` service. The VDD uses this technique to determine which pages have been accessed and need to be updated in the virtual display of a windowed MS-DOS box.

A linear address in a paging operating system such as VMM is decoded shown in Figure 3.2. Each PTE is 4 bytes in length and contains the access bits and physical address of the page. To examine the PTEs of the first megabyte of the active virtual machine, use page numbers in the range 0 to 10Fh. Page numbers of other virtual machines are computed using the CB_High_Linear field in the control block of the respective VM.

Given a pointer to a memory block in a VM, a VxD can use the Map_Flat service to translate this address to a flat offset. Shifting this address right by 12 gives you the page number. To determine if pages in a hooked V86 range have been accessed or if data has been written to these pages use the following code:

```
        VMMCall      _CopyPageTable, <guHookedPagesStart,\
                             guNumHookedPages,\
                             <OFFSET32 aPageBuf>, 0>
        mov    ecx, guNumHookedPages

Check_Accessed_Or_Dirty:
      test   dword ptr aPageBuf[ ecx ], P_ACC or P_DIRTY
      jz     SHORT Next_Page
      Trace_Out "Page #ECX of hooked range is dirty or has been\
accessed"
```

```
Next_Page:
        loop   Check_Accessed_Or_Dirty
```

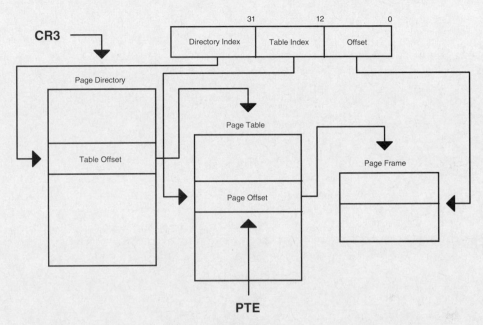

Figure 3.2
Decoding a linear address to a physical address

Allocating Selectors

A VxD can allocate selectors in the GDT or in a VM's LDT using the `_Allocate_GDT_Selector` and `_Allocate_LDT_Selector` services. Two descriptor double-words are required when allocating selectors. VMM provides the `_BuildDescriptorDWORDs` service to generate these double-words:

```
        VMMCall _BuildDescriptorDWORDs, < dwLinAddr, cbSize,\
                                          RW_Data_Type, 0, 0>
        VMMCall Allocate_GDT_Selector, <edx, eax, 0>
```

The following equates are useful when building descriptor double-words:

```
; Common definitions for segment and control descriptors

D_PRES                  segment is present in memory

D_NOTPRES               segment not present

D_DPL0                  descriptor privilege level definitions
D_DPL1
```

```
D_DPL2
D_DPL3

D_SEG                segment descriptor (application type)

D_CTRL               control descriptor (system type)

D_GRAN_BYTE          limit in byte granularity

D_GRAN_PAGE          limit in page granularity

D_DEF16                    default operation size is 16 bits (code)

D_DEF32                    default operation size is 32 bits (code)


; Definitions specific to segment descriptors

D_CODE               code segment

D_DATA               data segment

D_RX                 if code, readable

D_X                  if code, executable only

D_W                  if data, writeable

D_R                  if data, read only

D_ACCESSED           segment accessed bit


; Useful segment definitions

RW_Data_Type         present R/W data segment

R_Data_Type          read-only data segment

Code_Type            code segment
```

Instance Pages

The MMGR manages instance data for VMs. *Instance data* is a range in V86 address space that VMM maintains separately for each VM. It is used frequently for MS-DOS and some TSRs.

For example, if an MS-DOS device driver maintains an input buffer, it may be useful to have the buffered input directed to the VM that was active when the buffer was filled. In this case, the VxD would query the device driver for the buffer address and maximum size and add an instance data area as shown here:

```
// Define instance data for instance data manager

INSTDATASTRUC  Instance_Area = { NULL, NULL,
                                 NULL, NULL,
                                 ALWAYS_Field } ;
```

```
// Specify instanced area as provided by DOS driver.

Instance_Area.dwInstLinAddr = pInputBuffer ;
Instance_Area.dwInstSize = dwBufferSize ;
if (!VMM_AddInstanceItem( &Instance_Area, 0 ))
    goto DI_FatalError ;
```

Mapping Memory into Multiple VMs

When writing VxDs for use with "Windows-aware" TSRs, it may be necessary to allocate a block of memory that is global to all VMs, that is, a memory block with a V86 address mapped to the same physical memory in all VMs. The `_Allocate_Global_V86_Data_Area` service performs this type of allocation as shown here:

```
// Allocate a global V86 data area of 512 bytes

if (NULL ==
      (gdwGlobalArea =
          vmmAllocateGlobalV86DataArea( 512,
                                         GVDADWordAlign )))
{
   vmmDebugOut( "Failed to allocate global V86 data area!\r\n" ) ;
   return ( FALSE ) ;
}

vmmTraceOutParam( "Allocated global area at #EAX\r\n",
                gdwGlobalArea ) ;
```

The `_Allocate_Global_V86_Data_Area` service accepts the following flags:

GVDADWordAlign	Aligns the block on a doubleword boundary.
GVDAHighSysCritOK	Informs the services that the VxD can handle a block that is allocated from high MS-DOS memory, such as UMBs or XMS. (Win 3.1 only)
GVDAInquire	Returns the size in bytes of the largest block that can be allocated, given the requested alignment restrictions. (Win 3.1 only)
GVDAInstance	Creates an instance data block, allowing the VxD to maintain separate blocks for each VM.
GVDAPageAlign	Aligns the block on a page boundary.
GVDAParaAlign	Aligns the block on a paragraph boundary.
GVDAReclaim	Unmaps the physical pages in the block when mapping the system null page into the block. The physical pages are added to the free list when this value is specified. Only applies to blocks allocated on a page boundary.

	If this flag is not specified, it is up to the virtual device to reclaim these pages.
GVDAWordAlign	Aligns the block on a word boundary.
GVDAZeroInit	Fills the allocated block with zeros.

In the VMEMTRAP sample, an unassigned V86 area is located and assigned to the virtual device. Pages are allocated for each new VM and "instanced" pages are simulated, using hooked V86 pages and a page-fault handler. Using the **_AllocateGlobalV86-DataArea** service specifying the **GDVAInst** accomplishes the same thing in a single service call, with the exception that a specific V86 range cannot be specified. The VMEMTRAP sample on the enclosed diskette is designed to demonstrate the techniques necessary to manage contention of memory mapped devices.

_AllocateGlobalV86DataArea has limitations. For example, you cannot hook the page fault handler or modify the page bits of the V86 linear range returned by this service. Windows 3.x does not provide an interface to allow VxDs to monitor access of these pages other than viewing the page table entry access bits. A virtual device must provide an additional interface to manage VM contention of these pages using software interrupts or the VxD's API.

Page Protection

As stated in the preceding section, VMM's support for monitoring access to a given V86 address space is limited. Page protection can be implemented with pages assigned to a device using the **_Assign_Device_V86_Pages** service, but these pages are usually only available when memory is not already mapped into the reserved ROM addresses. Because of upper memory blocks (UMBs) implemented by most 386 memory managers, this region is usually already claimed by VMM. Also, the normal accessible regions of V86 memory (between **_GetFirstV86Page** and **_GetLastV86Page**) are off limits to a VxD using the API provided by VMM.

An unsupported method of providing page protection is to modify the page table entries (PTEs) directly and hook the **Invalid_Page_Fault** handler. The PTE contains the page frame address in the upper 20 bits (4k page aligned), and the lower 12 bits provide access restriction and accessed and/or dirty information.

Entry 0 in the page directory contains the physical address of the page table for the V86 address space of the active VM. By modifying these page table entries, you can modify the access rights to a given page in V86 address space.

You must use caution when accessing the page tables directly. Modifying not-present page tables or incorrectly modifying page access bits will cause the system to crash. In other words, "Ok, here's your weapon, first point it at your foot before pulling the trigger!"

Page protection is risky business when it is not directly supported by the host operating system, but some implementations require such information about how a VM is behaving. Take note!! You can guarantee that anything that you do now to provide this mechanism may not be supported in future releases of Windows. Use this information at your own risk and version bind your code to the Microsoft Windows 3.1 VMM.

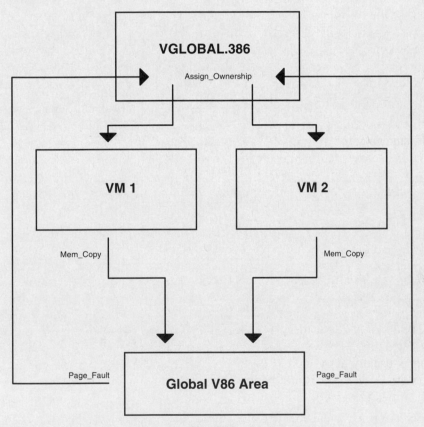

Figure 3.3
Possible design of TSR to VxD communication

The VGLOBALD sample on the enclosed diskette demonstrates the allocation of a global V86 data area that would be suitable for a TSR and VxD to use for communication in multiple VMs. If you run this sample under the debugging version of WIN386.EXE you should notice that, when new VMs are created and the System VM does not have access to the pages that are hooked using this page protection scheme, VMM will "gripe" about the not-present page within the V86 page range. You may decide to modify the page table entries to match WIN386 expectations before creating a new VM.

V86MMGR

V86MMGR provides an interface for VxDs to map protected-mode data buffers to V86-interfaces. When a virtual device translates an API which transfers data using pointers to data blocks from protected mode applications to DOS-mode device drivers, it needs to implement services provided by V86MMGR to translate these buffers to a V86 addressable memory. Also, DOS device drivers that update buffers asynchronously require memory to be mapped into global V86 address space.

For example, Int 21h commonly uses buffers referenced by DS:DX. The DOSMGR virtual device provides automatic buffer translation for most of these APIs by hooking Int 21h and translating the protected mode addresses so that DOS can understand the request without additional work required by the protected-mode application. Additionally, VNETBIOS provides buffer mapping for NetBIOS data packets using V86MMGR services. These buffers are updated as the result of interrupt processing.

V86MMGR provides two types of services: buffer mapping and buffer translation. The mapping services update the page tables in all VMs so that the buffer is in global V86 space. The translation services copy a buffer to a V86 copy buffer and use the copy buffers address to communicate with the DOS device driver code. The mapping services should be used only when the buffers will be updated asynchronously. Do not use the mapping services in place of the translation services to avoid copying the buffer's data — it is faster to copy data to and from a translation buffer than to map a buffer into multiple virtual machines.

V86MMGR does not directly support the mapping or translation of buffers referenced by pointers within a structure. The VxD is responsible for translating or mapping the buffer using V86MMGR services; it updates the structure to contain a valid V86 pointer and then passes the call to the DOS device driver.

When a VxD requires V86MMGR services, it must inform V86MMGR how many pages are required by using the `V86MMGR_Set_Mapping_Info` service. This service call must be made during initialization, preferably during `Sys_Critical_Init` processing. Alternatively, the VxD can call this service during `Device_Init`, if the VxD has an `Init_Order` less than `V86MMGR_Init_Order`.

When a call to the DOS device has been intercepted by the VxD, the VxD should determine whether the call is from V86 mode or protected mode. When a V86 call is trapped, buffer translation is not necessary, but mapping for asynchronously updated buffers may be necessary if the buffer is not located in global V86 address space determined by using the `_TestGlobalV86Mem` service.

To map pages to DOS addressable memory, a VxD calls **V86MMGR_Map_Pages** with the linear address and number of bytes to map. The returned linear address is guaranteed to be in the first megabyte and in global V86 address space. A map handle is also returned by this service. When the mapping region is no longer required, it is freed using the **V86MMGR_Free_Page_Map_Region** service with the map handle that was returned by **V86MMGR_Map_Pages**.

To translate a protected-mode buffer to V86 addressable memory, a VxD calls **V86MMGR_Allocate_Buffer** with the linear address of the buffer to translate and the number of bytes to allocate. If specified, this service copies data to the new buffer. Translation buffers are allocated in a "stack" fashion. In other words, the last buffer allocated must be the first buffer freed. When the translation buffer is no longer required, the **V86_Free_Buffer** service is used.

The following code fragment demonstrates how a software interrupt buffer is translated from a protected-mode to a real-mode driver:

```
;
; On entry Client_DS:Client_DX points to a buffer that is
; filled asynchronously and needs to be napped globally.
; Eat the PM interrupt and reflect it to V86 mode.
;
; When the DOS device driver has completed the data
; transfer, the pages must be unmapped using the
; V86MMGR_Free_Page_Map_Region service.
;

BeginProc PM_Translate

        pushad
        test    [ebx.CB_VM_Status], VMStat_PM_Exec
        jz      SHORT PT_Bail
        VMMCall Simulate_Iret
        Map_Flat esi, DS, DX
        movzx   ecx, [ebp.Client-CX]
        VxDCall V86MMGR_Map_Pages
        mov     hPageMap, esi
        shl     edi, 12
        shr     di, 12


        ;
        ; Simulate the interrupt to V86
        ;

        Push_Client_State
        Begin_Nest_V86_Exec
        mov     [ebp.Client_DX], di
        shr     edi, 16
        mov     [ebp.Client_DS], di
        mov     eax, Trapped_INT
        VMMCall Exec_Int
        VNNCakk End_Nest_Exec
```

```
        Pop_Client_State
        clc


PT_Bail:
        Debug_Out "Failure: Call not from protected mode!"
        stc

PT_Exit:
        popad
        ret

EndProc PM_Translate
```

V86MMGR provides a number of macros to define a script for use with the
V86MMGR_Xlat_API service. A VxD defines a translation script in its data segment using
these translation macros and calls the V86MMGR service to execute the script. This
provides the VxD with a way to reduce the code size of V86 translation services and to use
the optimized routines in V86MMGR.

The translation scripts are terminated by **Xlat_API_Exec_Int** or **Xlat_API_Jmp_To_**
Proc. When the **V86MMGR_Xlat_API** service executes one of these commands, control
returns to the VxD after the command has been executed. The following sample code
demonstrates the use of these macros to translate a null-terminated string for a call to a
DOS device driver:

```
;
; This code demonstrates a simple translation of a NULL
; terminated string in DS:SI to a local V86 buffer.
;

VxD_DATA_SEG
Xlat_ASCIIZ_Script:
        Xlat_API_ASCIIZ        ds, si
        Xlat_API_Exec_Int      60h
VxD_DATA_ENDS

VxD_CODE_SEG
BeginProc Translate_Int60h_Buffer

        mov    edx, OFFSET32 Xlat_ASCIIZ_Script
        VxDJmp V86MMGR_Xlat_API

EndProc Translate_Int60h_Buffer
VxD_CODE_ENDS
```

Chapter 4

V86/PM VxD API

A VxD can export an API to protected-mode and V86 mode applications, extending the capabilities of a Windows or MS-DOS driver using supervisor code. For example, the VCD provides an interface to the Windows communications driver (COMM.DRV) to acquire a COM port. The COMM driver queries the VCD for the availability of a given port. If the port is in use by an MS-DOS application, the VCD returns failure. This API allows the COMM.DRV to provide intelligent information regarding the availability of COM ports to the calling application and provides a mechanism to manage device contention.

A VxD declares the API support by defining API procedure entry points in the DDB (see Chapter 1). In the following example, **VSIMPLED_V86_API_Proc** and **VSIMPLED_PM_ API_Proc** procedures are the entry points for the API from V86 mode and protected mode, respectively. Additionally, the VxD must declare the device ID, as supplied by Microsoft.

```
Declare_Virtual_Device        VSIMPLED, VSIMPLED_MAJOR_VER,\
                              VSIMPLED,_MINOR_VER,\
                              VSIMPLED_Control_Proc,\
                              VSIMPLED_Device_ID,\
                              Undefined_Init_Order,\
                              VSIMPLED_V86_API_Proc,\
                              VSIMPLED_PM_API_Proc
```

An application acquires the entry point of the VxD by using Int 2Fh with AX=1684h and BX=VxD Device ID:

```
;
; Obtain the VxD entry point, if NULL, VxD is not present.
;

     mov    ax, 1684h             ; get VxD API entry point
     mov    bx, VSIMPLED_Device_ID
     int    2fh
     mov    word ptr dwVxDEntry, di
     mov    word ptr dwVxDEntry + 2, es
```

When this entry point is called by the application, the call is dispatched to the VxD, where it processes the request and returns control to the calling application.

Prior to requesting the VxD entry point from VMM, the application should first determine whether Windows/386 (VMM) is present. A Windows application can use the GetWinFlags() API. A DOS application needs to use Int 2Fh, AX=1600h interface to determine whether VMM is present:

```
mov    ax, 1600h                 ; Enhanced Windows Check
int    2fh
test   al, 7fh                   ; VMM (Win386) present?
jz     Not_Win386
```

The Faulting Mechanism and API Dispatch

If calling ring-0 VxD code directly from ring 3 seems too good to be true, you should be interested in how this call is dispatched to the VxD. When the Int 2Fh request is processed, the VMM allocates a callback address in the VM's address space. When the VM calls this address, the code generates a fault, a ring transition results, and the fault is dispatched to VMM's fault handler.

VMM determines the operation mode of the VM by testing the status flags in the VM control block. It determines whether the call was made from V86 or protected mode and then dispatches the call at ring 0 to the appropriate handler, as declared in the DDB.

The Client Register Structure

When the API entry points are called, the EBP register points to the Client_Register_ Structure (CRS):

```
typedef struct tagCRS_32
{
   DWORD  Client_EDI ;
   DWORD  Client_ESI ;
   DWORD  Client_EBP ;
   DWORD  dwReserved_1 ;              // ESP at pushall
   DWORD  Client_EBX ;
   DWORD  Client_EDX ;
```

```
    DWORD   Client_ECX ;
    DWORD   Client_EAX ;
    DWORD   Client_Error ;          // DWORD error code
    DWORD   Client_EIP ;
    WORD    Client_CS ;
    WORD    wReserved_2 ;           // (padding)
    DWORD   Client_EFlags ;
    DWORD   Client_ESP ;
    WORD    Client_SS ;
    WORD    wReserved_3 ;           // (padding)
    WORD    Client_ES ;
    WORD    WReserved_4 ;           // (padding)
    WORD    Client_DS ;
    WORD    wReserved_5 ;           // (padding)
    WORD    Client_FS ;
    WORD    wReserved_6 ;           // (padding)
    WORD    Client_GS ;
    WORD    wReserved_7 ;           // (padding)

    DWORD   Client_Alt_EIP ;
    WORD    Client_Alt_CS ;
    WORD    wReserved_8 ;           // (padding)
    DWORD   Client_Alt_EFlags ;
    DWORD   Client_Alt_ESP ;
    WORD    Client_Alt_SS ;
    WORD    wReserved_9 ;           // (padding)
    WORD    Client_Alt_ES ;
    WORD    WReserved_10 ;          // (padding)
    WORD    Client_Alt_DS ;
    WORD    wReserved_11 ;          // (padding)
    WORD    Client_Alt_FS ;
    WORD    wReserved_12 ;          // (padding)
    WORD    Client_Alt_GS ;
    WORD    wReserved_13 ;          // (padding)

} CRS_32, *PCRS_32 ;
```

The parameters to the API call, as set by the calling application, are contained in the CRS, and the current VM handle is in EBX.

A VxD usually defines a jump table to the specific API functions that perform the requested action and return the results to the API handler that reflects the results in the CRS. The following example code demonstrates how functions are dispatched from a VxD API procedure entry point:

```
;**************************************************************
;                  D E V I C E   D A T A
;**************************************************************

VxD_DATA_SEG

DOSXFER_PM_Call_Table LABEL DWORD
        dd      OFFSET32        DOSXFER_Get_Version
        dd      OFFSET32        DOSXFER_PM_Enable_CallBacks
        dd      OFFSET32        DOSXFER_PM_Copy_Data
```

```
Max_DOSXFER_PM_Service    equ     ($ - DOSXFER_PM_Call_Table) / 4

VxD_DATA_ENDS

;*****************************************************************
;                   E X P O R T E D   A P I
;*****************************************************************

BeginProc DOSXFER_PM_API_Proc, PUBLIC

        Trace_Out "In DOSXFER_PM_API_Proc"

        VMMCall Test_Sys_VM_Handle
IFDEF DEBUG
        jz      SHORT @f
        Debug_Out "DOSXFER_PM_API_Proc not from SYS VM"
@@:
ENDIF
        jnz     SHORT DOSXFER_PM_Call_Bad
        movzx   eax, [ebp.Client_DX]              ; function in DX
        cmp     eax, Max_DOSXFER_PM_Service
        jae     SHORT DOSXFER_PM_Call_Bad
        and     [ebp.Client_EFLAGS], NOT CF_Mask ; clear carry
        call    DOSXFER_PM_Call_Table[ eax * 4 ] ; call service
        jc      SHORT DOSXFER_PM_API_Failed
        ret

DOSXFER_PM_Call_Bad:
IFDEF DEBUG
        Debug_Out "Invalid function #EAX on DOSXFER_PM_API_Proc"
ENDIF

DOSXFER_PM_API_Failed:
        or      [ebp.Client_EFLAGS], CF_Mask     ; set carry
        ret

EndProc DOSXFER_PM_API_Proc
```

Examining and Modifying Information of the Active VM

Changes made in the CRS by the API handler are reflected to the VM when VMM returns control. This is the primary communication channel between code executing in the VM and the API handlers. VMM defines three structures for the CRS: One references the registers with 32-bit definitions (EAX), another for 16-bit registers (AX), and the last for 8-bit register access (AH and AL).

Modification of the client registers is made easy using these structure definitions:

```
;
; Copy the data structure to the VM and return the results
; of the function.
; EBX = VM handle, EBP = -> CRS
```

```
;
        Map_Flat edi, ES, DI
        lea     esi, gDataStruc
        mov     ecx, size DATASTRUCT
        shr     ecx, 1
        rep     movsw
        adc     cl, cl
        rep     movsb
        mov     [ebp.Client_CX], size DATASTRUCT
        mov     [ebp.Client_AX], 1                ; SUCCESS!
        and     [ebp.Client_EFlags], NOT( CF_Mask )   ; clc
```

A VxD may also update a buffer referenced in the CRS by obtaining a flat address using the mapping services discussed in Chapter 3.

Creating a Dual-Mode API

By setting both the V86 and PM API entry points in the DDB to the same handler, a VxD can provide the same services to all VMs and reduce the amount of code of duplicate dispatch functions. To determine the operating mode of the calling VM, the VxD queries the execution status of the VM using the status flags of the VM control block. By testing **CB_VM_Status** for **VMStat_PM_Exec**, a VxD can determine whether a VM is calling from V86 or protected mode:

```
;
; Determine the execution mode of the VM.
;
        test    [ebx.CB_VM_Status], VMStat_PM_Exec
        jz      SHORT API_VM_In_V86
        test    [ebx.CB_VM_Status], VMStat_PM_Use32
        jz      SHORT API_VM_In_PM16

API_VM_InPM32:
        Debug_Out "VM calling from 32-bit protect mode."
        ret

API_VM_In_V86:
        Debug_Out "VM calling from V86 mode."
        ret

API_VM_In_PM16:
        Debug_Out "VM calling frm 16-bit protected mode."
        ret
```

Note: In Windows 3.x, calling VxD procedures through VxD API calls from 32-bit code segments in the System VM can cause unexpected results when the offset of the return address of the calling routine is greater than 0xFFFF. This is a problem with the way that VMM determines the "32-bitness" of the calling application. The System VM is flagged for 16-bit protected mode operation, because Krnl386.EXE is responsible for the switch to protected mode when the Windows GUI is started. Whether 32-bit segments are allocated within the System VM and code within these segments calls VxD APIs, VMM determines that the calling application is 16-bit because of the VM flags. The return address is assumed to be 16 bits and is truncated. This is also a problem for protected-mode software interrupts hooked by a VxD. The only current work-around is to guarantee that the code calling the VxD has a return address with an offset less than 0xFFFF.

Callbacks and Hooking Existing DOS Devices

Callbacks are used indirectly when defining a VxD API. However, a VxD can also allocate a callback entry point that, when called by a VM, switches control to the associated callback procedure in the VxD.

Callbacks can be used to simulate DOS devices that return a pointer to a jump table by allocating a global V86 table and stuffing the address of the callback allocated using `Allocate_V86_Call_Back` service into this table. A segment and offset are returned that directs any calls to this routine to the VxDs callback procedure. The CRS reflects the current state of the VM when the callback entry point was called by the VM. A VxD can also provide a "chaining" interface to hooked software interrupts by using these services.

A VxD with "carnal" knowledge of a DOS device driver can intercept calls to this device by using the `Install_V86_Break_Point` service. This service patches the memory at the requested address with a call to the break point. When the break point is executed, the VxD can process the VM request as necessary and then return control by "bumping" the IP to the next instruction or by using `Simulate_Far_Jmp` to move the `Client_CS: Client_IP` to the correct address.

SECTION II

Advanced Topics

Chapter 5

Nested Execution

The *nested execution* services of VMM provide a controlled environment in which a VxD can cause a redirection of the execution path in a VM. A VxD saves the client registers, begins a nested execution block forcing a VM into V86 or protected mode, calls the necessary services to set up stack frames, and then resumes the VM execution. When the VM returns, the nested execution block is ended and the client registers are restored. Using this technique, a VxD can force the execution of code in TSRs, DOS applications, and even Windows procedures.

When calling routines in a VM other than the current VM, you may need to schedule a VM event to force a specific VM to become active. You may also need to determine the execution status of the VM and wait for critical sections to be completed, interrupts to be enabled, and so on. In these cases, you can use the `Call_Priority_VM_Event` service and begin the nested execution when the event is processed.

Simulating Software Interrupts

As demonstrated in Chapter 3, a VxD can simulate software interrupts to a VM using the `Simulate_Int` or `Exec_Int` services. Simulated interrupts are subject to being trapped by other VxDs and will respond exactly as if a VM executed the software interrupt in application code. Additionally, a VxD that has hooked a protected-mode interrupt can affect the caller's stack to "eat the interrupt" in protected mode by using a non-nested `Simulate_Far_Iret` and then reflect it to V86 mode by using nested execution services.

Note that when a VxD simulates calls to a VM and the execution has returned to the VxD, the VxD must copy the results from the CRS before restoring the client's state:

```
;
; Simulate a software interrupt to the current VM
;

        Push_Client_State
        VMMCall Begin_Nest_V86_Exec
        mov     [ebp.Client_AX], 4257h   ; specific function
        mov     [ebp.Client_BX], 4C57h   ; subfunction
        mov     eax, 60h
        VMMCall Simulate_Int
        VMMCall Resume_Exec
        VMMCall End_Nest_Exec
        movzx   eax, [ebp.Client_AX]              ; get return value
        Pop_Client_State
```

What magic occurs in this code that allows a VxD to simulate an interrupt call in a VM? The `Push_Client_State` macro allocates space on the stack and copies the current CRS to this block. `Begin_Nest_V86_Exec` modifies the VM state so that the execution block occurs in V86 mode. `Simulate_Int` builds an IRET frame and modifies the client's stack and CS:(E)IP to call the interrupt handler. `Resume_Exec` forces VMM to complete event processing and then resumes the execution of the VM. When the VM completes the execution block, control returns to the VxD and the `End_Nest_Exec` restores the VM's execution state. The `Pop_Client_State` macro restores the client's registers, as saved on the stack.

Calling Windows Functions from a VxD

The techniques used to simulate software interrupts to a VM can be extended to call functions in the System VM. There are a few restrictions when calling Windows functions or functions provided by Windows DLLs:

- The function must be able to handle reentrancy. Many Windows functions are not reentrant. `PostMessage()` and its derivatives are safe, as are a few other Windows multimedia services.

- The code segment of the function must be present. The Windows Kernel does not support not-present segment faults when reentered. Because a VxD can not determine when the Windows Kernel is executing code, the segment must always be present (or non-discardable).

- If DOS or BIOS is used for paging, the function code must be page-locked in memory. Because DOS and BIOS are not reentrant, a page-fault cannot be resolved if DOS or BIOS code is currently executing in any VM.

- The safest segmentation for a function called by a VxD is in a FIXED code segment of a DLL. Calling application code is dangerous and is not recommended.

To call Windows functions, you must use a helper application or DLL to provide the procedure address to the VxD. The VxD can then use the nested execution services to simulate a far call to the procedure in the System VM. If a VM context switch is required (if the current VM is other than the System VM), the VxD must schedule a VM event to call the procedure. The following code sample calls the Windows PostMessage() function from a VxD assuming the PostMessage function pointer was obtained from the application or DLL):

```
;=================================================================
;
;    VSIMPLED_NotifyApp
;
;       This routine notifies the Windows application through a
;       call to the PostMessage() API.
;
;    ENTRY:
;       EDX: contains the lParam of the message
;
;    USES:
;       FLAGS
;
;=================================================================
BeginProc VSIMPLED_NotifyApp, High_Freq

        VMMCall Test_Sys_VM_Handle
        je      SHORT VSIMPLED_PostEvent

NA_Schedule:
        push    ebx
        mov     eax, High_Pri_Device_Boost
        VMMCall Get_Sys_VM_Handle
        mov     ecx, PEF_Wait_For_STI OR PEF_Wait_Not_Crit
        mov     esi, OFFSET32 VSIMPLED_PostEvent
        xor     edi, edi
        VMMCall Call_Priority_VM_Event
        pop     ebx
        ret

EndProc VSIMPLED_NotifyApp
```

```
;==================================================================
;
;    VSIMPLED_PostEvent
;
;    Called by the priority VM event dispatch routine or
;    directly if System VM was already active.
;
;    ENTRY:
;       EBX: The system VM handle
;       EBP: Client register structure
;       EDX: Reference data
;
;    USES:
;       EAX, EDX, FLAGS
;
;==================================================================

BeginProc VSIMPLED_PostEvent

        Trace_Out "In VSIMPLED_PostEvent"

        cmp     lpPostMessage, 0            ; Q: ptr == NULL?
        je      SHORT PE_Exit               ;    Y: can't call

        Push_Client_State
        VMMCall Begin_Nest_Exec

        mov     ax, NotifyWnd               ; handle to window
        VMMCall Simulate_Push
        mov     ax, NotifyMsg               ; notification msg
        VMMCall Simulate_Push
        xor     ax, ax
        VMMCall Simulate_Push               ; wParam is NULL
        mov     eax, edx
        shr     eax, 16
        VMMCall Simulate_Push               ; lParam is ref data
        mov     eax, edx
        VMMCall Simulate_Push

        movzx   edx, WORD PTR [lpPostMessage]
        mov     cx, WORD PTR [lpPostMessage + 2]

        VMMCall Simulate_Far_Call           ; call PostMessage()
        VMMCall Resume_Exec
        VMMCall End_Nest_Exec
        Pop_Client_State
PE_Exit:
        ret

EndProc VSIMPLED_PostEvent
```

Calling Code in a TSR at Ring 0

In Windows 3.1, the VPICD added services that allow a Windows driver to provide interrupt service routines callable at ring 0. This means a Windows device driver to provide a common code base for hardware interrupt servicing. This technique can be implemented by other VxDs to call routines in a VM directly from ring 0, as shown in Figure 5.1.

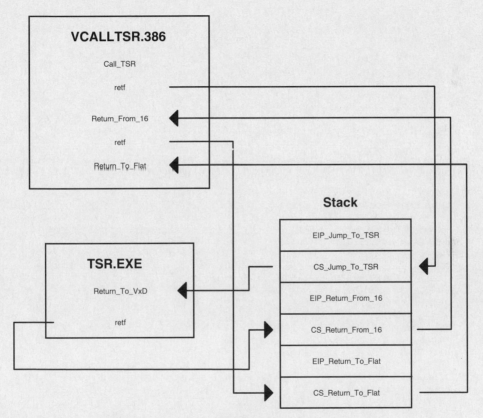

Figure 5.1
Possible design of calling a TSR directly (at ring 0) from a VxD

The technique to call TSR code from ring 0 is actually quite simple. A VxD provides an API that allows a V86 or PM application to register a procedure as a "direct" callback procedure. Ring 0 16-bit GDT selectors are built to access code and data of the callback procedure. When the required event occurs, the VxD calls the callback procedure by setting up a far return frame, including a 32-flat far return address to a return-to-flat procedure and a 16:16 far return address to a return-from-16 procedure in the VxD. The

VxD then performs a far return kicking out to the 16-bit code in the TSR. When the TSR has completed processing, the far return kicks back to the return-from-16 procedure in the VxD. The last remaining issue is to return to 32-flat model by using a final far return to the return-to-flat procedure.

This method makes some assumptions of the way TSRs are loaded in the system:

- The TSR is loaded before Windows is started and is therefore global to all VMs.

- The GDT selectors are based on the low linear address of the TSR. Because the TSR is global in all VMs, this mapping must remain constant in all page tables.

- If the code was specific to a VM, a priority VM event would be required to make the VM active before calling the code directly at ring 0.

- Using this scheme, the stack is provided by VMM and is a Use32 segment. Stack parameter passing is not valid unless the TSR uses 32-bit references to the stack (ESP and EBP). The TSR code should not attempt to change SS.

The following code fragments demonstrate the technique of calling TSR code (16-bit code) at ring 0. In Sys_Critical_Init, the GDT selectors used for the call to the TSR are allocated. For this sample, a global timeout is used to initiate the calls to the TSR.

```
;--------------------------------------------------------------------
;
;       VCALLTSR_Sys_Critical_Init
;
;       DESCRIPTION:
;           Allocates necessary GDT selectors.
;
;       ENTRY:
;           EBX = handle to Sys VM
;           EDX = reference data from real-mode init
;
;       EXIT:
;           Carry clear if no error, otherwise set if failure.
;
;       USES:
;           Flags
;
;--------------------------------------------------------------------

BeginProc VCALLTSR_Sys_Critical_Init

        Trace_Out "VCALLTSR: Sys_Critical_Init"

        pushad

;
; Note:
;
```

```
; An assumption is made that CS:0 is the base of the TSR.
; Since we don't have a segment size, we'll assume 1 page,
; but this could be handled by using a pointer to a structure
; within the TSR obtained from Exec_Int instead of using
; Real_Mode_Init to gather the information.
;

        mov       eax, edx
        movzx     edx, ax
        mov       dwTSR_Ring0_EIP, edx
        shr       eax, 16
        shl       eax, 4

        push      eax                               ; save address

        VMMCall  _BuildDescriptorDWORDS, < eax, <P_SIZE - 1>,\
                                          Code_Type,\
                                          <D_DEF16 + D_DPL0>,\
                                          BDDExplicitDPL >
        VMMCall  _Allocate_GDT_Selector, < edx, eax, 0 >
        or        eax, eax
        jnz       SHORT SCI_GotCSSel
        pop       eax
        jmp       SHORT SCI_Failure

SCI_GotCSSel:
        mov       dwTSR_Ring0_CS, eax

        pop       eax                               ; restore address

        VMMCall  _BuildDescriptorDWORDS, < eax, <P_SIZE - 1>,\
                                          RW_Data_Type,\
                                          <D_DEF16 + D_DPL0>,\
                                          BDDExplicitDPL >
        VMMCall  _Allocate_GDT_Selector, < edx, eax, 0 >
        or        eax, eax
        jz        SHORT SCI_Failure
        mov       dwTSR_Ring0_DS, eax

        VMMCall  _BuildDescriptorDWORDS, < <OFFSET32 VCT_Switch>,\
                                          VCT_Switch_Size,\
                                          Code_Type,\
                                          <D_DEF32 + D_DPL0>,\
                                          BDDExplicitDPL >
        VMMCall  _Allocate_GDT_Selector, < edx, eax, 0 >
        or        eax, eax
        jz        SHORT SCI_Failure
        mov       wTSR_Switch_To_Flat_CS, ax

        mov       eax, 500                          ; 500 ms timeout
        xor       edx, edx                          ; no data
        mov       esi, OFFSET32 VCALLTSR_TimeOut
        VMMCall  Set_Global_Time_Out
        mov       hTimeOut, esi
```

```
        popad
        clc
        ret

SCI_Failure:

        ;
        ; Free any allocated selectors and exit
        ;

        mov     eax, dwTSR_Ring0_CS
        or      eax, eax
        jz      SHORT SCI_Failure_TryDS
        VMMCall _Free_GDT_Selector, <eax, 0>

SCI_Failure_TryDS:
        mov     eax, dwTSR_Ring0_DS
        or      eax, eax
        jz      SHORT SCI_Failure_TryFlat
        VMMCall _Free_GDT_Selector, <eax, 0>

SCI_Failure_TryFlat:
        movzx   eax, wTSR_Switch_To_Flat_CS
        or      eax, eax
        jz      SHORT SCI_Failure_Exit
        VMMCall _Free_GDT_Selector, <eax, 0>

SCI_Failure_Exit:
        popad
        stc
        ret

EndProc VCALLTSR_Sys_Critical_Init
```

When the timeout procedure is called, the stack frames are created to call the TSR code directly. When the TSR returns the VxD unwraps the stack to get back to 32-bit flat model:

```
;-------------------------------------------------------------------
;
;   VCALLTSR_TimeOut
;
;   DESCRIPTION:
;       Event handler for global timeout. Calls TSR code directly
;       from ring 0.
;
;   ENTRY:
;       EBX = Current VM handle
;       ECX = additional ms since timeout
;       EDX = reference data
;       EBP = -> CRS
;
;   EXIT:
;       Reschedules time-out.
```

```
;
;   USES:
;       All registers.
;
;------------------------------------------------------------------

BeginProc VCALLTSR_TimeOut

        pushad

        mov     hTimeOut, 0                         ; clear handle

        Trace_Out "Setting up stack frames to call TSR."


        ;
        ; This stack frame is so we can get back to flat model.
        ;

        push    cs                                  ; save CS
        mov     eax, OFFSET32 VCALLTSR_Back_To_Flat
        push    eax                                 ; save EIP


        ;
        ; This stack frame will get us back to 32-bit code in
        ; the VxD and is addressable via 16:16 for the TSR.
        ;

        push    ds                                  ; save off DS
        push    dwTSR_RETF_From_16


        ;
        ; This is the stack frame used to get us to the TSR
        ; code. Additionally, DS is setup with a R/W pointer
        ; to the same base address.
        ;

        mov     eax, dwTSR_Ring0_DS
        mov     ds, ax
        push    cs:dwTSR_Ring0_CS
        push    cs:dwTSR_Ring0_EIP
        retf                                        ; go to the TSR

VCT_Switch:
        pop     ds                                  ; restore DS
        retf                                        ; return to flat

VCT_Switch_Size equ ($ - VCALLTSR_Switch_To_Flat) - 1

VCALLTSR_Back_To_Flat:

        Trace_Out "Back in flat model. Return from TSR = #AX"

        ;
```

```
        ; Reschedule time out event
        ;

        mov     eax, 500                              ; 500 ms timeout
        xor     edx, edx                              ; no data
        mov     esi, OFFSET32 VCALLTSR_TimeOut
        VMMCall Set_Global_Time_Out
        mov     hTimeOut, esi

        popad
        ret

EndProc VCALLTSR_TimeOut
```

Chapter 6

I/O Trapping

I/O protection is a powerful feature provided by the 80386/80486 chipset. When the Current Privilege Level (CPL) is less than or equal to the I/O privilege level (IOPL), the following instructions can be executed:

```
IN          input
INS         input string
OUT         output
OUTS        output string
CLI         clear interrupt-enable flag
STI         set interrupt-enable flag
```

If CPL is less than or equal to IOPL in protected mode, the processor allows the I/O operation to proceed. If CPL is greater than IOPL or if the processor is operating in virtual 8086 mode, the I/O permissions bitmap (IOPM) is used to determine whether access to the port is allowed. Because MS-DOS VMs run in virtual 8086 mode and a Windows application has a CPL of 3 (for Windows 3.1) and IOPL is 0, the I/O permissions bitmap is always used in these cases to determine whether access to the port is valid.

VMM keeps a copy of the IOPM for each VM (it is associated with the TSS and other task information). VxDs can enable or disable access to ports by modifying the IOPM using VMM services. Also, it is possible to trap ports in one VM and allow access to the hardware directly in another VM.

The `Install_IO_Handler` and `Install_Mult_IO_Handlers` services install handlers that are called when the GP fault handler has determined that I/O to the associated port has caused the fault. VMM provides the `Enable_Local_Trapping`, `Enable_Global_Trapping`, `Disable_Local_Trapping`, and `Disable_Global_`

`Trapping` services to modify the IOPM of virtual machines to enable and disable access to the I/O ports.

I/O trapping is the primary method used to manage device contention. By allowing only one VM access to a hardware device address space, the VxD can manage accesses by other VMs. For cases of contention, a VxD can simulate the device I/O and submit the actual hardware request when the hardware is free, ignore the hardware access, and return as though the hardware did not exist or crash the VM attempting to access the hardware.

A VxD can simulate hardware that does not exist by virtualizing the device using a finite state machine (or other similar method) and returning the appropriate information to the requesting application.

Trapping and Dispatching I/O

To trap I/O addresses, a VxD uses the `Install_IO_Handler` or `Install_Mult_IO_Handlers` services of VMM. These services are only available during device initialization.

These services associate a callback (or table of callbacks) with an I/O port (or table of I/O ports). By default, global trapping is enabled, any access to the trapped ports causes a fault, and the associated callback procedure is called.

An I/O table has the following format:

```
VxD_IDATA_SEG

Begin_VxD_IO_Table VTRAPIOD_Port_Table

        VxD_IO   TRAPIO_IDX,    VTRAPIOD_IO_Index_Reg
        VxD_IO   TRAPIO_DATA,   VTRAPIOD_IO_Data_Reg

End_VxD_IO_Table VTRAPIOD_Port_Table

VTRAPIOD_Port_Table_Entries equ (($-VTRAPIOD_Port_Table)-\
   (SIZE VxD_IOT_Hdr)) / (SIZE VxD_IO_Struc)

VxD_IDATA_ENDS
```

This table uses offsets from the base I/O address as the port address. When the base address of the hardware has been determined, the VxD can update the I/O table and install the handlers:

```
;----------------------------------------------------------------
;
;    VTRAPIOD_Device_Init
;
```

```
;    DESCRIPTION:
;        Non critical system initialization procedure.
;
;    ENTRY:
;        EBX = Sys VM handle
;
;    EXIT:
;        CLC if everything's A-OK, otherwise STC
;
;    USES:
;        Flags.
;
;-----------------------------------------------------------------

BeginProc VTRAPIOD_Device_Init

        Trace_Out "VTRAPIOD: Device_Init"

        pushad

        ;
        ; Build an I/O port table for Install_Mult_IO_Handlers
        ; using the base address.
        ;

        mov     ecx, VTRAPIOD_Port_Table_Entries
        mov     esi, OFFSET32 VTRAPIOD_Port_Table
        mov     edx, VTRAPIOD_Base_IO

DI_Install_IO_Handlers:
        mov     edi, esi                ; save a copy in EDI
        add     esi, (size VxD_IOT_Hdr)

DI_Bump_IO_Loop:
        add     [esi.VxD_IO_Port], dx   ; add port base to offset
        add     esi, (size VxD_IO_Struc)
        loop    DI_Bump_IO_Loop

        ;
        ; Tell VMM to trap ports.
        ;

        VMMcall Install_Mult_IO_Handlers
ifdef DEBUG
        jnc     SHORT DI_Exit
        Debug_Out "VTRAPIOD: cannot trap ports!!"
endif

DI_Exit:
        popad
        ret

EndProc VTRAPIOD_Device_Init
```

When an I/O port within the given range has been accessed, the fault handler dispatches to the associated I/O handler. For this example, the index register simply stores the index if valid (on write) or returns the current index (on read):

```
;-----------------------------------------------------------------
;
;    VTRAPIOD_IO_Index_Reg
;
;    DESCRIPTION:
;        Handles IO trapping.
;
;        This is a virtual R/W index register.
;
;    ENTRY:
;        EBX = VM Handle.
;        ECX = Type of I/O
;        EDX = Port number
;        EBP = Pointer to client register structure
;
;    EXIT:
;        EAX = data input or output depending on type of I/O
;
;    USES:
;        FLAGS
;
;-----------------------------------------------------------------

BeginProc VTRAPIOD_IO_Index_Reg, High_Freq

        Dispatch_Byte_IO Fall_Through, <SHORT IIR_Out>

        mov     al, bIndex
        clc
        ret

IIR_Out:
        cmp     al, VTRAPIOD_Max_Index
        ja      SHORT IIR_Exit
        mov     bIndex, al

IIR_Exit:
        clc
        ret

EndProc VTRAPIOD_IO_Index_Reg
```

The one drawback with this simple I/O trapping interface is that there is a single global virtual device. Multiple VMs can simultaneously (well, almost simultaneously) access this device and may inadvertently affect the processing of another VM by switching the index register while a different VM is updating an indexed data register. This is commonly referred to as *device contention*, and this VxD must be improved to properly handle contention between VMs. The next below discusses this topic in greater detail.

Device Contention Management

When multiple virtual machines attempt to access the same hardware interface and device contention is not handled by a VxD, the VMs probably interact with the hardware in such a way that all the hardware sees is gibberish.

To avoid these problems, a VxD implements one of the following methods of device contention:

- A VxD can completely virtualize the hardware interface, buffer the requests, and submit them when the hardware is free.

- A VxD can allow only one VM to access the hardware at a time. The hardware will not be visible to other VMs until the hardware is released by the owner.

- The VM can be terminated for attempting to access the hardware. (Not the most user-friendly or recommended method.)

The most commonly used method is to allow only one VM to access the hardware at a time. Other VMs cannot access the hardware until it has been released by the owner.

To implement this form of device contention, all I/O ports for the hardware device are trapped. When a VM accesses a trapped port, the handler routine checks to see whether the device has been assigned to a VM. If a contention is detected, the VxD may display a warning message using the Shell VxD's API and then return with carry set for all reads and writes to the hardware. If there is no current owner, the VxD assigns the device to the VM and disables the I/O trapping for the VM using the `Disable_Local_Trapping` service. When the VM terminates or when the hardware is explicitly released by the VM, the VxD re-enables the trapping for the VM, using the `Enable_Local_Trapping` service, and clears the owner status of the hardware.

The following sample code is contention management in its simplest form:

```
;-------------------------------------------------------------
;
;    VCONTEND_Check_Owner
;
```

```
;    DESCRIPTION:
;        Checks the current VM owner; if none, assigns
;        device to VM. If the VM is an owning VM, returns
;        carry clear, otherwise it returns carry set.
;
;    ENTRY:
;        EBX = VM Handle.
;
;    EXIT:
;        CLC if owner OK, or STC if contention
;
;    USES:
;        FLAGS
;
;-----------------------------------------------------------------

BeginProc VCONTEND_Check_Owner, High_Freq

        push    eax
        mov     eax, hOwnerVM
        or      eax, eax
        jz      SHORT CO_Assign_To_VM
        cmp     eax, ebx
        jne     SHORT CO_Failure

CO_Success:
        pop     eax
        clc
        ret

CO_Assign_To_VM:
        mov     hOwnerVM, ebx
        jmp     SHORT CO_Success

CO_Failure:
        pop     eax
        stc
        ret

EndProc VCONTEND_Check_Owner

;-----------------------------------------------------------------
;
;    VCONTEND_IO_Index_Reg
;
;    DESCRIPTION:
;        Handles IO trapping.
;
;        This is a virtual R/W index register.
;
;    ENTRY:
;        EBX = VM Handle.
;        ECX = Type of I/O
;        EDX = Port number
```

```
;        EBP = Pointer to client register structure
;
;   EXIT:
;        EAX = data input or output depending on type of I/O
;
;   USES:
;        FLAGS
;
;----------------------------------------------------------------

BeginProc VCONTEND_IO_Index_Reg, High_Freq

        call    VCONTEND_Check_Owner
        jc      SHORT IIR_Exit

        Dispatch_Byte_IO Fall_Through, <SHORT IIR_Out>

        mov     al, bIndex
        clc
        ret

IIR_Out:
        cmp     al, VCONTEND_Max_Index
        ja      SHORT IIR_Exit
        mov     bIndex, al
        clc

IIR_Exit:
        ret

EndProc VCONTEND_IO_Index_Reg
```

Note that with this method of contention management, the hardware remains in the state the last owning VM left it in. You may decide to define an initial state for a VM in the VM control block and update the state when the VM releases the hardware. When a VM acquires the hardware, the state would be copied from the VM's control block to the hardware.

Simulating Hardware

As demonstrated in the preceding code fragments, it is possible to simulate (or virtualize) hardware through the use of trapped I/O interfaces. The Windows 3.1 Device Driver Kit contains sources to VxDs that simulate hardware such as the Virtual DMA Device and the Virtual COMM Device. You should investigate these sources for examples of more complex interfaces.

VxDs can use these techniques to translate common hardware interfaces to new or improved hardware interfaces and maintain the backward compatibility of the older platforms for MS-DOS applications.

To fully virtualize a hardware interface, your VxD may need to incorporate IRQ virtualization and/or DMA virtualization. These topics are covered in Chapters 7 and 8, respectively.

Chapter 7

IRQ Virtualization

The Virtual Programmable Interrupt Controller Device (VPICD) provides an interface to hook (virtualize) IRQs, query information about the state of a hooked IRQ, simulate hardware interrupts to VMs, share interrupts, and handle interrupts in the System VM with a single ISR interface using the bimodal interrupt interface.

During initialization, the VPICD configures the PICs (slave and master), hooks the IDT entries, and establishes default handling for non-virtualized IRQs. The PICs are virtualized to all VMs. When a VM masks an interrupt, it is communicating with the VPICD and does not perform I/O directly to the PIC. VPICD provides services to affect the physical state of the PICs. It is strongly recommended that VxDs use this interface to change the physical state of a virtualized IRQ.

IRQ virtualization is recommended for hardware devices that use hardware interrupts as a form of communication with device drivers. There are several reasons for this recommendation:

- IRQ virtualization is a requirement for proper device contention management.

- Some devices require immediate interrupt servicing. Interrupt latency caused by non-virtualized interrupt handling in an ISR in either a TSR or Windows device driver do not satisfy this requirement.

- VPICD's default IRQ handling is sometimes inappropriate for devices that intend to be "Windows-GUI-only" oriented. IRQs that are unmasked prior to starting Windows are designated as "global." Global interrupts are not appropriate for this implementation.

The most common complaint of interrupt processing under Windows is the interrupt latency issue introduced by simulating interrupts to VMs. Additionally, you may be interested in monitoring interrupt response from a hardware device before simulating the interrupt to a VM. In these cases, IRQ virtualization is required.

Default VPICD Handling

Before discussing IRQ virtualization in detail, we need to explain the default operation of VPICD when an interrupt is not virtualized. By default, all IRQs are "virtualized" by VPICD. If the interrupt was unmasked prior to starting Win386 (or the special case of IRQ 9), the default owner is global. Otherwise, no default owner exists.

The default hardware interrupt procedure (Hw_Int_Proc) simulates an interrupt to the current VM if the IRQ is unowned. When the IRQ is global, VPICD simulates the interrupt to the current critical section owner or the current VM, if there is no critical section owner. Also, interrupts simulated for global IRQs are nested in the VM until the nesting has been "unwound", but non-owned interrupts are always simulated to the current VM in all circumstances.

When an interrupt is simulated to a VM (by a default IRQ handler or using the `VPICD_Set_Int_Request` service), the VM priority is boosted and the IRET procedure is hooked to notify the IRET procedure when the interrupt has been completed. These events only occur when the IRQ is not nested.

End-of-Interrupt results when the VM issues an EOI to the virtual PIC. The default EOI handler clears the virtual interrupt request and performs a physical EOI using the `VPICD_Clear_Int_Request` and `VPICD_Phys_EOI` services respectively.

By default each unowned or global interrupt procedure has a timeout of 500ms. A VM timeout is scheduled to watch the interrupt processing time in a VM. If the ISR in the VM does not service the interrupt within the specified timeout period, VPICD continues execution as though the ISR had issued an IRET. The timeout is canceled when the VM issues an IRET (or the last IRET in a nested block).

VPICD simulates a level-triggered PIC. That is, when a virtual EOI occurs another interrupt will be simulated immediately unless the virtual interrupt request has been cleared by the `VPICD_Clear_Int_Request` service.

IRQ Virtualization and Sharing

IRQ Virtualization

A VxD can change the default behavior of interrupt processing by virtualizing the IRQ using the `VPICD_Virtualize_IRQ` service. The VxD fills the following structure and calls this service to obtain an IRQ handle:

```
VPICD_IRQ_Descriptor STRUC
VID_IRQ_Number          dw      ?
VID_Options             dw      0
VID_Hw_Int_Proc         dd      ?
VID_Virt_Int_Proc       dd      0
VID_EOI_Proc            dd      0
VID_Mask_Change_Proc    dd      0
VID_IRET_Proc           dd      0
VID_IRET_Time_Out       dd      500
VPICD_IRQ_Descriptor ENDS
```

Some of the elements of this structure require further detail:

- `VID_Hw_Int_Proc` contains a pointer to the procedure called when hardware interrupts occur for the specified IRQ. (Required)

- `VID_Virt_Int_Proc` contains a pointer to the procedure called when interrupts are simulated to the VM for this IRQ. (Optional)

- `VID_EOI_Proc` contains a pointer to the procedure called when the hardware interrupt service routine in the VM issues an EOI to the PIC. (Optional)

- `VID_Mask_Change_Proc` contains a pointer to the procedure called when the VM changes the mask status of the IRQ on the PIC. (Optional)

- `VID_IRET_Proc` contains a pointer to the procedure called when the VM IRETs (or the last IRET of a nested block) from the simulated interrupt. This procedure is also called when a timeout occurs when a VM is servicing an interrupt. (Optional)

- `VID_IRET_Time_Out` is the timeout value for a VM to service an interrupt. When the timeout occurs, VPICD reacts as though the VM issued an IRET with the exception that the interrupt has not been physically serviced. (Optional, default is 500ms)

A VxD must virtualize an interrupt during device initialization. It is recommended that the VxD virtualize the interrupt during Sys_Critical_Init if you are using IRQ 9 to avoid problems introduced when interrupts occur between the Sys_Critical_Init and Device_Init control messages.

The following sample code demonstrates the use of VPICD services to virtualize an IRQ:

```
;===================================================================
;                     I N I T   D A T A
;===================================================================

VxD_IDATA_SEG

VIRQD_IRQ_Descriptor VPICD_IRQ_Descriptor <,,\
                                OFFSET32 VIRQD_Hw_Int_Proc,,\
                                OFFSET32 VIRQD_EOI_Proc,,,>
VxD_IDATA_ENDS

;===================================================================
;                     I N I T   C O D E
;===================================================================

VxD_ICODE_SEG

;-------------------------------------------------------------------
;
;   VIRQD_Device_Init
;
;   DESCRIPTION:
;       Non critical system initialization procedure.
;
;   ENTRY:
;       EBX = Sys VM handle
;
;   EXIT:
;       CLC if everything's A-OK, otherwise STC
;
;   USES:
;       Flags.
;
;-------------------------------------------------------------------

BeginProc VIRQD_Device_Init

        Trace_Out "VIRQD: Device_Init"

        push    eax
        push    edi

        mov     edi, OFFSET32 VIRQD_IRQ_Descriptor
        mov     [edi.VID_IRQ_Number], VIRQD_Interrupt
        VxDCall VPICD_Virtualize_IRQ
ifdef DEBUG
        jnc     SHORT @F
        Debug_Out "VIRQD: Unable to virtualize IRQ"
        jmp     SHORT DI_Exit
@@:
else
        jc      SHORT DI_Exit
endif
        mov     hVirtIRQ, eax
```

```
DI_Exit:
        pop     edi
        pop     eax
        ret

EndProc VIRQD_Device_Init

VxD_ICODE_ENDS
```

When the hardware interrupt occurs, the following procedures simulate the interrupt to the current VM and clear the interrupt when the ISR issues an EOI to the virtual PIC:

```
;====================================================================
;    H A R D W A R E    I N T E R R U P T    P R O C E D U R E S
;====================================================================
VxD_LOCKED_CODE_SEG
;--------------------------------------------------------------------
;
;    VIRQD_Hw_Int_Proc
;
;    DESCRIPTION:
;        Hardware interrupt handler. Called by VPICD.
;
;    ENTRY:
;        EAX = IRQ handle
;        EBX = current VM handle
;
;    EXIT:
;        CLC if processed, STC otherwise.
;
;    USES:
;        Flags.
;
;--------------------------------------------------------------------

BeginProc VIRQD_Hw_Int_Proc, High_Freq

        Trace_Out "<i"

        VxDCall VPICD_Set_Int_Request

        clc
        ret

EndProc VIRQD_Hw_Int_Proc

;--------------------------------------------------------------------
;
;    VIRQD_EOI_Proc
;
;    DESCRIPTION:
;        Hardware interrupt handler. Called by VPICD.
;
```

```
;   ENTRY:
;       EAX = IRQ handle
;       EBX = current VM handle
;
;   EXIT:
;       Nothing.
;
;   USES:
;       Nothing.
;
;--------------------------------------------------------------

BeginProc VIRQD_EOI_Proc, High_Freq

        Trace_Out "i>"

        VxDCall VPICD_Clear_Int_Request
        VxDCall VPICD_Phys_EOI

        ret

EndProc VIRQD_EOI_Proc


VxD_LOCKED_CODE_ENDS
```

Note that services called during the processing of the Hw_Int_Proc procedure must be declared asynchronous (see Chapter 2 for a complete list of asynchronous services). If a VxD requires the use of a non-asynchronous service to continue interrupt processing, the VxD must schedule a global event to continue. The debug version of WIN386.EXE notifies you when you attempt to call a non-asynchronous service during interrupt processing. Heed the warnings of VMM, lest your ignorance cause the system to crash.

Shared IRQ Procedures

If the hardware platform supports shared interrupts (Micro Channel Architecture) or the device is using an ISA shared interrupt strategy, the IRQ can be virtualized specifying the **VPICD_Opt_Can_Share** flag in the **VID_Options** element of the **VPICD_IRQ_Descriptor** structure. When the hardware interrupt is dispatched to the Hw_Int_Proc, the VxD should determine whether the interrupt was generated by the associated hardware device and, if so, process the interrupt and return with carry clear. If the interrupt was not generated by the supported hardware, the VxD should return immediately with carry clear. VPICD will continue to walk the shared interrupt list until a VxD responds with carry set.

Note that the VxD cannot assume that subsequent calls to other callback procedures specified in the IRQ descriptor structure are the result of an interrupt for the associated hardware device. The VxD should set a flag when it has simulated an interrupt to a VM and test against this flag when notifications from VPICD are processed. When the VxD processes the EOI_Proc it should clear the flag, perform the necessary EOI procedures, and then return.

Dispatching IRQs to a VM

The example below demonstrates a very simple IRQ virtualization. The `VIRQD_Hw_Int_Proc` simply sets the interrupt request for the current VM and returns. When the ISR performs an EOI to the PIC, the `VIRQD_EOI_Proc` clears the interrupt request and performs a physical EOI.

When a VxD requests an interrupt for a VM using the `VPICD_Set_Int_Request` service, the interrupt simulation may not occur immediately. There are several conditions that do not allow an interrupt to be simulated immediately:

- Interrupts are disabled in the VM.

- The virtual IRQ is masked in the VM.

- A higher priority virtual IRQ is already in service.

- The virtual machine is suspended.

In these cases, the interrupt is simulated as soon as the conditions are met.

Note that using `VPICD_Set_Int_Request` does not guarantee that an interrupt will be simulated to a VM. For example, if a VM has masked and never unmasks the IRQ, the interrupt will not be simulated. Additionally, a call to `VPICD_Clear_Int_Request` before the interrupt has been simulated prevents the VM from receiving the interrupt.

The example also does not demonstrate proper techniques when processing hardware interrupts for device contention management. The `VIRQD_Hw_Int_Proc` should be expanded to first determine whether an owner VM exists and then simulate the interrupt to that VM, as follows:

```
;-----------------------------------------------------------------
;
;   VIRQD_Hw_Int_Proc
;
;   DESCRIPTION:
;       Hardware interrupt handler. Called by VPICD.
;       Simulates the interrupt to the hardware owner or
;       to the current VM if unowned.
;
;   ENTRY:
;       EAX = IRQ handle
;       EBX = current VM handle
```

```
;
;    EXIT:
;        CLC if processed, STC otherwise.
;
;    USES:
;        EBX, Flags.
;
;-------------------------------------------------------------------

BeginProc VIRQD_Hw_Int_Proc, High_Freq

        Trace_Out "<i"
        cmp       hOwnerVM, 0
        je        SHORT HIP_SetIt
        mov       ebx, hOwnerVM

HIP_SetIt:
        VxDCall VPICD_Set_Int_Request

        clc
        ret

EndProc VIRQD_Hw_Int_Proc
```

Servicing Interrupts in a VxD

To reduce the interrupt latency of servicing a hardware device contained in ISR code of a VM, a VxD can service interrupts directly during processing of the Hw_Int_Proc procedure. In cases where a steady stream of data is processed, the VxD should buffer the information from the hardware device and provide the information to the owning VM in chunks.

A Hw_Int_Proc for servicing an interrupt directly might be similar to this:

```
;-------------------------------------------------------------------
;
;    VIRQD_Hw_Int_Proc
;
;    DESCRIPTION:
;        Hardware interrupt handler. First, EOI the PIC
;        so we avoid missing another IRQ generated by the
;        device. Call a procedure elsewhere in the VxD to
;        service the hardware device and then return.
;
;    ENTRY:
;        EAX = IRQ handle
;        EBX = current VM handle
;        Interrupts are disabled.
;
;    EXIT:
;        CLC if processed, STC otherwise.
;
```

```
;   USES:
;       EBX, Flags.
;
;----------------------------------------------------------------

BeginProc VIRQD_Hw_Int_Proc, High_Freq

        Trace_Out "<i>"
        VxDCall VPICD_Phys_EOI
        call    VIRQD_Service_Hardware
        clc
        ret

EndProc VIRQD_Hw_Int_Proc
```

In this example, `VIRQD_Hw_Int_Proc` does not set the interrupt request for the VM. **The VIRQ_Service_Hardware** procedure may set an interrupt request to the owning VM when a threshold has been reached. This is strictly determined by the requirements of your hardware and the maximum amount of CPU load you wish to generate. The VxD could also use some other form of communication to a driver in a VM, such as nested execution or updating global memory buffers.

Additionally, the `VIRQ_EOI_Proc` would not perform a physical EOI of the PIC. Its only requirement would be to clear the interrupt request status for the VM if simulated interrupts are used to communicate with the VM's device driver.

Note that interrupt simulation is an expensive procedure. Ring transitions and VM context switches are often a result of interrupt simulation, and reducing simulated interrupt generation will help reduce the total burden of the CPU.

Bimodal Interrupt Handlers

Bimodal interrupt handlers are a new feature of the Windows 3.1 VPICD that allows a Windows device driver (or DLL) to service interrupts without waiting for VPICD to simulate an interrupt to the System VM and can avoid the associated delays of VM focus changes and VM event processing. Interrupt latency can be reduced using these services while maintaining a common code base for the ISR under Standard and Enhanced Mode Windows. Note that servicing interrupts directly in a VxD (as discussed in the preceding section) yields minimal interrupt latency.

The following services are available through the PM API of the VPICD to install and remove bimodal interrupt handlers:

```
VPICD_API_Get_Ver             retrieve the VPICD version
VPICD_Install_Handler             install a bimodal IRQ handler
VPICD_Remove_Handler              remove a bimodal IRQ handler
```

The VPICD API can only be accessed via the protected mode API entry point. It is not available to V86 VMs. To access the VPICD API, a VM obtains the API entry point:

```
VPICD_Device_ID            EQU     0003h
VPICD_API_Get_Ver          EQU     0000h
VPICD_Install_Handler      EQU     0001h
VPICD_Remove_Handler       EQU     0002h
VPICD_Call_At_Ring0        EQU     0003h

        xor    di, di
        mov    es, di
        mov    ax, 1684h                   ; get API entry point
        mov    bx, VPICD_Device_ID         ;    of the VPICD
        int    2fh
        mov    word ptr lpVPICDEntry, di
        mov    word ptr lpVPICDEntry + 2, es
        mov    ax, es
        or     ax, di
        jz     SHORT No_VPICD_API
```

Under Windows 3.0, the VPICD entry point will be NULL, because it does not support any API functionality. If the entry point is not NULL, VPICD's version can be obtained:

```
Get_VPICD_Version:
        mov    ax, VPICD_API_Get_Ver
        call   dword ptr lpVPICDEntry
        jc     SHORT VPICD_Error
        cmp    ax, 30Ah
        jbe    SHORT VPICD_Error
```

A DLL installs and removes a bimodal IRQ handler using the **VPICD_API_Install** and **VPICD_API_Remove** functions respectively:

```
Install_Bimodal_Handler:
        les    di, lpBIS                   ; pointer to BIS struct.
        mov    ax, VPICD_Install_Handler
        call   dword ptr lpVPICDEntry
        jc     SHORT VPICD_Error

Remove_Bimodal_Handler:
        les    di, lpBIS                   ; pointer to BIS struct.
        mov    ax, VPICD_Remove_Handler
        call   dword ptr lpVPICDEntry
        jc     SHORT VPICD_Error
```

In these routines, the Bimodal_Int_Struc (BIS) is referenced. This structure has the following format:

```
Bimodal_Int_Struc    STRUC
       BIS_IRQ_Number        dw      ?
       BIS_VM_ID             dw      0
       BIS_Next              dd      ?
       BIS_Reserved1         dd      ?
       BIS_Reserved2         dd      ?
       BIS_Reserved3         dd      ?
       BIS_Reserved4         dd      ?
       BIS_Flags             dd      0
       BIS_Mode              dw      0
       BIS_Entry             dw      ?
       BIS_Control_Proc      dw      ?
                             dw      ?
       BIS_User_Mode_API     dd      ?
       BIS_Super_Mode_API    dd      ?
       BIS_User_Mode_CS      dw      ?
       BIS_User_Mode_DS      dw      ?
       BIS_Super_Mode_CS     dw      ?
       BIS_Super_Mode_DS     dw      ?
       BIS_Descriptor_Count        dw      ?
Bimodal_Int_Struc    ENDS
```

The field definitions of this structure are detailed as follows:

BIS_IRQ_Number   VPICD installs a bimodal interrupt for the IRQ specified by this field when the **VPICD_Install_Handler** API is called.

BIS_VM_ID   Contains the current VM ID when the interrupt handler specified by **BIS_Entry** is called.

BIS_Next   Currently not used by the Windows 3.1 VPICD.

BIS_Flags   Must be set to zero.

BIS_Mode   Set to 0 to indicate user mode or 4 to indicate supervisor mode. This value can be used as an offset to obtain the appropriate user-mode or super-mode BIS API handler. (Set by VPICD when calling the procedures defined by the **BIS_Entry** and **BIS_Control_Proc** offsets.)

```
       mov    bx, es:[di.BIS_Mode]               ; mode 0=user, 4=super
       call   es:[bx][di.BIS_User_Mode_API]
```

BIS_Entry   Specifies the offset of the ISR from the CS specified in the **BIS_User_Mode_CS** field. When VPICD calls the interrupt handler for interrupt servicing, ES:DI points to this structure. (Filled by caller for the call to `VPICD_Install_Handler`.)

BIS_Control_Proc   Specifies the offset of the control procedure from the CS specified in the `BIS_User_Mode_CS` field. The control procedure is currently not used by the Windows 3.1 VPICD, but should point to a dummy control procedure that performs a far return. (Filled by the caller for `VPICD_Install_Handler`.)

BIS_User_Mode_API   Specifies the far address of the user-mode API procedure entry point. (Filled by VPICD after a call to `VPICD_Install_Handler` API.)

BIS_Super_Mode_API   Specifies the far address of the supervisor mode API procedure entry point. (Filled by VPICD after a call to the `VPICD_Install_Handler` API.)

BIS_User_Mode_CS   Specifies the selector of the user-mode code segment of the interrupt handler. The `BIS_Entry` and `BIS_Control_Proc` offsets must be relative to the code selector specified by this field. (Filled by caller for `VPICD_Install_Handler`.)

BIS_User_Mode_DS   Specifies the selector of the user-mode data segment of the interrupt handler. The Bimodal_Int_Struc structure should be located in this segment. (Filled by caller for `VPICD_Install_Handler`.)

BIS_Super_Mode_CS   VPICD stores the GDT alias of the user-mode CS selector in this field after a call to `VPICD_Install_Handler`.

BIS_Super_Mode_DS   VPICD stores a GDT alias of the user mode CS selector in this field after a call to `VPICD_Install_Handler`.

BIS_Descriptor_Count   Specifies the number of `EBIS_Sel_Struc` structures immediately following the `Bimodal_Int_Struc` structure. VPICD creates a GDT alias for each of the selectors in the structures that follow.

```
EBIS_Sel_Struc STRUC
      EBIS_User_Mode_Sel  dw      ?
                          dw      ?
      EBIS_Super_Mode_Sel dw      ?
EBIS_Sel_Struc ENDS
```

`EBIS_User_Mode_Sel`	User mode selector
`EBIS_Super_Mode_Sel`	GDT alias of selector created by VPICD after a call to `VPICD_Install_Handler`.

VPICD automatically creates GDT aliases for the ISR code and data segments as specified in `BIS_User_Mode_CS` and `BIS_User_Mode_DS`, respectively. Additionally, the caller can request that VPICD create GDT aliases for a number of selectors specified by `BIS_Descriptor_Count`. The user-mode selectors are filled in an array of the `EBIS_Sel_Struc` structures immediately following the `Bmodal_Int_Structure`. The associated GDT aliases are returned in the `EBI_Super_Mode_Sel` element of each of the `EBIS_Sel_Struc` structures. For example, the Windows 3.1 COMM driver uses this functionality to create GDT aliases of the receive and transmit queues.

A DLL creates a Bimodal_Int_Struc and fills the appropriate fields. When the IRQ occurs, VPICD calls the ISR directly at ring 0, regardless of the current VM. On entry to the ISR, the CS is set to the GDT alias of the ISR code segment and ES:DI is set to the GDT alias of the Bimodal_Int_Struc. If this structure is located in the data segment, you can make the data addressable by moving ES into DS.

The ISR executes at ring 0 (CPL=0) through a 16-bit GDT code segment alias. As with calling TSR code directly from a VxD, the provided stack is a Use32 segment and parameter passing must reference the stack using 32-bits (ESP and EBP). The ISR cannot switch to a different stack unless a ring 0 stack selector is created. Note that a DLL cannot legally create such a selector.

The ISR must return from the procedure with a far return and carry clear if the IRQ was serviced or carry set if the IRQ was not serviced. When the ISR is called directly by VPICD, it must not manipulate the PIC directly. Instead, VPICD provides services through the `BIS_Super_Mode_API` procedure to perform these operations:

```
BIH_API_EOI        EQU    0000h
BIH_API_Mask       EQU    0001h
BIH_API_Unmask            EQU    0002h
BIH_API_Get_Mask   EQU    0003h
BIH_API_Get_IRR    EQU    0004h
BIH_API_Get_ISR    EQU    0005h
BIH_API_Call_Back  EQU    0006h
```

`BIH_API_EOI`	Equivalent to calling `VPICD_Phys_EOI`.

`BIH_API_Mask`	Equivalent to calling the `VPICD_Physically_Mask` service.
`BIH_API_Get_IRR`	Equivalent to calling the `VPICD_Test_Phys_Request` service. Returns carry set if the physical interrupt request is set.
`BIH_API_Get_ISR`	Retrieves the in-service state of the IRQ. Returns with carry set if the IRQ is in service.
`BIH_API_Call_Back`	Uses the Call_Priority_VM_Event service to schedule an event for the target VM specified BX. When the event callback is processed, VPICD will use nested execution services to simulate a far call to the address specified by CX:DX.

The `BIH_API_Call_Back` procedure is useful for calling routines that do not have GDT aliases or that must be executed in a specific VM. A common use of this service is to call a routine in the driver that posts a message using the PostMessage() Windows API.

Note: VMM schedules event services to process the callback in the specified VM. The callback is *not* executed synchronously. A driver should not post more than one event without notification that the event has been processed. If multiple events are posted without verifying that outstanding callbacks already exist, the VMM event services may run out of resources and crash the system.

Chapter 8

Virtualized DMA

The Virtual DMA Device (VDMAD) provides services that allow a VxD to take control of a DMA channel. A VxD using these services can intercept the DMA requests and modify the VM state causing the VM to believe that the request completed. Also, it is possible to translate or modify the VM's request before the physical state of the DMA controller is updated. Additionally, by using these services, a VxD can add another level of hardware contention management or indirectly replace portions of VDMAD's default handling.

All DMA channels are virtualized by VDMAD to map DMA requests by drivers to the physical hardware. VDMAD validates the memory region supplied by the driver, and if necessary, allocates the region from an internal DMA buffer.

Certain restrictions imposed by the DMA controller require the region management of VDMAD[1] :

- The DMA controller can only understand contiguous physical memory addresses.

- The DMA controller can not cross 64k boundaries, because the page register does not auto increment.

- The DMA controller has an address limit of 16 MB.

VDMAD breaks up requests into partial DMA transfers to satisfy these requirements. DMA buffers submitted using the auto-init mode of the DMA controller cannot be broken; consequently, these requests must be submitted with regions adhering to the restrictions.

---

[1] For simplicity, this discussion only reference the hardware with the lowest common denominator, the 8253 DMA controller. Other controllers may support advanced features, but for proper coverage by your VxD, this controller interface constrains the functionality of the DMA interface.

For this reason, auto-init-mode DMA requires special memory management on behalf of the device driver.

Note that this discussion does not cover advanced DMA topics, such as bus-mastering devices and DMA controllers supporting scatter-gather.

Physical State *vs*. Virtual State

As a VM programs the DMA controller, the controller's virtual state is updated, but state is not submitted to the hardware until the VM unmasks the channel. This is important to remember when you are debugging drivers using DMA. To display the channel status, use the debug version of Win386 supplied with VxD-Lite and query VDMAD.

After the VM has unmasked the channel, VDMAD attempts to lock the memory region, as programmed by the VM. If it is unsuccessful, VDMAD buffers the DMA transfer and modifies the DMA controller's physical state.

VDMAD uses the `VPICD_Hw_Int_Proc` service to provide a watchdog event to poll for the DMA controller's terminal count when non-auto-init-mode DMA transfers are requested. When the DMA controller has completed the request, the necessary buffers are updated (if a read operation was requested and buffers were allocated) and the VM's virtual DMA state is updated to reflect the completed transfer.

A VxD can modify the DMA controller's virtual and physical states using the `VDMAD_Set_Virt_State` and `VDMAD_Set_Phys_State` services, which are usually incorporated with a handle of DMA channel that has been virtualized by a VxD.

DMA Virtualization

A VxD uses DMA virtualization to add functionality to the base support of VDMAD. A VxD can use this virtualization to change the virtual state before the request is submitted to the hardware. To virtualize a DMA channel, a VxD uses the `VDMAD_Virtualize_` `Channel` service:

```
;
; Tell VDMAD that we want to know about this
; DMA controller.
;

  xor     eax, eax
  mov     [gdwDMAHandle], eax

  movzx   eax, gbDMAChannel
  mov     esi, OFFSET32 VSIMPLED_Virtual_DMA_Trap
```

```
VxDCall VDMAD_Virtualize_Channel
mov     [gdwDMAHandle], eax
jc      SHORT VDC_Exit_Failure
```

When a VM has changed the virtualized DMA controller's mask state, it calls the supplied procedure, in this case VSIMPLED_Virtual_DMA_Trap.

The VxD can modify the virtual state of the VM and then call the default handler, **VDMAD_Default_Handler**, to allow VDMAD to continue the region management as follows:

```
;-----------------------------------------------------------------
;    VSIMPLED_Virtual_DMA_Trap
;
;    DESCRIPTION:
;        Forces DMA_block_mode and then calls the default
;        DMA handler.
;
;-----------------------------------------------------------------

BeginProc VSIMPLED_Virtual_DMA_Trap, High_Freq

   VxDCall VDMAD_Get_Virt_State
   test    dl, DMA_requested
   jz      SHORT VDT_Exit
   test    dl, DMA_masked
   jnz     SHORT VDT_Exit

   ; Force block mode DMA, channel is requested and
   ; unmasked by the VM.

   and     dl, NOT (DMA_mode_mask)
   or      dl, DMA_block_mode

   xor     dh, dh
   VxDCall VDMAD_Set_Virt_State

VDT_Exit:
   VxDCall VDMAD_Default_Handler
   ret

EndProc VSIMPLED_Virtual_DMA_Trap
```

If necessary, a VxD can handle the actual DMA buffer translation and program the physical state of the DMA controller. This type of virtualization requires the use of the VDMAD buffer copy and region management services (listed in Appendix A).

Additionally, a VxD can translate the DMA request to a replacement interface, such as those supplied by the PCMCIA hardware implementations. Again, the VxD must virtualize the DMA channel and process the notifications from VDMAD.

Although some of the buffer management details are discussed in the next section, you should investigate the VDMAD sources provided in the Microsoft Windows 3.1 Device Driver Kit for code samples and to develop a better understanding of the operation of VDMAD.

DMA Region Mapping

As already mentioned, the primary purpose of VDMAD is to buffer DMA requests and to map the regions to memory accessible by the DMA controller. DMA region mapping is automatically performed by VDMAD on a non-virtualized channel when the DMA channel is unmasked. A VxD virtualizing a DMA channel can use these services without additional code overhead simply by calling the **VDMAD_Default_Handler**. When a non-standard interface is implemented, some or all of the region mapping services of VDMAD will be needed.

To request a DMA buffer from VDMAD and copy information from a VM to this buffer, the VxD uses the **VDMAD_Request_Buffer** and **VDMAD_Copy_To_Buffer** services:

```
;
; Request a buffer from VDMAD and copy from VM
; On entry, EAX is DMA handle, EBX is VM handle.
;

VxDCall VDMAD_Get_Virt_State
push    edx                           ; save mode for later
push    ebx                           ; save VM for later

; ESI = linear address
; ECX = count
; DL/DH = mode/flags

test    dl, DMA_requested
jnz     SHORT Buffer_New

test    dl, DMA_masked
jnz     SHORT Buffer_CleanUp

VxDCall VDMAD_Request_Buffer
jc      SHORT Error_No_Buffer

; EDX now contains the physical address of
; the DMA buffer..

test    dl, DMA_type_read
jz      SHORT Dont_Copy

; EBX = buffer handle
; ESI = linear region
; ECX = size
```

```
; EDI = offset

xor     edi, edi
VxDCall VDMAD_Copy_To_Buffer
jc      SHORT Error_Copy
```

To prepare the hardware state, the VxD updates the region information and programs the physical state to the DMA controller. The VxD starts DMA transfer by unmasking the channel:

```
Dont_Copy:
   pop     ebx
   VxDCall VDMAD_Set_Region_Info
   pop     edx
   VxDCall VDMAD_Set_Phys_State

   ; Unmask the DMA channel to begin the transfer

   VxDCall VDMAD_UnMask_Channel
```

Note that these code fragments are very simple and incomplete. For instance, the VxD does not check to see whether the region can be locked by using the **VDMAD_Lock_DMA_Region** service before requesting the buffer from VDMAD.

When a DMA channel is unmasked using the **VDMAD_UnMask_Channel** service, the ownership of the DMA channel is assigned to the requesting VM. VDMAD sets up the watchdog event to modify the virtual channel state when the terminal count is reached for non-auto-init-mode transfers. When the watchdog event determines that the channel has reached terminal count, VDMAD virtually masks it. If the operation was a DMA write operation, the buffer is copied to the VM's linear address, as supplied with **VDMAD_Set_Region_Info**. The virtual count register is updated, the channel is physically masked, and the channel owner is set to NULL.

Avoiding VDMAD Interference

VDMAD always attempts to complete the DMA transfer when the channel has been unmasked by using the **VDMAD_UnMask_Channel** service. To completely control the DMA channel in your VxD, you can virtualize the DMA channel using a NULL handling procedure and then program the DMA controller directly from your VxD. VDMAD will continue to trap the I/O range for the controller but will not update the physical state. Alternatively, you can provide a virtual DMA handling procedure and program the controller directly by using the virtual controller state information as provided by VDMAD. When using this implementation, you must avoid VDMAD services that affect the physical state or make assumptions about the ownership of the channel. Also, you need to resolve contention by other VMs in your procedure. Consult the VDMAD sources for further details.

Chapter 9

VKD and Keyboard Processing

The Virtual Keyboard Driver (VKD) provides an interface to the keyboard that allows a VxD to trap for hot keys, simulate keystrokes into a VM, and simulate a paste operation from a supplied buffer into a VM. This interface can be used to force certain actions in a VxD or to serve as form of communication between a VxD and an active application in a VM.

Hot Keys

Hot keys are registered with the VKD through the **VKD_Define_Hot_Key** service. Hot keys are enabled and disabled on a per-VM basis using the **VKD_Local_Enable_Hot_Key** and **VKD_Local_Disable_Hot_Key** services when the Local_Key flag is specified, as follows:

```
;
; Define hot keys for ctrl-pgup and ctrl-pgdn
;

    mov     al, 49h                   ; page-up
    mov     ah, ExtendedKey_B
    ShiftState <SS_Toggle_mask + SS_Either_Ctrl>, <SS_Ctrl>
    mov     cl, CallOnPress + CallOnRepeat + Local_Key
    mov     esi, OFFSET32 VSIMPLED_Hot_Key_Handler
    xor     edx, edx
    xor     edi, edi
    VxDCall VKD_Define_Hot_Key
    jc      SHORT Exit_Failure
    mov     ghhkCtrlPgUp, eax

    mov     al, 51h                   ; page-down
```

```
    mov     ah, ExtendedKey_B
    ShiftState <SS_Toggle_mask + SS_Either_Ctrl>, <SS_Ctrl>
    mov     cl, CallOnPress + CallOnRepeat + Local_Key
    mov     esi, OFFSET32 VSIMPLED_Hot_Key_Handler
    xor     edx, edx
    xor     edi, edi
    VxDCall VKD_Define_Hot_Key
    jc      SHORT Exit_Failure
    mov     ghhkCtrlPgDn, eax
```

To disable these keys by default, use the **VKD_Local_Disable_Hot_Key** service
during the **Sys_VM_Init** and **VM_Critical_Init** message processing:

```
VSIMPLED_Sys_VM_Init LABEL NEAR
BeginProc VSIMPLED_VM_Critical_Init

    mov     eax, ghhkCtrlPgUp
    VxDCall VKD_Local_Disable_Hot_Key
    mov     eax, ghhkCtrlPgDn
    VxDCall VKD_Local_Disable_Hot_Key
    clc
    ret

EndProc VSIMPLED_VM_Critical_Init
```

Once a hot key has been enabled in a VM the VxD receives a notification from VKD
whenever the hot key is pressed and processes it accordingly:

```
BeginProc VSIMPLED_Hot_Key_Handler

    push    eax

    ; Turn off hot key mode in case we're going
    ; to expand this to force keys. Don't want
    ; to be in hot key mode when forcing keys
    ; to a VM.

    VxDCall VKD_Cancel_Hot_Key_State

    cmp     al, 49h
    jne     SHORT HK_PgDn

    ;
    ; Ctrl-PgUp pressed...
    ;

    Trace_Out "Control-PgUp pressed in VM #EBX"
    jmp     SHORT HK_Exit

HK_PgDn:

    ;
    ; Ctrl-PgDn pressed...
```

```
    ;
    Trace_Out "Control-PgDn pressed in VM #EBX"

HKKH_Exit:
    pop      eax
    ret

EndProc VSIMPLED_Hot_Key_Handler
```

Simulating Keystrokes to VMs

VKD provides services to force keys to a VM's keyboard buffer, so that the VM reacts as the key had been pressed on the physical keyboard. The buffer passed to the **VKD_Force_Keys** service contains actual keyboard scan codes, such as the "key down," "key repeat," and "key up" codes.

```
;
; This code snippet just forces PgDn and PgUp
; to the VM in place of Ctrl-PgDn and Ctrl-PgUp.
;

ForceKey_Buffer_Down label byte
    db      51h, D1h
ForceKey_Buffer_Down_Len equ $-ForceKey_Buffer_Down

ForceKey_Buffer_Up label byte
    db      49h, C9h
ForceKey_Buffer_Up_Len equ $-ForceKey_Buffer_Up

BeginProc VSIMPLED_Hot_Key_Handler

    push     eax

    ; Don't want to be in hot key mode
    ; when forcing keys to a VM.

    VxDCall VKD_Cancel_Hot_Key_State

    cmp      al, 49h
    jne      SHORT HK_PgDn


    ;
    ; Ctrl-PgUp pressed...
    ;

    Trace_Out "Control-PgUp pressed in VM #EBX"

    mov      ecx, ForceKey_Buffer_Up_Len
    lea      esi, ForceKey_Buffer_Up_Len
    jmp      SHORT HK_ForceEm
```

```
HK_PgDn:

   ;
   ; Ctrl-PgDn pressed...
   ;

   Trace_Out "Control-PgDn pressed in VM #EBX"
   mov      ecx, ForceKey_Buffer_Down_Len
   lea      esi, ForceKey_Buffer_Down

HK_ForceEm:
   VxDCall VKD_Force_Keys
IFDEF DEBUG
   jnc      SHORT @F
   Debug_Out "VKD_Force_Keys failed!"

@@:
ENDIF
   pop      eax
   ret

EndProc VSIMPLED_Hot_Key_Handler
```

Using the force keys service is quite simple, but determining which scan codes to send is probably the most time-consuming part of using this interface. To make determing the scan codes simpler, I have created a simple utility that watches INT 9h and displays the keystrokes to the screen until you press the <ESC> key. The code for the KEYDISP utility can be found on the accompanying disk in the ASM\KEYDISP directory.

Chapter 10

Writing VxDs in C

The concept of writing VxDs in 'C' has been widely misunderstood. Writing VxDs in 'C' is not impossible -- on the contrary, you can do it without a great deal of grief. Forget everything anyone has every told you about writing VxDs in 'C' and open your mind. VxDs wrtten in 'C' are the wave of the future, not just a passing fad.

VMM does not look in the object code of VxDs for magical embedded notations to determine whether the code was generated by a 'C' compiler or the magical MASM 5.10B assembler. When a good 386 32-bit 'C' compiler generates the necessary code, the LINK386 linker will link the objects and generate a proper executable, which can be called a VxD.

The main hurdle to overcome when writing VxDs in 'C' is that a great portion of VMM services require either parameter passing using registers or that the mystical dynalinking macro must be used to generate the code to call VxD or VMM services. Additionally, services declared by VxDs are created with tables hidden by the VMM.INC macros and the actual procedure entry points are renamed with a new prefix. But that doesn't mean that it's time to give up and return to assembly, only that you may not be able to write all of your VxD in 'C'. Some assembly may be required: I affectionately refer to this as MASM-tape. I'll provide the MASM-tape on the accompanying disk and some instruction and you can begin writing VxDs in 'C' almost immediately, assuming you have the rest of the necessary tools. I have been successful using the WATCOM C/386 V9.5 compiler to generate flat 32-bit code. The samples included on the diskette were created using this compiler.

The limitations and restrictions of writing a VxD in 'C' include the following?

• because most VxDs have been written in assembly, interfacing to these VxDs requires external procedures written in assembly.

- Some of the debugging functionality (call logging, for example) is not available to VxD procedures written in 'C'.

- Testing and debugging is more difficult, because you must rely on the compiler code generation instead of an assembler.

Segment Attributes

VxD segments require the following specific attributes:

- All code and data segments are USE32 with the exception of the Real Mode Initialization segment, which is the only USE16 segment in the VxD executeable (excluding the stub executable).

- Initialization code and data are defined by the **_ITEXT** and **_IDATA** segments, respectively. These code segments have the segment class definition of **ICODE**.

- Pageable code and data are defined by the **_TEXT** and **_DATA** segments and have a segment class definition of **PCODE**.

- Locked code and data are defined by the **_LTEXT** and **_LDATA** segments and have a segment class definition of **LCODE**.

- Because VxDs require flat model, the 'C' compiler in question must be able to generate 32-bit flat model code.

Most compilers support the **#pragma code_seg** and **#pragma data_seg** directives. The following directives will define the necessary segments and classes:

```
// code and data segment directives for init code
#pragma code_seg( "_ITEXT", "ICODE" )
#pragma data_seg( "_IDATA", "ICODE" )

// code and data segment directives for pageable code
#pragma code_seg( "_TEXT", "PCODE" )
#pragma data_seg( "_DATA", "PCODE" )

// code and data segment directives for locked code
#pragma code_seg( "_LTEXT", "LCODE" )
#pragma data_seg( "_LDATA", "LCODE" )
```

When developing the samples in 'C' for this book, I experienced problems with the WATCOM C/386 compiler using the **#pragma code_seg** directive and was forced to use command line options to define the segment and class names (see the sample makefiles for more information). Also, some 'C' compilers may not support multiple segment declarations in a single module. You may be required to create one module for initialization code and data, another for locked code and data and another for pageable code and data.

A 'C'-callable Wrapper for VMM

A VxD entry point is defined in the Device Declaration Block (DDB) as defined in Chapter 1. The DDB is exported using a .DEF file. A typical export is as follows:

```
EXPORTS
        VSIMPLED_DDB @1
```

In order to maintain compatibility with this naming convention, the compiler must not generate the 'C'-style underscore prefix. The WATCOM C/386 compiler provides an option for disabling this namiing convention.

The DDB structure, as defined using 'C', is as follows:

```
#define DDK_Version 0x30A

typedef struct tagVxD_Desc_Block
{
   DWORD   DDB_Next ;                    // VMM reserved field
   WORD    DDB_SDK_Version  ;            // VMM reserved field
   WORD    DDB_Req_Device_Number ;       // Required device number
   BYTE    DDB_Dev_Major_Version ;       // Major device number
   BYTE    DDB_Dev_Minor_Version ;       // Minor device number
   WORD    DDB_Flags ;                   // Flags init calls complete
   BYTE    DDB_Name[ 8 ] ;               // Device name
   DWORD   DDB_Init_Order ;              // Initialization Order
   DWORD   DDB_Control_Proc ;            // Offset of control procedure
   DWORD   DDB_V86_API_Proc ;            // Offset of API procedure
   DWORD   DDB_PM_API_Proc ;             // Offset of API procedure
   DWORD   DDB_V86_API_CSIP ;            // CS:IP of API entry point
   DWORD   DDB_PM_API_CSIP ;             // CS:IP of API entry point
   DWORD   DDB_Reference_Data ;          // Ref. data from real mode
   DWORD   DDB_Service_Table_Ptr ;       // Pointer to service table
   DWORD   DDB_Service_Table_Size ;      // Number of services

} DDB ;
```

The following example declares a DDB within a 'C' module:

```
#include <vmm.h>
#include "vsimpled.h"

#pragma data_seg( "_LDATA", "CODE" )

//================================================================
//      V I R T U A L   D E V I C E   D E C L A R A T I O N
//================================================================
```

```
DDB VSIMPLED_DDB = { NULL,                    // must be NULL
                     DDK_Version,             // DDK_Version
                     VSIMPLED_Device_ID,      // Device ID
                     VSIMPLED_Major_Ver,      // Major Version
                     VSIMPLED_Minor_Ver,      // Minor Version
                     NULL,
                     "VSIMPLED",
                     Undefined_Init_Order,
                     (DWORD) vmmwrapVxDControlProc,
                     NULL,
                     NULL,
                     NULL,
                     NULL,
                     NULL,
                     NULL,
                     NULL } ;
```

To provide an interface to the register parameters for VxD control procedures, an assembly wrapper is necessary. This procedure creates a 'C' stack frame and calls the associated procedure as defined in a dispatch table:

```
//
// This table is used by the vmmwrapVxDControlProc defined
// in VMMWRAP.ASM. It lists the messages and associated
// dispatch functions, it must be terminated with -1 and NULL.
//

DISPATCHINFO alpVxDDispatchProcs[] =
   { Create_VM,            VSIMPLED_Create_VM,
     Sys_Critical_Init,    VSIMPLED_Sys_Critical_Init,
     Device_Init,          VSIMPLED_Device_Init,
     -1,                   NULL } ;
```

When the VxD control procedure is called by VMM, the vmmwrapVxDControlProc (provided by VMMWRAP.ASM) walks this table and dispatches the system message to the associated procedure. Note that vmmwrapVxDControlProc uses a linear search algorithm; consequently, the least-frequent system events should be located at end of the table. Some of the dispatch functions have slightly different prototypes, not listed here becausse the sample sources demonstrate their use and the VMMWRAP.ASM code is well documented.

The following code excerpt demonstrates a VxD initialization procedure as written in 'C':

```
#pragma data_seg( "_IDATA", "ICODE" )

//================================================================
//                        I C O D E
//================================================================

//----------------------------------------------------------------
```

```
//   BOOL VSIMPLED_Device_Init
//
//   Description:
//       This is a non-system critical initialization procedure.
//       IRQ virtualization, I/O port trapping, and VM control
//       block allocation can occur here.
//
//       Again, the same return value applies... TRUE for success,
//       FALSE for error notification.
//
//   Parameters:
//       DWORD hVM
//           System VM handle
//
//       PSTR pCmdTail
//           pointer to WIN.COM's command tail
//
//       PCRS_32 pCRS
//           pointer to System VM client register structure
//
//
//   History:    Date       Author       Comment
//               3/ 9/93    BryanW       Wrote it.
//
//-----------------------------------------------------------------
BOOL CDECL VSIMPLED_Device_Init
(
    DWORD   hVM,
    PSTR    pCmdTail,
    PCRS_32 pCRS
)
{

    UNUSED_PARAM( hVM ) ;
    UNUSED_PARAM( pCmdTail ) ;
    UNUSED_PARAM( pCRS ) ;

    vmmTraceOut( "VSIMPLED_Device_Init\r\n" ) ;

    return ( TRUE ) ;

} // end of VSIMPLED_Device_Init()
```

Wrapping VxD Services

As mentioned earlier, VxD service calls to other VxDs or VMMs use the Int 20h dynalink interface. Embedding this code throughout your VxD is inefficient, and some form of 'C' to assembly interface is necessary with some services because of register parameter passing.

VMMWRAP.ASM defines a large number of 'C' callable routines that convert stack parameters into the correct register parameter interfaces used by the various services and return the results of the service call. For example, the VMM service `List_Create` uses the ECX, EAX, and ESI registers to define a node size and flags and to return a handle to the list. It then becomes necessary to provide an C-callable interface:

```
;-----------------------------------------------------------------
;
;    DWORD PASCAL vmmListCreate( UINT uNodeSize, UINT uFlags )
;
;    DESCRIPTION:
;        Creates a new list structure.
;
;    PARAMETERS:
;        UINT uNodeSize
;
;        UINT uFlags
;            Specifies the creation flags, it can be a
;            combination of the following values:
;
;                LF_Alloc_Error, LF_Async, LF_Use_Heap
;
;    RETURN VALUE:
;        DWORD
;            handle to the list or NULL if failure
;
;-----------------------------------------------------------------

BeginProc vmmListCreate, PUBLIC

        uFlags            equ      [ebp + 8]
        uNodeSize         equ      [ebp + 12]

        push    ebp
        mov     ebp, esp

        push    esi
        push    ecx
        mov     ecx, uNodeSize
        mov     eax, uFlags

        VMMCall List_Create
        pop     ecx
        mov     eax, esi
        pop     esi
        jnc     SHORT VLC_Exit
        xor     eax, eax

VLC_Exit:
        pop     ebp
        ret     8

EndProc vmmListCreate
```

A VxD in 'C' can then call this service as follows:

```
// Create a list with elements of the type NODE
hList = vmmListCreate( sizeof( NODE ), 0 ) ;
```

Thunking Callbacks

A thunk is a piece of assembly code that fronts your 'C' procedure to map registers as passed by VMM to a 'C' stack frame and then calls your procedure. A thunk also converts the 'C' return value to the expected return value for the callback. Callbacks are used by VMM and other VxDs for notification and event processing. For example, when a V86 page is hooked, a page fault handler in the VxD is called to resolve the fault.

A thunk is created "on the fly" by a thunking procedure. Given a procedure address, a thunking procedure copies the base code, patches the necessary offsets, and returns a pointer to this piece of code. An advantage to using flat model code here is that a VxD can reference code and data with the same offset. Creating executable code with a simple heap allocation is easy, because selector restrictions are not an issue. For example, the following will create a procedure thunk for a generic VMM event callback:

```
;-------------------------------------------------------------
;
;    EVENTPROC PASCAL vmmwrapThunkEventProc( EVENTPROC pProc )
;
;    DESCRIPTION:
;        Creates a procedure thunk for VxD generic event callbacks.
;
;    PARAMETERS:
;        DWORD pProc
;            pointer to callback procedure, must have the form:
;                VOID CDECL EventProc( DWORD hVM,
;                                      DWORD dwRefData,
;                                      PCRS_32 pCRS )
;
;    RETURN VALUE:
;        EVENTPROC
;            pointer to thunk or NULL if failure
;
;-------------------------------------------------------------

BeginProc vmmwrapThunkEventProc, PUBLIC

        pCRS    equ     [ebp]
        pProc   equ     [ebp + 8]

        push    ebp
        mov     ebp, esp
```

```
        call    Allocate_Procedure_Thunk
        jc      SHORT VEProc_Failure
        jmp     SHORT VEProc_CreateThunk

;==================
; Begin thunk code

EventThunk label    byte

        push    pCRS
        push    edx                                 ; uPage
        push    ebx                                 ; hVM

        call    $
EventThunkCallAddr equ $-EventThunk
        add     esp, 12                             ; fixup for CDECL
        ret

EventThunkSize      equ     $-EventThunk
;
;End thunk code
;==================

VEProc_CreateThunk:
        push    ecx
        push    edi
        push    esi

        ;
        ; Copy the thunk...
        ;

        lea     esi, EventThunk
        mov     edi, eax
        mov     ecx, EventThunkSize
        cld
        shr     ecx, 1
        rep     movsw
        adc     cl, cl
        rep     movsb


        ;
        ; Fix it up...
        ;

        push    eax
        add     eax, EventThunkCallAddr
        mov     esi, eax
        sub     esi, 4
        sub     eax, pProc
        neg     eax
        mov     dword ptr [esi], eax
        pop     eax
```

```
        pop     esi
        pop     edi
        pop     ecx
        jmp     SHORT VEProc_Exit


VEProc_Failure:
        xor     eax, eax

VEProc_Exit:
        pop     ebp
        ret     4

EndProc vmmwrapThunkEventProc
```

To avoid page faults while executing thunk code, allocate a non-pageable memory block for a thunk table on the first call to **Allocate_Procedure_Thunk**. To simplify thunk allocation management, the allocation routine uses a fixed, maximum thunk size; this routine could be improved to be more memory efficient. The actual thunk code is embedded in the specific thunk allocation procedure. After the memory allocation for the thunk has been performed, the thunk code is copied and patched with the correct offset to the caller's provided procedure address. Thunks should be created only once per procedure, as follows:

```
// NOTE!!! pVMEMTRAP_PFault is a global pointer to the
// Page_Fault procedure thunk.

if (!pVMEMTRAP_PFault)
{
   if (pVMEMTRAP_PFault =
          vmmwrapThunkV86PHProc( VMEMTRAP_PFault ))
   else
   {
      vmmDebugOut( "Could not allocate Page_Fault thunk!\r\n" ) ;
      return ( FALSE ) ;
   }
}
vmmHookV86Page( wPage, pVMEMTRAP_PFault ) ;
return ( TRUE ) ;
```

Service Tables

Service tables are best left to assembly. Although it is possible to create a service table using 'C', there are many restrictions:

- Predefined services for replacement system drivers (such as VDD, VCD, etc.) almost always use register parameter passing. An assembly front end must be used for these procedures. There is no need to create a service table in C for these cases.

- VMM.INC uses the '@' prefix for the actual procedure name. It also generates a service number for each of the listed services. Your "public" header file must provide these definitions and your service names must be distinct from the service number defintions.

- VMM.INC creates debugging calls to watch for VMM reentrancy of non-asynchronous services. These services will not be available to your VxD's service procedures if they are written in 'C'.

A service table can be declared in 'C' as follows:

```
#define VSIMPLED_Get_Version (VSIMPLED_Device_ID) << 16 + 0x0000
#define VSIMPLED_Get_Info    (VSIMPLED_Device_ID) << 16 + 0x0001

DWORD CDECL I_VSIMPLED_Get_Version( VOID ) ;
BOOL CDECL I_VSIMPLED_Get_Info( PINFOSTRUCT ) ;

SERVICETABLE VSIMPLED_ServiceTable =
{
   I_VSIMPLED_Get_Version,
   I_VSIMPLED_Get_Info
}
```

The service table *must* be located in the locked data segment. The DDB should be contain a pointer to service table and number of services declared.

If your VxD is replacing a standard VxD, such as the Virtual Display Driver, a service interface already exists. To support this interface and to allow the VxD service procedures to be written in 'C', the service entry points are thunked using a macro, such as the following to provide an interface to the register parameters:

```
Service_Thunk   MACRO   Service_Name, Type

IFNB <Type>
   IFIDNI <Type>, <ASYNC_SERVICE>
      BeginProc Service_Name, ASYNC_SERVICE
   ELSE
      %OUT ERROR: Service_Thunk <Type> parameter must be\
ASYNC_SERVICE or undefined
      .err
   ENDIF
ELSE
   BeginProc Service_Name, SERVICE
ENDIF
      EXTRN   _&Service_Name:NEAR

IFDEF DEBUG
      Debug_Out 'In &Service_Name'
ENDIF
      pushad
      pushfd
```

```
        push    esp
        cCall   _&Service_Name
        add     esp, 4
        popfd
        popad
        ret

    EndProc Service_Name

        ENDM
```

The service thunks are defined as follows using the macro:

```
VXD_CODE_SEG

Service_Thunk    VDD_Get_Version
Service_Thunk    VDD_PIF_State
Service_Thunk    VDD_Get_GrabRtn
Service_Thunk    VDD_Hide_Cursor
Service_Thunk    VDD_Set_VMType
Service_Thunk    VDD_Get_ModTime
Service_Thunk    VDD_Set_HCurTrk
Service_Thunk    VDD_Msg_ClrScrn
Service_Thunk    VDD_Msg_ForColor
Service_Thunk    VDD_Msg_BakColor
Service_Thunk    VDD_Msg_TextOut
Service_Thunk    VDD_Msg_SetCursPos
Service_Thunk    VDD_Query_Access

;
; New services for 3.1
;

Service_Thunk    VDD_Check_Update_Soon

VXD_CODE_ENDS
```

The service table is defined as usual:

```
.xlist
        INCLUDE VMM.INC

        PUBLIC VDD_Service_Table
        Create_VDD_Service_Table EQU True

        INCLUDE VDD.INC
.list
```

Finally, a service procedure written in 'C' uses a pointer reference to the registers, as provided by the thunk, to access the parameters:

```
//-------------------------------------------------------------
//
//   VOID VDD_PIF_State
```

```
//
//   Description:
//       Informs VDD about PIF bits for newly created VM.
//
//   Parameters:
//       PREGS pRegs
//          pRegs -> ebx = VM handle
//          pRegs -> ax = PIF bits
//
//   Return (VOID):
//       Nothing.
//
//-----------------------------------------------------------------

VOID CDECL VDD_PIF_State
(
    PREGS              pRegs
)
{

    PVDDCB   pVMCB ;

    if (vmmTestSysVMHandle( pRegs -> ebx ))
        wPIFSave = (WORD) pRegs -> eax ;
    else
    {
        pVMCB = (PVDDCB) (pRegs -> ebx + dwVidCBOff) ;
        if (pVMCB -> VDD_PIF != (WORD) pRegs -> eax)
        {
            pVMCB -> VDD_PIF = (WORD) pRegs -> eax ;
            VDD_TIO_SetTrap( pRegs -> ebx, pVMCB ) ;
        }
    }

} // VDD_PIF_State()
```

VSIMPLED Sources in 'C'

The VSIMPLED VxD introduced in Chapter 1 has been rewritten in 'C' to demonstrate some of the techniques discussed in this chapter:

VSDINIT.C

```
//-----------------------------------------------------------------
//
//   Module: vsdinit.c
//
//   Purpose:
//       Init code and data for VSIMPLED.
//
//   Development Team:
//       Bryan A. Woodruff
//
```

```
//   History:    Date        Author      Comment
//               3/14/93     BryanW      Wrote it.
//
//----------------------------------------------------------------
//
//          Copyright (c) 1993 Woodruff Software Systems.
//                      All Rights Reserved.
//
//----------------------------------------------------------------

#include <vmm.h>
#include "vsimpled.h"

#pragma data_seg( "_IDATA", "ICODE" )

//================================================================
//                      I C O D E
//================================================================


//----------------------------------------------------------------
//   BOOL VSIMPLED_Sys_Critical_Init
//
//   Description:
//
//   On entry, interrupts are disabled. Critical initialization
//   for this VxD should occur here. For example, we can read
//   settings from VMM's cached copy of the SYSTEM.INI and act
//   set up our VxD as appropriate.
//
//   This procedure is called when the VxD_Control_Proc
//   dispatches the Sys_Critical_Init notification from VMM.
//
//   We can notify VMM of success or failure by returning TRUE or
//   FALSE.
//
//   Parameters:
//      DWORD hVM
//          System VM handle
//
//      DWORD dwRefData
//          reference data passed from real-mode init
//
//      PSTR pCmdTail
//          pointer to WIN.COM's command tail
//
//      PCRS_32 pCRS
//          pointer to System VM client register structure
//
//   History:    Date        Author      Comment
//               3/ 9/93     BryanW      Wrote it.
//
//----------------------------------------------------------------

BOOL CDECL VSIMPLED_Sys_Critical_Init
```

```
(
    DWORD    hVM,
    DWORD    dwRefData,
    PSTR     pCmdTail,
    PCRS_32  pCRS
)
{
    UNUSED_PARAM( hVM ) ;
    UNUSED_PARAM( dwRefData ) ;
    UNUSED_PARAM( pCmdTail ) ;
    UNUSED_PARAM( pCRS ) ;

    vmmDebugOut( "VSIMPLED_Sys_Critical_Init\r\n" ) ;
    return ( TRUE ) ;

} // end of VSIMPLED_Sys_Critical_Init()

//-----------------------------------------------------------------
//   BOOL VSIMPLED_Device_Init
//
//   Description:
//       This is a non-system critical initialization procedure.
//       IRQ virtualization, I/O port trapping, and VM control
//       block allocation can occur here.
//
//       Again, the same return value applies: TRUE for success,
//       FALSE for error notification.
//
//   Parameters:
//       DWORD hVM
//           System VM handle
//
//       PSTR pCmdTail
//           pointer to WIN.COM's command tail
//
//       PCRS_32 pCRS
//           pointer to System VM client register structure
//
//
//   History:    Date       Author       Comment
//               3/ 9/93    BryanW       Wrote it.
//
//-----------------------------------------------------------------
BOOL CDECL VSIMPLED_Device_Init
(
    DWORD    hVM,
    PSTR     pCmdTail,
    PCRS_32  pCRS
)
{

    UNUSED_PARAM( hVM ) ;
    UNUSED_PARAM( pCmdTail ) ;
```

```
   UNUSED_PARAM( pCRS ) ;

   vmmTraceOut( "VSIMPLED_Device_Init\r\n" ) ;

   return ( TRUE ) ;

} // end of VSIMPLED_Device_Init()

//----------------------------------------------------------------
//  End of File: vsdinit.c
//----------------------------------------------------------------
```

VSIMPLED.C

```
//----------------------------------------------------------------
//
//   Module: vsimpled.c
//
//   Purpose:
//      A simple VxD written in 'C'.
//
//   Development Team:
//      Bryan A. Woodruff
//
//   History:    Date        Author        Comment
//               3/ 9/93     BryanW        Wrote it.
//
//----------------------------------------------------------------
//
//          Copyright (c) 1993 Woodruff Software Systems.
//                     All Rights Reserved.
//
//----------------------------------------------------------------

#include <vmm.h>
#include "vsimpled.h"

#pragma data_seg( "_LDATA", "CODE" )

//================================================================
//        V I R T U A L   D E V I C E   D E C L A R A T I O N
//================================================================

DDB VSIMPLED_DDB = { NULL,                      // must be NULL
                     DDK_Version,               // DDK_Version
                     VSIMPLED_Device_ID,        // Device ID
                     VSIMPLED_Major_Ver,        // Major Version
                     VSIMPLED_Minor_Ver,        // Minor Version
                     NULL,
                     "VSIMPLED",
                     Undefined_Init_Order,
                     (DWORD) vmmwrapVxDControlProc,
```

```
                        NULL,
                        NULL,
                        NULL,
                        NULL,
                        NULL,
                        NULL,
                        NULL } ;

//
// This table is used by the vmmwrapVxDControlProc.
// It lists the messages and associated dispatch functions. It
// must be terminated with -1 and NULL.
//

DISPATCHINFO alpVxDDispatchProcs[] =
    { Sys_Critical_Init,    VSIMPLED_Sys_Critical_Init,
      Device_Init,          VSIMPLED_Device_Init,
      Create_VM,            VSIMPLED_Create_VM,
      -1,                   NULL } ;

//-----------------------------------------------------------------
//  BOOL CDECL VSIMPLED_Create_VM( DWORD hVM, PCRS_32 pCRS )
//
//  Description:
//    Notification when VMs (other than system VM) are created.
//
//  Parameters:
//     hVM
//        VM handle
//
//     pCRS
//        pointer to client register structure
//
//  History:    Date      Author      Comment
//              3/ 9/93   BryanW      Wrote it.
//
//-----------------------------------------------------------------

BOOL CDECL VSIMPLED_Create_VM( DWORD hVM, PCRS_32 pCRS )
{
    UNUSED_PARAM( hVM ) ;
    UNUSED_PARAM( pCRS ) ;

    vmmTraceOut( "VSIMPLED_Create_VM\r\n" ) ;

    return ( TRUE ) ;

} // end of VSIMPLED_Create_VM()

//-----------------------------------------------------------------
//  End of File: vsimpled.c
//-----------------------------------------------------------------
```

Chapter 11

Using the Debugging Services

Debugging services are some of the most important, but least used, services of the VMM. The debugging services provide important feedback during the operation of your VxD. The debug version of WIN386, through the debugger interface, provides key information that can help you track down even the most difficult bugs. A better understanding of the debug services and VMM's debugging interface can save you time and frustration.

Debug Strings

The most commonly used macros are Debug_Out and Trace_Out which expand to calls to the **Out_Debug_String** service. Debug_Out also embeds an INT 1 in the code to cause a debugger break after displaying the string.

Debug trace strings are useful when you are tracking the last action before a crash or the watching execution path of code. Trace_Out is particularly well-suited to this. Debug_Out is most commonly used when an assertion fails or some other unexpected event occurs.

In Windows 3.1, the Mono_Out and Mono_Out_At macros call the **Out_Mono_String** service to display a string on the monochrome display. The **Out_Mono_String** service offers you a fast memory write so you don't have to wait for the serial port when using the WDEB386 debugger. This is excellemt for high frequency debug strings in such places as interrupt handlers.

The Queue_Out macro calls the **Queue_Debug_String** service, which queues a message string until it is retrieved by the **.lq** command from the debugger interface. This is useful when multiple debug traces are occuring and scrolling from view. The Queue_Out macro lets you to record events and display them at your convenience.

Assertions

The DEBUG.INC header file includes a few useful assertions that are only available in a debug build of your VxD. Some of these services may not be available in the retail build of WIN386. See Appendix A for details.

Assert_VM_Handle	Verifies that the provided register or memory location contains a valid VM handle.
Assert_Cur_VM_Handle	Verifies that the provided register or memory location contains the current VM handle.
Assert_Client_Ptr	Verifies that the provided register or memory location points to the client register structure of the current VM.
Assert_Ints_Disabled	Verifies that interrupts are disabled.
Assert_Ints_Enabled	Verifies that interrupts are enabled.

Extended Debug Commands

Extended debug commands are available in the debug version of WIN386 through the .VMM command from a debugger prompt. The following menu appears when you invoke this command:

```
V M M    D E B U G    I N F O R M A T I O N A L    S E R V I C E S

[A]   System time
[B]   Time-slice information/profile
[C]   Dyna-link service profile information
[D]   Reset dyna-link profile counts
[E]   I/O port trap information
[F]   Reset I/O profile counts
[G]   Turn procedure call trace logging on
[H]   V86 interrupt hook information
[I]   PM interrupt hook information
[J]   Reset PM and V86 interrupt profile counts
[K]   Display event lists
[L]   Display device list
[M]   Display V86 break points
[N]   Display PM break points
[O]   Display interrupt profile
[P]   Reset interrupt profile counts
[Q]   Display GP fault profile
[R]   Reset GP fault profile counts
[S]   Toggle Adjust_Exec_Priority Log AND DISPLAY
[T]   Reset Adjust_Exec_Priority Log info
[U]   Toggle verbose device call trace
```

```
[V]  Fault Hook information
Enter selection or [ESC] to exit:
```

The information available through this interface is quite extensive and specific to VMM. For example, the time slice command displays the following:

```
# VMs scheduled = 02
# idle VMs = 01
Time-Slice focus VM = 804A1000
Scheduled VM     = 804A1000

Time slice size = 00000014
Timer period    = 14

804A1000 background
    Fgd=0064, Bkgd=0032, %CPU=71(dec), Tick Weight=00000016,
Total=00004EB6
8071E000 background high-pri-bkgd idle
    Fgd=0064, Bkgd=0028, %CPU=28(dec), Tick Weight=00000038,
Total=00000DC8
```

Additionally, the following additional dot (.) commands are available in the debug version of VMM:

```
.VM [#] ------ Displays complete VM status
.VC [#] ------ Displays the current VMs control block
.VH ---------- Displays the current VM handle
.VR [#] ------ Displays the registers of the current VM
.VS [#] ------ Displays the current VM's virtual mode stack
.VL ---------- Displays a list of all valid VM handles
.T  ---------- Toggles the trace switch
.S  [#] ------ Displays short logged exceptions starting at #
.SL [#] ------ Displays long logged exceptions
.LQ ---------- Display queue outs from most recent
.DS ---------- Dumps the protected mode stack with labels
.MH [handle] - Displays Heap information
.MM [handle] - Displays Memory information
.MV ---------- Displays VM Memory information
.MS PFTaddr -- Display PFT info
.MF ---------- Display Free List
.MI ---------- Display Instance data info
.ML LinAddr -- Display Page table info for given linear address
.MP PhysAddr - Display ALL Linear addrs that map the given addr
.MD ---------- Change debug MONO paging display
.MO ---------- Set a page out of all present pages
.VMM --------- Menu VMM state information
.<dev_name> -- Display device specific info
```

One of the most useful commands is the exception tracing option. To turn tracing on, use the `.T` command:

```
##.t
start tracing

##.s
stop tracing
exceptions logged = 00000C9D
00000C9D: OUT   804A1000 02 EI VMM   800E097E
00000C9C: 0050  804A1000 02 EI VMM   800E097E
00000C9B: 0006  804A1000 02 EI V86 2586:2230
00000C9A: OUT   804A1000 02 DI V86 C803:0A05
00000C99: 0006  804A1000 03 EI V86 2586:2230
00000C98: OUT   804A1000 03 DI V86 FFFF:0BEB
00000C97: 0006  804A1000 04 DI V86 265F:14A0
00000C96: OUT   804A1000 04 EI V86 D800:04A1
00000C95: 001A  804A1000 04 EI V86 D800:04A1 INT  1A      00000004
00000C94: OUT   804A1000 04 EI V86 D800:04A1
00000C93: 001A  804A1000 04 EI V86 D800:04A1 INT  1A      0000008C
00000C92: OUT   804A1000 04 EI V86 0486:0EF0
00000C91: 0050  804A1000 04 EI V86 0486:0EF0 INT  50      00000308
00000C90: OUT   804A1000 04 DI V86 1024:0F3C
00000C8F: 0013  804A1000 03 EI V86 FFFF:0BEB INT  13      00000308
00000C8E: OUT   804A1000 02 DI V86 B1AD:0031
00000C8D: 002A  804A1000 02 DI V86 B1AD:0031 INT  2A      00008200
00000C8C: OUT   804A1000 02 DI V86 C803:0A05
00000C8B: 0006  804A1000 02 EI V86 2586:2230
00000C8A: OUT   804A1000 02 DI V86 B1AD:0031
00000C89: 002A  804A1000 02 DI V86 B1AD:0031 INT  2A      00008200
```

The exception log shows 0xC9B exceptions during the short period that the system is allowed to run. To display details about an exception, use the .sl command:

```
##.sl c8b
stop tracing
Show exception 00000C8B
00000C8B: 0006  804A1000 02 EI V86 2586:2230

V86 Fault 0006   VM_Handle = 804A1000       00000C8B
AX=00007000   CS=2586  IP=00002230  FS=0000
BX=00000005   SS=0BCC  SP=00000190  GS=0000       TIME=00000096:1930
CX=0000001A   DS=9E9B  SI=0000003F  BP=0000201A
DX=0000001A   ES=0000  DI=00004000  FL=00033202
```

This fault occured in V86 mode and was an invalid opcode (exception 6). To learn why an invalid opcode occur, we need to look at the dissassembly:

```
##u &2586:2230
&2586:00002230 6380fc90     arpl    word ptr [bx+si+90fc],ax
```

Obviously, an arpl is not a valid V86 instruction. This arpl instruction is really a V86 break point. To demonstrate that this assumption is valid and to find the owner, we can use the **M** command (Display V86 break points) in the VMM debugging interface:

```
  CS:IP      Hit Count   Ref Data   Procedure
2586:2230    00002D76    00000031   @Resume_Exec + 2a
```

The owner of this break point is the the **Resume_Exec** service, which probably means that this fault was generated as the result of V86 nested execution in the VM.

As you can see, using of the debug version of WIN386 is essential to tracking down problems with your VxD. Some additional helpful debugging tips:

- Always run the debug version of WIN386.EXE during your development and test cycle, however painful it may be. Although this version may be slower, it is much more informative than the retail version. The debug version of VMM will let you know when you've done bad things to the system.

- Use the debug string services to output information during essential operations of your VxD. Watch for return codes and use **Debug_Out** when something unexpected occurs.

- If you suspect that code in a particular VM is causing problems with your VxD, use the **.VL** and **.VM** commands to display the VM status and then set a break point at the current CS:IP. Restart the system and trace through the VM's code.

- Become familar with the **P** (step into) and **T** (trace into) commands of the WDEB386 debugger or similar commands in your favorite debugger. Watching the code as it executes (especially with nested execution) is essential to locating problems.

- Never treat a system hang as the end of the world. Restart the system, turn on exception tracing, reproduce the problem, and break into the debugger. You should find that the exception tracing will assist in pin-pointing the problem. Once you become familiar with the fault sequences under normal operation of the system, you should be able to look at an exception log and find the areas of interest.

- Load the symbols for the debugger, including WIN386.SYM and any core components of the Windows GUI that may be of interest, such as KRNL386.SYM. Once you've located an address that may be causing problems, you can locate the nearest symbol by using the **LN** (list near symbols) debugger command.

SECTION III

Putting It All Together

Chapter 12

VCOMMD Design Notes

Unfortunately, some of the best example programs are not themselves terribly usable. That holds for the example here: While it is useful as a teaching tool, I strongly recommend against actually using it in your system.

The following program virtualizes the COM1 port. One of the biggest problems with WIN386 today is the multitude of hardware cards, mostly used for communication of one type or another (modem, fax, network, tape,and so forth), that attempt to run without a VxD. I chose this topic in the hope that, by focusing on this particular problem, more hardware vendors will provide VxDs for their cards.

This driver does not fully replace the VCD. It virtualizes the COMM port and can be used instead of the VCD by DOS apps. However, it does not include the calls required to support Windows COMM drivers, so it cannot be used by Windows programs that talk to the Windows COMM API.

Design

To determine the goals of our COMM device. We need to virtualize the COMM port. If at all possible, we want to allow several applications to use the port simultaneously. Many applications should be able to read the state of the port and even set the communication parameters, even if they are not going to talk over the line.

We can fully virtualize all of the ports except for the actual data port. Because we cannot virtualize the actual data port, we have to make sure that only one application can talk on the line at any given time. If two try to talk at the same time, we have to let the user decide which application can use the port.

We also need to reflect interrupts into the proper VM, which is an expensive operation, so we want to make sure that we only do it if absolutely necessary. We can establish this by watching the value that the application writes to the Interrupt Enable Register and by trapping when the application does an EOI. Also, since emulation has so much overhead, we need to define a new interface that is directly callable from DOS, Windows, and other VxDs, is designed to allow block I/O (which is much faster than handling things on a byte-by-byte basis), and implements an open and close on the port so that we know when an app is done with the port. This eliminates the need to handle contention problems.

So, while we emulate to support existing applications, we also create a new API that works a lot more efficiently in a WIN386 world. If you write the only code that touches your card, then you should consider creating just the new interface. In this case, you still want to trap on your ports, so that other applications cannot write to them by mistake.

The Code

Declare_Virtual_Device sets up our VxD. RS232_DEVICE_ID is an identification number Microsoft has assigned to me personally; do not use it in any of your own VxDs. I use this same number for other VxDs I write about. The init order is set to VCD_Init_Order+1, so that RS232 loads before VCD, allowing us to get the IRQ and ports instead of VCD.

VidComIrq

VidComIrq is the data structure required by VPICD_Virtualize_IRQ to grab the IRQ. ComHwInt is called on each IRQ that comes in. Because we reflect the IRQ into a VM, we need ComEoi. ComEoi is called when the VM does an EOI. We then do a VPICD_Phys_EOI.

Finally, when we are reflecting interrupts to a VM, we want to be careful to not use up all of their stack. Therefore, rather than simulating another IRQ when the VM does an EOI, we wait until their IRQ handler does an iret, completely unusing the stack, before we send in another one. We use ComIret, which is called after the VM does an iret to emulate the next pending IRQ.

When VPICD receives an interrupt, it masks the interrupt off and sends an EOI. It then reflects the IRQ to our VxD. When we do a VPICD_Phy_EOI, the VPICD unmasks the interrupt. This has two important ramifications. First, another interrupt can then occur immediately, and we can see it as soon as we unmask it. Second, if we never EOI, the interrupt is never unmasked, and we never see it again.

The Buffers

When a byte comes in on the data port, we want to read it before the next data byte overwrites it. A VM cannot always respond this quickly. While we usually must be able to reflect data to the VM as fast as it comes in, we can't do this on every byte, something like the argument on polling versus. using an interrupt to handle an asynchronous line. Therefore, all reads and writes are done within the VxD using buffers. All port emulation read and writes also go to the buffers. Both the read and write buffers are circular buffers. If the read and write pointers point to the same location, the buffer is empty. There is no buffer overrun check because a check would create the possibility of losing old or new data: If we ignore the problem, we lose old data. The result is the same — the program still runs but data is lost. (Granted, we lose more data this way, but if we lose any data, we are generally in trouble.) This eliminates the performance hit of checking the buffer size on each read and write.

The read buffer needs of three bytes for each data byte received. For each data byte, we first read the two status registers and store them. We then read the data byte and store it. We read the status bytes first so that the line status shows the data byte. By saving all three bytes, the calling application can get the status for each data byte.

Other Data

Next comes a number of jmp tables. These are used at various places within the code to quickly jmp to the proper function.

bInVmIrq is a count of how many IRQs sent to the VM have not yet returned. Sending several at once is not a problem, as long as we don't overflow the VM's stack. This count should never go over 2.

bIntEnb holds the value of the Interrupt Enable Register as set by the VM that owns the port. Regardless of the value set, the hardware always has bits 0011b set. If the app in the VM has not set these bits, we do not want the performance hit of emulating an IRQ. Therefore, we use the values in bIntEnb to see whether we need to reflect an IRQ.

ComSysCritInit

We do all of our initialization during Sys_Critical_Init. This allows us to get on the IRQ and ports while no interrupts are occurring. We first use Allocate_Device_CB_Area to get some per VM data. We can then access this data by adding the returned value to the VM handle.

Next we take over the eight COM1 I/O ports. If we cannot take over all of them, we return with carry set, which tells WIN386 not to load our VxD. If we don't own all of the ports, we are in conflict with another VxD (this is why VCD will fail to load if you load this VxD).

Following that, we take over IRQ4. In a commercial VxD, both the port numbers and the IRQ should be able to be overridden by values in system.ini. You can read system.ini by using Get_Profile_String. This allows you to change settings if the board is reconfigured. Once we have both the ports and the IRQ, we know we can run.

Now, we hook interrupts 21h, 23h, and 24h, so that we can take ownership of the port away from a VM if it terminates. While interrupts 23h and 24h do not guarantee that an app has terminated, an app can terminate in this manner.

Finally, we initialize the COM hardware, turning the interrupts on and enabling the transmit and receive interrupts.

Port Trapping

Trapping is where half the work of emulating the port occurs (the other half is the IRQ emulation). ComIoPortTrap is the common entry point. If the call comes from the VM that owns the port, the logic is quite simple.

First we call Emulate_Non_Byte_IO. If we get a request for non-byte I/O (word, dword, string), this macro breaks it into byte-sized calls. Since I don't foresee anyone actually using these calls, I use the emulate macro. If an app is likely to do a string of 512 bytes, you will want to handle it yourself. The overhead of Emulate_Non_Byte_IO is significant.

Next, we clear the direction flag. (If we don't we will get annoying, time-consuming intermittent bug.)

Then, if we don't take the jmp, we build the jmp vector offset. This takes into account the sizes of the read and write tables, as well as the specific values of ECX for reads and writes. We then jmp to the proper function, so that the ret from that function will take us directly back to WIN386.

Any call, jmp, or ret flushes the on-board cache on the 386 & 486, so we want to minimize these. Conditional jmps that are not taken do not flush the cache. That's why ComIoPortTrap has a single jmp for the common code path throughout this code. Generally, emulation code is never fast enough, so you do everything you can to speed it up.

If the calling VM doesn't own the port, we need to decide what to do. If no one owns the port, we can assign it to the calling VM. It would probably be better to assign the port to the first VM that accessed the data port; instead it is assigned to the first app to hit the port at all. We then initialize the port to the values we were holding in our instance data. If the app has written those values (while another app owned the port), it expects the hardware to be in a certain configuration. If someone else owns the port, we fake it, providing it is not a data read/write, by reflecting it back to the port-specific function which handles this. The one exception is I/O to 3F8h, when it is set to be the baud rate instead of the data port. That is handled in-line.

If we have a data I/O and someone else owns the port, we have to decide who gets it. If the owner app used the new API, they keep the port. This not only gives apps an incentive to use the new API but leaves the API with the app that will free up its use as soon as it is done. Use a contention prompt when you think the owner may be done but are not sure.

Otherwise, we put up a contention MessageBox using SHELL_Resolve_Contention. This call puts up a box asking the user to pick between the two VMs by using their window titles to ID them (which usually both read MS-DOS Prompt). If the user picks the new one, the ownership is switched. The one that is not picked is marked as FAILED so we don't keep prompting every time it tries to read/write a byte.

IoRead

In IoRead8 all input goes through the buffer. Therefore, the first thing we do is look for bytes in the buffer. If the buffer is empty, we return a 0; otherwise, we get the data byte from the buffer, inc the read pointer to the next set of data, and return the byte. Notice that we only take a conditional jmp if the pointer wrapped. This eliminates jmps from the common code path. We only get to IoRead8 if the DLAB bit is off (its the data byte). ComIoPortTrap handles virtualizing the low byte baud rate in 3F8h.

IoRead9 is doubly tricky. If the DLAB bit is set in register 3FBh, then register 9 is the high byte of the baud rate. If it is not set, it is the bitmap of the interrupts we have enabled. If it is the interrupts, we have to return the values the app set, which may be different from the actual values since we force the transmit and receive interrupts on.

First we test to see whether we own the port. If not, we jmp to the end of the function to return the information from our instance data. On a write to 3F9h, we save these values so we return what the app expects. If DLAB is set, we read the port and return the value. If DLAB is not set, we return the value in bIntEnb so that the app receives the valueit expects.

IoReadA is completely faked. We know which IRQ we sent down to the app and return the appropriate value. If we did not send an IRQ down, we either return 001b (receive IRQ) if we have data or return nothing if we do not. IoReadB and IoReadC, on the other hand, are both quite simple. If the app owns the port, we read from the hardware. If not, we read from the instance data.

IoReadD returns the line status. It tells us whether we can read or write a byte and whether there are any errors. If the calling app owns the port, we return data from the read buffer. If the read buffer is empty, we read the actual port. But if the calling app does not own the port, we return 00011110b which tells the app that the transmit buffer is full (the app cannot write), the receive buffer is empty (the app cannot read), and all error bits are on. This seems to be the best way to get the point across to the app that it is not going to have any luck with this port.

IoReadE is straightforward. If the calling app does not own the port, we use our instance data. If it does own the port, we get the data from the read buffer. If the read buffer is empty, we read from the hardware.

IoReadPort (used only for port F) just reads from the hardware if the calling app owns the port. If the caller does not own the port, it returns 0. This port is undefined for the 8250, so we can't virtualize it.

IoWrite

IoWrit8 copies the data to the write buffer and increments its pointer. Again, it uses two jmps if the pointer wrapped to avoid jmps when the pointer does not wrap. If the output buffer was empty, we call IrqTransmit to send the byte to the hardware.

IoWrit9, like IoRead9, is tricky. If the write is from an app that does not own the port, we copy the value to the instance data for that VM. We do this for both the interrupt enable and the high-baud registers (both of which use this port). We use the instance data for the line control register to determine whether DLAB is set. If the app owns the port, and it is writing to the interrupt enable register, we save the value in bIntEnb and then 'or' it with 0011b. This forces an IRQ to receive empty and transmit full, which we need for our buffering code. We then write the byte to the hardware.

IoWritB and IoWritC are both quite simple. If the calling app does not own the port, we copy the value to the instance data for that VM. If the app does own the port, we write to the hardware. IoWritPort (used for ports A, D, E, and F) goes directly to the port if the calling app owns the port. Writing to these ports is undefined for the 8250, so we cannot virtualize it.

IRQ Trapping

We trap the IRQ for two reasons. First, we need to see the interrupts when the transmit buffer is empty or the receive buffer is full for our buffering. Second, we need to reflect the interrupts down to the app that owns the port if it has enabled the interrupts that come in. When the interrupt handler is called, interrupts are off. We want to turn them on as soon as possible, because there may be other IRQs. When we turn them on, our IRQ remains masked until we call VPICD_Phys_EOI, so we do not need to worry about being re-entered. Since we do not need interrupts off for any reason, the first instruction is an STI.

On calls to us, the direction flag is in an unknown state. We clear it so that mov instructions will increment the pointers.

In ComHwInt we determine the correct handler to call based on the value in port 3FAh. We use this value to determine which offset in IrqTabl to jmp to. We jmp so that the ret in the called function returns directly back to WIN386.

In IrqReceive we first go into a loop that reads the data port until it is empty. We loop because the 16550 has a 16-byte FIFO and we could get multiple bytes. Doing this in this loop is much faster than getting each IRQ invividually. We read the status ports first so that the line status will show that we have a data byte. After reading in the data, we call VPICD_Phys_EOI, which causes the IRQ to be unmasked (remember, it has already been EOIed). Its critical to do this as soon as possible so that we can get to the next interrupt quickly. This separates talking to the port from virtualizing it.

Now we need to virtualize the IRQ down to the VM. We only do this if we are not already in the middle of reflecting an IRQ. We also make sure we have data in our buffer. Finally, we don't reflect it if the app didn't turn on that interrupt. We then call VPICD_Set_Int_Request, which attempts to reflect the IRQ immediately, otherwise it will reflect it as soon as possible.

Finally, if we have set up a callback function, we set up an event to call the app back. We need to set up an event because we received the IRQ as an asynchronous event, limiting what we can do. We may not even be in the proper VM (remember, a VxD is always running in a VM, but which particular VM it is running on can change). If a fast response is critical, you may want to use Critical_Section_Boost instead of Cur_Run_VM_Boost.

IrqTransmit works basically the same way as IrqReceive. IrqModemStaus and IrqLineStatus are used merely to reflect the interrupts down to the VM. Our driver itself doesn't care about these.

VmCallBack is very simple. We pass a parameter in EAX which is the appropriate value in port 3FAh, letting the called app know whether the callback is due to a non-empty receive buffer or an empty transmit buffer. We then put the callback address in CX:EDX and use the Simulate_Far_Call to set up the stack and Resume_Exec to make the call. Don't forget the Client_State and Nest_Exec calls — without them it will not work.

ComEoi is called when the app does an EOI sends an EOI to the PIC. We have to call VPICD_Clear_Int_Request to end the IRQ in that VM.

ComIret is called after the IRQ handler in a VM has completed the iret call in the interrupt handler called when we called VPICD_Set_Int_Request. At this point we call VPICD_Set_Int_Request if we have data in our buffers and the app wants the IRQs. We do it here so that we do not eat up the app's stack by having IRQs come in on top of each other.

Com_Api_Proc

Com_V86_API_Proc and Com_PM_API_Proc are the entry points when a real or protected mode app calls us via the int 2F call. In the initial functions, we have to convert any pointers to flat 32-bit pointers. We then jmp to Com_API_Proc.

Com_API_Proc copies the values for ECX and EDX that the app passed us to ECX and EDX and then calls the appropriate function. On return, it copies EAX, ECX, and EDX back to the client area on the stack, so that, on return, the calling app gets these return values. The actual calls here are simple. ComOpen and ComClose give apps a way to ask for the port and relinquish it when they are done. This eliminates the need for a contention MessageBox and for guessing when an app is done with the port.

ComRead and ComWrite essentially copy their data from and into the buffers and return. Doing read/writes of blocks of data is faster than emulating on a byte-by-byte basis and avoids buffer overruns.

VM Creation and Destruction

ComVmTerminate is called every time a VM is terminated. When a VM owns the port, it obviously will not need it any more, so we clear the ownership and call-back address.

ComVmCreate is called every time a VM is created (except the system VM). On creation, we set the instance data to 1200,n,8,1.

ComInt21 and ComInt23_24 are used to determine when to take away ownership of a port. If a program exits, we want to take away its ownership. An app can end with to an int 23 or int 24. It can also end with an int 21, function 4Ch, 31h, or 00h. We take away ownership on an EXEC call.

The Total VxD

When you first look at the total VxD it may seem overwhelming. But if you break it into its component pieces, it becomes easy. The trick is to build the pieces one at a time.

First, build the core code that will talk to the hardware. Once you get this to work, decide which is more critical, the new API or the emulation, and build in that part. Then, build the other. As you do this, you need to keep a couple of things in mind.

First, it is absolutely critical that your VxD performs all communication to the physical hardware. Do not let even the smallest part of it be handled directly by an application. For example, port 3FFh is undefined for the 8250. My VxD emulates it and only allows the app that owns the port to access it, rather than assuming that no one will access it. By the same token, port 3FBh is called very rarely, and I probably could have not trapped it. In that case, another VM could have written to it, changing the behavior of the port, and I would never know. Thus, you handle all of the hardware from your VxD for both speed and security reasons.

Create a new API using the direct call in capability. It is much more efficient than trapping ports, interrupts, an so on. While you will still emulate the old API, you will have a much more efficient approach for new code. Also, try to minimize the number of times you have to make calls. Don't make calls to write one byte at a time—have a call to write a block of data. In most situations, you can write 1 to 4 K as quickly as one byte.

Your emulation must average a certain speed, depending on what you are doing. However, if at 9600 baud the buffers in this VxD slowly fill up, its average speed is slower than 9600 baud. Your either have is to make your emulation faster or live with the limits. Generally you should find that there is only so much you can do to speed up emulation. Emulating a port is a big hit, and emulating an IRQ is a gigantic hit. Compared to real mode, emulation speed versus actual hardware speed is a difference in orders of magnitude. However, in this case, all is not lost. First, you can also trap software interrupts, which is faster than trapping ports and generally eliminates the need for IRQ emulation. In the example of this driver, we could trap int 14h. Unfortunately, most applications don't use int 14h, but we could be faster with those that do. Second, in the case of the this VxD, while we talk to a 8250, we could emulate a 16550 with a FIFO buffer. On an IRQ, an app can read multiple bytes, eliminating the IRQs for all those bytes. By the same token, just because you are written for a specific device does not mean you can't emulate another device more efficiently.

Chapter 13

Win-Link Design and Implementation Notes

Now it's time to look at how you can use VxDs to pull tricks in the real world. We'll use Win-Link as an example. As with many real-world projects, I had several reasons for writing this program.

The first part arose when I was having lunch with a number of other authors shortly before the launch of Windows 3.1. They complained that Windows was not 32-bit and was not pre-emptively multi-tasked, while OS/2 was. I immediately set about to refute this. Although little known at the time, Windows 3.1 did have support in it for 32-bit programs. Granted it was minimal and required assembler at first but it did exist (and it is what Win32 uses).

But that left OS/2 as the pre-emptively multi-tasked O/S. So I pointed out that the DOS boxes were pre-emptively multi-tasked under Windows. If a Windows app could talk to a DOS app in a DOS box and have the DOS app do the heavy work, then the Windows app would essentially be multi-tasked.

It made an interesting argument. Almost everyone at lunch was willing to concede that a Windows app could be multi-tasked. But it made me wonder how this could be implemented.

At the same time, there were a couple of features of Windows 3.1 that I found frustrating. When I am in a DOS box and type the name of a Windows program, it tells me that I need Windows to run it. Well, what does it think is running? When typing in the name of a Windows EXE from a DOS box, I want it to run that EXE. I also found the title of DOS boxes a little less than desirable. ALT-TABing through five windows, all called **MS-DOS Prompt**, usually did not tell me which DOS box was running Brief. I wanted the name of the program. And while I was at it, I had one more pet peeve: You can only print from one DOS box or Windows at a time. The DOS boxes don't spool their printing — they are dedicated to it until the printing completes. Yet Windows has a nice spooler. Everything was there — I just wanted the DOS boxes to print to the Windows spooler. Then all the DOS boxes could print simultaneously — and do it quickly to the spooler.

Out if this came Win-Link, so named because it linked Windows and DOS applications. Win-Link is essentially two programs in one. First, it provides Interprocess Communication between Windows and DOS boxes as well as shared memory. Second, it extends the User Interface of Windows by (1) launching Windows applications (and additional DOS boxes) from a DOS box, (2) listing the running program as the title of a Windows DOS box, and (3) sending all printer output from DOS boxes to the WIndows spooler.

Implementing this was a killer. First of all, a number of the major concepts had not been tried before. While everything should have worked, only one implementation that actually did. In addition, there were a myriad of little details necessary to getting it right. Because the code intercepted calls in every DOS box and made asynchronous calls to Windows, every detail had to be right or the entire system would hang. or worse.

This chapter laysout the basic capabilities of the program to give you a clear picture of what the code is trying to accomplish. Then it details the specific logic used to implement each of these pieces, building on the previous pieces where appropiate. Finally, it walks through and explains the actual code. This chapter does not try to teach you anything general about writing VxDs. Instead, by concentrating on the specifics of a piece of real-world code that pulls a number of interesting hacks, you can learn from it by example.

The System

How does a Windows or DOS app know which DOS box it wants to send a message to? When a DOS box is launched, there is no way to identify it, so each DOS app must register itself with Win-Link when it starts up and unregister itself when it is exiting. An application can also make a call to get the VM handle for an application based on its ID. Therefore, a Windows or DOS application can launch a DOS application and keep polling until it finds the registered application (it needs to keep polling because the new DOS box needs enough time slices to start up and execute the app to the point it registers itself).

We know how a Windows app can launch a DOS box. However, how does a DOS app launch another DOS box (as opposed to spawning a process)? We add a call allowing a DOS app to launch another DOS app. The parameters are similiar to spawning, but instead of spawning in the same VM, Win-Link starts a new VM and runs the app.

Next we need a way to pass messages back and forth. On the Windows side we already have a system, so we merely give DOS boxes a way to call PostMessage. In the other direction, and for between DOS boxes, we have our own message queue. It has three calls, MsgPost to post a message to a VM, MsgPeek to look at a message sent to a VM, and MsgRead to read a message posted to a VM. Unlike Windows messages, these messages can't send pointers, because they are in different address spaces. So we provide two ways to pass blocks of data between VMs. MsgMemCopy copies data from memory in one VM to memory in another VM. MsgMemCopy automatically knows whether the each of the VMs is in V86 or protected mode and interprets the segment/selector appropriately. There are calls to allocate and free LDTs/GDTs for memory in a VM. While real-mode DOS applications cannot access these selectors, Windows apps as well as protected-mode DOS apps can. So a DOS app can pass a LDT to the Windows app to some of its memory. Then both applications can access the memory. These calls give applications a way to communicate with each other between VMs.

Two other sets of calls are provided to DOS applications. Win-Link provides a call to let a DOS application set its Window title. For example, when Brief running, having B is preferrable to **MS-DOS Prompt**, `Brief - [filename.c]` is even nicer. Win-Link also provides a set of calls for printing. While DOS printer output is captured fairly efficiently, again all Win-Link can show for a print job is the name of the application printing the job. By adding a call to open the job, the application can display the name of the document being printed in the Windows spooler. Also, Win-Link generally has to guess when a print job has ended. This can be fixed by adding a call at the end of a job.

Finally, there are the DOS calls Win-Link intercepts. Win-Link intercepts all EXEC calls. On these calls Win-Link determines whether the program being executed is a Windows application. If so, Win-Link checks it against a list of files to execute as DOS apps. If the application is not on that list, Win-Link executes the program from Windows instead of from DOS.

The exception list is there for two reasons. There is no way to differentiate between bound OS/2 applications and Windows applications, so any bound OS/2 app must be on the exception list. Also, some applications have a complete DOS app as their Windows dos-stub program, and you may wish to run the DOS stub.

Win-Link intercepts all output sent to LPT 1 via int 17h. We do not intercept print I/O directly to the port, nor do we intercept printers on other ports. But all output written to LPT 1 at the DOS level eventually gets to int 17h so that output is intercepted.

Printing a file performed via the PRINT command or programatically using PRINT's int 2Fh calls is also intercepted. But printing a file is intercepted at the command level, so that just the file name is passed to Win-Link, which is much more efficient than intercepting the calls to int 17h. When a file prints, the file name is the job name in the Windows print spooler. When a file prints to int 17h, the name of the program is the name of the job. When a program uses the Win-Link call to name a print job, it will be the name the program gave it.

EXEC, TERMINATE, and some other calls are tracked to determine the name of the program running in the DOS box. This name is then matched against a list, which expands predefined names to different names. For example, B changes to Brief. This name is then set as the title of the Window for the DOS box.

The Approach

Win-Link is composed of three parts: (1) Win-Link, a Windows application, (2) Win-IPC, a VxD, and (3) raw.drv, a printer driver. Win-Link and Win-IPC provide the functionality we need. A VxD cannot make Windows calls and a Windows app cannot make VxD calls, so the two programs work together. Raw.drv is needed for printing because many printer drivers in Windows do not implement the PASSTHROUGH escape call.

The primary data structure is called VMDATA and is in both win_link.h and win_ipc.inc. One of these structures exists for each VM, including the system VM. These are set up in a linked-list so that Win-Link or Win-IPC can walk through all the VM's instances of the structure. This gives the VxD full access, with little effort, to any VM data. In addition, the first element is a LDT selector:offset that points to the structure, valid in the system VM. This provides an easy way for Win-IPC to give Win-Link a pointer to the structure for any VM.

In general, Win-IPC or Win-Link changes values in this structure and then sends a message to the other telling it what to look at in the structure. Following is a brief description of each element of the structure.

```
VmData struc
        VmLdt       dd      0
        VmHandle    dd      0
        PrnSem      dd      0
        MsgSem      dd      0
        TimeHdl     dd      0
        LinkNext    dd      0
        LdtNext     dd      0
        pPsp        dd      0
        MsgGet      dd      0                ; Next Message to read
        MsgPut      dd      0                ; Next free spot
        MsgLast     dd      0                ; Next == Free -> empty
        PrntNum     dw      0
        hDc         dw      0
        iPrnErr     dw      0
        iStr        dw      0
```

```
          hWnd        dw      0
          wFlags      dw      0
          BufCnt      dw      0
          PrntBuf     db      SIZE_PRNT_BUF dup (0)
          sXtra       db      0, 0
          MsgArr      db      ((size DosMsg) * MAX_DOS_MSG) dup (?)
          sPsp        db      9 dup (0), 0
          sProgName   db      31 dup (' '), 0
          sTitle      db      80 dup (0)
          sExec       db      129 dup (0), 0
          sCmdLine    db      129 dup (0), 0
          sPrntStr    db      129 dup (0), 0
VmData ends
```

- **VmLdt**, a pointer to the structure in this VM. The LDT pointer is only valid in the context of the system VM (not the VM this structure is for).

- **VmHandle** is the hVM, as defined by WIN386 for this VM. This value is needed by a number of the VxD functions.

- **PrnSem** and **MsgSem** are semaphores created for the life of the VM. PrnSem is used for handling int 17h printing, and MsgSem is used to implement an internal SendMessage mechanism (the public interface only supports PostMessage). These semaphores exist for the life of the VM because they are frequently used.

- **TimeHdl** is used when a time-out intercepting int 17h printing is set. This value is non-zero only when a timer event has been set.

- **LinkNext** is a flat 32-bit offset to the next VM's VMDATA structure. This value can be used in Win-IPC in any VM to walk to the next VM's structure.

- **LdtNext** is a selector:offset LDT pointer valid in the system VM only. This value can be used in Win-Link to walk to the next VM's structure.

- **pPsp** is a flat 32-bit offset to the PSP of the application presently running in that VM. As a flat 32-bit pointer it is only accessed by Win-IPC.

- **MsgNext**, **MsgFree**, and **MsgEnd** are flat 32-bit offsets into MsgArr. They are used to track the queue of messages posted to DOS VMs. MsgNext is the location of the next message to read. MsgFree is the location where the next message will be written (that is, an available location). MsgEnd points to the byte after the end of MsgArr.

- **PrntNum** is the number of bytes presently in PrntBuf. When this value exceeds **SIZE_PRINT_BLOCK**, the data in PrntBuf is written to the spooler.

- **hDc** is the printer DC for the data presently being redirected from int 17h to the Windows print spooler. This value is 0 if there is presently nothing to print (and therefore no DC open).

- **iPrnErr** is the value returned when an app in a VM calls int 17h to get the LPT status.

- **iStr** is the listbox index of this VM's print job. Each print job is listed in the Win-Link dialog box, and this value is used to delete the job when it has completed printing.

- **hWnd** is the handle to the Window for this DOS box. Determining this is not an exact science, and the handle may be wrong. It is also initially 0 until a guess can be made as to its value.

- **wFlags** is a bitmap of a number of flags. These flags set which of the interception capabilities (such as, exec Windows apps from DOS or print redirection to the spooler) are on.

- **BufCnt** is used when data is sent to the print spooler. The first 2 bytes of the buffer are the length of the data in the rest of the buffer. Therefore, we don't pass the address of PrntBuf. Instead, we set BufCnt to the value of PrntNum and pass the address of BufCnt.

- **PrntBuf** holds that data intercepted from int 17h. If every byte intercepted by Win-IPC were posted to Win-Link, the overhead of the message posting would bring the system to its knees. Therefore, once 1K of data has been intercepted, Win-Link is notified to write the data to the spooler.

- **MsgArr** holds the messages posted to DOS VMs. These messages are held until read by the app in a DOS VM. This is a static array — once it is out of space no more messages may be posted until some are read.

The following elements are used to pass data for certain messages. This data is only considered valid between the time when the message is sent to when it is processed. The data is placed here instead of in the message because pointers cannot be passed in a message.

- **sPsp** is a zero-terminated string of the program name in the selected PSP in this VM. This string is pulled from the MCB of the PSP and is here because Win-Link cannot access pPsp.

- **sProgName** is the name of the VM set by the Register call. A DOS app Registers itself to name a VM and another DOS or Windows app, then finds the hVM of the registered DOS app by searching for the named VM.

- **sTitle** is the title to set for this VM's window. This is the value pulled from sPsp or passed when a DOS app sets its title. Translations made by Win-Link (such as B to Brief) are handled by Win-Link when it receives the message telling it to use this value.

- **sExec** is the file presently being exec'ed. This is used if a program is a Windows executable and a message is then passed to Win-Link to exec the program. Win-Link determines whether the program is on the list of programs not to exec from Windows. This is also used when DOS apps are launched by creating a new DOS box.

- **sCmdLine** is the command line for sExec. The command lines are kept separate because at times Win-IPC and Win-Link need to know only the file name.

- **sPrntStr** is the name of a file sent to PRINT to be printed.

Handling VM Creation

Before getting into how we implement any specific piece of Win-IPC/Win-Link, we need to discuss what we do on VM creation. Creation is the platform on which we can provide all our capabilities.

When creating the system VM, we _Allocate_Device_CB_Area for the VMDATA structure for each VM and interrupt we need to intercept (17h, 21h, 23h, 24h, & 2Fh).

```
BeginProc WinIpc_Sys_Critical_Init

      ; Allocate per/VM instance data
      VMMCall  _Allocate_Device_CB_Area, <<size VmData>, 0>
      cmp    eax, 0
      je     short sci10              ; No memory - do nothing
      mov    [CbVmData], eax
      and    [SysFlags], not MEM_OFF

      ; Set up the System VM data
      mov    eax, ebx
      call   GetVmData
      mov    [esi.VmHandle], ebx
      VMMcall  Get_Sys_VM_Handle       ; Save System VM
      mov    [SysVm], ebx

sci10: clc
      ret
EndProc WinIpc_Sys_Critical_Init

BeginProc WinIpc_Dev_Init

      ; Hook interrupts
      mov    eax, 17h                 ; Sit on int 17
      mov    esi, OFFSET32 WinIpc_Int_17
```

```
        VMMcall Hook_V86_Int_Chain
        mov    eax, 21h                    ; Sit on int 21
        mov    esi, OFFSET32 WinIpc_Int_21
        VMMcall Hook_V86_Int_Chain
        mov    eax, 23h                    ; Sit on int 23
        mov    esi, OFFSET32 WinIpc_Int_23
        VMMcall Hook_V86_Int_Chain
        mov    eax, 24h                    ; Sit on int 24
        mov    esi, OFFSET32 WinIpc_Int_24
        VMMcall Hook_V86_Int_Chain
        mov    eax, 2Fh                    ; Sit on int 2F
        mov    esi, OFFSET32 WinIpc_Int_2F
        VMMcall Hook_V86_Int_Chain

        clc
        ret
EndProc WinIpc_Dev_Init
```

For each additional VM created we do a little more. First, we need to initialize VMDATA by performing the following steps:

1. We zero out all the data (thereby handling all elements that need to be set to 0).

2. We set the VmHandle (it is EBX on entry) and MsgNext, MsgFree, and MsgEnd. We can now accept messages posted to this VM.

3. We set pPsp to the PSP for the VM. This way we know that pPsp is valid in the rest of our code.

4. We create the MsgSem and PrnSem semaphores. This allows us to assume these exist in the rest of our code as well as avoid the processor overhead of constantly creating and freeing them.

5. We create a LDT selector:offset to point to the VMDAT structure that is good in the system VM.

6. We insert this VMs VMDATA structure into the linked list of all the VM's VMDATA structures. We do this for both LinkNext and LdtNext.

```
BeginProc WinIpc_VM_Create

        test   [SysFlags], MEM_OFF
        jnz    vmc10                   ; Turned off - do nothing
        ; Get & zero-fill VmData
        mov    eax, ebx
        call   GetVmData
        mov    edi, esi
        xor    eax, eax
        mov    ecx, (size VmData) / 4
        rep    stosd

        ; Init VmData
```

```
        mov     [esi.VmHandle], ebx
        lea     ecx, [esi].MsgArr
        mov     [esi].MsgGet, ecx
        mov     [esi].MsgPut, ecx
        mov     eax, MAX_DOS_MSG - 1
        mov     edx, size DosMsg
        mul     edx
        add     eax, ecx
        mov     [esi].MsgLast, eax

        ; Get the PSP (via SDA) location
        Push_Client_State
        VMMcall Begin_Nest_Exec
        mov     [ebp.Client_AX], 5D06h
        mov     eax, 21h
        VMMcall     Exec_Int
        movzx   edx, [ebp.Client_DS]
        shl     edx, 4
        movzx   eax, [ebp.Client_SI]
        add     edx, eax
        add     edx, [ebx.CB_High_Linear]
        add     edx, 10h
        mov     [esi].pPsp, edx

        VMMcall End_Nest_Exec
        Pop_Client_State

        xor     ecx, ecx                    ; Set up Msg semaphore
        VMMcall Create_Semaphore
        jc      vmc10
        mov     [esi].MsgSem, eax
        xor     ecx, ecx                    ; Set up Prn semaphore
        VMMcall Create_Semaphore
        jc      vmc10
        mov     [esi].PrnSem, eax

        ; Create LDT so Win-Link can access structure
        SizeVmData EQU (size VmData)
        VMMcall _BuildDescriptorDWORDs  <esi, SizeVmData, RW_Data_Type,
D_GRAN_BYTE, 0>
        VMMcall _Allocate_LDT_Selector  <[SysVm], edx, eax, 1, 0>
        rol     eax, 16
        mov     [esi.VmLdt], eax

        ; Build linked-list
        ; Do this last so we are only in the list if 1) We are all
        ; filled in & 2) We were able to set up semaphores, etc.
        mov     edi, esi
        mov     eax, [SysVm]
        call    GetVmData
        mov     eax, [esi.LinkNext]
        mov     [edi.LinkNext], eax
        mov     [esi.LinkNext], edi
```

```
        mov    eax, [esi.LdtNext]
        mov    [edi.LdtNext], eax
        mov    eax, [edi.VmLdt]
        mov    [esi.LdtNext], eax

        ;... see next listing
        ; We now send a msg to set the title. We do this here
        ; so we get the message before another VM is created; we
        ; just grab the first free VM in Windows.
        PostPm [SysVm], [SysWnd], MSG_DOS_TITLE, 0, [edi.VmLdt]

vmc10: clc
        ret
EndProc WinIpc_VM_Create
```

At this point we still have two remaining tasks before we are fully ready for the new VM. The easy one is setting the title of the DOS box. The difficult one is, determining the handle of the Window for this VM and we can't set the title until we know the hWnd.

Be warned that the method covered here is not completely foolproof. It seems to work about 98 percent of the time. It runs into trouble largely when a bunch of DOS boxes are launched in a row, so that we have several hVM <-> hWnd resolutions pending.

Implementation

We start implementation by posting a message to Win-Link telling it to set the title for this VM. It does this by posting MSG_DOS_TITLE to Win-Link. However, if hWnd is NULL, Win-Link (in the function DosTitle) performs some special processing. This processing exists only for this first call to DosTitle:

```
        ; We now send a msg to set the title.
        PostPm [SysVm], [SysWnd], MSG_DOS_TITLE, 0, [edi.VmLdt]

vmc10: clc
        ret
EndProc WinIpc_VM_Create
```

If we are running under Windows 3.1, we set a hook and post a message back to Win-IPC. We cover what this does in a moment because it has no effect until we complete the rest of the processing in DosTitle.

We next walk through all Windows whose class is tty (the class of all DOS box windows). We also check that this window is a DOS box, although this may be merely paranoia on my part. Once we find a tty window, we check whether it is already registered to another of our VMs. If so, we keep looking. If not, we assume that it belongs to this VM.

If you are following along in the code you'll notice we also passed in a NULL text string and you will set a potentially wrong hWnd to the title. However, because the string is NULL, the text will not be set — DosTitle actually is two separate functions wrapped in one for historical reasons — I originally attempted to get the hWnd by other means.

```
        // We walk the list of top windows looking for one of class tty
        hWnd = FindWindow ("tty", NULL);

        while (hWnd)
                {
                // See if its a DOS box
                GetClassName (hWnd, sBuf, 5);
                if (StrCmp (sBuf, "tty"))
                        goto NextWin;
                if (! IsWinOldApTask (GetWindowTask (hWnd)))
                        goto NextWin;

                // See if we already have this one
                fpVmOn = fpVmData;
                do
                        {
                        if (fpVmOn->hWnd == hWnd)
                                goto NextWin;
                        if (! (fpVmOn = fpVmOn->LdtNext))
                                break;
                        }
                while (fpVmOn != fpVmData);

                // We have it!
                fpVmData->hWnd = hWnd;

                // Get the next window
NextWin:
                hWnd = GetWindow (hWnd, GW_HWNDNEXT);
                }
        // We failed
        fpVmData->hWnd = (HWND) -1;
```

Now we have a hVM == hWnd pairing. But this was merely a guess. This is where the hook comes in. We have hooked all messages being sent to any window — a very expensive hook but quite necessary. We then posted a message to Win-IPC. The message causes _MsgShellEvent in Win-IPC to be called. In _MsgShellEvent we make a VxD call to SHELL_Event. SHELL_Event allows us to send a Windows message to a DOS box window by specifying its hVM, which we do know. So we post a message with a constant in uMsg to ID the message and the selector to VmData (we make use of the fact that all our LDT pointers have an offset of 0) in wParam. In our hook filter proc we look for any message with this message number. When we see it, we set that hWnd as the hWnd for our VM. Finally, we post a message to ourselves. When we receive this message we remove the hook. Once the hook is removed, we no longer impose any overhead on the system. We have the correct hWnd unless someone else sent the same message number between the time we installed the hook and the time SHELL_Event got the message back to us. We now have our hWnd and are initialized for the VM just created.

```
// ... in DosTitle
      if (uVer >= 0x030A)
            if (iHookCnt++ == 0)
            hhookMsgFilterHook = SetWindowsHook (WH_GETMESSAGE,
(HOOKPROC)lpfnMsgFilterProc);
      PostMessage (hDlg, MSG_EVENT_ON, 0, fpVmData->VmHandle);

      // ... In main DlgProc
                  case MSG_EVENT_ON :
                        dShellEvent (lParam);
                        break;
                  case MSG_EVENT_OFF :
                        if (--iHookCnt == 0)
                              UnhookWindowsHook (WH_GETMESSAGE,
(HOOKPROC)lpfnMsgFilterProc);
                        break;

// HOOK Call-backs
LRESULT CALLBACK _export __loadds MsgFilterFunc (int nCode, WORD
wParam, DWORD lParam )
{
      if (((MSG __far *) lParam)->message == 0x6969)
            HandleEvent (lParam);
      return (0);
}

void __loadds HandleEvent (long lParam)
{
      VMDATA _far *pVmData;
      pVmData = PTR (((MSG __far *) lParam)->wParam, 0);
      if (! SelOk ((void _far *) pVmData, sizeof (VMDATA)))
            return;
      pVmData->hWnd = ((MSG __far *) lParam)->hwnd;
      PostMessage (hMainDlg, MSG_EVENT_OFF, 0, 0);
}

; WIN_IPC.386 dShellEvent
_MsgShellEvent  proc

      push    ebx
      mov     eax, [ebp.Client_ECX]
      mov     ebx, eax
      call    GetVmData
      mov     ecx, 6969h
      movzx   eax, word ptr [esi.VmLdt + 2]
      xor     esi, esi
      xor     edx, edx
      VxDcall         SHELL_Event
```

```
        pop     ebx

        ret
_MsgShellEvent  endp
```

Registering DOS Apps

We now need to determine which VM is running our DOS app. To do this Win-IPC provides a call in which a DOS app passes a name to our VmData structure. Another app can Query and Win-IPC will walk the VmData structs to find the one with the matching name.

Internal Message Passing

Message posting is the most difficult part of the system. This section discusses how Win-Link and Win-IPC post and send messages to each other. The next section will discuss how applications can post messages, and that functionality makes use of the basic message passing. However, this section only discusses the internal messaging used by Win-Link and Win-IPC.

Win-Link to Win-IPC

When messages pass from Win-Link to Win-IPC a Windows application is calling a VxD. This is always safe — if it wasn't Windows would not be receiving any time slices. All messages from Win-Link to Win-IPC are sent as opposed to posted. This is because it is much easier to send than to post and there is no need for posted messages. All parameters are passed in registers. Win-Link then calls the far-call address it received when it initially called int 2Fh with AX=1684h. This calls the entry point in Win-IPC with these registers set.

```
; EAX: uMsg = Message to post to Win-IPC
; ECX: lParam1 = first long param
; EDX: lParam2 = second long param

CallVxd MACRO       uMsg, lParam1, lParam2
        mov     ecx, lParam1
        mov     edx, lParam2
        mov     eax, uMsg
```

```
        xor     ebx, ebx
        call    dword ptr [WinIpcAddr]
        ENDM
```

This gets a message to **WinIpc_PM_Api_Proc** in Win-IPC. A jump table is used to go to the handler for the specific message passed in. Because this is also the entry point other Windows applications use to call Win-IPC, the procedure first checks to make sure the passed-in message is a legit number for a Windows application. It does this by using the message number as an offset into the table **PmOkTable**, which is a table of bytes. If a byte is 0, then the message is not legal; if it is -1, it is legitimate. At the same time the procedure also makes sure that the message number is within the range of handled messages.

```
BeginProc WinIpc_PM_API_Proc

        movzx   eax, [ebp.Client_AX]
        cmp     eax, (NumPmOk - 1)
        ja      short pap10
        and     eax, 0FFh
        mov     al, [PmOkTable + eax]
        cmp     al, 0
        je      short pap20

pap10:  call    DefMsgProc
        ret

pap20:  mov     [ebp.Client_AX], ERR_UNKNOWN_MSG
        ret                              ; exit error

EndProc WinIpc_PM_API_Proc
```

DefMsgProc is even simpler. It first looks to see if Win-IPC is on. If the flag **MEM_OFF** in **SysFlags** is set, the Win-IPC is turned off. In this case, DefMsgProc does nothing and refuses to handle any messages. DefMsgProc then jmps to the appropiate handler from MsgDispTable. This is a quick way to get to the correct message. We jump instead of call because that saves us a ret when we are done.

```
DefMsgProc  proc

        test    [SysFlags], MEM_OFF              ; Are we running?
        jz      short dmp20
        mov     [ebp.Client_AX], ERR_NO_VM_MEMORY
        ret

dmp20:  movzx   eax, [ebp.Client_AX]            ; Get the message
        jmp     [MsgDispTable + 4 * eax]

DefMsgProc  endp
```

Whichever function is called then executes and returns. When it returns, the return goes back to Win-Link, with the return value passed in AX.

Win-IPC to Win-Link

We want to post messages to Win-Link whenever possible so that we can be in Win-IPC when Windows is in a non-reentrant state. As a matter of fact, almost any time we are in Win-IPC, Windows, and therefore Win-Link, is in a non-reentrant state. This means we cannot make a call to Win-Link from Win-IPC. There is one exception to this rule. **PostMessage** in Windows was specifically designed to be fully re-entrant. So the one connection we have from Win-IPC to Win-Link is the ability to call PostMessage.

There is still one minor concern. We do not want to call PostMessage if the Windows VM is in the critical section or has interrupts off. This is not an absolute requirement, but it is part of being a good neighbor. Taking the time to post a message while a Windows app (or DLL, more likely) is in a critical section can delay that application enough to cause it major harm — and bring the system down. We also have to wait until the Windows VM can be scheduled. An immediate call would go into the current VM, which quite possibly is not the Windows VM. Therefore, when **LinkMsgProc** returns, the message may not yet have been posted. So we have to get a temporary structure to hold our message until we can post it to Windows. Otherwise, the message could be overwritten as soon as LinkMsgProc returned.

SendMessage

The function LinkMsgProc is used for both posting and sending messages. The following code is an abbreviated version showing just those parts relevant to PostMessage. The parameter checking is not displayed here, either. For a full discussion of the code, see the discussion of SendMessage that follows.

```
LinkMsgProc   proc

        ; Get a VmMsg struct
dmp70: mov     cx, [VmMsgAlloc]
       mov     edi, [VmMsgOff]
       mov     eax, [ebp.Client_EBX]
dmp80: xchg    [edi.Handle], eax
       cmp     eax, 0
       je      short dmp90
       xchg    [edi.Handle], eax
       add     edi, size VmMsg
       loop    dmp80
       mov     [ebp.Client_AX], ERR_MSG_FULL
       ret
```

```
            ; edi points to a VMMSG struct
dmp90: mov     eax, [ebp.Client_EAX]               ; save message
       mov     [edi.lParam1], eax
       mov     eax, [ebp.Client_EDX]
       mov     [edi.lParam2], eax
       mov     eax, [ebp.Client_ECX]
       mov     [edi.lWndMsg], eax
       mov     [edi.VmOff], esi

       ; lets generate the call-back
       mov     eax, Low_Pri_Device_Boost
       push    ebx
       mov     ebx, [esi.VmHandle]
       mov     ecx, PEF_Wait_For_STI or PEF_Wait_Not_Crit
       mov     edx, edi
       mov     esi, OFFSET32 HandleCallBack
       VMMcall     Call_Priority_VM_Event
       pop     ebx

       mov     edx, [edi.Rtn]                       ; rtn regs & Client_regs
       mov     [ebp.Client_EDX], edx
       mov     eax, ERR_NONE
       mov     [ebp.Client_EAX], eax

       ret

LinkMsgProc   endp
```

This code has not necessarily posted a message. It has merely saved it in the structure and set up a call to **HandleCallBack**. If the Windows VM had interrupts on and was not in a critical section, HandleCallBack was called before **Call_Priority_VM_Event** returned. Either way, HandleCallBack has been, or shortly will be, executed.

HandleCallBack first pushes the client state so it can modify the VM's registers. It then moves the message values to the client registers on the stack. These are the values the registers will have when **Resume_Exec** is called. HandleCallBack then sets up a nested execution call to _dMsgProc in Win-Link. This code makes a call to PostMessage to get the message posted. On return from Resume_Exec, the message is posted, assuming that there was room in the queue for it. Finally, the VMMSG struct is marked as free and the client registers are taken off the stack. When HandleCallBack returns, it has returned the VM to its original state.

```
HandleCallBack   proc
     Push_Client_State

     mov     edi, edx                    ; Get pointer
     mov     eax, [edi.lParam1]          ; Set up registers
     mov     [ebp.Client_EAX], eax
     mov     eax, [edi.lParam2]
     mov     [ebp.Client_EDX], eax
     mov     eax, [edi.lWndMsg]
```

```
        mov     [ebp.Client_ECX], eax
        mov     [ebp.Client_EBX], edi

        mov     edx, [SysCallBack]
        mov     cx, dx                    ; Call the sucker
        shr     edx, 16
        VMMcall         Begin_Nest_Exec
        VMMcall         Simulate_Far_Call
        VMMcall         Resume_Exec
        VMMcall         End_Nest_exec

        mov     eax, [ebp.Client_EAX]          ; save rtn value
        mov     [edi.Rtn], eax
        mov     [edi.Handle], 0        ; Mark VmMsg avail

        Pop_Client_State
        ret
HandleCallBack   endp
```

Win-Link

On the Win-Link side, the message has to be posted via the Windows **PostMessage** API. This is not as trivial as merely passing our parameters to PostMessage. Unfortunately, in a number of send messages we need to pass two DWORDs as well as a WORD. Since the standard Windows message does not have this capacity, we have to build it in. Because we use the same code to post and send, we must build into post also. Also, Win-Link maintains another array of message strucs that hold the incoming message. The actual message posted to Win-Link is a pointer to this structure.

```
_dMsgProc  proc far

        push    si
        push    ds
        push    bp
        push    0
        mov     bp, sp

        push    ax
        push    cx
        mov     ax, _DATA
        mov     ds, ax
        mov     cx, NUM_MSG
        mov     si, offset _DATA:MsgData

mp10:   mov     ax, 0FFFFh
        xchg    ds:[si.InUse], ax
        cmp     ax, 0
        je      mp20
        add     si, size VXDMSG
        loop    mp10
        IntTest
```

```
        pop     cx
        pop     ax
        jmp     mp30

mp20:   pop     cx
        pop     ax
        mov     dword ptr ds:[si.mWnd], ecx
        mov     dword ptr ds:[si.mwParam], eax
        mov     ds:[si.mlParam], edx
        mov     ds:[si.mEDI], ebx

        push    ds:[MainWnd]
        push    MSG_WIN_IPC
        push    0
        push    ds
        push    si

        call    PostMessage

mp30:   add     sp, 2
        pop     bp
        pop     ds
        pop     si
        ret

_dMsgProc   endp
```

This pushes the message into the Windows message queue. We have to look at what happens when it pops out the other end.

For this we look at the function MainDlgProc in win_link.c. Again, we abbreviate it to show just the PostMessage code. We find that we post a plain old Windows message, so we go back into the message queue.

```
    case MSG_WIN_IPC :
      pVxdMsg = (VXDMSG _far *) lParam;

      // Lots of SendMessage code...

      PostMessage (pVxdMsg->hWnd, pVxdMsg->uMsg, pVxdMsg->wParam,
pVxdMsg->lParam);
      pVxdMsg->InUse = 0;
      break;
```

This is not necessarily the best way to handle a post; but it works.

SendMessage to Win-Link

To get from SendMessage to Win-Link, we merely add two additional pieces to the puzzle. First, in LinkMsgProc we block on a semaphore after posting the message. This semaphore is then unblocked by a call Win-Link makes after the message has been processed.

Because of this semaphore, it is critical that we do not send a message from the Windows VM. If we do we will block the Windows VM, and if the Windows VM is blocked it will never execute the code to unblock the semaphore.

The second addition to the code involves returning a value. The main reason to call SendMessage instead of PostMessage is that you need to know the return value from SendMessage. So we start with LinkMsgProc again. We add a semaphore, block on after setting an event to HandleCallBack, and destroy the semaphore when we have unblocked. We create and destroy the semaphore on a per-message basis for two reasons. First, there can be multiple SendMessages, so we can't use a single semaphore. Second, a SendMessage is a pretty rare event, so the overhead is not a killer.

The handle to the semaphore is included in the message structure. The handle is needed by Win-Link to make a call back to Win-IPC, telling it to unblock that semaphore. We first check to see whether IPC is turned on or off. If it is turned off we do not accept any messages. Then we check to see whether we are sending a message from a Windows app to a Windows app. There is no reason for that to go through us, so we don't allow it. Next we get the VmData struct for the receiving VM. GetVmData returns a pointer to VmData in ESI. This also assures us that we are sending a message to a VM that exists.

We now check to make sure we have an address to call in the Windows VM to get to PostMessage. The flag IPC_OFF should be set if this is NULL, but I like to be paranoid in cases like this. We then go into the code we saw before to get a VMMSG struct. This struct holds our passed-in message parameters, the semaphore we use to block, and the return value from the SendMessage call. This data is allocated to this message until the semaphore is unblocked at the end of ListMsgProc.

```
LinkMsgProc   proc

        ; We have a message to post/send.
        ; We can't send a msg from Windows to Windows!!

dmp40: test   [SysFlags], IPC_OFF              ; Are we running?
       jz     short dmp50
       mov    [ebp.Client_AX], ERR_NO_WIN_APP
       ret

dmp50: cmp    ebx, [SysVm]               ; Win Msg to WinMsg?
       jne    short dmp60
       cmp    ebx, [ebp.Client_EBX]
       jne    short dmp60
       mov    [ebp.Client_AX], ERR_WIN_TO_WIN
       ret

dmp60: mov    eax, [ebp.Client_EBX]          ; Get destination VM
       call   GetVm
       jc     short dmp65
```

```
        call    GetVmData

        cmp     [SysCallBack], 0
        jne     short dmp70
dmp65:  mov     [ebp.Client_AX], ERR_UNKNOWN_VM
        ret


        ; Get a VmMsg struct
dmp70:  mov     cx, [VmMsgAlloc]
        mov     edi, [VmMsgOff]
        mov     eax, [ebp.Client_EBX]
dmp80:  xchg    [edi.Handle], eax
        cmp     eax, 0
        je      short dmp90
        xchg    [edi.Handle], eax
        add     edi, size VmMsg
        loop    dmp80
        mov     [ebp.Client_AX], ERR_MSG_FULL
        ret
```

Here is where we start to differentiate because we are sending a message. First we create a semaphore, and this value is stored in our VMMSG structure. Following that, we set up the rest of the structure and then set up an event to call HandleCallBack, just as we did in PostMessage.

```
dmp90:  test    [ebp.Client_EAX], FLAG_SEND_MSG  ; send?
        jz      short dmp110
        xor     ecx, ecx                         ; Set up a semaphore
        VMMcall Create_Semaphore
        jnc     short dmp100
        mov     [ebp.Client_AX], ERR_NO_SEMAPHORE
        ret

dmp100: mov     [edi.SendSem], eax

dmp110: mov     eax, [ebp.Client_EAX]            ; save message
        mov     [edi.lParam1], eax
        mov     eax, [ebp.Client_EDX]
        mov     [edi.lParam2], eax
        mov     eax, [ebp.Client_ECX]
        mov     [edi.lWndMsg], eax
        mov     [edi.VmOff], esi

        ; lets generate the call-back
        mov     eax, Low_Pri_Device_Boost
        push    ebx
        mov     ebx, [esi.VmHandle]
        mov     ecx, PEF_Wait_For_STI or PEF_Wait_Not_Crit
        mov     edx, edi
        mov     esi, OFFSET32 HandleCallBack
        VMMcall         Call_Priority_VM_Event
        pop     ebx
```

```
        mov     edx, [edi.Rtn]                      ; rtn regs & Client_regs
```

The rest of the function is send-specific. The semaphore is blocked to stop LinkMsgProc from returning until after the semaphore is unblocked. In the meantime, before or after the semaphore is blocked, HandleCallBack calls Win-Link, which processes the message. When the message has been processed, Win-Link makes a call to Win-IPC, passing the semaphore and return value. This call in Win-IPC sets the return value in the VMMSG struct and clears the semaphore.

The end result of this is that when Wait_Semaphore returns, the return value of the SendMessage is in EDI.Rtn. All that is left to do is to destroy the semaphore, free up the VMMSG struct, and return the result from SendMessage.

Note that the value is returned in DX. AX is always the status returned from the call so that you can differentiate between a 1 returned from SendMessage and an error code of 1.

```
        test    [ebp.Client_EAX], FLAG_SEND_MSG  ; send?
        jz      short dmp130

dmp120:     mov     eax, [edi.SendSem]
        mov     ecx, Block_Svc_Ints or Block_Enable_Ints
        VMMcall     Wait_Semaphore                      ; block until sent

        mov     eax, [edi.SendSem]
        VMMcall     Destroy_Semaphore         ; destroy it
        mov     edx, [edi.Rtn]                ; rtn regs & Client_regs
        mov     [edi.Handle], 0               ; Mark VmMsg avail

dmp130:     mov     [ebp.Client_EDX], edx
        mov     eax, ERR_NONE
        mov     [ebp.Client_EAX], eax

        ret

LinkMsgProc endp
```

So what happens differently in HandleCallBack? Nothing! There is a different code path for a SendMessage to a VM other than the system VM, but a SendMessage to the system VM is identical to a PostMessage. The same goes for _dMsgProc in Win-Link.

Which brings us to MainDlgProc. I have shown the full code for handling a message from Win-IPC, but the part executed when we send a message from Win-IPC to Win-Link is the part that creates the SendDlg struct and passes that. So all the messages we send to Win-Link are sent from the MSG_WIN_IPC case back to MainDlgProc, with all the variables passed in a struct that lParam points to. The return value to be passed back is set in that struct. When the internal SendMessage call returns, we call dPostMsg, passing the return value and a pointer to the VMMSG struct that is holding the sent message on the Win-IPC side. This call sets the return value in VMMSG and clears the semaphore. Finally, the VXDMSG struct is freed. At this point the message has been processed, but we still need to go back to Win-IPC, pass the return value, and clear the semaphore.

```
  case MSG_WIN_IPC :
    pVxdMsg = (VXDMSG _far *) lParam;

    if (pVxdMsg->wFlags & 0x0001)
       {
       if (pVxdMsg->hWnd != hDlg)
          lRtn = SendMessage (pVxdMsg->hWnd, pVxdMsg->uMsg, pVxdMsg-
>wParam, pVxdMsg->lParam);
       else
          {
          SendDlg.lParam = pVxdMsg->lParam;
          SendDlg.wParam = pVxdMsg->wParam;
          SendDlg.lRtn = 0;
          SendMessage (pVxdMsg->hWnd, pVxdMsg->uMsg, 0, (long) (LPVOID)
&SendDlg);
          lRtn = SendDlg.lRtn;
          }

       dPostMsg (_MSG_SEND_RTN, lRtn, pVxdMsg->lEDI);
       }

    else
       PostMessage (pVxdMsg->hWnd, pVxdMsg->uMsg, pVxdMsg->wParam,
pVxdMsg->lParam);

    pVxdMsg->InUse = 0;
    break;
```

The message _MSG_SEND_RTN works its way through the dispatching code and ends up at _MsgSendRtn. _MsgSendRtn checks to make sure the passed-in pointer is good, then places the return value in VMMSG and clears (signals) the semaphore. This causes the Block_Semaphore in LinkMsgProc to return with the original SendMessage call.

```
_MsgSendRtn  proc

        ; Check edi (points to VmMsg, good handle)
        mov     edi, [ebp.Client_EDX]
        mov     ecx, [VmMsgOff]
        cmp     edi, ecx
        jb      short msr10

        mov     eax, size VmMsg
        mul     [VmMsgAlloc]
        add     eax, ecx
        cmp     edi, eax
        jae     short msr10
        cmp     ebx, [edi.Handle]
        jne     short msr10
```

```
      ; Its ok - save the rtn value & turn semaphore off
      mov   eax, [ebp.Client_ECX]
      mov   [edi.Rtn], eax
      mov   eax, [edi.SendSem]
      VMMcall      Signal_Semaphore

msr10: ret
_MsgSendRtn   endp
```

We have thus sent a message from Win-IPC to Win-Link. Definitely not a trivial undertaking, but not terribly complicated or convoluted.

Other Design Considerations

PostMessage is coded to be totally re-entrant, but it does have one blind spot: PostMessage itself is not re-entrant. In other words, you can call PostMessage when any other code in Windows is being executed, but you cannot call PostMessage when PostMessage is executing.

The only time this comes up is when you post a message in an interrupt handler in your VxD and while the message is being posted, another interrupt comes in so that you post again. Using PostMessage under these conditions causes the first message to disappear. This is not a good idea anyway — you would probably max out the message queue under such a design.

You need to make sure that any memory touched by Win-Link while in _dMsgProc is locked down in physical memory. Again, because we can call this at any time, the code and data used cannot be swapped out to disk. If it were, you would use whatever happened to be there instead or fault, depending on the state of the system at the time. That is why Win-Link locks down its code and data when it starts. It is not necessary to lock the entire program down (I did it because Win-Link is small model), but it is critical that *every* byte of code and data that you touch at this time is locked down.

Message Passing Between VMs

Message passing between applications takes three forms: (1) DOS app to Windows app, (2) Windows App to DOS app, and (3) DOS app to DOS app (between different VMs). And after trying several approaches to this kind of message passing, I settled on allowing only posting, not sending. This eliminates all the re-entrancy problems that send messages cause. In addition, Win-IPC does not call a DOS box with a message. A DOS box has to poll. This is less efficient but is a lot safer. And with shared memory you can add code to set a flag before posting a message.

DOS to DOS, Windows to DOS

Posting to a DOS app involves three functions, MsgPost, MsgPeek, and MsgRead in win_ipc.asm. To post a message to a DOS app the calling app will call MsgPost. MsgPost will then place the passed parameters in a DOSMSG struct that is held in an array in the VmData for the receiving VM. This is an array of a set size (just like a Windows app), so the first test is to make sure that space exists in the array. If it does not, the post will fail. If there is room, the message is stored in the structure and the structure pointer MsgLast is incremented to the next slot. We have now posted the message to the queue.

If the DOS app receiving the message calls MsgRead, it is blocked on a semaphore. We signal the semaphore to free it up. If MsgRead has not been called yet, it is called to read the message. Because we already signaled the semaphore, when MsgRead calls Block_Semaphore it returns instantly.

Finally, we boost the execution priority of the receiving VM. The theory behind this is that this VM has been waiting for the message. We now want to give it a boost so it can get started processing the message. Depending on your application, you may prefer not to include this step. It gives you a faster response but makes Windows freeze for a moment.

In the following code fragment I have removed the part that handles messages posted to a Windows app. This is the code that handles posting to a DOS app.

```
MsgPost  proc

mp10:  call   GetVmData                  ; ESI = VmData of dest VM

       ; Do we have room in the message array???
       ; NO if Write == Read-1 OR (Read == MsgArr
       ; AND Write == last element)
       mov    eax, size DosMsg
       mov    edi, [esi].MsgGet
       sub    edi, eax
       cmp    edi, [esi].MsgPut          ; Write == Read-1?
       je     short mp90                 ; YES

       lea    edx, [esi].MsgArr
       cmp    [esi].MsgGet, edx          ; Read == MsgArr?
       jne    short mp20                 ; NO
       mov    eax, [esi].MsgLast
       cmp    eax, [esi].MsgPut          ; AND Write == last
       je     short mp90

       ; OK we can store it
mp20:  mov    edi, [esi].MsgPut
       mov    ax, [ebp.Client_CX]
       mov    [edi].dWnd, ax
       mov    ax, [ebp.Client_CXh]
       mov    [edi].dMsg, ax
```

```
            mov     ax, [ebp.Client_DI]
            mov     [edi].dwParam, ax
            mov     eax, [ebp.Client_EDX]
            mov     [edi].dlParam, eax

            ; inc free, roll it if past end
            add     [esi].MsgPut, size DosMsg
            mov     eax, [esi].MsgLast
            cmp     [esi].MsgPut, eax
            jbe     short mp30
            lea     eax, [esi].MsgArr
            mov     [esi].MsgPut, eax

            ; Signal read we have a message
mp30:       mov     eax, [esi.MsgSem]
            VMMcall Signal_Semaphore

            ; Boost the execution priority of the guy we call
            ; so it gets the message ASAP.
            mov     eax, Low_Pri_Device_Boost
            VMMcall Adjust_Exec_Priority

mp40:       mov     [ebp.Client_EAX], ERR_NONE
            ret

mp90:       mov     [ebp.Client_EAX], ERR_MSG_FULL
            ret

MsgPost   endp
```

We now have a message in the queue for a DOS VM. There are two calls to handle getting the message to the DOS app. The first call is MsgPeek. When a DOS app calls MsgPeek, it gets a copy of the next message in the queue. If there is no message, Release_Time_Slice is called and a no-message error is returned. This call assumes MsgPeek is only called in an idle loop. If you make this call to check for an abort message, you might want to remove the Release_Time_Slice.

```
MsgPeek   proc

            mov     eax, ebx
            call    GetVmData               ; ESI = VmData of VM

            ; do we have one?
            mov     edi, [esi].MsgGet
            cmp     edi, [esi].MsgPut
            je      short mpk90

            ; Lets fill it in
            mov     eax, [ebp].Client_EDX
            call    V86ToPmPtr
            mov     esi, edi
            mov     edi, eax
```

```
        mov     ecx, (size DosMsg) / 2
        rep     movsw

        mov     [ebp.Client_EAX], ERR_NONE
        ret

mpk90:  VMMcall Release_Time_Slice
        mov     [ebp.Client_EAX], ERR_NO_MSG
        ret

MsgPeek  endp
```

The second call is MsgRead. Although MsgPeek will return the contents of the next message, MsgRad actually removes a message from the queue. The first step is to call Wait_Semaphore. If there are no messages in the queue, this call blocks until MsgPost is called, putting a message in the queue and signaling the semaphore. Next, the message is filled in and the pointer **MsgGet** is incremented to the next location in the queue. The message is then returned.

```
MsgRead  proc

        mov     eax, ebx
        call    GetVmData               ; ESI = VmData of VM

        ; Lets block if there are no messages
        mov     eax, [esi.MsgSem]
        mov     ecx, Block_Svc_Ints or Block_Enable_Ints
        VMMcall       Wait_Semaphore

        ; Lets fill it in
mr10:   Save    <esi>
        mov     eax, [ebp].Client_EDX
        call    V86ToPmPtr
        mov     esi, [esi].MsgGet
        mov     edi, eax
        mov     ecx, (size DosMsg) / 2
        rep     movsw
        Restore       <esi>

        ; inc next, roll it if past end
        add     [esi].MsgGet, size DosMsg
        mov     eax, [esi].MsgLast
        cmp     [esi].MsgGet, eax
        jbe     short mr20
        lea     eax, [esi].MsgArr
        mov     [esi].MsgGet, eax

mr20:   mov     [ebp.Client_EAX], ERR_NONE
        ret

MsgRead  endp
```

DOS to Windows

Posting a message from a DOS app to a Windows app piggybacks on the internal message passing system. The DOS app needs to know the handle of the Windows app it is posting to. Then it just calls our internal PostMessage routine, passing it the message parameters. The message is then passed to Win-Link, which posts the message. The following code shows just the to Windows part of MsgPost.

```
MsgPost   proc

        mov     eax, [ebp.Client_EBX]
        call    GetVm
        jc      short mp05
        cmp     eax, [SysVm]
        jne     short mp10

        PostPm [SysVm], [ebp.Client_CX], [ebp.Client_CXh],
[ebp.Client_DI], [ebp.Client_EDX]
        mov     [ebp.Client_EAX], ERR_NONE
        ret

mp05:   mov     [ebp.Client_EAX], ERR_UNKNOWN_VM
        ret

mp10:   ; post to DOS app code ...

MsgPost   endp
```

Shared Memory and Copying Data Between VMs

Posting messages has a couple of disadvantages: It has a high overhead, it has a high latency (slow response time), and it has a queue limit. Most of all, you cannot pass pointers, just data in the registers themselves. Therefore we need calls to let us share memory. This capability comes to us in three calls, which let us copy data from one VM to another and give us pointers in one VM to data in another VM. Unfortunately, the pointer trick only works in protected-mode apps. A protected-mode app can get a pointer to data in a real mode app, but, because a real-mode app uses segments instead of selectors, this is a one-way street. The real-mode DOS app cannot get a pointer to memory in a Windows application.

Copying Memory

The MsgMemCopy function copies data from any VM to any other VM. It assumes that any VM other than the system VM is a real-mode address. The code for this is very simple:

the pointers are converted to flat 32-bit pointers and the data is then copied. The function V86ToPmPtr converts the pointer/VM pairs to the flat 32-bit offsets.

```
V86ToPmPtr     proc

      Save     <edx>
      cmp      ebx, [SysVm]
      jne      short vtp20

      Save     <ecx>
      push     eax
      shr      eax, 16
      VMMcall _SelectorMapFlat <[SysVm], EAX, 0>
      pop      edx

      cmp      eax, -1
      je       short vtp10

      and      edx, 0FFFFh
      add      eax, edx
      Restore <ecx,edx>
      clc
      ret

vtp10: Restore <ecx,edx>
      stc
      ret

vtp20: movzx    edx, ax
      shr      eax, 12
      and      eax, 0FFFF0h
      add      eax, edx
      add      eax, [ebx.CB_High_Linear]

      Restore <edx>
      clc
      ret

V86ToPmPtr     endp
```

GetVm performs a very simple function. If the passed-in value in EAX is 0, GetVm returns the system VM in EAX. Otherwise, it leaves EAX alone, assuming it is the handle to a VM. In debug mode GetVm validates the VM handle. Thus, it is a way to convert any passed-in VM handle from our system that maps a handle of 0 to the system VM, and in debug mode validates the handle.

```
GetVm  proc

      or       eax, eax
      jnz      short gv10
      mov      eax, [SysVm]
```

```
gv10:   Save    <ebx>
        mov     ebx, eax
        VMMcall         Validate_VM_Handle
        Restore         <ebx>

        ret
GetVm   endp
```

This function is not affected by what VM is currently running. However, the memory at both ends of this copy had better be locked down. The error-checking code has been removed from the following to make the sample clearer.

```
MsgMemCopy   proc

        Save    <ebx>

        ; Get the params
        mov     eax, [ebp.Client_EBX]
        call    GetVm
        mov     ebx, eax

        mov     eax, [ebp.Client_ESI]
        call    V86ToPmPtr
        mov     esi, eax

        mov     eax, [ebp.Client_EDX]
        call    GetVm
        mov     ebx, eax

        mov     eax, [ebp.Client_EDI]
        call    V86ToPmPtr
        mov     edi, eax

        mov     ecx, [ebp.Client_ECX]
        Restore         <ebx>

        ; Copy the dwords
        Save    <ecx>
        shr     ecx, 2
        rep     movsd
        Restore         <ecx>
        and     ecx, 03h
        jz      short mmc30
        rep     movsb

mmc30:  mov     [ebp.Client_EAX], ERR_NONE
        ret

MsgMemCopy   endp
```

Ldt and Gdt Pointers

The pairs of calls to create and free LDT and GDT pointers are: MsgMemLdt, MsgMemFreeLdt, MsgMemGdt, and MsgMemFreeGdt. We discuss only the LDT calls here. The GDT calls are similiar except that you do not need to specify in which sector VM will be used.

MsgMemLdt first verifies that the VM where the memory is located is good. It then calls V86ToPmPtr to get the flat offset of the memory location. It next tests the limit. Because we are returning a 16:16 pointer, we have to ensure that the limit does not exceed 64K. Finally, we verify that the VM that will use the returned LDT pointer is legit.

We use the pair of calls _BuildDescriptorDWORDs and _Allocate_LDT_Selector to create a LDT pointer from the passed-in parameters.

```
MsgMemLdt  proc

    Save    <ebx>

    mov     eax, [ebp.Client_EDX]
    call    GetVm
    jc      short mm130
    mov     ebx, eax

    ; Get flat address
    mov     eax, [ebp.Client_EDI]
    call    V86ToPmPtr
    jc      short mm130
    mov     esi, eax

    ; Get the limit
    mov     edi, [ebp.Client_ECX]
    test    edi, 0FFF00000h
    jnz     short mm130

    mov     eax, [ebp.Client_EBX]
    call    GetVm
    jc      short mm130
    mov     ebx, eax

    ; Create it
    VMMcall         _BuildDescriptorDWORDs <esi, edi, RW_Data_Type,
D_GRAN_BYTE, 0>
    VMMcall         _Allocate_LDT_Selector <ebx, edx, eax, 1, 0>

    Restore         <ebx>
    mov     [ebp.Client_AX], ax
    ret

mm130: Restore         <ebx>
    mov     [ebp.Client_EAX], 0
```

```
        ret

MsgMemLdt   endp
```

Freeing an LDT is even easier. Again, because a VM handle of 0 needs to be converted we call GetVm. Then we call **_Free_LDT_Selector** to free the LDT.

Whether you use LDTs or GDTs, the free call is critical. There are only 8K of GDTs in the entire system and only 8K of LDTs in each VM. If you have a leak where you allocate and don't free pointers, you will bring the system to its knees sooner or later.

```
MsgMemFreeLdt   proc

        Save    <ebx>

        mov     eax, [ebp.Client_EBX]
        call    GetVm
        jc      short mf120
        mov     ebx, eax

        movzx   edx, word ptr [ebp.Client_EDX]
        VMMcall _Free_LDT_Selector <ebx, edx, 0>

        Restore <ebx>
        mov     [ebp.Client_EAX], 0
        ret

mf120:  Restore <ebx>
        mov     [ebp.Client_EAX], ERR_UNKNOWN_VM
        ret

MsgMemFreeLdt   endp
```

Launching a DOS box

A Windows app can launch a DOS or Windows app with no help from us. The trick is for a DOS app to launch a Windows app or another DOS box.

This is painfully easy. The DOS app sends a message to Win-Link, which calls DosExec in Win-Link. This call passes a file to exec and a run parameter. This file can be a DOS or Windows app.

Win-Link will then call **WinExec** to launch the app. The app is launched in the mode specified. If the mode is SW_HIDE, the app is launched but you will not even see an icon for it.

```
void DosExec (HWND hDlg,LONG lParam)
{
BYTE _far *fpsFile;
```

```
SENDDLG _far *fpSendDlg;
VMDATA _far *fpVmData;

  fpSendDlg = (SENDDLG _far *) lParam;
  fpVmData = (VMDATA _far *) fpSendDlg->lParam;
  fpsFile = fpVmData->sExec;

  if (WinExec (fpsFile, fpSendDlg->wParam) <= 32)
      fpSendDlg->lRtn = 0L;
  else
    fpSendDlg->lRtn = -1L;

  *(fpVmData->sExec) = 0;
}
```

Launching Windows Applications from DOS

We now come to the initial instigation for the Win-Link program. In a window at the DOS prompt you type the name of a Windows app and it returns saying, **"This program requires Microsoft Windows."**

And the initial thought I always had was: What do you think is running? Granted this was partially a problem with wording — I have seen some applications that will sense if Windows is running and, if it is, gives you a better message. But still, Windows is running and I want it to start up my Windows app, even if I type the command from the DOS command line. So we will now go through this process.

The first step is to intercept the int 21h call to exec a DOS program. (Note: all the following code fragments show just the necessary parts to catch the DOS exec. I have also removed the special case code for win.com.) If you type win at the ODS command prompt, Win-Link had some special handling. This is remnant from Windows 3.0 days when Windows would let you start Windows in a DOS box.

The first thing we do is open the .EXE file. We have to be careful here because if share is loaded and this is a Windows EXE that is already running, we will get a sharing violation. So we also have an int 24h hooker to catch the violation. This stops it from appearing in the DOS box.

```
BeginProc WinIpc_Int_24

      mov     eax, ebx
      call    GetVmData

      test    [esi.wFlags], I24_ON
      jz      short i24_10

      mov     [ebp.Client_AL], 3
```

```
        clc
        ret

i24_10:      stc
        ret

EndProc WinIpc_Int_24
```

If the open fails, we check the return code. If it is a sharing violation, we pass it on to Win-Link to try and exec because the odds are pretty good that its a Windows app. If it is a different error we pass it on to DOS for a try.

If the open succeeded, we next read to see if it is a New Executable format file. Unfortunately all this means is it is not real mode. However, there is no way to tell if it's a Windows or OS/2 application.

If the file does not have the NE signature, we pass it on to DOS. Up to this point our hit has been minimal. Yes we did an open, but DOS will open the same file again so all we did is get it in the cache sooner.

```
BeginProc WinIpc_Int_21

i21_70: cmp   [ebp.Client_AX], 4B00h          ; EXEC, func 0?
        jne   i21_160

        test  [SysFlags], EXEC_OFF             ; EXEC off?
        jnz   i21_160

        Push_Client_State
        VMMcall Begin_Nest_Exec

        push  edi                              ; local vars
        push  esi                              ; local vars
        sub   esp, size DiStk
        mov   edi, esp
        mov   [edi.hVm], ebx

        movzx edx, [ebp.Client_ES]             ; get offset to cmd line
        shl   edx, 4
        movzx eax, [ebp.Client_BX]
        add   edx, eax
        add   edx, [ebx.CB_High_Linear]

        movzx eax, word ptr [edx+4]
        shl   eax, 4
        movzx edx, word ptr [edx+2]
        add   edx, eax
        add   edx, [ebx.CB_High_Linear]
        mov   [edi.pCmd], edx

        movzx edx, [ebp.Client_DS]             ; get offset to file
name
```

```
        shl     edx, 4
        movzx   eax, [ebp.Client_DX]
        add     edx, eax
        add     edx, [ebx.CB_High_Linear]
        mov     [edi.pFn], edx

        or      [esi.wFlags], I24_ON
        mov     eax, 3D20h                      ; open file
        VxDint 21h
        jnc     short i21_110                   ; NO error on open
        and     [esi.wFlags], not I24_ON
        cmp     al, 5                           ; file locked?
        jne     i21_150                         ; NO - leave it to DOS
        jmp     i21_120

i21_110:        and     [esi.wFlags], not I24_ON
        mov     [edi.hFile], ax
        mov     ebx, eax

        mov     eax, 3F00h                      ; read MZ
        mov     ecx, 2
        lea     edx, [edi]+RwBuf
        VxDint 21h
        jc      i21_140
        cmp     word ptr [edi.RwBuf], 5A4Dh
        jne     i21_140

        mov     eax, 4200h                      ; seek to offset
        xor     ecx, ecx
        mov     edx, 3Ch
        VxDint 21h
        jc      i21_140

        mov     eax, 3F00h                      ; read offset
        mov     ecx, 4
        lea     edx, [edi]+RwBuf
        VxDint 21h
        jc      i21_140

        movzx   edx, word ptr [edi.RwBuf]       ; Seek to new EXE
        movzx   ecx, word ptr [edi.RwBuf+2]
        mov     eax, 4200h
        VxDint 21h
        jc      i21_140

        mov     eax, 3F00h                      ; read NE
        mov     ecx, 2
        lea     edx, [edi]+RwBuf
        VxDint 21h
        jc      i21_140
        cmp     word ptr [edi.RwBuf], 454Eh
        jne     i21_140

        mov     bx, [edi.hFile]                 ; close file
```

```
        mov     eax, 3E00h
        VxDint 21h
```

Ok, we may have a Windows app, so we copy the file name and command line into our structure and send a message to Win-Link. Win-Link will return a 0 if it launched the program successfully. In that case we return, eating the interrupt call. This will return the DOS box back to the DOS prompt.

If Win-Link returns non zero, then it could not launch the app. In that case we return with carry set and the interrupt is passed on to DOS. DOS then attempts to launch the application.

```
i21_120:        mov     ebx, [edi.hVm]
        mov     eax, ebx
        call    GetVmData

        push    edi
        push    esi

        mov     edi, [edi].pFn
        lea     esi, [esi].sExec          ; copy fn
        xchg    esi, edi
        mov     ecx, 128 / 4
        rep     movsd

        pop     esi
        pop     edi
        push    edi
        push    esi

        mov     edi, [edi].pCmd           ; copy command line
        lea     esi, [esi].sCmdLine
        xchg    esi, edi
        mov     ecx, 128 / 4
        rep     movsd

        pop     esi
        pop     edi

        mov     edx, [esi.VmLdt]
        Save    <edi,esi>
        SendPm [SysVm], [SysWnd], MSG_WIN_EXEC, 0, edx

        Restore <esi,edi>
        mov     ebx, [edi.hVm]

        cmp     edx, 0            ; WinExec OK?
        jne     short i21_150

        add     esp, size DiStk
        pop     esi
        pop     edi
```

```
        VMMcall        End_Nest_Exec
        Pop_Client_State

        clc                            ; return done
        ret

i21_140: mov bx, [edi.hFile]          ; close file
        mov    eax, 3E00h
        VxDint 21h

i21_150: mov ebx, [edi.hVm]

        add    esp, size DiStk
        pop    esi
        pop    edi
        VMMcall End_Nest_Exec
        Pop_Client_State

i21_160: stc                          ; return continue chain
        ret

EndProc WinIpc_Int_21
```

When the message is sent to Win-Link, it processes it in ExecFile. We first look to see if this file is in a list of files that are to not be launched. This list includes bound OS/2 apps, apps that have both a real DOS program as their stub, and any other EXEs that have a NE header that you do not wish to launch. These files are tracked by file name only, not the full path. So we compare just the file name.

We then find the drive and directory of the file being executed. This is the directory it is in because command.com walks the path, but for each attempt it passes EXEC the fully qualified file name to run. We set that drive and directory as the default drive and directory. This way an application is run from its own directory. Experience has shown me that this is the best drive to use.

Now we're ready to try it. We call LoadModule because we only want to launch Windows apps and not DOS apps. A DOS app should stay in its own VM. LoadModule can only exec a Windows app. LoadModule gives us a return value which we then pass back as our return value. Obtaining this return value is the reason we needed a SendMessage instead of a PostMessage.

Finally, we restore the default drive and directory.

```
void ExecFile (HWND hDlg,WORD wParam,DWORD lParam)
{
BYTE _far *fpsBase, _far *fpsFile;
SENDDLG _far *fpSendDlg;
VMDATA _far *fpVmData;
FARPROC lpProcAbout;
int iNum;
```

```
LOADMOD LoadMod;
WORD wCmdShow[2];
BYTE sBuf[FILE_MAX+2], sCwd[FILE_MAX+2];

  fpSendDlg = (SENDDLG _far *) lParam;
  fpVmData = (VMDATA _far *) fpSendDlg->lParam;
  fpsBase = fpVmData->sExec;
  fpsFile = fStrEnd (fpsBase);
  while ((fpsFile >= fpsBase) && (*fpsFile != '\\') &&
         (*fpsFile != '/') && (*fpsFile != ':'))
    fpsFile--;
  fpsFile++;

  // see if in our no-no list
  fpSendDlg->lRtn = 0L;
  if ((iNum = (int) SendDlgItemMessage (hDlg, DLG_NO_EXEC,
        LB_FINDSTRING, 0, (LONG) fpsFile)) >= 0)
    {
    SendDlgItemMessage (hDlg, DLG_NO_EXEC, LB_GETTEXT,
        iNum, (LONG) (LPSTR) sBuf);
    if (! fStriCmp (sBuf, fpsFile))
      fpSendDlg->lRtn = 0xFFFFFFFFL;
    }

  if (fpSendDlg->lRtn != 0)
    {
    *(fpVmData->sExec) = 0;
    return;
    }

  // Save the current dir & set the current dir to the dir
  // the program is in. After the exec - we restore the cur dir
  _getdcwd (toupper (*fpsBase) - 'A' + 1, sCwd, FILE_MAX);
  fStrnCpy (sBuf, fpsBase, FILE_MAX);
  iNum = Min (fpsFile - fpsBase, FILE_MAX);
  if ((iNum > 3) && (sBuf[iNum-1] == '\\'))
    iNum--;
  sBuf [iNum] = 0;

  // Set default drive & dir
  _dos_setdrive (toupper (sBuf[0]) - 'A' + 1, (unsigned *) &iNum);
  _chdir (sBuf);

  fpsFile = fpVmData->sCmdLine;
  *(fpsFile + (*fpsFile) + 1) = 0;

  LoadMod.wEnvSeg = 0;
  LoadMod.dwRes = 0;
  LoadMod.lpCmdLine = fpsFile + 1;
  LoadMod.lpCmdShow = wCmdShow;
  wCmdShow[0] = 2;
  wCmdShow[1] = SW_SHOWNORMAL;

  if (LoadModule (fpsBase, &LoadMod) <= (HINSTANCE) 32)
```

```
    fpSendDlg->lRtn = -1L;
  *(fpVmData->sExec) = 0;

  // Back to the old drive & dir
  _dos_setdrive (toupper (sCwd[0]) - 'A' + 1, (unsigned *) &iNum);
  _chdir (sCwd);
}
```

The DOS Box Title, Print Intercepting, and Everything

We have covered a significant part of Win-Link. Unfortunately (or fortunately depending on your point of view), this book is not tittled *The Complete Guide to the Win-Link Sources.*

The DOS box title tracking is fairly straightforward. Whenever Win-IPC believes that the running application has changed, it sets the title to the string found in the memory arena for the currently selected PSP.

The one weird thing here is you can't track the set PSP call because there are usually TSRs or device drivers that temporarily change it. You will find that the title constantly changes as you sit at the DOS prompt.

The print intercepting is probably the most complicated part of the entire program. It involves intercepting various interrupts, time-outs, and its own printer driver. A thorough discussion of it could be a book by itself. And, unfortunately, I do not have permission to include the sources to the raw printer driver. However, all RAW.DRV does is properly implement the PASSTHROUGH escape command; most 3.1 printer drivers also do that.

The rest of Win-Link is pretty dull. There is the code to handle the dialog box and the other details of a standard Windows program. I hope by explaining how a commercial program works, I have provided a different viewpoint into VxDs than you get from sample programs. I also hope that if you ever have to write a program like this that the code presented here will give you a head start. I can tell you from experience that attacking this for the first time is not the best way to learn about VxDs.

SECTION 4

VMM and VxD Service Reference

Appendix A

Service Interface Reference

This appendix contains an alphabetic listing of the VMM and system VxDs services and macros.[1]

VMM Service Reference

_AddFreePhysPage

```
include vmm.inc

VMMcall _AddFreePhysPage, <PhysPgNum, nPages, flags>

mov     [PagesAdded], eax       ; 0 = none, 1 = some, 2 = all
```

The **_AddFreePhysPage** service adds one or more physical pages to the free memory pool. Virtual devices use this service to add pages that the Windows loader could not find, but that the virtual device did find. For example, the V86MMGR device adds any unused physical pages it finds when using the Global EMM Import function of a 386 LIMulator.

This service is only available during initialization and only in Windows version 3.1 and later.

Parameters

PhysPgNum

Specifies the physical page number of the first page to add. The page number must be greater than or equal to 110h; only extended memory pages may be added to the pool.

------

[1]Reprinted with permission of Microsoft Corporation.

The specified pages must be read/write physical memory pages, and must be available for use at any time.

nPages

Specifies the number of physical pages to add.

flags

Specifies the operation flags. This parameter must be set to 0.

Return Value

The EAX register contains one of the following values:

Value	Meaning
0	None of the specified physical pages were added to the free pool.
1	Some, but not all, of the specified physical pages were added.
2	All of the specified physical pages were added.

Comments

A virtual device must not attempt to use pages once it has added them to the free pool, or attempt to add pages that are already available to the system.

This service returns an error if the number of pages to add exceeds the limit of the internal data structure the system uses the manage the free pool. The internal data structure is allocated during initialization and cannot be modified.

Uses

EAX

See Also

_GetFreePageCount

_Add_Global_V86_Data_Area

```
include vmm.inc

VMMcall _Add_Global_V86_Data_Area, <LinAddr, nBytes, flags>

or      eax, eax        ; nonzero if added, zero if error
jz      not_added
```

The **_Add_Global_V86_Data_Area** service adds a region to the list of regions available for allocation as global V86 data areas.

This service is only available during initialization, and only for Windows version 3.1 or later.

Parameters

LinAddr

Specifies the linear address of the first byte of the region. This address must be less than 100000h, and must not lie between the first and last V86 page for the specified virtual machine.

nBytes

Specifies the size in bytes of the region.

flags

Specifies the operation flags. This parameter must be set to 0.

Return Value

The EAX register contains a nonzero value if the service is successful. Otherwise, EAX contains zero to indicate an error such as an invalid region specification.

Comments

This service supports virtual devices, such as the virtual MS-DOS manager and the V86MMGR device, which can manage high memory above the last V86 page. The service lets these devices add available regions which would otherwise go unused. Typically, such regions are nonpage-aligned fragments which cannot be used for normal operations requiring page-aligned memory.

Calls to this service should be made during processing of the **Sys_Critical_Init** message. Virtual devices should not wait for the **Device_Init** or **Init_Complete** messages since most of the allocation of global V86 data areas is done while processing the **Device_Init** message.

If this service adds a region that is above the last V86 page, virtual devices should not attempt to allocate the region until the **Sys_Critical_Init** message has been processed.

Uses

EAX

See Also

_Allocate_Global_V86_Data_Area

_AddInstanceItem

```
include vmm.inc

VMMcall _AddInstanceItem, <<OFFSET32 InstStruc>, flags>

or      eax, eax        ; nonzero if added, zero if error
jz      not_added
```

The **_AddInstanceItem** service identifies a region of instance data in the V86 address space.

Parameters

InstStruc

Points to an **InstDataStruc** structure containing information about the block of memory to instance.

flags

Specifies the operation flags. This parameter must be set to 0.

Return Value

The EAX register contains a nonzero value if the service is successful. Otherwise EAX contains zero to indicate an error.

Comments

To prevent errors, a virtual device must not change the location and content of any **InstDataStruc** structures until after the system has completed its initialization. To achieve this, a virtual can either staticly allocate the structures in its INIT data segment or dynamically allocate the structures on the system heap using the **_HeapAllocate** service. If the structures are in the INIT data segment, the system automatically frees the structure when it reclaims the INIT segment space. If the structures are in the system heap, the virtual device must free the structures using the **_HeapFree** service while processing the **Sys_VM_Init** message.

If a virtual device the structures on the system heap, it must not attempt to reallocate the structure before system initialization has completed since this invalidates the structure address.

Only one, contiguous region of instance data can be identified with each structure. The virtual device can cut down the call overhead and data space requirements by coalescing adjacent blocks of instance data and identifying the coalesced blocks as a single instance item.

Uses

EAX

Adjust_Exec_Priority

```
include vmm.inc

mov     eax, PriorityBoost      ; signed integer
mov     ebx, VM                 ; VM handle
VMMcall Adjust_Exec_Priority
```

The **Adjust_Exec_Priority** service raises or lowers the execution priority of the specified virtual machine. The service adds the specified boost to the virtual machine's current execution priority.

Parameters

PriorityBoost

Specifies a positive or negative priority boost for the virtual machine. This parameter must be a value such that when added to the current execution priority, the result is within the range Reserved_Low_Boost to Reserved_High_Boost.

The following lists some common priority boost values:

Value	Meaning
Reserved_Low_Boost	Reserved for use by system.
Cur_Run_VM_Boost	The time-slice scheduler uses this value to force a virtual machine to run for its allotted time-slice.
Low_Pri_Device_Boost	Virtual devices use this value for events that need timely processing but are not time critical.
High_Pri_Device_Boost	Virtual devices use this value for events that need timely processing but should not circumvent operations that have a critical section boost.
Critical_Section_Boost	The system uses this value for virtual machines specified in a call to the Begin_Critical_Section service.
Time_Critical_Boost	Virtual devices use this value for events that must be processed even when another virtual machine is in a critical section. For example, VPICD uses this when simulating hardware interrupts.
Reserved_High_Boost	Reserved for use by system.

VM

Specifies the handle identifying the virtual machine.

Return Value

This service has no return value.

Comments

Since the nonsuspended virtual machine with the highest execution priority is always the current virtual machine, this service causes a task switch under two circumstances:

1.   The execution priority of the current virtual machine is lowered (EAX is negative), and there is another virtual machine with a higher priority that is not suspended.

2.   The execution of a nonsuspended virtual machine which is not the current virtual machine is raised (EAX is positive) higher than the current virtual machine's execution priority.

Even if the current virtual machine is in a critical section, a task switch will still occur if the priority of another nonsuspended virtual machine is raised higher than the current virtual machine's priority. However, this will only occur when a virtual machine is given a time-critical boost, for example, to simulate a hardware interrupt.

It is often more convenient to call the **Call_Priority_VM_Event** service than to call this service directly.

Uses

Flags

See Also

Begin_Critical_Section, **Call_Priority_VM_Event**

Adjust_Execution_Time

```
include vmm.inc

mov     eax, Time        ; number of milliseconds
mov     ebx, VM          ; VM handle
VMMcall Adjust_Execution_Time
```

The **Adjust_Execution_Time** service adjusts the amount of execution time a virtual machine is granted with each time slice. Virtual devices, such as the virtual COM device, use this service to temporarily boost the priority of a virtual machine, such as when the virtual machine is receiving an unusually high number of interrupts.

Parameters

Time

Specifies a signed integer value representing the number of milliseconds to add or subtract from the current time-slice granularity value.

VM

Specifies a handle identifying the virtual machine to adjust.

Return Value

This service has no return value.

Comments

This service has the same effect on all virtual machines regardless of their time-slice priority. If the specified virtual machine is not on the time-slice list, this service returns immediately (does nothing). This service never forces a nonrunnable virtual machine to execute. A virtual machine not already in the background cannot be forced to run in the background by boosting its execution time.

This service can increase or decrease the execution time for a virtual machine. However, decreasing execution time is not recommended because it defeats the purpose of multitasking. Virtual devices should avoid using this service.

Uses

Flags

See Also

Get_Time_Slice_Granularity, **Set_Time_Slice_Granularity**

_Allocate_Device_CB_Area

```
include vmm.inc

VMMcall _Allocate_Device_CB_Area, <nBytes, flags>

or      eax, eax        ; zero if error
jz      not_allocated

mov     [Offset], eax   ; offset from start of control block
```

Uses

EAX, EDX

See Also

_Allocate_LDT_Selector, _Free_GDT_Selector

_Allocate_Global_V86_Data_Area

```
include vmm.inc

VMMcall _Allocate_Global_V86_Data_Area, <nBytes, flags>

or      eax, eax        ; zero if error
jz      error
mov     [Address], eax  ; ring-0 linear address of block
```

The **_Allocate_Global_V86_Data_Area** service allocates a block of memory from the global V86 data area. The block is for exclusive use by the virtual device. Virtual devices use this service to allocate memory for device-specific objects which must be accessible to both the virtual device and software running in the virtual machine.

This service is only available during initialization.

Parameters

nBytes

Specifies the number of bytes to allocate. This parameter should be a multiple of 4096.

flags

Specifies the operation flags. This parameter can be a combination of the following values:

Value	Meaning
GVDAWordAlign	Aligns block on a word boundary. If no alignment value is given, the service aligns the block on a byte boundary.
GVDADWordAlign	Aligns block on a doubleword boundary. If no alignment value is given, the service aligns the block on a byte boundary.
GVDAParaAlign	Aligns block on a paragraph (16-byte) boundary. If no alignment value is given, the service aligns the block on a byte boundary.

GVDAPageAlign	Aligns block on a page (4 kilobyte) boundary. If no alignment value is given, the service aligns the block on a byte boundary.
	The GVDAWordAlign, GVDADWordAlign, GVDA-ParaAlign, and GVDAPageAlign values are mutually exclusive.
GVDAInstance	Creates an instance data block allowing the virtual device to maintain different values in the block for each virtual machine. If this value is not given, the service creates a global block in which the same data is available to all virtual machines.
GVDAZeroInit	Fills the block with zeros. If this value is not given, the initial content of the block is undefined.
GVDAReclaim	Unmaps any physical pages in the block while mapping the system nul page into the block. The service places unmapped physical pages in the free list. This value only applies if the GVDAPageAlign value is also given. If this value is not given, the service ignores any physical pages it unmaps. It is up to the virtual device to reclaim these pages.
	The GVDAReclaim and GVDAInstance values are mutually exclusive.
GVDAInquire	Returns the size in bytes of the largest block that satisfies the requested alignment but does not require the first V86 page to be moved. The nBytes parameter is not used if this value is specified
	A virtual device typically uses this value, while processing the **Init_Complete** message, to allocate portions of the global V86 data area that might otherwise go unused. The GVDAInquire value is only available for Windows version 3.1 or later.
GVDAHighSysCritOK	Informs the service that the virtual device can manage a block that resides in high MS-DOS memory. The service allocates from high MS-DOS memory only if such memory is available (for example, implemented

as XMS UMBs) and the virtual device specifies this value. A virtual device can use this value only while processing the **Sys_Critical_Init** message.

When first allocated, a block in high MS-DOS memory may not be immediately usable since memory supporting the area may not yet have been mapped. The system maps the memory for the area sometime during the **Sys_Critical_Init** message, but there is no guarantee as to when.

The GVDAHighSysCritOK value is only available for Windows version 3.1 or later.

All other values are reserved.

Return Value

The EAX register contains the ring-0 linear address of the block if the service is successful. Otherwise, EAX contains zero to indicate an error such as insufficient memory to satisfy the request.

If GVDAInquire is given, EAX contains the size in bytes of the largest block that satisfies the request, but that does not move the first V86 page. EAX contains zero if all such requests move the first V86 page.

Comments

If this service returns an error, the virtual device should consider this a fatal error and respond accordingly.

The size returned when the GVDAInquire value is given may be less than a reasonable minimum. For instance, if GVDAPageAlign is specified, the return size may be less than 4096. It is up to the virtual device to check for this.

For blocks allocated with GVDAInstance, this service calls automatically calls the **_AddInstanceItem** service.

The **_Allocate_Global_V86_Data_Area** service is not available and must not be called if the virtual device has allocated a temporary block using the **_Allocate_Temp_V86_Data_Area** service. The virtual device must free the block before it can call the **_Allocate_Global_V86_Data_Area** service.

If GVDAReclaim is not given, the virtual device should reclaim the physical addresses of any unmapped physical pages and map the pages to other addresses. A virtual device reclaims the physical addresses by using the **_CopyPageTable** service to retrieve the page table entries for the system virtual machine. The virtual device can then use the **_PhysIntoV86** service to map the physical pages into the V86 address space.

Uses

EAX

See Also

_CopyPageTable, **_PhysIntoV86**

_Allocate_LDT_Selector

```
include vmm.inc

VMMcall _Allocate_LDT_Selector, <VM, DescDWORD1, DescDWORD2,\
                                 Count, flags>
```

The service creates a new selector or selectors and adds them to the Local Descriptor Table (LDT) for the specified virtual machine.

Parameters

VM

Specifies a handle identifying the virtual machine to receive the selectors.

DescDWORD1

Specifies the high four bytes of the descriptor for the selector. This parameter contains the high 16 bits of the base address, the high 4 bits of the limit, and the status and type bits.

DescDWORD2

Specifies the low four bytes of the descriptor for the selector. This parameter contains the low 16 bits of the base address and limit.

Count

Specifies the number of contiguous LDT selectors to allocate if the flags parameter does not specify the ALDTSpecSel value. Otherwise, this parameter specifies the LDT selector to allocate.

flags

Specifies the operation flags. This parameter can be the following value:

Value	Meaning
ALDTSpecSel	Allocates the LDT selector specified by the Count parameter. The service copies the descriptor data to the specified LDT entry and returns the selector. If the LDT selector is already allocated, the service returns an error value instead.
	If this value is not given, the service allocates the number of selectors specified by Count.

All other values are reserved.

Return Value

If the service is successful, the EAX and EDX registers contain the following values:

Register	Description
EAX	Contains the new selector. If Count is greater than 1, EAX contains only the first selector. The second selector is EAX+8, the third EAX+16, and so on. The high 16 bits of the selector is always zero.
EDX	Contains the selector for and the size of the local descriptor table (LDT). The low 16 bits contains the selector for the LDT, and the high 16 bits contains the size of the LDT expressed as the number of selectors in the table.

The EAX and EDX registers contain zero to indicate an error such as an invalid descriptor value, the LDT is full, an invalid virtual machine handle, or selector already allocated.

Comments

A virtual device can use the selector of the LDT to directly edit the selectors in the LDT. However, a virtual device should use the **_SetDescriptor** service to change an LDT selector rather than edit the LDT.

This service sets the RPL of the selector to the DPL of the selector set in the *DescDWORD1* parameter.

LDT selectors are only valid when the virtual machine for which they are created is the current virtual machine. However, a virtual device can use the **_SelectorMapFlat** service to examine the region described by a LDT selector in virtual machines which are not the current virtual machine.

Although this service can create multiple selectors, the **_Free_LDT_Selector** service cannot free multiple selectors. Multiple selectors must be freed individually.

When this service creates multiple selectors, it gives each selector the same descriptor values. It does not change the base address for each selector. It is up to the virtual device to edit the selectors, and assign appropriate base addresses.

Virtual devices should not rely on specific hard-coded LDT selectors, and therefore, they should avoid using the ALDTSpecSel value.

Uses

EAX, EDX

See Also

_Allocate_GDT_Selector, _Free_LDT_Selector

Allocate_PM_Call_Back

```
include vmm.inc

mov     edx, OFFSET32 RefData    ; reference data
mov     esi, OFFSET32 Callback   ; callback procedure to call
VMMcall Allocate_PM_Call_Back

jc      error
mov     [CallbackAddr], eax      ; offset for callback
```

The Allocate_PM_Call_Back service installs a callback procedure that protected-mode applications can call to execute code in a virtual device. The service returns a callback address, specified as selector:offset pair. When protected-mode applications call this address, the system passes control to the callback procedure specified by the Callback parameter.

Virtual devices typically use this service to allow software running in a virtual machine to call APIs provided by the virtual device.

Parameters

RefData

Points to reference data to be passed to the callback procedure.

Callback

Points to the callback procedure to install. See the Comments section for more information about the procedure.

Return Value

If the carry flag is clear, the EAX register contains the address of the callback procedure. Otherwise, the carry flag is set to indicate that the callback procedure could not be installed.

Comments

The system calls the callback procedure as follows:

```
mov     ebx, VM                     ; current VM handle
mov     edx, OFFSET32 RefData       ; points to reference data
mov     ebp, OFFSET32 crs           ; points to Client_Reg_Struc
call    [Callback]
```

The *VM* parameter is a handle identifying the current virtual machine. The *RefData* parameter points to the reference data supplied when the callback procedure was installed, and *crs* points to a **Client_Reg_Struc** structure containing the register values for the virtual machine.

Uses

EAX, Flags

See Also

Allocate_V86_Call_Back

_Allocate_Temp_V86_Data_Area

```
include vmm.inc

VMMcall _Allocate_Temp_V86_Data_Area, <nBytes, flags>
or      eax, eax        ; zero if error
jz      error
mov     [Address], eax  ; address of temporary block
```

The **_Allocate_Temp_V86_Data_Area** service allocates a block of memory from the global V86 data area. The block is for exclusive use by the virtual device during system initialization only. A virtual device typically allocates a temporary block to serve as a buffer for calls to MS-DOS or BIOS functions. A virtual device makes such calls using the **Simulate_Int** service.

This service is only available during initialization.

Parameters

nBytes

Specifies the number of bytes to allocate.

flags

Specifies the operation flags. This parameter must be set to 0.

Return Value

The EAX register contains the ring-0 linear address of the block if the service is successful. Otherwise, EAX contains zero to indicate an error such as insufficient memory to satisfy the request or temporary area already allocated.

Comments

This service always aligns the temporary block on a paragraph boundary and fills the block with zeros.

Virtual devices must free the temporary block as soon as possible. The system provides only one temporary data area, therefore only one temporary block can be allocated at a time. Attempts to allocate a temporary block when it is already allocated will result in an error.

Uses

EAX

See Also

_Free_Temp_V86_Data_Area

Allocate_V86_Call_Back

```
include vmm.inc

mov      edx, OFFSET32 RefData    ; reference data
mov      esi, OFFSET32 Callback   ; callback procedure to call
VMMcall  Allocate_V86_Call_Back

jc       error
mov      [CallbackAddr], eax      ; segment:offset for callback
```

The **Allocate_V86_Call_Back** service installs a callback procedure that V86 mode applications can call to execute code in a virtual device. The service returns a callback address, specified as segment:offset pair. When V86 mode applications call this address, the system passes control to the callback procedure specified by the *Callback* parameter.

Virtual devices typically use this service to allow software running in a virtual machine to call APIs provided by the virtual device.

Parameters

RefData

> Points to reference data to be passed to the callback procedure.

Callback

> Points to the callback procedure to install. See the "Comments" section for more information about the procedure.

Return Value

If the carry flag is clear, the EAX register contains the address of the callback procedure. Otherwise, the carry flag is set to indicate that the callback procedure could not be installed.

Comments

The system calls the callback procedure as follows:

```
mov     ebx, VM                   ; current VM handle
mov     edx, OFFSET32 RefData      ; points to reference data
mov     ebp, OFFSET32 crs          ; points to Client_Reg_Struc
call    [Callback]
```

The *VM* parameter is a handle identifying the current virtual machine. The *RefData* parameter points to the reference data supplied when the callback procedure was installed, and crs points to a **Client_Reg_Struc** structure containing the register values for the virtual machine.

Uses

EAX, Flags

See Also

Allocate_PM_Call_Back

_Assign_Device_V86_Pages

```
include vmm.inc

VMMcall _Assign_Device_V86_Pages, <VMLinrPage, nPages,\
                                VM, flags>

or      eax, eax                  ; nonzero if assigned
jz      not_assigned
```

The **_Assign_Device_V86_Pages** service assigns to a virtual device one or more pages of the V86 address space.

Parameters

VMLinrPage

Specifies the linear page number of the first page of V86 address space to assign. The page number must be in the range 0 through 10Fh.

nPages

Specifies the number of pages to assign. All pages to assign must be within the V86 address space. If any a page is already assigned, this service returns an error value.

VM

Specifies a handle identifying a virtual machine. If this parameter is a valid handle, the assignments apply only to the specified virtual machine. If this parameter is zero, the assignments apply to all virtual machines.

flags

Specifies the operation flags. This parameter must be set to 0.

Return Value

The EAX register contains a nonzero value if the service is successful. Otherwise, EAX contains zero to indicate an error such as a specified page already assigned or an invalid page range.

Comments

A virtual device can make global assignments at any time, including during device initialization. For global assignments, the VM parameter must be zero. The virtual device must not attempt to assign a page that is already assigned. A virtual device can make local assignments only after device initialization is complete.

Uses

EAX

See Also

_DeAssign_Device_V86_Pages

Begin_Critical_Section

```
include vmm.inc

mov     ecx, Flags              ; flags for servicing interrupts
VMMcall Begin_Critical_Section
```

The **Begin_Critical_Section** service causes the current virtual machine to enter a critical section. Only one virtual machine can own the critical section at a time. If a virtual machine calls this service while another virtual machine owns the critical section, the calling virtual machine will block until the critical section is released.

Parameters

Flags

Specifies actions to take when interrupts occur while the virtual machine is blocked waiting for the critical section. This parameter can be a combination of the following values:

Value	Meaning
Block_Svc_Ints	Service interrupts in the virtual machine even if the virtual machine is blocked.
Block_Svc_If_Ints_Locked	Service interrupts in the virtual machine even if the virtual machine is blocked and the VMStat_V86IntsLocked flag is set.
Block_Enable_Ints	Service interrupts in the virtual machine even if the virtual machine does not currently have interrupts enabled. This forces interrupts to be enabled. This value is only relevant if either Block_Svc_Ints or Block_Svc_If_Ints_Locked is set.

The Block_Poll value is reserved and must not be used with this service.

Return Value

This service has no return value.

Comments

The system maintains a count of claims for critical sections and releases the critical section only when an equal number of **Begin_Critical_Section End_Critical_Section** services have been called.

When the critical section is first claimed, the system boosts the execution priority of the current virtual machine by the Critical_Section_Boost value (as described for the **Adjust_Exec_Priority** service). While a virtual machine is in a critical section, the system will switch to another task only if the virtual machine blocks on a semaphore or the other task has a time-critical operation, such as simulating hardware interrupts.

Uses

Flags

See Also

Adjust_Exec_Priority, **End_Critical_Section**

Begin_Nest_Exec

```
include vmm.inc

VMMcall Begin_Nest_Exec
```

The **Begin_Nest_Exec** service starts a nested execution block. This service is used in conjunction with the **End_Nest_Exec** service to create a nested execution block in which a virtual device may call the **Exec_Int** and **Resume_Exec** services. Virtual devices use these services to call software in the virtual machine.

Parameters

This service has no parameters.

Return Value

The **Client_CS** and **Client_IP** registers contain a break point used by nested execution services.

Comments

While in a nested execution block, a virtual device may call the **Exec_Int** and **Resume_Exec** services any number of times.

If one of these calls changes the virtual machine registers, these changes are also made to the client state. Before creating the nested execution block, a virtual device should save the client state by using the **Save_Client_State** service. After ending the nested execution block, a virtual device should restore the client state by using the **Restore_Client_State** service.

This service forces the virtual machine into protected-mode execution if there is a protected-mode application running in the current virtual machine. Otherwise, the virtual machine remains in V86 mode. The **End_Nest_Exec** service restores the virtual machine to its mode prior to the call to **Begin_Nest_Exec**.

If the execution mode changes to protected mode, this service automatically switches the virtual machine to the locked protected-mode stack and **End_Nest_Exec** switches it back. This allows most devices to change execution modes without worrying about demand paging issues.

Example

The following example shows a nested call to the MS-DOS function Get Version (Interrupt 21h, Function 30h):

```
VMMcall  Begin_Nest_Exec           ; Start nested execution
mov      [ebp.Client_AH], 30h      ; 30h = Get MS-DOS Version #
mov      eax, 21h                  ; Execute an Int 21h in the
VMMcall  Exec_Int                  ; current VM to call DOS
VMMcall  End_Nest_Exec             ; End of nested exec calls
```

This example copies the MS-DOS version to the **Client_AH** and **Client_AL** registers.

Uses

Client_CS, **Client_IP**, Flags

See Also

Begin_Nest_V86_Exec, **End_Nest_Exec**, **Exec_Int**, **Restore_Client_State**, **Resume_Exec**, **Save_Client_State**, **Set_PM_Exec_Mode**, **Set_V86_Exec_Mode**

Begin_Nest_V86_Exec

```
include vmm.inc

VMMcall Begin_Nest_V86_Exec
```

The **Begin_Nest_V86_Exec** service sets the current virtual machine to V86 mode and prepares the virtual machine for nested execution. This service is used in conjunction with the **End_Nest_Exec** service to create a nested execution block in which a virtual device may call the **Exec_Int** and **Resume_Exec** services. Virtual devices use these services to call software in the virtual machine.

Parameters

This service has no parameters.

Return Value

The **Client_CS** and **Client_IP** registers contain a break point used by nested execution services.

Comments

When in a nested execution block, a virtual device may call the **Exec_Int** and **Resume_Exec** services any number of times.

This service should only be used by virtual devices that convert protected-mode calls into V86 calls. For example, the virtual MS-DOS manager uses this service to map calls to MS-DOS functions (Interrupt 21h) issued by protected-mode programs into calls to MS-DOS functions in V86 mode.

This service saves the current execution mode of the virtual machine and **End_Nest_Exec** restores the mode.

Uses

Client_CS, **Client_IP**, Flags

See Also

Begin_Nest_Exec, **End_Nest_Exec**

Begin_Reentrant_Execution

```
include vmm.inc

VMMcall Begin_Reentrant_Execution

mov     [Count], ecx        ; reentrancy count
```

The **Begin_Reentrant_Execution** service starts reentrant execution. Virtual devices use this service when hooking VMM faults (reentrant processor exceptions) so that they may call nonasynchronous VMM or virtual device services or execute a virtual machine.

Most virtual devices have no reason to use this service. Do not use this service to avoid scheduling events on hardware interrupts.

Parameters

This service has no parameters.

Return Value

The ECX register contains the old reentrancy count. This count must be passed to the **End_Reentrant_Execution** service.

Uses

ECX, Flags

Return Value

The EAX register contains the low doubleword of the descriptor and the EDX register contains the high doubleword of the descriptor.

Comments

Virtual devices must not rely on the privilege level at which protected-mode applications run. When creating selectors for protected-mode applications, a virtual device should specify the BDDExplicitDPL value. This provides a convenient way to build descriptors without knowing the protection level for protected-mode applications.

Uses

EAX, EDX

See Also

_Allocate_GDT_Selector, **_Allocate_LDT_Selector**

Build_Int_Stack_Frame

```
include vmm.inc

mov     cx, Segment         ; code segment of routine to call
mov     edx, Offset         ; offset of routine to call
VMMcall Build_Int_Stack_Frame
```

The **Build_Int_Stack_Frame** service prepares the current virtual machine to execute an interrupt routine. This service saves the current **Client_CS**, **Client_IP**, and **Client_Flags** registers on the virtual machine's stack and sets the **Client_CS** and **Client_IP** registers to the address of the interrupt routine specified by the *Segment* and *Offset* parameters. When execution resumes in the virtual machine (such as when the **Resume_Exec** service is called), the virtual machine executes the interrupt routine. The interrupt routine continues to run until it executes an iret instruction.

Parameters

Segment

Specifies the segment address or segment selector for the code segment containing the interrupt routine.

Offset

Specifies the offset of interrupt routine. If the specified code segment is a 16-bit segment, the high word of this parameter must be 0.

Return Value

This service has no return value.

Example

The following example executes the interrupt routine in the code segment specified by My_Segment at the offset My_Offset:

```
VMMcall Begin_Nest_Exec
mov     cx, [My_Segment]
mov     edx, [My_Offset]
VMMcall Build_Int_Stack_Frame
VMMcall Resume_Exec
VMMcall End_Nest_Exec
```

Uses

Client_CS, Client_EIP, Client_ESP, Client_Flags, Flags

See Also

Simulate_Far_Call

Call_Global_Event

```
include vmm.ino

mov     esi, OFFSET32 EventCallback ; callback procedure
mov     edx, OFFSET32 RefData       ; reference data
VMMcall Call_Global_Event

mov     [Event], esi                ; event handle
```

The **Call_Global_Event** service either calls the event callback procedure immediately, or schedules a global event. This service schedules the event if the virtual device is processing a hardware interrupt that interrupted the VMM. In all other cases, the service calls the callback procedure without scheduling an event.

This is an asynchronous service.

Parameters

EventCallback

Points to the callback procedure. See the "Comments" section for more information about the procedure.

RefData

Points to reference data to be passed to the event callback procedure.

Return Value

The ESI register is zero if the service calls the callback procedure. Otherwise, the ESI register contains the event handle. The event handle can be used in subsequent calls to the **Cancel_Global_Event** service to cancel the event.

Comments

If the service schedules a global event, the system calls the event callback procedure immediately before the returning from the current interrupt. Any virtual machine can process the event, so the system does not switch tasks before calling the procedure.

The callback procedure can carry out any actions, and use any VMM services. The system calls the event callback procedure as follows:

```
mov     ebx, VM                  ; current VM handle
mov     edx, OFFSET32 RefData    ; points to reference data
mov     ebp, OFFSET32 crs        ; points to a Client_Reg_Struc
call    [EventCallback]
```

The *VM* parameter is a handle identifying the current virtual machine, *RefData* points to reference data supplied by the virtual machine that scheduled the event, and *crs* points to a **Client_Reg_Struc** structure containing the contents of the virtual machine's registers.

The callback procedure can modify EAX, EBX, ECX, EDX, ESI, and EDI.

Uses

Flags

See Also

Cancel_Global_Event, **Schedule_Global_Event**

Call_Priority_VM_Event

```
include vmm.inc

mov     eax, PriorityBoost       ; priority boost (can be 0)
mov     ebx, VM                  ; VM handle
mov     ecx, Flags               ; option flags
mov     edx, OFFSET32 RefData    ; points to reference data
mov     esi, OFFSET32 EventCallback ; points to event callback procedure
mov     edi, TimeOut             ; number of ms for time-out
VMMcall Call_Priority_VM_Event

mov     [Event], esi             ; handle or zero if called
```

The **Call_Priority_VM_Event** service either calls the callback procedure immediately or schedules a priority event for the specified virtual machine. This service schedules the event if the virtual device is processing a hardware interrupt that interrupted the VMM, or the current virtual machine is not the specified virtual machine, or the *Flags* parameter

Th
out

Th

Th

```
mov
mov
mov
cal:
```

Th
occ
the

Th
sch
con

The

Uses

Fla

See Al

Ad
Int:

Call_

```
incl

mov
mov
mov
VMMc

mov
```

The
sch
the
curr
call:

specifies the PEF_Always_Sched value. In all other cases, the service calls the callback procedure and returns without scheduling an event.

This is an asynchronous service.

Parameters

PriorityBoost

Specifies a positive or negative priority boost for the virtual machine. This parameter must be a value such that when added to the current execution priority the result is within the range Reserved_Low_Boost to Reserved_High_Boost. This parameter can be 0 if no boost is necessary.

The following lists some common priority boost values:

Value	Meaning
Reserved_Low_Boost	Reserved for use by system.
Cur_Run_VM_Boost	The time-slice scheduler uses this value to force a virtual machine to run for its allotted time-slice.
Low_Pri_Device_Boost	Virtual devices use this value for events that need timely processing, but are not time critical.
High_Pri_Device_Boost	Virtual devices use this value for events that need timely processing, but should not circumvent operations that have a critical section boost.
Critical_Section_Boost	The system uses this value for virtual machines specified in a call to the Begin_Critical_Section service.
Time_Critical_Boost	Virtual devices use this value for events that must be processed even when another virtual machine is in a critical section. For example, VPICD uses this when simulating hardware interrupts.
Reserved_High_Boost	Reserved for use by system.

VM

Specifies a handle identifying the virtual machine to process the event.

Flags

Specifies how to carry out the event. This parameter can be a combination of the following values:

Uses

Flags

See Also

Call_When_Not_Critical, **Call_When_Task_Switched**

Call_When_Not_Critical

```
include vmm.inc

mov     esi, CritSecCallback    ; callback procedure
mov     edx, RefData            ; reference data
VMMcall Call_When_Not_Critical
```

The **Call_When_Not_Critical** service installs a critical-section callback procedure. The system calls this procedure whenever a virtual device releases the critical section.

Parameters

CritSecCallback

Points to the callback procedure to install. See the "Comments" section for more information about the procedure.

RefData

Points to reference data to pass to the callback procedure.

Return Value

This service has no return value.

Comments

The system does not execute the callback until the current virtual machine's execution priority is less than the Critical_Section_Boost value even if the current virtual machine is not in a critical section. This allows a virtual device to release the critical section and process any simulated interrupts before the system calls the callback procedure.

Virtual devices can install any number of callback procedures, but the system calls only the most recent procedure on the list when the critical section is released. The system removes the callback procedure from the list as it calls the procedure.

The system calls the callback procedure as follows:

```
mov     ebx, VM                 ; current VM handle
mov     edx, OFFSET32 RefData    ; reference data
mov     ebp, OFFSET32 crs        ; Client_Reg_Struc structure
call    [CritSecCallback]
```

The *VM* parameter specifies a handle identifying the current virtual machine, *RefData* points to reference data from the virtual device that installed the callback, and the *crs* parameter points to a **Client_Reg_Struc** structure containing the registers of the current virtual machine.

The callback procedure can carry out any operation and can modify EAX, EBX, ECX, EDX, ESI, EDI, and Flags.

It is more convenient to use the **Call_Priority_VM_Event** service than to call this service directly.

Uses

Flags

See Also

Call_When_Idle, **Call_When_Task_Switched**

Call_When_Task_Switched

```
include vmm.inc

mov     esi, TaskSwitchCallback     ; callback procedure
VMMcall Call_When_Task_Switched
```

The **Call_When_Task_Switched** service installs a task-switched callback procedure. The system calls this procedure whenever it carries out a task switch. This service should be used sparingly and the callback procedure should be optimized for speed.

Parameters

TaskSwitchCallback

Points to the callback procedure to install. See the "Comments" section for more information about the procedure.

Return Value

This service has no return value.

Comments

Some virtual devices must save the state of a hardware device every time a task switch occurs and restore the hardware state for the virtual machine that is about to be run. However, virtual machine events can often be used in place of using this service.

Virtual devices can install any number of callback procedures. The system calls each one in the order installed, until all procedures have been called.

The system calls the callback procedure as follows:

```
mov     eax, OldVM              ; previous VM handle
mov     ebx, VM                 ; current VM handle
call    [CritSecCallback]
```

The *OldVM* parameter specifies a handle identifying the previous virtual machine (just prior to the task switch), and *VM* specifies a handle identifying the current virtual machine.

The callback procedure can carry out any operation and can modify EAX, EBX, ECX, EDX, ESI, EDI, and Flags.

Uses

Flags

See Also

Call_When_Idle, **Call_When_Not_Critical**

Call_When_VM_Ints_Enabled

```
include vmm.inc

mov     edx, OFFSET32 RefData    ; points to reference data
mov     esi, OFFSET32 Callback   ; points to callback procedure
VMMcall Call_When_VM_Ints_Enabled
```

The **Call_When_VM_Ints_Enabled** service installs a callback procedure that the system calls whenever the virtual machine enables interrupts. This service calls the callback procedure immediately if interrupts are already enabled. Virtual devices use this service to receive notification when the virtual machines enables interrupts.

Parameters

RefData

Points to reference data to be passed to the callback procedure.

Callback

Points to the callback procedure. See the "Comments" section for more information about the procedure.

Return Value

This service has no return value.

Comments

It is usually more convenient to use the **Call_Priority_VM_Event** service instead of calling this service directly. However, this service is faster.

The system calls the callback procedure as follows:

```
mov     ebx, VM                     ; current VM handle
mov     edx, OFFSET32 RefData       ; points to reference data
mov     ebp, OFFSET32 crs           ; points to a Client_Reg_Struc
call    [Callback]
```

The *VM* parameter is a handle identifying the current virtual machine, *RefData* points to the reference data specified when the callback procedure was installed, and *crs* points to a **Client_Reg_Struc** structure containing the register values for the virtual machine.

The callback procedure may use EAX, EBX, ECX, EDX, ESI, EDI, and Flags.

Uses

Client_Flags, Flags

See Also

Call_When_Idle, **Call_When_Not_Critical**, **Call_When_Task_Switched**

Call_When_VM_Returns

```
include vmm.inc

mov     eax, TimeOut                ; ms until time out
mov     edx, OFFSET32 RefData       ; points to reference data
mov     esi, OFFSET32 Callback      ; callback procedure to install
VMMcall Call_When_VM_Returns
```

The **Call_When_VM_Returns** service installs a callback procedure that receives control when a virtual machine executes the iret instruction for the current interrupt.

Parameters

TimeOut

Specifies the number of milliseconds to wait before calling the callback procedure. The time-out occurs only if the iret instruction is not executed before the specified time elapses. If this parameter is positive, the system calls the callback when time elapses. If this parameter is negative, the system calls the callback when time elapses and calls it again when the iret instruction is executed. If this parameter is zero, the system ignores the time-out.

RefData

> Points to reference data to be passed to the callback procedure.

Callback

> Points to the callback procedure to install. See the "Comments" sectionfor more information about this procedure.

Return Value

This service has no return value.

Comments

A virtual device typically uses this service in a callback procedure that it installed using the **Hook_V86_Int_Chain** service. This service directs the system to replace the return address for the interrupt with the address of the callback procedure. That is, the system pushes the callback procedure address on the stack when it creates the stack frame for the interrupt. The system then passes the interrupt to the virtual machine.

When the virtual machine executes the iret instruction, the callback procedure receives control and can carry out tasks. After the callback procedure returns, the system restores the original interrupt return address and execution continues as if returning from the interrupt.

The system calls this callback procedure as follows:

```
mov     ebx, VM                 ; current VM handle
mov     edx, OFFSET32 RefData   ; points to reference data
mov     ebp, OFFSET32 crs       ; points to a Client_Reg_Struc
call    [Callback]
```

The *VM* parameter is a handle identifying the current virtual machine. The *RefData* parameter points to the reference data supplied when the callback procedure was installed, and *crs* points to a **Client_Reg_Struc** structure containing the register values for the virtual machine.

If the system calls the callback procedure as a result of a time-out, it sets the carry flag before calling the procedure. If the system calls the callback a second time (once for a time-out and once for the iret instruction), the system sets the zero flag before calling the procedure.

Uses

Client_CS, **Client_EIP**, Flags

See Also

Hook_V86_Int_Chain

Cancel_Global_Event

```
include vmm.inc

mov     esi, Event          ; event handle
VMMcall Cancel_Global_Event
```

The **Cancel_Global_Event** service cancels an event that was previously scheduled using the **Schedule_Global_Event** or **Call_Global_Event** service. A virtual device must not attempt to cancel an event if the callback procedure for the event has already been called.

Parameters

Event

> Specifies a handle identifying the event to cancel. This parameter can be zero to indicate that no event should be canceled.

Return Value

This service has no return value.

Comments

The event callback procedure typically sets the event handle to zero so that subsequent calls by the virtual machine to this service do not cause errors.

See Also

Call_Global_Event, **Schedule_Global_Event**

Cancel_Priority_VM_Event

```
include vmm.inc

mov     esi, Event              ; priority event handle

VMMcall Cancel_Priority_VM_Event
```

The **Cancel_Priority_VM_Event** service cancels an event that was previously scheduled using the **Call_Priority_VM_Event** service. A virtual device must not attempt to cancel an event if the callback procedure for the event has already been called.

Parameters

Event

Specifies a handle identifying the event to cancel. This parameter can be zero to indicate that no event should be canceled.

Return Value

This service has no return value.

Comments

The event callback procedure typically sets the event handle to zero so that subsequent calls by the virtual machine to this service do not cause errors.

This service cancels any priority boost associated with the event even if the PEF_Dont_Unboost value was specified when the event was scheduled.

Do not use this service to cancel events scheduled using the **Call_VM_Event** or **Schedule_VM_Event** services. You must cancel virtual machine events using the **Cancel_VM_Event** service.

Uses

Flags, ESI

See Also

Call_Priority_VM_Event

Cancel_Time_Out

```
include vmm.inc

mov     esi, TimeOut     ; time-out handle
VMMcall Cancel_Time_Out
```

The **Cancel_Time_Out** service cancels a time-out that was scheduled using the **Set_VM_Time_Out** or **Set_Global_Time_Out** service.

Parameters

TimeOut

Specifies a handle identifying the time-out to cancel. If this parameter is zero, the service returns immediately (does nothing).

Return Value

This service has no return value.

Comments

This service makes the time-out handle invalid; the virtual device must not attempt to use the handle in subsequent calls to services.

Uses

Flags

See Also

Set_Global_Time_Out, **Set_VM_Time_Out**

Cancel_VM_Event

```
include vmm.inc

mov     ebx, VM         ; VM handle
mov     esi, Event      ; event handle
VMMcall Cancel_VM_Event
```

The **Cancel_VM_Event** service cancels an event that was previously scheduled using the **Schedule_VM_Event** or **Call_VM_Event** service. A virtual device must not attempt to cancel an event if the callback procedure for the event has already been called.

Parameters

VM

Specifies a handle identifying the virtual machine for which the event is to be canceled.

Event

Specifies a handle identifying the event to cancel. This parameter can be zero to indicate that no event should be canceled.

Return Value

This service has no return value.

Comments

The event callback procedure typically sets the event handle to zero so that subsequent calls by the virtual machine to this service do not cause errors.

Do not use this service to cancel events scheduled using the **Call_Priority_VM_Event** service. You must cancel priority events using the **Cancel_Priority_VM_Event** service.

Uses

Flags

See Also

Call_VM_Event, Schedule_VM_Event

Claim_Critical_Section

```
include vmm.inc

mov      eax, Claims      ; times to claim critical section
mov      ecx, Flags       ; flags for servicing interrupts
VMMcall Claim_Critical_Section
```

The Claim_Critical_Section service increments the claim count by the specified value. It has the same effect as calling the Begin_Critical_Section service repeatedly.

Parameters

Claims

Specifies the number of times to claim the critical section. Zero is a valid number, but is ignored.

Flags

Specifies actions to take when interrupts occur while the virtual machine is blocked waiting for the critical section. This parameter can be a combination of the following values:

Value	Meaning
Block_Svc_Ints	Service interrupts in the virtual machine even if the virtual machine is blocked.
Block_Svc_If_Ints_Locked	Service interrupts in the virtual machine even if the virtual machine is blocked *and* the VMStat_V86IntsLocked flag is set.
Block_Enable_Ints	Service interrupts in the virtual machine even if the virtual machine does not currently have interrupts enabled. This forces interrupts to be enabled. This value is only relevant if either Block_Svc_Ints or Block_Svc_If_Ints_Locked is set.

The Block_Poll value is reserved and must not be used with this service.

Return Value

This service has no return value.

Uses

Flags

See Also

Adjust_Exec_Priority, Begin_Critical_Section, End_Critical_Section

Clear_Mono_Screen

```
include vmm.inc

VMMcall Clear_Mono_Screen
```

The **Clear_Mono_Screen** service clears the secondary display screen by filling it with spaces, and setting character attributes to normal.

Parameters

This service has no parameters.

Return Value

This service has no return value.

Comments

This service has no effect in the retail version of Windows. It is intended to be used with the debugging version.

Uses

Flags

See Also

Out_Mono_Chr

Close_VM

```
include vmm.inc

mov     eax, TimeOut     ; ms to wait before failing close
mov     ebx, VM          ; handle of VM to close
```

```
mov     ecx, Flags        ; action to take
VMMcall Close_VM
```

The **Close_VM** service attempts to close the virtual machine, allowing all virtual devices an opportunity to clean up before the virtual machine terminates.

This service is only available in Windows version 3.1 and later.

Parameters

TimeOut

Specifies the number of milliseconds the service must wait before calling the **NukeVM** service to force the virtual machine to close.

VM

Specifies a handle identifying the virtual machine to close.

Flags

Specifies whether to return to the caller while closing the virtual machine. This parameter can be a combination of the following values:

Value	Meaning
CVF_Continue_Exec	Return to the virtual machine after scheduling the closing event even if the virtual machine is being closed.

All other values are reserved.

Return Value

This service has no return value.

Comments

Whenever possible, a virtual device should use this service instead of the the **Nuke_VM** or **Crash_Cur_VM** service.

Uses

Flags

Convert_Boolean_String

```
include vmm.inc

mov     edx, OFFSET32 String        ; points to Boolean string
VMMcall Convert_Boolean_String
```

```
jc      not_valid                      ; carry set if not valid
mov     [Result], eax                  ; 0 if false, -1 if true
```

The **Convert_Boolean_String** service converts a string representing a Boolean value and returns either -1 or 0 to indicate that the string is true or false.

This service is available during initialization only.

Parameters

String

Points to the null-terminated string representing a Boolean value. The service recognizes at least the following Boolean string values:

String	Meaning
0	False
1	True
False	False
No	False
Off	False
On	True
True	True
Yes	True

Return Value

The carry flag is clear if the string represents a valid Boolean value. In this case, the EAX register contains either 0 if the string evaluates to false, or -1 if the string evaluates to true. The carry flag is set if the specified string is not valid.

Uses

Flags, EAX

See Also

Convert_Decimal_String, **Convert_Fixed_Point_String**, **Convert_Hex_String**

Convert_Decimal_String

```
include vmm.inc

mov      edx, OFFSET32 String        ; points to decimal string
VMMcall Convert_Decimal_String

mov      [Value], eax                ; decimal value
mov      [TermChar], edx             ; -> terminating character
```

The **Convert_Decimal_String** service converts a string representing a decimal number into a value. The service also returns a pointer to the character in the string that marked the end of the decimal number.

This service is only valid during initialization.

Parameters

String

Points to the null-terminated string to convert. The string can be any combination of decimal digits and may preceded by a plus sign (+) or minus sign (-) to indicate a positive or negative value.

Return Value

The EAX register contains the value of decimal string, and the EDX register contains the address of the character in the string that terminated the decimal value.

Comments

If the string is empty or does not contain a valid decimal integer, **Convert_Decimal_String** returns zero, and the EDX register continues to point to the first character in the string.

Uses

EAX, EDX, Flags

See Also

Convert_Boolean_String, **Convert_Fixed_Point_String**, **Convert_Hex_String**

Convert_Fixed_Point_String

```
include vmm.inc

mov      ecx, Places     ; number of decimal places
mov      edx, String     ; points to string to convert
VMMcall Convert_Fixed_Point_String
```

```
mov     [Value], eax    ; fixed-point value
mov     [TermChar], edx ; pointer to terminating character
```

The **Convert_Fixed_Point_String** service converts a string representing a fixed-point number into a fixed-point value. This service also returns a pointer to the character in the string that marked the end of the number.

This service is only valid during initialization.

Parameters

Places

> Specifies the number of digits after the decimal point to convert. If a fixed-point number has extra digits, the service skips over the digits without calculating them into the fixed-point value.

String

> Points to the null-terminated string to convert. The "Comments" section describes the format of the string.

Return Value

The EAX register contains the normalized value of fixed-point number; the actual value is computed as EAX * 10 ** (-Places). The EDX register contains the address of the character in the string marking the end of the fixed-point number.

Comments

A fixed-point number is a decimal number that consists of an integer, a fraction, or a combination of integer and fraction. The integer can be any combination of decimal digits and may be preceded by a plus sign (+) or a minus sign (-) to indicate a positive or negative fixed-point value. The fraction can be any combination of decimal digits but must be preceded with a decimal point (.).

Uses

EAX, EDX, Flags

See Also

Convert_Boolean_String, **Convert_Decimal_String**, **Convert_Hex_String**

Convert_Hex_String

```
include vmm.inc

mov      edx, OFFSET32 String         ; -> hexadecimal string
VMMcall Convert_Hex_String

mov      [Value], eax                 ; value of string
mov      [TermChar], edx              ; -> terminating character
```

The **Convert_Hex_String** service converts a string representing a hexadecimal number into a value. The service also returns a pointer to the character in the string that marked the end of the hexadecimal number.

This service is only valid during initialization.

Parameters

String

Points to the null-terminated string to convert. The string can be any combination of hexadecimal digits (0-9, A-F), and may terminated with an uppercase or lowercase letter H.

Return Value

The EAX register contains the value of the hexadecimal string and the EDX register contains the address of the character in the string that terminated the hexadecimal value. If a letter H terminates the number, EDX contains the address the character immediately following the H.

Uses

Flags

See Also

Convert_Boolean_String, **Convert_Decimal_String**, **Convert_Fixed_Point_String**

_CopyPageTable

```
include vmm.inc

VMMcall _CopyPageTable, <LinPgNum, nPages,\
                        <OFFSET32 PageBuf>, flags>

mov      [Copied], eax     ; nonzero if copied, zero otherwise
```

The **_CopyPageTable** service copies one or more page-table entries to the specified buffer. Virtual devices, such as the virtual DMA device, use this service to analyze the mapping of linear to physical addresses.

Parameters

LinPgNum

Specifies the number of the first page table entry to copy. This parameter must be in the range 0 through 0FFFFFh. Numbers in the range 0 through 10Fh specify pages in the 1 megabyte V86 address space of the current virtual machine. Page numbers for other virtual machines can be computed using the CB_High_Linear field in the control block of each virtual machine.

nPages

Specifies the number of page table entries to copy.

PageBuf

Points to buffer to receive the page table entries. This buffer must be large enough to receive the specified number of entries. Each entry is 4 bytes.

flags

Specifies the operation flags. This parameter must be set to 0.

Return Value

The EAX register contains a nonzero value if the copy is successful. Otherwise, it contains zero indicating that at least one of the specified page table entries was in a region where the corresponding page directory entry is not present.

Comments

This service copies the page table, so writing to the buffer does not affect the content of the actual page table. The system does not update the buffer when changes to the actual page table are made, so no guarantees are made about the length of time the information in the buffer remains accurate.

Uses

EAX

Crash_Cur_VM

```
include vmm.inc

VMMcall Crash_Cur_VM
```

The **Crash_Cur_VM** service abruptly terminates the current VM. A virtual device should call this service when a catastrophic error has occured in the VM, such as executing an illegal instruction or attempting to program a piece of hardware in a way incompatible with the device virtualization.

If the system VM is the current VM, Windows exits with a fatal error without explicitly crashing the other VMs.

Parameters

This service has no parameters.

Return Value

This service does not return.

Create_Semaphore

```
include vmm.inc

mov      ecx, TokenCount     ; initial token count
VMMcall Create_Semaphore

jc       error               ; carry set if semaphore not created
mov      [Semaphore], eax    ; semaphore handle
```

The **Create_Semaphore** service allocates memory for and initializes a new semaphore.

Parameters

TokenCount

Specifies the initial count of tokens.

Return Value

The carry flag is clear and the EAX register contains the semaphore handle if the function is successful. Otherwise, the carry flag is set to indicate an error.

Uses

EAX, Flags

See Also

Destroy_Semaphore, **Signal_Semaphore**, **Wait_Semaphore**

_DeAssign_Device_V86_Pages

```
include vmm.inc

VMMcall _DeAssign_Device_V86_Pages, <VMLinrPage, nPages,\
                                     VM, flags>

or      eax, eax        ; nonzero if unassigned, zero if error
jz      not_unassigned
```

The **_DeAssign_Device_V86_Pages** service unassigns a region in the V86 address space which was previously assigned using the **_Assign_Device_V86_Pages** service.

Parameters

VMLinrPage

Specifies the linear page number of the first page to unassign. The page number must be in the range 0 through 10Fh.

nPages

Specifies the number of pages to unassign. All pages to unassign must be within the V86 address space. If any a page is not assigned, this service returns an error value.

VM

Specifies a handle identifying a virtual machine. If this parameter is a valid handle, the service unassigns pages previously assigned to the virtual machine. If this parameter is zero, the service unassigns pages that were previously assigned to all virtual machines.

flags

Specifies the operation flags. This parameter must be set to 0.

Return Value

The EAX register contains a nonzero value if the service was successful. Otherwise, EAX contains zero to indicate an error such as a page in the range already unassigned or an invalid page range.

Comments

This service only works after device initialization is complete.

A virtual device must not attempt to unassign pages that have not yet been assigned, or attempt to globally unassign pages that were only locally assigned.

Uses

EAX

See Also

_Assign_Device_V86_Pages

Destroy_Semaphore

```
include vmm.inc

mov      eax, Semaphore        ; semaphore handle
VMMcall Destroy_Semaphore
```

The **Destroy_Semaphore** service destroys the specified semaphore.

Parameters

Semaphore

Specifies the handle of the semaphore to delete.

Return Value

This service has no return value.

Uses

Flags

See Also

Create_Semaphore

Disable_Global_Trapping

```
include vmm.inc

mov      edx, Port             ; I/O port number
VMMcall Disable_Global_Trapping
```

The **Disable_Global_Trapping** service disables I/O port trapping for the specified I/O port. This applies to every virtual machine.

This service must not be used unless an I/O callback procedure has been installed for the given port using the **Install_IO_Handler** or **Install_Mult_IO_Handlers** service during initialization.

Parameters

Port

> Specifies the number of the I/O port for which global trapping is to be disabled.

Return Value

This service has no return value.

Comments

The system applies to current global trapping state to each new virtual machine as it is created. When the system first starts, global trapping is enabled by default.

Uses

Flags

See Also

Enable_Global_Trapping, Install_IO_Handler, Install_Mult_IO_Handlers

---

Disable_Local_Trapping

```
include vmm.inc

mov      ebx, VM          ; VM handle
mov      edx, Port        ; I/O port number
VMMcall  Disable_Local_Trapping
```

The **Disable_Local_Trapping** service disables I/O port trapping for the specified I/O port. This applies only to the specified virtual machine.

This service must not be used unless an I/O callback procedure has been installed for the given port using the **Install_IO_Handler** or **Install_Mult_IO_Handlers** service during initialization.

Parameters

VM

> Specifies a handle identifying the virtual machine for which to disable I/O trapping.

Port

> Specifies the number of the I/O port for which trapping is disabled.

Return Value

This service has no return value.

Uses

Flags

See Also

Enable_Local_Trapping, Install_IO_Handler, Install_Mult_IO_Handlers

Disable_VM_Ints

```
include vmm.inc

VMMcall Disable_VM_Ints
```

The **Disable_VM_Ints** service disables interrupts during virtual machine execution for the current virtual machine. This has the same effect as the virtual machine executing a cli instruction.

Parameters

This service has no parameters.

Return Value

This service has no return value.

Uses

Flags

See Also

Enable_VM_Ints

Enable_Global_Trapping

```
include vmm.inc

mov     edx, Port           ; I/O port number
VMMcall Enable_Global_Trapping
```

The **Enable_Global_Trapping** service enables I/O port trapping for the specified port. This applies to every virtual machine.

This service must not be used unless an I/O callback procedure has been installed for the given port using the **Install_IO_Handler** or **Install_Mult_IO_Handlers** service during initialization.

Parameters

Port

Specifies the number of the I/O port for which global trapping is to be enabled.

Return Value

This service has no return value.

Comments

The system applies to current global trapping state to each new virtual machine as it is created. When the system first starts, global trapping is enabled by default.

Uses

Flags

See Also

Disable_Global_Trapping, **Install_IO_Handler**, **Install_Mult_IO_Handlers**

Enable_Local_Trapping

```
include vmm.inc

mov      ebx, VM        ; VM handle
mov      edx, Port      ; I/O port number
VMMcall Enable_Local_Trapping
```

The **Enable_Local_Trapping** service enables I/O port trapping for the specified port. This applies to the specified virtual machine only.

This service must not be used unless an I/O callback procedure has been installed for the given port using the **Install_IO_Handler** or **Install_Mult_IO_Handlers** service during initialization.

Parameters

VM

Specifies a handle identifying the virtual machine for which to enable I/O trapping.

Port

Specifies the number of the I/O port for which trapping is enabled.

Return Value

This service has no return value.

Uses

Flags

See Also

Disable_Local_Trapping, Install_IO_Handler, Install_Mult_IO_Handlers

Enable_VM_Ints

```
include vmm.inc

VMMcall Enable_VM_Ints
```

The **Enable_VM_Ints** service enables interrupts during virtual machine execution for the current virtual machine. This has the same effect as the virtual machine executing an sti instruction.

Parameters

This service has no parameters.

Return Value

This service has no return value.

Comments

Virtual devices use this service to permit callback procedures installed by the **Call_When_Ints_Enabled** or **Call_Priority_VM_Event** service to be called. The system does not call these callback procedures immediately. Instead it waits until the next event occurs. This means the virtual machine's state does not change while this service executes.

Uses

Flags

See Also

Call_Priority_VM_Event, Call_When_VM_Ints_Enabled, Disable_VM_Ints

End_Crit_And_Suspend

```
include vmm.inc

VMMcall End_Crit_And_Suspend
jc       not_released              ; carry set if not released
```

The **End_Crit_And_Suspend** service releases the critical section and immediately suspends the current virtual machine. Virtual devices use this service to block a virtual machine until another virtual machine can process an event.

Parameters

This service has no parameters.

Return Value

The carry flag is clear if this service is successful. Otherwise, the carry flag is set to indicate an error.

Comments

This service releases the critical section only if the virtual machine has claimed the section once. This service returns an error if the system could not suspend the virtual machine, or could not release the critical section because the claim count was not 1. In such cases, the service does not decrement the claim count and the critical section is not released.

Example

The following example uses this service to display a dialog box in the system virtual machine. The Show_Dialog_Box procedure enters a critical section to prevent the **Call_Priority_VM_Event** service from switching to the system virtual machine immediately. It then calls **End_Crit_And_Suspend** which blocks the current virtual machine. The Show_Dialog_Event procedure runs in the system virtual machine and actually displays the dialog box.

When it is finished it resumes the virtual machine that called Show_Dialog_Box by calling the **Resume_VM** service.

```
Show_Dialog_Box:
    VMMcall Get_Crit_Section_Status
    jc      Cant_Do_It      ; critical section already claimed

    VMMcall Begin_Critical_Section
    mov     eax, Low_Pri_Device_Boost
    VMMcall Get_System_VM_Handle
    mov     ecx, 11b
    mov     edx, OFFSET32 Dialog_Box_Data_Strucure
```

```
        mov     esi, OFFSET32 Show_Dialog_Event
        VMMcall Call_Priority_VM_Event
        VMMcall End_Crit_And_Suspend
        jc      Did_Not_Work
        ; When End_Crit_And_Suspend returns the dialog box
        ; will have been displayed

Show_Dialog_Event:
        ; Call Windows to display the dialog box

        mov     ebx, [Suspended_VM_Id]
        VMMcall Resume_VM
        jc      Error
        ret
```

Uses

Flags

See Also

End_Critical_Section, Resume_VM, Suspend_VM

End_Critical_Section

```
include vmm.inc

VMMcall End_Critical_Section
```

The **End_Critical_Section** service releases the critical section if the current virtual machine owns the section and the claim count is zero.

Parameters

This service has no parameters.

Return Value

This service has no return value.

Comments

This service decrements the claim count and releases the critical section if the new count is zero. Since releasing the critical section lowers the execution priority of the current virtual machine, this service causes a task switch if a nonsuspended virtual machine has higher priority.

Uses

Flags

See Also

Begin_Critical_Section, End_Crit_And_Suspend

End_Nest_Exec

```
include vmm.inc

VMMcall End_Nest_Exec
```

The **End_Nest_Exec** service ends a nested execution block. This service is used in conjunction with the **Begin_Nest_Exec** or **Begin_Nest_V86_Exec** service to create a nested execution block in which virtual devices may call the **Exec_Int** and **Resume_Exec** services.

Parameters

This service has no parameters.

Return Value

The **Client_CS** and **Client_IP** registers contain the original values saved by when the nested execution block was created.

Comments

A virtual device must end all nested execution blocks before returning to the virtual machine manager.

This service restores the execution mode to the mode prior to the start of the nested execution block. It also restores the **Client_CS** and **Client_IP** registers, but does not restore any other client registers. A virtual device should save and restore these registers using the **Save_Client_State** and **Restore_Client_State** macros.

Uses

Client_CS, **Client_IP**, Flags

See Also

Begin_Nest_Exec, **Begin_Nest_V86_Exec**, **Restore_Client_State**, **Save_Client_State**

End_Reentrant_Execution

```
include vmm.inc

mov     ecx, Count      ; reentrancy count
VMMcall End_Reentrant_Execution
```

The **End_Reentrant_Execution** service ends reentrant execution. Virtual devices use this service in conjunction with the **Begin_Reentrant_Execution** service. A virtual device that calls **Begin_Reentrant_Execution** must call this service before returning.

Parameters

Count

Specifies the reentrancy count previously returned by the **Begin_Reentrant_Execution** service.

Return Value

This service has no return value.

Uses

Flags

See Also

Begin_Reentrant_Execution

End_Use_Locked_PM_Stack

```
include vmm.inc

VMMcall End_Use_Locked_PM_Stack
```

The **End_Use_Locked_PM_Stack** service unlocks the protected-mode stack. This service decrements the locked-stack counter and restores the previous stack of the virtual machine if the counter is zero. To unlock the stack, a virtual device must call this service once for each call made to the **Begin_Use_Locked_PM_Stack** service.

Parameters

This service has no parameters.

Return Value

If locked-stack counter is zero, the **Client_SS**, **Client_SP**, and **Client_EIP** registers contain the original values before the **Begin_Use_Locked_PM_Stack** service was called. Otherwise, these registers remain unchanged.

Uses

Flags

See Also

Begin_Use_Locked_PM_Stack

Exec_Int

```
include vmm.inc

mov     eax, Interrupt       ; number of interrupt to execute
VMMcall Exec_Int
```

The **Exec_Int** service simulates the specified interrupt and resumes execution of the virtual machine. This service may only be called in a nested execution block created using the **Begin_Nest_Exec** or **Begin_Nest_V86_Exec** service.

Parameters

Interrupt

Specifies the number of the interrupt to simulate.

Return Value

This service has no return value.

Comments

When in a nested execution block, this service can be called any number of times.

This service is comparable to combining the **Simulate_Int** and **Resume_Exec** services.

Uses

Flags

See Also

Begin_Nest_Exec, **Begin_Nest_V86_Exec**, **Resume_Exec**, **Simulate_Int**

Exec_VxD_Int

```
include vmm.inc

push    dword ptr Interrupt      ; interrupt to execute
VMMcall Exec_VxD_Int
```

The **Exec_VxD_Int** service executes the specified software interrupt. Virtual devices uses this service to call MS-DOS or BIOS functions outside the context of a nested execution block.

Parameters

Interrupt

Specifies the number of the interrupt to execute.

Return Value

One or more registers may contain return values depending the function of the specified interrupt.

Comments

Before calling this service, a virtual device must set registers to values that are appropriate for the specified software interrupt. This service supports all MS-DOS and BIOS functions that are supported in protected mode programs.

This service does not change the client registers and flags, so there is no need for the virtual device to save and restore the client register structure. This service also pops the interrupt number from the stack.

Examples

The following examples calls the MS-DOS function Get Version (Interrupt 21h, Function 30h):

```
mov     ax, 3000h
push    dword ptr 21h
VMMcall Exec_VxD_Int
mov     [Major], al      ; major MS-DOS version
mov     [Minor], al      ; minor MS-DOS version
```

See Also

VxDInt

Fatal_Error_Handler

```
include vmm.inc

mov     esi, <MsgPtr>       ; points to message to display
mov     eax, <ErrFlags>     ; exit flags
VMMcall Fatal_Error_Handler
```

The **Fatal_Error_Handler** service terminates Windows by informing all initialized virtual devices that is an unrecoverable error has occurred and returning to real mode (optionally printing an error message). A virtual device should call or jump to this service when it detects a fatal error.

Parameters

MsgPtr

Points to a zero-terminated string specifying the message to display. If this parameter is 0, no message is displayed.

ErrFlags

Specifies the exit flags. It can be a combination of the following values:

Value	Meaning
EF_Hang_On_Exit	Hangs the system on a fatal exit.

All other values are reserved.

Return Value

This service does not return.

Uses

All registers

See Also

Fatal_Error, **Fatal_Memory_Error**

Fatal_Memory_Error

```
include vmm.inc

VMMcall Fatal_Memory_Error
```

The **Fatal_Memory_Error** service terminates Windows and displays an error message indicating that there was not enough memory to initialize one or more virtual devices. A virtual device should call this service during intialization if there is not enough memory to initialize.

Parameters

This service has no parameters.

Return Value

This service does not return.

Comments

This service uses the **Fatal_Error_Handler** service to terminate Windows.
Fatal_Memory_Error sets the exit flags to zero before calling the **Fatal_Error_
Handler**.

Uses

All registers

See Also

Fatal_Error_Handler

_Free_GDT_Selector

```
include vmm.inc

VMMcall _Free_GDT_Selector, <Selector, flags>

or      eax, eax               ; nonzero if freed, zero if error
jz      not_freed
```

The **_Free_GDT_Selector** service frees a GDT selector previously allocated using the
_Allocate_GDT_Selector service.

Parameters

Selector

Specifies the selector to free. This parameter must have been previously created using
the **_Allocate_GDT_Selector** service.

flags

Specifies the operation flags. This parameter must be set to 0.

Return Value

The EAX register contains a nonzero value if the service is successful. Otherwise, EAX
contains zero to indicate an error such as an invalid selector.

Comments

Certain system selectors cannot be freed since they are required for Windows operation.
This service ignores the RPL bits of the selector.

Uses

EAX

See Also

_Allocate_GDT_Selector, _Free_LDT_Selector

_Free_LDT_Selector

```
include vmm.inc

VMMcall _Free_LDT_Selector, <VM, Selector, flags>
```

The **_Free_LDT_Selector** service frees a LDT selector previously allocated using the **_Allocate_LDT_Selector** service.

Parameters

VM

Specifies a handle identifying the virtual machine to which the selector belongs.

Selector

Specifies the selector to free. This parameter must have been previously created using the **_Allocate_LDT_Selector** service.

flags

Specifies the operation flags. This parameter must be set to 0.

Return Value

The EAX register contains a nonzero value if the service is successful. Otherwise, EAX contains zero to indicate an error, such as an invalid selector or an invalid virtual machine handle.

Comments

This service ignores the RPL bits of the selector.

Uses

EAX

See Also

_Allocate_LDT_Selector, _Free_GDT_Selector

_Free_Temp_V86_Data_Area

```
include vmm.inc

VMMcall _Free_Temp_V86_Data_Area

or      eax, eax        ; nonzero if freed, zero if error
jz      not_freed
```

The **_Free_Temp_V86_Data_Area** service frees the temporary block previously allocated using the **_Allocate_Temp_V86_Data_Area** service.

This service is only available during initialization.

Parameters

This service has no parameters.

Return Value

The EAX register contains a nonzero value if the service is successful. Otherwise, EAX contains zero to indicate an error such as the temporary area not allocated.

Comments

The **_Allocate_Global_V86_Data_Area** service is not available while a temporary block is allocated. The virtual device must free the block before the **_Allocate_Global_V86_Data_Area** service can be called.

This service invalidates the address of the temporary block. Attempting to use the address can cause a system crash.

Uses

EAX

See Also

_Allocate_Temp_V86_Data_Area

_GetAppFlatDSAlias

```
include vmm.inc

VMMcall _GetAppFlatDSAlias

mov     [FlatData], eax         ; read-only GDT selector
```

The **_GetAppFlatDSAlias** service returns a ring-3, read-only, GDT selector that provides access to the same memory as the system's ring-0 data segment selector. Virtual devices use this service to support protected-mode APIs that let protected-mode applications read from the same memory as the virtual device.

Parameters

This service has no parameters.

Return Value

The EAX register contains the selector.

Comments

Since more than one virtual device may use this selector, a virtual device must never attempt to free the selector using the **_Free_GDT_Selector** service. Also, a virtual device should not attempt to create a read/write selector using this selector. If a virtual device requires an application to write to any portion of system memory, the virtual device should build its own selector with a base and limit that specifies just the memory the application must modify.

Uses

EAX

See Also

_Free_GDT_Selector

_GetFirstV86Page

```
include vmm.inc

VMMcall _GetFirstV86Page

mov     [FirstPage], eax        ; first page of V86 memory
```

The **_GetFirstV86Page** service returns the page number of the first page in the current virtual machine.

Parameters

This service has no parameters.

Return Value

The EAX register contains the page number of the first page.

Comments

The first page in a virtual machine moves during virtual device initialization, so the page number returned by this service during initialization will not be valid at any later time.

Uses

EAX

See Also

_GetLastV86Page

Get_Config_Directory

```
include vmm.inc

VMMcall Get_Config_Directory

mov     [WinDir], edx        ; points to the Windows directory
```

The **Get_Config_Directory** service returns a pointer to a null-terminated string that specifies the fully qualified path of the directory containing the Windows configuration files. Virtual devices use this service to locate files such as SYSTEM.INI.

This service is available during initialization only.

Parameters

This service has no parameters.

Return Value

The EDX register points to the null-terminated string specifying the configuration directory. If the WINDIR environment variable is defined when Windows starts, EDX points to the value associated with WINDIR regardless of whether it specifies the actual directory where SYSTEM.INI is found.

Comments

The string returned by this service always ends with a backslash (\).

Uses

EDX, Flags

Get_Cur_PM_App_CB

```
include vmm.inc

mov     ebx, VM              ; handle of VM
```

```
VMMcall Get_Cur_PM_App_CB

mov     [ControlBlock], edi     ; address of app control block
```

The **Get_Cur_PM_App_CB** services returns a pointer to the application control block for a protected-mode application.

Parameters

VM

Specifies a handle identifying the virtual machine in which the protected-mode application is running.

Return Value

The EDI register contains the address of the application control block.

Uses

EDI

Get_Crit_Section_Status

```
include vmm.inc

VMMcall Get_Crit_Section_Status

mov     [VM], ebx          ; VM handle of owner
mov     [Claims], ecx      ; # of times critical section claimed
jc      high_priority      ; pri is Critical_Section_Boost or >
```

The **Get_Crit_Section_Status** service returns the claim count and owner of the critical section.

Parameters

This service has no parameters.

Return Value

The ECX register contains the critical section claim count, and the EBX register contains the handle identifying the virtual machine owning the critical section. If the ECX register is 0, the EBX register contains the handle of the current virtual machine.

The carry flag is set if the current virtual machine has an execution priority greater than or equal to **Critical_Section_Boost**, such as during a hardware interrupt simulation.

Comments

Windows 3.1 sometimes delays releasing the critical section until events are processed. This service causes the system to complete any delayed releases before the service returns the status. This may cause a task switch if another virtual machine has a delayed release.

If a virtual device must ensure that it owns the critical section to auccessfully complete an operation, it should call this service to make sure that the critical section status is up to date.

This is not an asynchronous service; it must not be called at interrupt time.

Uses

Flags

See Also

Get_Crit_Status_No_Block

Get_Crit_Status_No_Block

```
include vmm.inc

VMMcall Get_Crit_Status_No_Block

mov     [VM], ebx        ; VM handle of owner
mov     [Claims], ecx    ; # of times critical section claimed
jc      high_priority    ; pri is Critical_Section_Boost or >
```

(Version 3.1 only)

The **Get_Crit_Status_No_Block** service returns the claim count and handle of the owner of the critical section. Unlike the **Get_Crit_Section_Status** service, this service returns immediately (without blocking) even if a delayed request to release the critical section is pending.

Parameters

This service has no parameters.

Return Value

The ECX register contains the critical section claim count, and the EBX register contains the handle identifying the virtual machine owning the critical section. If the ECX register is 0, the EBX register contains the handle of the current virtual machine.

The carry flag is set if the current virtual machine has an execution priority greater than or equal to **Critical_Section_Boost**, such as during a hardware interrupt simulation.

Comments

In some cases, this service may indicate that the critical section is currently owned even when it will be released before returning to the virtual machine.

This is an asynchronous service; it may be called at interrupt time.

Uses

Flags

See Also

End_Critical_Section, **Get_Crit_Section_Status**

Get_Cur_VM_Handle

```
include vmm.inc

VMMcall Get_Cur_VM_Handle

mov     [VM], ebx          ; current VM handle
```

The **Get_Cur_VM_Handle** service returns the handle to the currently running virtual machine.

This is an asynchronous service.

Parameters

This service has no parameters.

Return Value

The EBX register contains the handle of the current virtual machine.

Uses

EBX, Flags

See Also

Get_Sys_VM_Handle, **Test_Cur_VM_Handle**

Get_Debug_Options

```
include vmm.inc

mov     al, Char            ; debugging option
VMMcall Get_Debug_Options
```

The **Get_Debug_Options** service sets the zero flag if the given character was specified as a command-line debugging option when Windows was started.

This service is available during initialization only.

Parameters

Char

Specifies the debugging option to check for.

Return Value

If the zero flag is set, the character was specified on the command line.

Comments

This service has no effect in the retail version of Windows. It is intended to be used with the debugging version.

Uses

Flags

See Also

Test_Debug_Installed

_GetDemandPageInfo

```
include vmm.inc

VMMcall _GetDemandPageInfo, <<OFFSET32 DemandInfo>, flags>
```

The **_GetDemandPageInfo** service retrieves information used for demand paging, copying the information to the specified structure. This service is for exclusive use by the virtual paging device.

Parameters

DemandInfo

Points to a **DemandInfoStruc** structure containing information for demand paging.

flags

> Specifies the operation flags. This parameter must be set to 0.

Return Value

This service has no return value.

Uses

Flags

_GetDescriptor

```
include vmm.inc

VMMcall _GetDescriptor, <Selector, VM, flags>

mov     ecx, eax            ; zero in eax and edx if error
or      ecx, edx
jz      error

mov     [DescDWORD1], edx   ; high doubleword of descriptor
mov     [DescDWORD2], eax   ; low doubleword of descriptor
```

The **_GetDescriptor** service retrieves a copy of the descriptor associated with the given LDT or GDT selector.

Parameters

Selector

> Specifies a GDT or LDT selector.

VM

> Specifies a handle identifying the virtual machine to which the specified LDT selector belongs. The service ignores this parameter if Selector is a GDT selector. Otherwise, the handle must be valid for LDT selectors.

flags

> Specifies the operation flags. This parameter must be set to 0.

Return Value

The EAX register contains the low doubleword of the descriptor and the EDX register contain the high doubleword of the descriptor. Both EAX and EDX contain zero to indicate an error, such as an invalid selector or an invalid virtual machine handle.

Comments

This service ignores the high 16-bits of the Selector parameter; the 80386 CPU often sets these bits to random values when doubleword operations are performed on segment registers.

This service ignores the RPL bits of the selector.

Uses

EAX, EDX

See Also

_BuildDescriptorDWORDs, **_SetDescriptor**

_Get_Device_V86_Pages_Array

```
include vmm.inc

VMMcall _Get_Device_V86_Pages_Array, <VM, <OFFSET32 ArrayBuf>,\
                                     flags>

or      eax, eax        ; nonzero if retrieved, zero if error
jz      not_retrieved
```

The **_Get_Device_V86_Pages_Array** service retrieves a copy of the assignment array used by the **_Assign_Device_V86_Pages** and **_DeAssign_Device_V86_Pages** services. Virtual devices use the assignment array to determine which regions of the V86 address space are currently assigned, and which are available.

Parameters

VM

Specifies a handle identifying the virtual machine to retrieve the assignment array for. If this parameter is zero, the service retrieves the global assignment array.

ArrayBuf

Points to the 36-byte buffer that receives the assignment array.

flags

Specifies the operation flags. This parameter must be set to 0.

Return Value

The EAX register contains a nonzero value if the service is successful. Otherwise, it contains zero to indicate an error such as an invalid virtual machine handle.

Comments

The assignment array consists of 110h bits with each bit representing a single page in the V86 address space. If a bit is 1, the corresponding page is assigned. If a bit is 0, the corresponding page is not assigned.

The global assignment array does not indicate which pages are available. A page is available for global assignment only if it is neither globally nor locally assigned. To determine whether a page is available for global assignment, a virtual device must check the global assignment array, and then check the assignment arrays for each virtual machine.

Uses

EAX

See Also

_Assign_Device_V86_Pages, _DeAssign_Device_V86_Pages

GetDOSVectors

```
include vmm.inc

VMMcall GetDOSVectors

mov     [Int23], eax   ; V86 address of original Int23 handler
mov     [Int24], edx   ; V86 address of original Int24 handler
```

The **GetDOSVectors** service returns the Interrupt 23h and Interrupt 24h vectors as originally set by MS-DOS for the Windows virtual machine manager. When Windows starts, the VMM changes the original Interrupt 23h and 24h vectors to the addresses of its own handlers. When a virtual machine starts, the virtual MS-DOS manager resets these vectors to the original handlers using this service to retrieve the original addresses.

Virtual devices must not use this service; this service is reserved for exclusive use by the virtual MS-DOS manager.

Parameters

This service has no parameters.

Return Value

The EAX register contains the V86-mode address (segment:offset) for the MS-DOS Interrupt 23h handler, and the EDX register contains the V86-mode address (segment:offset) for the MS-DOS Interrupt 24h handler.

Uses

EAX, EDX

See Also

Get_PSP_Segment

Get_Environment_String

```
include vmm.inc

mov     esi, OFFSET32 Variable   ; environment variable
VMMcall Get_Environment_String

jc      not_found                ; carry set if not found
mov     [Value], edx             ; -> value of env. variable
```

The **Get_Environment_String** service returns the value of the specified environment variable.

This service is only available during initialization.

Parameters

Variable

Points to a null-terminated string specifying the name of an MS-DOS environment variable. This service is not sensitive to case, so the name may be given in any combination of uppercase and lowercase letters.

Return Value

The carry flag is clear and the EDX register points to a null-terminated string specifying the value of the environment variable if the service is successful. Otherwise, the carry flag is set to indicate that the environment variable could not be found.

Comments

Environment variables, set using the MS-DOS set command, are a limited resource. Although some virtual devices use environment variables as a way to set operating parameters, this is not recommended unless the variable is used by a set of programs, MS-DOS device drivers, and virtual devices.

Uses

EDX, Flags

Get_Execution_Focus

```
include vmm.inc

VMMcall Get_Execution_Focus
mov     [Focus], ebx            ; handle of VM with focus
```

The **Get_Execution_Focus** service returns the handle of the virtual machine currently having the execution focus. This virtual machine is called the foreground virtual machine.

Parameters

This service has no parameters.

Return Value

The EBX register contains the handle of virtual machine that currently has the execution focus.

Uses

EBX, Flags

See Also

Set_Execution_Focus

Get_Exec_Path

```
include vmm.inc

VMMcall Get_Exec_Path

mov     [Path], edx      ; points to full path of WIN386.EXE
mov     [Length], ecx    ; number of chars including last \
```

The **Get_Exec_Path** service returns a null-terminated string that specifies the full path of the Windows virtual machine manager (WIN386.EXE). Virtual devices often use this service to locate executable files that are not in directories specified by the PATH environment variable.

This service is only available during initialization.

Parameters

This service has no parameters.

Return Value

The EDX register points to a null-terminated string specifying the full path of the VMM. The ECX register contains a count of characters up to and including the last backslash (\).

Uses

ECX, EDX

Get_Fault_Hook_Addrs

```
include vmm.inc

mov     eax, Interrupt      ; interrupt number
VMMcall Get_Fault_Hook_Addrs
```

The **Get_Fault_Hook_Addrs** service returns addresses of the V86 mode, protected-mode, and VMM fault handlers for a specified fault.

Parameters

Interrupt

Specifies the interrupt number of the fault to check.

Return Value

If the carry flag is clear, the EDX, ESI, and EDI registers contain the addresses described in the following list. Otherwise, the carry flag is set to indicate an error such as an invalid interrupt number.

Register	Description
EDX	Contains the address of the fault handler installed by a V86 mode application. This register contains zero if no handler has been installed.
ESI	Contains the address of the fault handler installed by a protected-mode application. This register contains zero if no handler has been installed.
EDI	Contains the address of a fault handle installed by the VMM. This register contains zero if no handler has been installed.

Comments

A virtual device cannot get the hook address for the Non-Maskable Interrupt (Interrupt 2). It must use the **Get_NMI_Handler_Addr** and **Set_NMI_Handler_Addr** services to hook Interrupt 2.

Uses

Flags

See Also

Get_NMI_Handler_Addr, Set_NMI_Handler_Addr

_GetFreePageCount

```
include vmm.inc

VMMcall _GetFreePageCount, <flags>

mov     dword ptr [FreePages], eax      ; free pages
mov     dword ptr [LockablePages], edx  ; lockable pages
```

The **_GetFreePageCount** service returns the number of pages in the free list. This service also returns the number of free pages that can be allocated as locked pages. Virtual devices can allocate free pages using the **_PageAllocate** service.

Parameters

flags

Specifies the operation flags. This parameter must be set to 0.

Return Value

The EAX register contains the count of free pages, and the EDX register contains the count of pages available for allocation as locked pages.

Comments

In a demand-paged virtual memory system such as Windows, the number of free pages is usually very close to 0, so the count of pages available for locking is usually a better indicator of available memory. However, virtual devices must not rely on the count of free pages being less than or equal to the count of pages to lock. No guarantees can be made about the length of time the information returned by this service remains accurate.

Uses

EAX, EDX

See Also

_PageAllocate

_GetGlblRng0V86IntBase

```
include vmm.inc

VMMcall _GetGlblRng0V86IntBase

mov      [Address], eax        ; address for ring-0 V86
                               ; interrupt handlers
```

The **_GetGlblRng0V86IntBase** service returns the linear address used to manage ring-0 global V86 interrupt handlers.

This service is only available during initialization, and only available for Windows version 3.1 or later.

Parameters

This service has no parameters.

Return Value

The EAX register contains the linear address of the ring-0 handler.

Comments

Ring-0 global V86 interrupt handlers require segment selectors that permit execution in protected mode at ring 0. Furthermore, the selectors must represent memory that is not subject to page faults. Page faults are a potential problem because part of the global code or data for a ring-0 V86 interrupt handler may overlap with the noninstanced part of an instance data page.

This service returns the linear address of the start of a V86 address space in which instance data pages are always present. The linear address is a duplicate of the V86 address 0:0 in the system virtual machine. The size of this duplicate mapping is 1 megabyte plus 64 kilobytes. This address space includes the xMS HMA (pages 100h-10Fh). The system sets up the duplicate mapping after all virtual devices have processed the **Sys_Critical_Init** message. The A20 state of the system virtual machine, or any other virtual machine, has no effect on the mapping used for this address space. The physical (global) HMA is always mapped in this address space. Thus, A20 is effectively always on (HMA always enabled).

Virtual devices that use this address space must wait until the **Device_Init** or **Init_Complete** message to request the address. This service returns zero if a virtual device attempts to retrieve the address while processing the **Sys_Critical_Init** message. If a virtual device needs the address sooner than receipt of the **Device_Init** message, the virtual device can use a base address of 0 to build the selectors. It can then edit the selectors when it processes the **Device_Init** message, changing the base address to the correct location by adding in the return value from this service.

Ring-0 global V86 interrupt handlers may only access global memory.

Instance data does not work properly in this address space. The local part of this address space is mapped with the system nul page.

Uses

EAX

Get_Last_Updated_System_Time

```
include vmm.inc

VMMcall Get_Last_Updated_System_Time

mov     [SysTime], eax          ; system time in milliseconds
```

The **Get_Last_Updated_System_Time** service returns the time in milliseconds since Windows was started. This service is accurate to approximately 50 milliseconds.

This is an asynchronous service.

Parameters

This service has no parameters.

Return Value

The EAX register contains the elapsed time in milliseconds since Windows started.

Comments

This service does not detect rollover of the clock which occurs every 49 1/2 days. If a virtual device is sensitive to rollover, it should schedule a time-out every 30 days

Although the **Get_System_Time** service is more accurate than this service, **Get_System_Time** must call the timer device to update the clock so it is slower than **Get_Last_Updated_System_Time**.

Uses

EAX, Flags

See Also

Get_System_Time

Get_Last_Updated_VM_Exec_Time

```
include vmm.inc

VMMcall Get_Last_Updated_VM_Exec_Time

mov     [ExecTime], eax     ; time in milliseconds that
                            ; VM has run
```

The **Get_Last_Updated_VM_Exec_Time** service returns the amount of time that the current virtual machine has run. This service is accurate to approximately 50 milliseconds.

This is an asynchronous service.

Parameters

This service has no parameters.

Return Value

The EAX register contains the execution time for the current virtual machine.

Comments

When the system creates a virtual machine, it sets the execution time for the virtual machine to zero. The system increases the execution time only when the virtual machine actually runs. Therefore the execution does not reflect the length of time the virtual machine has existed, but indicates the amount of time the current virtual machine has run.

Uses

EAX, Flags

See Also

Get_VM_Exec_Time

_GetLastV86Page

```
include vmm.inc

VMMcall _GetLastV86Page

mov     [LastPage], eax     ; last page in V86 memory
```

The **_GetLastV86Page** service returns the page number of the last page of V86 memory for the specified virtual machine.

This service is only available for Windows version 3.1 or later.

Parameters

This service has no parameters.

Return Value

The EAX register contains the page number of the last page in V86 memory.

Comments

The last page in V86 memory moves during initialization. Virtual devices that retrieve the last page when processing initialization messages must retrieve the page number again to use it later.

Uses

EAX

See Also

_GetFirstV86Page

Get_Machine_Info

```
include vmm.inc

VMMcall Get_Machine_Info

mov     [Major], AH        ; MS-DOS major version number
mov     [Minor], AL        ; MS-DOS minor version number
mov     [OEM], BH          ; MS-DOS OEM serial number
mov     [Model], BL        ; machine model byte
mov     [Type], EBX        ; machine type flags
                           ;     (high-order 16-bits)
mov     [SysConf], ECX     ; points to System
                           ;     Configuration Parameters
mov     [Equip], EDX       ; equipment flags
```

The **Get_Machine_Info** service returns information about the computer system that Windows is running on.

Parameters

This service has no parameters.

Return Value

The AX, EBX, ECX, and EDX registers contain the following information:

Register	Description
AH	MS-DOS major version number
AL	MS-DOS minor version number
BH	MS-DOS OEM serial number
BL	Machine model byte (from address F000:FFFE in system ROM)
EBX	Machine type flags (in the high-order 16-bits) as follows:

Value	Meaning
GMIF_80486	80486 processor
GMIF_PCXT	PCXT accelerator
GMIF_MCA	Micro Channel
GMIF_EISA	EISA

ECX	Ring 0 linear address to System Configuration Parameters (as returned from BIOS service Interrupt 15h, AH=C0h) Applies only to PS/2 or computers with extended BIOS. See the PS/2 BIOS documentation for details.
EDX	Equipment flags (as returned from Interrupt 11h)

Comments

The address returned in the ECX register points to a copy of the system configuration parameters because the actual parameters may have been moved into a buffer which is subject to page remapping.

Uses

EAX, EBX, ECX, EDX, Flags

Get_Mono_Chr

```
include vmm.inc

VMMcall Get_Mono_Chr
mov     byte ptr [Char], al        ; character value
mov     byte ptr [Attr], ah        ; character attribute
```

The **Get_Mono_Chr** service retrieves the character and attribute value at the current cursor position.

Parameters

This service has no parameters.

Return Value

The AL register contains the character value, and the AH register contains the character attribute.

Comments

This service has no effect in the retail version of Windows. It is intended to be used with the debugging version.

Uses

EAX, Flags

See Also

Out_Mono_Chr, Set_Mono_Cur_Pos

Get_Mono_Cur_Pos

```
include vmm.inc

VMMcall Get_Mono_Cur_Pos
mov     byte ptr [Column], dl        ; current column position
mov     byte ptr [Row], dh           ; current row position
```

The **Get_Mono_Cur_Pos** service retrieves the current cursor position for the secondary display.

Parameters

This service has no parameters.

Return Value

The DL register contains the column position value, and the AH register contains the row position.

Comments

This service has no effect in the retail version of Windows. It is intended to be used with the debugging version.

Uses

Flags

See Also

Set_Mono_Cur_Pos

Get_Name_Of_Ugly_TSR

```
include vmm.inc

VMMcall Get_Name_Of_Ugly_TSR

jz      no_ugly_TSR          ; zero set if no ugly TSRs present
mov     [Name], eax          ; first 4 characters of TSR name
mov     [Name+4], ebx        ; last 4 characters of TSR name
```

The **Get_Name_Of_Ugly_TSR** service returns the name of an uncooperative TSR. During its real-mode initialization, the virtual MS-DOS manager checks for and records the names of any TSRs that may prevent other MS-DOS programs from running. **Get_Name_Of_Ugly_TSR** checks the list and returns one of the TSR names (if any) so that virtual devices can determine whether they can successfully operate. Although more than one ugly TSR may be present in the list, the service chooses only one name to return.

This service is only available during initialization and only available for Windows 3.1 and later.

Parameters

This service has no parameters.

Return Value

The zero flag is set and the EAX and EBX registers are set to zero if no ugly TSRs are present. Otherwise, the zero flag is clear and the EAX register contains the first four characters of the TSR name, and the EBX register contains the last four characters.

Uses

EAX, EBX, Flags

Get_Next_Arena

```
include vmm.inc

mov     ecx, 0               ; must be zero
VMMcall Get_Next_Arena

mov     [Data], eax          ; data value
mov     [Flags], ecx         ; high MS-DOS memory flags
mov     [Memory], edx        ; points to array of
                             ;    Common_Memory_struc
```

The **Get_Next_Arena** service returns a pointer to an MS-DOS data structure.

Virtual devices must not use this service; it is intended for exclusive use by the virtual MS-DOS manager.

Parameters

This service has no parameters.

Return Value

The EAX, ECX, and EDX registers contain the following information:

Register	Description
EAX	Specifies a data value.
ECX	Specifies the high MS-DOS flags. It can be a combination of the following values:

Value	Meaning
GNA_HiDOSLinked	Set if high MS-DOS arenas were linked in when Windows was started.
GNA_IsHighDOS	Set if high MS-DOS arenas exist.

EDX	Points to an array of Common_Memory_struc structures specifying the addresses and sizes of high MS-DOS memory segments. Each element of the list has the following form:

```
Common_Memory_struc struc
  CM_seg   dw  ?   ; segment address of start
  CM_size  dw  ?   ; size in paragraphs
Common_Memory_struc ends
```

The last element of array contains zero.

Uses

EAX, ECX, EDX, and Flags

Get_Next_Profile_String

```
include vmm.inc

mov     edx, Profile    ; points to the previous entry value
mov     edi, Keyname    ; points to the entry name
VMMcall Get_Next_Profile_String

jc      no_next         ; carry set if there is no next value
mov     [Next], edx     ; points to entry value of next
                        ; profile string
```

The **Get_Next_Profile_String** service searches the SYSTEM.INI file for the first entry that follows the entry specified by the *Profile* parameter, and that has the given *Keyname*. This service returns a pointer to this next entry if it is found.

Virtual devices typically use this service if they have more than one entry having the same keyname. A virtual device retrieves the first string using the **Get_Profile_String** service, then uses **Get_Next_Profile_String** to retrieve all subsequent entries. In all cases, the virtual device must not modify the returned string.

Parameters

Profile

> Points to a null-terminated string specifying the value of the previous entry. The string must have been previously returned using the **Get_Profile_String** or **Get_Next_Profile_String** service.

Keyname

> Points to a null-terminated string identifying the keyname for the entry.

Return Value

If the carry flag is clear, the EDX register contains the address of the next string having the specified keyname. The carry flag is set if there are no more matching entries.

Uses

EDX, Flags

See Also

Get_Profile_String

Get_Next_VM_Handle

```
include vmm.inc

mov      ebx, VM              ; VM handle
VMMcall Get_Next_VM_Handle

mov      [NextVM], ebx        ; next VM handle
```

The **Get_Next_VM_Handle** service returns the handle of the next virtual machine in the virtual machine list maintained by the system. Although each virtual machine appears only once in the list, the order of the handles is not guaranteed. The list is circular, so a virtual device scanning the list should stop scanning when the latest handle returned is equal to the first handle returned.

Parameters

VM

> Specifies a handle identifying a virtual machine.

Return Value

The EBX register contains the handle of the next virtual machine in the list.

Example

The following example modifies the state of every virtual machine by using the **Get_Next_VM_Handle** service to retrieve handles of all valid virtual machines:

```
    VMMcall Get_Cur_VM_Handle

Scan_Loop:

  ; modify the VM state

    VMMcall Get_Next_VM_Handle
    VMMcall Test_Cur_VM_Handle
    jne     Scan_Loop
```

Uses

EBX, Flags

See Also

Get_Cur_VM_Handle, **Test_Cur_VM_Handle**

Get_NMI_Handler_Addr

```
    include vmm.inc

    VMMcall Get_NMI_Handler_Addr

    mov     [NMI], esi          ; offset to current NMI handler
```

The **Get_NMI_Handler_Addr** service returns the address of the current Non-Maskable Interrupt (NMI) handler.

Parameters

This service has no parameters.

Return Value

The ESI register contains the offset of current NMI handler.

Comments

If a virtual device needs to hook the Non-Maskable Interrupt it must first call this service to get and save the original NMI handler address. The virtual can then install the new NMI handler my using the **Set_NMI_Handler_Addr** service. The new handler should create an NMI handler chain by passing execution to the original NMI handler whenever it does not process the NMI.

Uses

ESI, Flags

See Also

Set_NMI_Handler_Addr

_GetNulPageHandle

```
include vmm.inc

VMMcall _GetNulPageHandle

mov     [NulPage], eax          ; handle of system nul page
```

The **_GetNulPageHandle** service returns the memory handle of the system nul page. This page is used to occupy regions of the address space which are unused but for which it is not desirable to cause a page fault when accessed. The system nul page can be mapped to multiple locations in the system, so its contents are always random.

Parameters

This service has no parameters.

Return Value

The EAX register contains the memory handle of the system nul page.

Uses

EAX

See Also

_MapIntoV86

Get_PM_Int_Type

```
include vmm.inc

mov     eax, Interrupt          ; number of interrupt to check
VMMcall Get_PM_Int_Type

mov     [Type], edx             ; 0 if trap gate, otherwise
                                ; interrupt gate
```

The Get_PM_Int_Type service determines whether a protected-mode interrupt vector is an interrupt gate or trap gate type interrupt.

Parameters

Interrupt

Specifies the number of the interrupt to check.

Return Value

The EDX register contains zero if the specified interrupt corresponds to a trap gate. The EDX register contains a nonzero value if the interrupt corresponds to an interrupt gate.

Comments

An interrupt through an interrupt gate automatically clears the interrupt flag bit to disable interrupts. Interrupts through a trap gate do not modify the interrupt bit. All protected-mode interrupts default to the trap gate type, but virtual devices such as the virtual PIC device, may change some trap gates to interrupt gates so that hardware interrupts disable interrupts. The virtual PIC device leaves software interrupts, such as Interrupt 21h, unchanged. This avoids an unnecessary ring transition by eliminating the need for the software interrupt handlers to execute an sti instruction.

Uses

EDX, Flags

See Also

Get_PM_Int_Vector, Set_PM_Int_Type

Get_PM_Int_Vector

```
include vmm.inc

mov      eax, Interrupt          ; number of interrupt to check
VMMcall Get_PM_Int_Vector

mov      [Segment], cx           ; segment selector for
                                 ;    interrupt routine
mov      [Offset], edx           ; offset to interrupt routine
```

The **Get_PM_Int_Vector** service returns the address of the interrupt routine for the specified protected-mode interrupt in the current virtual machine.

Parameters

Interrupt

Specifies the number of the interrupt to check.

Return Value

The CX register contains the segment selector of the interrupt routine, and the EDX register contains the offset of the interrupt routine. If the code segment is a 16-bit segment, the high word of the EDX register is zero.

The zero flag is set if the interrupt address points to the default interrupt handler; the flag is clear if a virtual device has hooked the interrupt.

Comments

The system maintains a protected-mode interrupt vector table for each virtual machine. By default, each table entry points to a protected-mode breakpoint procedure that reflects the interrupt to V86 mode.

Uses

ECX, EDX, Flags

See Also

Get_PM_Int_Type, Set_PM_Int_Vector

Get_Profile_Boolean

```
include vmm.inc

mov      eax, Default            ; default value
mov      esi, OFFSET32 Profile   ; points to section name
mov      edi, OFFSET32 Keyname   ; points to entry name
VMMcall Get_Profile_Boolean

jc       not_found               ; carry set if entry not found
```

```
jz      no_value          ; zero set if entry has no value
mov     [Value], eax      ; entry value is either 0 (false)
                          ;    or -1 (true)
```

The **Get_Profile_Boolean** service returns the value of a boolean-type entry in the SYSTEM.INI file. The *Profile* and *Keyname* parameters specify the section and entry to search.

This service is only available during initialization.

Parameters

Default

Specifies the default value to return if the entry is not found, or has no current value.

Profile

Specifies a null-terminated string identifying the section in the SYSTEM.INI file to search. If *Profile* is zero, the service searches the [386Enh] section.

Keyname

Points to a null-terminated string identifying the name of the entry to locate.

Return Value

If the carry and zero flags are clear, the specified entry is found and is a valid boolean-type string. In this case, the EAX register is set to -1 or 0 indicating that the entry value evaluates to true or false, respectively.

If the carry flag is clear and the zero flag is set, the specified entry exists but has no corresponding value. If the carry flag is set, the entry cannot be found or the entry does not represent a boolean-type value. In these cases, the EAX register is set to the *Default* value.

Comments

This service returns the *Default* value unless the value corresponding to the specified entry is a valid boolean-type string. A boolean-type string can be one of the following:

String	Meaning
0	False
1	True
False	False
N	False

No	False
Off	False
On	True
True	True
Y	True
Yes	True

Non-English versions of Windows may have language-specific additions to this list.

Uses

Flags

See Also

Get_Profile_Decimal_Int, **Get_Profile_Fixed_Point**, **Get_Profile_Hex_Int**

Get_Profile_Decimal_Int

```
include vmm.inc

mov     eax, Default            ; default value
mov     esi, OFFSET32 Profile   ; points to section name
mov     edi, OFFSET32 Keyname   ; points to entry name
VMMcall Get_Profile_Decimal_Int

jc      not_found               ; carry set if entry not found
jz      no_value                ; zero set if entry has no value

mov     [Value], eax            ; entry value
```

The **Get_Profile_Decimal_Int** service returns the value of a decimal-number entry in the SYSTEM.INI file. The *Profile* and *Keyname* parameters specify the section and entry to search.

This service is only available during initialization.

Parameters

Default

Specifies the default value to return if the entry is not found or has no current value.

Profile

Specifies a null-terminated string identifying the section in the SYSTEM.INI file to search. If *Profile* is zero, the service searches the [386Enh] section.

Keyname

Points to a null-terminated string identifying the name of the entry to locate.

Return Value

If the carry and zero flags are clear, the specified entry is found and is a valid decimal number. In this case, the EAX register is set to the value of the number.

If the carry flag is clear and the zero flag is set, the specified entry exists but has no corresponding value. If the carry flag is set, the entry cannot be found or the entry does not represent a valid decimal number. In these cases, the EAX register is set to the *Default* value.

Comments

A valid decimal number consists of one or more decimal digits and contains no embedded spaces or decimal points. The decimal number can be preceded with a plus sign (+) or minus sign (-) to indicate a positive or negative number, respectively.

Uses

Flags

See Also

Get_Profile_Boolean, **Get_Profile_Fixed_Point**, **Get_Profile_Hex_Int**

Get_Profile_Fixed_Point

```
include vmm.inc

mov     eax, Default            ; default value
mov     ecx, Places             ; number of digits after
                                ;      decimal point
mov     esi, OFFSET32 Profile   ; points to section name
mov     edi, OFFSET32 Keyname   ; points to entry name
VMMcall Get_Profile_Fixed_Point

jc      not_found               ; carry set if entry not found
jz      no_value                ; zero set if entry has no value

mov     [Value], eax            ; entry value
```

The **Get_Profile_Fixed_Point** service returns the value of a fixed-point-number entry in the SYSTEM.INI file. The *Profile* and *Keyname* parameters specify the section and entry to search for.

This service is only available during initialization.

Parameters

Default

Specifies the default value to return if the entry is not found or has no current value.

Places

Specifies the number of digits after the decimal point to convert. If fixed-point number has extra digits, the service ignores them.

Profile

Specifies a null-terminated string identifying the section in the SYSTEM.INI file to search. If *Profile* is zero, the service searches the [386Enh] section.

Keyname

Points to a null-terminated string identifying the name of the entry to locate.

Return Value

If the carry and zero flags are clear, the specified entry is found and is a valid fixed-point number. In this case, the EAX register is set to the normalized value of the number; the actual value is computed as EAX * 10 ** (-Places).

If the carry flag is clear and the zero flag is set, the specified entry exists but has no corresponding value. If the carry flag is set, the entry cannot be found or the entry does not represent a valid fixed-point number. In these cases, the EAX register is set to the *Default* value.

Comments

A valid fixed-point number is a decimal number that consists of an integer, a fraction, or a combination of integer and fraction. The integer can be any combination of decimal digits, and may be preceded by a plus sign (+) or a minus sign (-) to indicate a positive or negative fixed-point value.

The fraction can be any combination of decimal digits but must be preceded with a decimal point (.).

Uses

Flags

See Also

Get_Profile_Boolean, **Get_Profile_Decimal_Int**, **Get_Profile_Hex_Int**

Get_Profile_Hex_Int

```
include vmm.inc

mov     eax, Default          ; default value
mov     esi, OFFSET32 Profile ; points to section name
mov     edi, OFFSET32 Keyname ; points to entry name
VMMcall Get_Profile_Hex_Int

jc      not_found             ; carry set if entry not found
jz      no_value              ; zero set if entry has no value

mov     [Value], eax          ; entry value
```

The **Get_Profile_Hex_Int** service returns the value of a hexadecimal-number entry in the SYSTEM.INI file. The *Profile* and *Keyname* parameters specify the section and entry to search.

This service is only available during initialization.

Parameters

Default

Specifies the default value to return if the entry is not found or has no current value.

Profile

Specifies a null-terminated string identifying the section in the SYSTEM.INI file to search. If *Profile* is zero, the service searches the [386Enh] section.

Keyname

Points to a null-terminated string identifying the name of the entry to locate.

Return Value

If the carry and zero flags are clear, the specified entry is found and is a valid hexadecimal number. In this case, the EAX register is set to the value of the number.

If the carry flag is clear and the zero flag is set, the specified entry exists but has no corresponding value. If the carry flag is set, the entry cannot be found or the entry does not represent a valid hexadecimal number. In these cases, the EAX register is set to the *Default* value.

Comments

A valid hexadecimal number consist of any combination of hexadecimal digits (0-9, A-F), and can be terminated with the uppercase or lowercase letter H.

Uses

Flags

See Also

Get_Profile_Decimal_Int, Get_Profile_Fixed_Point, Get_Profile_Hex_Int

Get_Profile_String

```
include vmm.inc

mov      edx, OFFSET32 Default ; points to default string
                              ;       (optional)
mov      esi, OFFSET32 Profile ; points to section name
mov      edi, OFFSET32 Keyname ; points to entry name
VMMcall Get_Profile_String

jc       not_found            ; carry set if entry not found
mov      [Value], edx         ; points to entry value string
```

The **Get_Profile_String** service searches the SYSTEM.INI file for a specified entry and returns a pointer to a null-terminated string representing the entry value.

This service is only available during initialization.

Parameters

Default

Points to a null-terminated string to be returned if the entry is not found or has no current value.

Profile

Specifies a null-terminated string identifying the section in the SYSTEM.INI file to search. If *Profile* is zero, the service searches the [386Enh] section.

Keyname

Points to a null-terminated string identifying the name of the entry to locate.

Return Value

If the carry flag is clear, the EDX register contains the address of the null-terminated string representing the entry value. If the carry flag is set, the string cannot be found.

Comments

A virtual device must not modify the string pointed to by the EDX register. If modification is required, the virtual device must copy the string and modify the copy.

Uses

EDX, Flags

See Also

Get_Next_Profile_String

Get_PSP_Segment

```
include vmm.inc

VMMcall Get_PSP_Segment

mov     [PSP], eax            ; segment address of PSP
```

The **Get_PSP_Segment** service returns the segment address of program segment prefix (PSP) for the Windows virtual machine manager (WIN386.EXE). Virtual devices typically use this service to retrieve values from the PSP that can not be retrieve using the **Get_Exec_Path** and **Get_Environment_String** services.

This service is only available during initialization.

Parameters

This service has no parameters.

Return Value

The EAX register contains the segment address for the program segment prefix. The high word is always zero.

Comments

This service returns a segment address. To convert the segment address to an physical address, shift it left by 4 bits.

Uses

EAX, Flags

See Also

Get_Environment_String, **Get_Exec_Path**

GetSetDetailedVMError

```
include vmm.inc

mov     ebx, VM        ; VM Handle or 0 if Create_VM error
mov     ecx, GetSet    ; zero if get, nonzero zero if set
mov     eax, Error     ; error code if ecx nonzero
mov     edx, RefData   ; points to reference data
                       ;      if ecx nonzero
VMMcall GetSetDetailedVMError

jz      no_error_info  ; zero set if no error information

mov     [Error], eax   ; error code
mov     [RefData], edx ; reference data for the error code
```

The **GetSetDetailedVMError** service sets detailed error code for a virtual machine crash or start-up error.

This service is only available for Windows 3.1 or later.

Parameters

VM

Specifies a handle identifying the virtual machine. If this parameter is zero, the service gets or sets error information for the **Create_VM** message.

GetSet

Specifies which action tot take. If zero, the service retrieves error information. If nonzero, the service sets error information.

Error

Specifies the error code to set. This parameter is used only if GetSet is nonzero. There are the following error code values:

Value	Meaning
GSDVME_CrtNoMsg	Supress standard messages; the SHELL_Message service is used for custom messages.
GSDVME_DevNuke	Device-specific problem.
GSDVME_DevNukeHdwr	Device-specific problem caused by software running in the virtual machine.
GSDVME_InsMemEMS	Available EMS memory is less than requested; set by the virtual V86 mode memory manager.
GSDVME_InsMemV86	Insufficient V86 memory; set by the virtual V86 mode memory manager.

GSDVME_InsMemV86Hi	Insufficient high MS-DOS memory; set by the virtual MS-DOS manager.
GSDVME_InsMemVid	Insufficient base video memory; set by the virtual display device.
GSDVME_InsMemVM	Insufficient base virtual machine memory for control block or instance buffer.
GSDVME_InsMemXMS	Available XMS memory is less than requested; set by the virtual V86 mode memory manager.
GSDVME_InsV86Space	Available V86 address space is less than requested; set by the virtual V86 mode memory manager.
GSDVME_InvalFlt	Invalid fault.
GSDVME_InvalGpFlt	Invalid GP fault.
GSDVME_InvalInst	Attempt to execute an invalid instruction.
GSDVME_InvalPgFlt	Invalid page fault.
GSDVME_InsMemDev	Could not allocate base virtual machine memory for device.
GSDVME_NukeNoMsg	Suppress standard messages; the SHELL_Message service is used for custom messages.
GSDVME_OkNukeMask	Reserved for the exclusive use of the virtual MS-DOS manager.
GSDVME_PrivInst	Attempt to execute a privledged instruction.
GSDVME_UserNuke	User requested running virtual machine be terminated.

Error values that have the high word set to 2 are intended to be used when a virtual machine fails on start up.

RefData

Points to reference data to set. The reference data is an additional doubleword of data associated with an error. This parameter is used only if *GetSet* is nonzero. This parameter is zero if there is no associated reference data.

Return Value

If the zero flag is clear, the EAX register contains the error code and the EDX register contains the address of the reference data associated with the error code. The zero flag is set if the service found no detailed error information.

Uses

EAX, EDX, Flags

GetSet_HMA_Info

```
include vmm.inc

mov      ecx, Action          ; zero to get, nonzero to set
mov      dx, A20Enable        ; A20 enable count (if ecx
                              ;      is nonzero)
VMMcall GetSet_HMA_Info

mov      [NoGlobalHMA], eax   ; nonzero if no global HMA user
mov      [XMSCallAddr], ecx   ; loader XMS call address
mov      [A20Enable], edx     ; A20 enable count before
                              ;     Windows started
```

The **GetSet_HMA_Info** service returns and sets information related to the high-memory area (HMA) region.

This service lets the XMS driver (in the V86MMGR device) determine whether a global HMA user existed before Windows started and gives the driver access to the HMA enable count.

This service is always valid (not restricted to initialization).

Parameters

Action

Specifies whether to get or set information. If this parameter is zero, the service returns HMA information. Otherwise, it sets the information.

A20Enable

Specifies the A20 enable count to set for the Windows VMM loader. The service uses this parameter only if the Action parameter is nonzero.

Return Value

The EAX, ECX, and EX register contain the following HMA information:

Register	Description
EAX	Specifies whether a global HMA user is present. If this register is 0, Windows did not allocate the HMA meaning either there is a global HMA

user or there is no HMA. If this register is nonzero, Windows has allocated the HMA, meaning there is no global HMA user.

ECX   Specifies the V86-mode address (segment:offset) that Windows used to call the XMS driver when loading. The segment address is in the high 16 bits of the register.

EDX   Specifies the A20 enable count before Windows started.

Comments

The global HMA flag and loader XMS call address cannot be set.

Uses

EAX, ECX, EDX, Flags

_GetSysPageCount

```
include vmm.inc

VMMcall _GetSysPageCount, <flags>

mov     [SysPages], eax          ; count of system pages
```

The **_GetSysPageCount** service returns the current count of system pages. System pages are pages that have been allocated using the PG_SYS value.

Parameters

flags

Specifies the operation flags. This parameter must be set to 0.

Return Value

The EAX register contains the number of pages allocated as PG_SYS pages.

Comments

Although the return value often is equal to the size of the Windows virtual machine manager, virtual devices must not rely on this fact.

Uses

EAX

See Also

_GetFreePageCount, **_GetVMPgCount**

_GetSetPageOutCount

```
include vmm.inc

VMMcall _GetSetPageOutCount, <NewCount, flags>
```

The **_GetSetPageOutCount** service either sets or returns the page out count.

This service is for exclusive use by the virtual pageswap device.

Parameters

NewCount

>   Specifies the new page out count. This parameter is used only if the flag parameter is not set to the GSPOC_F_Get value.

flags

>   Specifies the operation flags. This parameter can be the following value:

Value	Meaning
GSPOC_F_Get	Returns the current value of the page out count; the *NewCount* parameter is ignored. If this value is not given, the service sets the value of the page out count to *NewCount*.

>   All other values are reserved.

Return Value

The EAX register contains the page out count if the GSPOC_F_Get value is given. Otherwise, this service has no return value.

Comments

This service allows the virtual pageswap device to manipulate a memory manager parameter associated with demand paging. This parameter is the page out ahead count. Whenever a page is paged out to satisfy a page in, the system pages out an additional PageOutCount-1 pages and puts the pages on the free list (if possible).

Uses

EAX

See Also

_PageOutDirtyPages

Get_System_Time

```
include vmm.inc

VMMcall Get_System_Time

mov     [SysTime], eax          ; system time in milliseconds
```

The **Get_System_Time** service returns the time in milliseconds since Windows started. This service is accurate to 1 millisecond.

This is an asynchronous service.

Parameters

This service has no parameters.

Return Value

The EAX register contains the elapsed time in milliseconds since Windows started.

Comments

This service does not detect rollover of the clock which occurs every 49 1/2 days. If a virtual device is sensitive to rollover, it should schedule a time-out every 30 days

Although the **Get_System_Time** service is more accurate than the **Get_Last_Updated_System_ Time** service, **Get_System_Time** must call the timer device to update the clock so it is slower than **Get_Last_Updated_System_Time**.

Uses

EAX, Flags

See Also

Get_Last_Updated_System_Time

Get_Sys_VM_Handle

```
include vmm.inc

VMMcall Get_Sys_VM_Handle

mov     [SysVM], ebx             ; system VM handle
```

The **Get_Sys_VM_Handle** service returns the handle for the system virtual machine.

This is an asynchronous service.

Parameters

This service has no parameters.

Return Value

The EBX register contains the system virtual machine handle.

Uses

EBX, Flags

See Also

Get_Cur_VM_Handle, **Test_Sys_VM_Handle**

Get_Time_Slice_Granularity

```
include vmm.inc

VMMcall Get_Time_Slice_Granularity

mov     [Granularity], eax          ; minimum time-slice in ms
```

The **Get_Time_Slice_Granularity** service returns the current time-slice granularity. This value specifies the minimum number of milliseconds a virtual machine runs before being rescheduled.

Parameters

This service has no parameters.

Return Value

The EAX register contains the time-slice granularity in milliseconds.

Uses

EAX, Flags

See Also

Get_Time_Slice_Info, **Get_Time_Slice_Priority**, **Set_Time_Slice_Granularity**

Get_Time_Slice_Info

```
include vmm.inc

VMMcall Get_Time_Slice_Info

mov     [Scheduled], eax     ; number of virtual machines
                             ;     scheduled
```

```
mov     [Current], ebx      ; handle of currently scheduled
                            ;    virtual machine
mov     [Idle], ecx         ; number of idle virtual machines
```

The **Get_Time_Slice_Info** service returns information about the number of virtual machines currently scheduled by the time-slicer, and the number of virtual machines that are idle.

This is an asynchronous service.

Parameters

This service has no parameters.

Return Value

The EAX, EBX and ECX registers contain the following information:

Register	Description
EAX	Contains the number of virtual machines scheduled.
EBX	Contains the handle of the currently scheduled virtual machine.
ECX	Contains the number of scheduled virtual machines that are currently idle.

Uses

EAX, EBX, ECX, Flags

See Also

Get_Time_Slice_Granularity, **Get_Time_Slice_Priority**

Get_Time_Slice_Priority

```
include vmm.inc

mov     ebx, VM             ; VM handle
VMMcall Get_Time_Slice_Priority

mov     [Flags], eax        ; flags from CB_VM_Status
mov     [Foreground], ecx   ; foreground time-slice priority
mov     [Background], edx   ; background time-slice priority
mov     [CPUTime], esi      ; percentage of total CPU time used
```

The **Get_Time_Slice_Priority** service returns the time-slice execution flags, the foreground and background priorities, and the percent of CPU usage for a specified virtual machine.

Parameters

VM

Specifies a handle identifying the virtual machine for which to retrieve information.

Return Value

The EAX, ECX, EDX, and ESI registers contain the following information:

Register	Description
EAX	Specifies status flags from the CB_VM_Status field in the virtual machine's control block. It can be one of the following values:

Value	Meaning
VMStat_Exclusive	Exclusive execution.
VMStat_Background	Background execution.
VMStat_High_Pri_Back	High-priority background execution.

Register	Description
ECX	Specifies the foreground time-slice priority. The high word is always 0.
EDX	Specifies the background time-slice priority. The high word is always 0.
ESI	Specifies the percentage of total CPU time used by the virtual machine.

Comments

The percentage of CPU time indicates the maximum amount of time the virtual machine can run. If the virtual machine releases its time slice, this actual amount of CPU time will be lower because the system grants the released time to other virtual machines.

Uses

EAX, ECX, EDX, ESI, Flags

See Also

Get_Time_Slice_Granularity, **Get_Time_Slice_Info**

Get_V86_Int_Vector

```
include vmm.inc

mov     eax, Interrupt        ; number of interrupt to check
VMMcall Get_V86_Int_Vector

mov     [Segment], cx         ; segment address for
                              ;     interrupt routine
mov     [Offset], edx         ; offset to interrupt routine
```

The **Get_V86_Int_Vector** service returns the address of the interrupt routine for the specified real-mode interrupt in the current virtual machine.

Parameters

Interrupt

Specifies the number of the interrupt to check.

Return Value

The CX register contains the segment address of the interrupt routine and the EDX register contains the offset of the interrupt routine (the high word is always zero).

Uses

ECX, EDX, Flags

See Also

Get_PM_Int_Vector, **Set_V86_Int_Vector**

_GetV86PageableArray

```
include vmm.inc

VMMcall _GetV86PageableArray, <VM, <OFFSET32 ArrayBuf>, flags>

or      eax, eax            ; nonzero if array retrieved,
                            ;    zero if error
jz      error
```

The **_GetV86PageableArray** service returns a copy of the bit array of pages whose behavior has been modified using the **_SetResetV86Pageable** service.

Virtual devices use this service to determine whether regions in the V86 address space in a virtual machine have had the normal lock and unlock behavior modified.

Parameters

VM

Specifies the virtual machine to examine.

ArrayBuf

Points to the buffer to receive the array. The array contains 100h bits (32 bytes), one bit for each page in the range 0 through 100h. If a bit is set, the lock and unlock behavior for the corresponding page is disabled. Otherwise, the behavior is enabled.

flags

Specifies the operation flags. This parameter must be set to 0.

Return Value

The EAX register contains a nonzero value if the service is successful. Otherwise, EAX contains zero to indicate an error such as an invalid virtual machine handle.

Comments

This service returns a bit array whose bits are all zero if the VMStat_PageableV86 value is not given in the CB_VM_Status field of the control block for the virtual machine.

Uses

EAX

See Also

_SetResetV86Pageable

Get_VM_Exec_Time

```
include vmm.inc

VMMcall Get_VM_Exec_Time

mov      [ExecTime], eax      ; time in ms that VM has run
```

The **Get_VM_Exec_Time** service returns the amount of time that the current virtual machine has run. This service is accurate to 1 millisecond.

This is an asynchronous service.

Parameters

This service has no parameters.

Return Value

The EAX register contains the execution time for the current virtual machine.

Comments

When the system creates a virtual machine, it sets the execution time for the virtual machine to zero. The system increases the execution time only when the virtual machine actually runs. This means the execution time indicates the amount of time the current virtual machine has run, not the length of time since it was created.

Although the **Get_VM_Exec_Time** service is more accurate than the **Get_Last_Updated_VM_Exec_Time** service, **Get_VM_Exec_Time** must call the timer device to update the clock so it is slower than **Get_Last_Updated_VM_Exec_Time**.

Uses

EAX, Flags

See Also

Get_Last_Updated_VM_Exec_Time

Get_VMM_Reenter_Count

```
include vmm.inc

VMMcall Get_VMM_Reenter_Count

jecxz   not_reentered            ; ecx is zero if VMM not
                                 ;    re-entered
mov     [Count], ecx             ; otherwise, number of times
                                 ;    re-entered
```

The **Get_VMM_Reenter_Count** service returns the number of times the VMM has been re-entered as a result of a hardware interrupt, page fault, or other processor exception. Virtual devices typically use this service to determine whether they can call nonre-entrant VMM services.

Parameters

This service has no parameters.

Return Value

The ECX register is zero if the VMM has not been re-entered. Otherwise, the ECX register specifies the number of times the VMM has been re-entered.

Comments

If this service returns a nonzero value, a virtual device may call only VMM services that are asynchronous. If a virtual must call other VMM services, the virtual device can schedule an event using a service such as **Schedule_Global_Event**. The system calls the event's callback procedure when all VMM services are available.

The **Call_Global_Event** and **Call_VM_Event** services call this service to determine whether the event callback procedure should be called immediately.

Uses

Flags

See Also

Call_Global_Event, Call_VM_Event, Schedule_Global_Event, Schedule_VM_Event

Get_VMM_Version

```
include vmm.inc

VMMcall Get_VMM_Version

mov     [Major], ah         ; major version number
mov     [Minor], al         ; minor version number
mov     [Debug], ecx        ; debug development
                            ;    revision number
```

The **Get_VMM_Version** service returns the version number for the Windows virtual machine manager (VMM).

Parameters

This service has no parameters.

Return Value

The carry flag is clear and the AX and ECX registers contain the following version number information:

Register	Description
AH	Specifies the major version number. For Windows 3.1, this number is 3.
AL	Specifies the minor version number. For Windows 3.1, this number is 10.
ECX	Specifies the debug development revision number.

Uses

EAX, Flags

_GetVMPgCount

```
include vmm.inc

VMMcall _GetVMPgCount, <VM, flags>
```

The **_GetVMPgCount** service returns the current count of pages allocated to a particular virtual machine.

Parameters

VM

Specifies a handle identifying the virtual machine to examine.

flags

Specifies the operation flags. This parameter must be set to 0.

Return Value

The EAX register contains the total number of pages allocated for the specified virtual machine, and the EDX register contains the count of pages which are allocated to this virtual machine but which are not mapped into the virtual machine's 1 megabyte address space.

Both EAX and EDX contain zero to indicate an error, such as an invalid virtual machine handle.

Comments

Virtual devices must not rely on the sum of the return values being the size (in pages) of the virtual machine.

Uses

EAX, EDX

See Also

_GetFreePageCount, _GetSysPageCount

_HeapAllocate

```
include vmm.inc

VMMcall _HeapAllocate, <nbytes, flags>

or      eax, eax            ; zero if error
jz      not_allocated
mov     [Address], eax      ; address of memory block
```

The **_HeapAllocate** service allocates a block of memory from the heap.

Parameters

nbytes

Specifies the size in bytes of the block to allocate. This parameter must not be zero.

flags

Specifies the allocation flags. It can be the following value:

Value	Meaning
HeapZeroInit	Fills the memory block with zeros. If this value is not given, the initial content of the memory block is undefined.

All other values are reserved.

Return Value

The EAX register contains the ring-0 address of the block if the service is successful. Otherwise, EAX contains zero to indicate an error such as insufficient memory to satisfy the request.

Comments

This service aligns allocated block on doubleword boundaries, however, the block size does not have to be a multiple of 4.

Since the system offers no protection on the heap, virtual devices must provide their own protection to prevent overrunning allocated blocks.

The system offers no compaction on the heap; all memory blocks on the heap are fixed. Virtual devices must not to use the heap in such a way as to severely fragment it.

Uses

EAX

See Also

_HeapFree, **_HeapReAllocate**

_HeapFree

```
include vmm.inc

VMMcall _HeapFree, <hAddress, flags>

or      eax, eax            ; nonzero if freed, zero if error
jz      not_freed
```

The **_HeapFree** service frees an existing memory block of heap.

Parameters

hAddress

> Specifies the address of the memory block to free. This address must have been previously returned from the **_HeapAllocate** or **_HeapReAllocate** service.

flags

> Specifies the operation flags. This parameter must be set to 0.

Return Value

The EAX register contains a nonzero value if the service is successful. Otherwise, EAX contains zero to indicate an error such as an invalid address.

Uses

EAX

See Also

_HeapAllocate, **_HeapReAllocate**

_HeapGetSize

```
include vmm.inc

VMMcall _HeapGetSize, <hAddress, flags>

or      eax, eax        ; zero if error
jz      error
mov     [Size], eax     ; size in byte of memory block
```

The **_HeapGetSize** service returns the size in bytes of an existing block of heap.

Parameters

hAddress

> Specifies the address of the memory block. This address must have been previously returned from the **_HeapAllocate** or **_HeapReAllocate** service.

flags

> Specifies the operation flags. This parameter must be set to 0.

Return Value

The EAX register contains the size in bytes of the block if the service is successful. Otherwise, EAX contains zero to indicate an error such as an invalid address.

Uses

EAX

See Also

_HeapAllocate

_HeapReAllocate

```
include vmm.inc

VMMcall _HeapReAllocate, <hAddress, nbytes, flags>

or      eax, eax        ; zero if error
jz      error
mov     [Address], eax  ; address of reallocated block
```

The **_HeapReAllocate** service reallocates or reinitializes an existing memory block.

Parameters

hAddress

Specifies the address of the memory block. This address must have been previously returned from the **_HeapAllocate** or **_HeapReAllocate** service.

nbytes

Specifies the new size in bytes of the reallocated block. This parameter must not be zero.

flags

Specifies the allocation flags. This parameter can be a combination of the following values:

Value	Meaning
HeapZeroInit	Fills any new bytes in the memory block with zeros. All existing bytes remain unchanged.
HeapZeroReInit	Fills all bytes, new and existing, with zeros.
HeapNoCopy	Does not preserve contents of existing bytes. If this value is not given, the service preserves the contents of

existing bytes by copying the contents of the old memory block into the new block.

All other values are reserved.

Return Value

The EAX register contains the ring-0 address of the new block if the service is successful. Otherwise, EAX contains zero to indicate an error such as insufficient memory to satisfy the request or an invalid address.

Comments

If this service is successful, it frees the old memory block, making the old address invalid. Virtual devices must never rely on the old and new addresses being the same. If this service returns an error, the old memory block is not freed and the old address remains valid.

Since the system offers no protection on the heap, virtual devices must provide their own protection to prevent overrunning allocated blocks.

The system offers no compaction on the heap; all memory blocks on the heap are fixed. Virtual devices must not not to use the heap in such a way as to severely fragment it.

Uses

EAX

See Also

_HeapAllocate, **_HeapFree**

Hook_Device_Service

```
include vmm.inc

mov      eax, Service              ; specifies the service
mov      esi, OFFSET32 HookProc    ; points to the hook
                                   ;     procedure to install
VMMcall  Hook_Device_Service

jc       not_installed            ; carry set if error
mov      [Real_Proc], esi
```

The **Hook_Device_Service** service allows one virtual device to monitor or replace the services of another virtual device or of the VMM itself.

Hook_Device_PM_API

```
include vmm.inc

mov     eax, ID                  ; device ID
mov     esi, OFFSET32 Callback  ; points to new API callback
VMMcall Hook_Device_PM_API
```

The **Hook_Device_PM_API** service installs an API callback procedure allowing a virtual device to intercept calls to the protected-mode API of another virtual device. This service is intended to support virtual devices that need to monitor calls to the APIs of other virtual devices. Most virtual devices will never need this service.

Parameters

ID

Specifies the identifier for the virtual device to monitor.

Handler

Points to the callback proecdure to install. See the "Comments" section for more information about the procedure.

Return Value

The carry flag is clear and the ESI register contains the address of the previous callback procedure if the service is successful. Otherwise, the carry flag is set to indicate the specified virtual device does not support an API.

Comments

The system calls the callback procedure whenever an application in a virtual machine calls the API for the specified virtual machine. The system calls the callback as follows:

```
mov     ebx, VM                  ; current VM handle
mov     ebp, OFFSET32 crs       ; points to Client_Reg_Struc
call    [Callback]
```

The *VM* parameter is a handle identifying the current virtual machine and *crs* points to a **Client_Reg_Struc** structure containing the regsiter values of the current virtual machine. Other registers contain the parameter values intended for the API.

The callback procedure can carry out tasks but eventually must pass execution to the previous API callback procedure, preserving the EBX and EBP registers when it calls.

Uses

ESI, Flags

See Also

Hook_Device_V86_API

Hook_PM_Fault

```
include vmm.inc

mov      eax, Interrupt          ; interrupt number for fault
mov      esi, OFFSET32 FaultProc ; points to a fault handler
VMMcall Hook_PM_Fault

jc       not_installed           ; carry set if not installed
mov      [Previous], esi         ; points to previous fault
                                 ;    handler (if any)
```

The **Hook_PM_Fault** service installs a fault handler procedure for protected mode. Virtual devices typically install fault handlers while processing the Sys_Critical_Init control message to handle faults, such as general protection faults, that the VMM's own fault handlers cannot handle. The VMM installs its fault handlers only after the Sys_Critical_Init control message. Virtual devices install fault handlers after Sys_Critical_Init to handle faults before the fault is passed to the VMM's fault handlers.

Parameters

Interrupt

Specifies the number of the interrupt for which to install the fault handler. The interrupt number cannot be 02h and must not be greater than 4Fh.

FaultProc

Points to the fault handler to install. See the "Comments" section for more information about this procedure.

Return Value

If the carry flag is clear, the ESI register contains the address of the previous fault handler. The register contains zero if there was no previous handler.

If the carry flag is set, the specified fault number is not valid and the handler is not installed.

Comments

A virtual device can install a fault handler while processing the Sys_Critical_Init control message or at a later time. Any fault handler a virtual device may install while processing the message receives a fault only after the VMM's own fault handlers have had a chance to process the fault.

The system disables interrupts and calls the fault handler as follows:

```
mov     ebx, VM                  ; current VM handle
mov     ebp, OFFSET32 crs        ; points to a Client_Reg_Struc
call    [FaultProc]
```

The *VM* parameter is a handle identifying the current virtual machine, and the *crs* parameter points to a **Client_Reg_Struc** structure containing the register values for the current virtual machine.

If the fault does not process the fault, it should pass the fault to the previous fault handler (if any), making sure that all registers are preserved (not just the registers containing input parameters).

If the fault handler processes the fault or if there is no previous fault handler, the handler should return without chaining by executing a near ret instruction (not an iret instruction).

The fault handler can modify EAX, EBX, ECX, EDX, ESI, and EDI.

Do not use this service to install a fault handler for the Non-Maskable Interrupt (NMI). Instead, a virtual device must use the **Get_NMI_Handler_Addr** and **Set_NMI_Handler_Addr** services.

Do not use this service to install handlers for hardware interrupts. Instead, a virtual device must use virtual PIC device services.

Uses

ESI, Flags

See Also

Hook_V86_Fault, **Hook_VMM_Fault**

Hook_V86_Fault

```
include vmm.inc

mov     eax, Interrupt           ; interrupt number for fault
mov     esi, OFFSET32 FaultProc  ; points to a fault handler
VMMcall Hook_V86_Fault

jc      not_installed            ; carry set if not installed
mov     [Previous], esi          ; points to previous fault
                                 ;     handler (if any)
```

The Hook_V86_Fault service installs a fault handler procedure for V86 mode. Virtual devices typically install fault handlers while processing the Sys_Critical_Init control message to handle faults, such as general protection faults, that the VMM's own fault handlers cannot handle. The VMM installs its fault handlers after the Sys_Critical_Init control message. Virtual devices install fault handlers after Sys_Critical_Init to handle faults before the fault is passed to the VMM's fault handlers.

Parameters

Interrupt

Specifies the number of the interrupt for which to install the fault handler. The interrupt number cannot be 02h and must not be greater than 4Fh.

FaultProc

Points to the fault handler to install. See the Comments section for more information about this procedure.

Return Value

If the carry flag is clear, the ESI register contains the address of the previous fault handler. The register contains zero if there was no previous handler.

If the carry flag is set, the specified fault number is not valid and the handler is not installed.

Comments

A virtual device can install a fault handler while processing the Sys_Critical_Init message or at a later time. Any fault handler a virtual device may install while processing the message receives a fault only after the VMM's own fault handlers have had a chance to process the fault.

The system disables interrupts and calls the fault handler as follows:

```
mov     ebx, VM                 ; current VM handle
mov     ebp, OFFSET32 crs       ; points to a Client_Reg_Struc
call    [FaultProc]
```

The *VM* parameter is a handle identifying the current virtual machine, and the *crs* parameter points to a **Client_Reg_Struc** structure containing the register values for the current virtual machine.

If the fault does not process the fault, it should pass the fault to the previous fault handler (if any), making sure that all registers are preserved (not just the registers containing input parameters).

If the fault handler processes the fault or if there is no previous fault handler, the handler should return without chaining by executing a near ret instruction (not an iret instruction).

The fault handler can modify EAX, EBX, ECX, EDX, ESI, and EDI.

Do not use this service to install a fault handler for the Non-Maskable Interrupt (NMI). Instead, a virtual device must use the **Get_NMI_Handler_Addr** and **Set_NMI_Handler_Addr** services.

Do not use this service to install handlers for hardware interrupts. Instead, a virtual device must use virtual PIC device services.

Uses

ESI, Flags

See Also

Hook_PM_Fault, **Hook_VMM_Fault**

Hook_V86_Int_Chain

```
include vmm.inc

mov     eax, Interrupt         ; number of interrupt to hook
mov     esi, OFFSET32 HookProc ; points to hook procedure
VMMcall Hook_V86_Int_Chain

jc      not_installed   ; carry set if procedure not installed
```

The **Hook_V86_Int_Chain** service installs a hook procedure that the system calls whenever the specified interrupt occurs. Virtual devices use this service to monitor software interrupts and simulated hardware interrupts in V86 mode.

This service is only available during initialization.

Parameters

Interrupt

Specifies the number of the interrupt for which to install the hook procedure.

HookProc

Points to the hook procedure. See the Comments section for more information about this procedure.

Return Value

The carry flag is clear if the hook procedure is installed. The carry flag is set to indicate an error such as an invalid interrupt number.

Comments

The system calls the hook procedure whenever the corresponding interrupt occurs, a virtual device calls the **Simulate_Int** service, or the system simulates a hardware interrupt. This means a hook procedure must make no assumptions about the origin of the interrupt.

The system calls the procedure as follows:

```
mov      eax, Interrupt        ; number of interrupt hooked
mov      ebx, VM               ; current VM handle
mov      ebp, OFFSET32 crs     ; points to a Client_Reg_Struc
call     [HookProc]

jc       pass_to_next          ; carry set if interrupt
                               ;    not serviced
```

The *Interrupt* parameter is the number of the current interrupt, *VM* is a handle identifying the current virtual machine, and crs points to a **Client_Reg_Struc** structure containing the register values of the current virtual machine. If the hook procedure services the interrupt, it must clear the carry flag to prevent the system from passing the interrupt to the next hook procedure.

Any number of virtual devices can install a hook procedure for a given interrupt. The system always calls the last hook procedure first. A hook procedure either services the interrupt or directs the system to pass the interrupt to the next hook procedure. If no hook procedure services the interrupt, the system reflects the interrupt to the virtual machine.

This service is recommended instead of hooking the V86 interrupt vector directly.

Uses

Flags

See Also

Set_V86_Int_Vector, Simulate_Int

Hook_V86_Page

```
include vmm.inc

mov      eax, PageNum              ; page number
mov      esi, OFFSET32 Callback    ; points to Address of
                                   ;    trap routine
VMMcall Hook_V86_Page
```

The **Hook_V86_Page** service install a callback procedure to handle faults for the specified page. Virtual devices, such as the virtual display device, use this service to detect when particular address ranges are accessed.

Parameters

Page

Specifies the number of the V86 page to install the callback procedure. This number must be within the range specified by the number of the last V86 page and 0FFh.

Callback

Points to the callback procedure to install. See the "Comments" section for more information about this procedure.

Return Value

The carry flag is clear if the service installs the callback procedure. Otherwise, the carry flag is set to indicate an error such as an invalid page number or the page is already hooked.

Comments

The system calls the callback procedure whenever a page fault occurs for the specified page regardless of the current virtual machine.

The system calls the callback as follows:

```
mov     eax, Page     ; faulting page number
mov     ebx, VM       ; current VM handle
call    [Callback]
```

The *Page* parameter specifies the number of the page that caused the page fault and *VM* is the handle of the current virtual machine. The EBP register does not point to a client register structure.

The callback procedure must either map physical memory into page causing the page fault or terminate the virtual machine. In unusual circumstances, the virtual device may need to map the system nul page into the faulting page.

Virtual devices must not rely on the contents of the CR2 (page fault) register. Instead, the callback procedure must use the *Page* parameter to determine which page caused the fault.

Uses

Flags

Hook_VMM_Fault

```
include vmm.inc

mov     eax, Interrupt            ; interrupt number for fault
mov     esi, OFFSET32 FaultProc   ; points to a fault handler
VMMcall Hook_VMM_Fault
```

```
jc       not_installed          ; carry set if not installed
mov      [Previous], esi        ; points to previous fault
                                ;     handler (if any)
```

The **Hook_VMM_Fault** service installs a fault handler procedure for the VMM. Virtual devices typically install fault handlers while processing the Sys_Critical_Init control message to handle faults, such as general protection faults, that the VMM's own fault handlers cannot handle. The VMM installs its fault handlers after the Sys_Critical_Init control message. Virtual devices install fault handlers after Sys_Critical_Init to handle faults before the fault is passed to the VMM's fault handlers.

Parameters

Interrupt

Specifies the number of the interrupt for which install the fault handler. The interrupt number cannot be 02h and must not be greater than 4Fh.

FaultProc

Points to the fault handler to install. See the Comments section for more information about this procedure.

Return Value

If the carry flag is clear, the ESI register contains the address of the previous fault handler. The register contains zero if there was no previous handler.

If the carry flag is set, the specified fault number is not valid and the handler is not installed.

Comments

A virtual device can install a fault handler while processing the Sys_Critical_Init message or at a later time. Any fault handler a virtual device may install while processing the message receives a fault only after the VMM's own fault handlers have had a chance to process the fault.

The system disables interrupts and calls the fault handler as follows:

```
mov      ebx, VM                ; current VM handle
mov      ebp, OFFSET32 stkfrm   ; points to VMM re-entrant
                                ;     stack frame
call     [FaultProc]
```

The *VM* parameter is a handle identifying the current virtual machine, and the *stkfrm* parameter points to the VMM re-entrant fault stack frame.

The fault handler may call asynchronous services only.

If the fault handler does not process the fault, it should pass the fault to the previous fault handler (if any), making sure that all registers are preserved (not just the registers containing input parameters).

If the fault handler processes the fault or if there is no previous fault handler, the handler should return without chaining by executing a near ret instruction (not an iret instruction).

The fault handler can modify EAX, EBX, ECX, EDX, ESI, and EDI.

Do not use this service to install a fault handler for the Non-Maskable Interrupt (NMI). Instead, a virtual device must use the **Get_NMI_Handler_Addr** and **Set_NMI_Handler_Addr** services.

Do not use this service to install handlers for hardware interrupts. Instead, a virtual device must use virtual PIC device services.

Uses

ESI, Flags

See Also

Hook_PM_Fault, Hook_V86_Fault

In_Debug_Chr

```
include vmm.inc

VMMcall In_Debug_Chr
mov     byte ptr [Char], al    ; character from debug device
```

The **In_Debug_Chr** service reads a character from the debugging device.

Parameters

This service has no parameters.

Return Value

The AL register contains the character read. If the ESCAPE key or CTRL+C key combination was pressed, the service sets the zero flag.

Comments

This service has no effect in the retail version of Windows. It is intended to be used with the debugging version.

Uses

EAX

See Also

Is_Debug_Chr

Install_IO_Handler

```
include vmm.inc

mov     esi, IOCallback       ; points to callback procedure
mov     edx, Port             ; I/O port number
VMMcall Install_IO_Handler

jc      not_installed         ; carry set if procedure
                              ;    not installed
```

The **Install_IO_Handler** service installs a callback procedure for I/O port trapping and enables trapping for the specified port. Only one procedure may be installed for a given port.

This service is only available during initialization.

Parameters

IOCallback

Points to the callback procedure. See the "Comments" for more information about the callback procedure.

Port

Specifies the I/O port to be trapped.

Return Value

The carry flag is clear if the service successfully installs the callback procedure. If the carry flag is set, a callback procedure is already installed for the specified port or the system limit for I/O callback procedures has been reached.

Comments

The system calls the callback procedure whenever a program in a virtual machine attempts to access the specified I/O port, and I/O trapping is enabled. The system calls the procedure as follows:

```
mov     ebx, VM               ; current VM handle
mov     ecx, IOType           ; type of I/O
mov     edx, Port             ; port number
mov     ebp, OFFSET32 crs     ; points to a Client_Reg_Struc
mov     eax, Data             ; output data
                              ;    (if I/O type is output)
```

```
call    [IOCallback]

mov     [Data], eax          ; input data (if I/O type is input)
```

The *VM* parameter specifies the current virtual machine, *Port* specifies the I/O port, and *crs* points to a **Client_Reg_Struc** structure containing the register contents for the current virtual machine.

The *IOType* parameter specifies the type of input or output operation requested and determines whether the callback procedure receives data in the EAX register or must return data in the EAX register. The *IOType* parameter can be a combination of the following values:

Value	Meaning
Byte_Input	Input a single byte; place in AL if String_IO not given.
Byte_Output	Output a single byte from AL if String_IO not given.
Word_Input	Input a word; place in AX if String_IO not given.
Word_Output	Output a word from AX if String_IO not given.
Dword_Input	Input a double word; place in EAX if String_IO not given.
Dword_Output	Output a double word from EAX if String_IO not given.
String_IO	Input or output a string. The high 16-bits specifies segment address of buffer containing the string to output or to receive the string input.
Rep_IO	Repeat the input or output string operation the number of times specified by the Client_CX field in the Client_Reg_Struc structure.
Addr_32_IO	Use 32-bit address offsets for input or output string operations. If this value is not given, the 16-bit offsets are used.
Reverse_IO	Decrement string address on each input or output operation. If this value is not given, the string address is incremented on each operation.

A virtual machine can disable trapping of a port for every or for specific virtual machines by using the **Disable_Global_Trapping** and **Disable_Local_Trapping** services.

Uses

Flags

See Also

Disable_Global_Trapping, **Disable_Local_Trapping**, **Install_Mult_IO_Handlers**

Install_Mult_IO_Handlers

```
include vmm.inc

mov      edi, OFFSET32 IOTable    ; points to an I/O table
VMMcall  Install_Mult_IO_Handlers

jnc      installed               ; carry clear if all
                                 ;   procedures installed
mov      [BadPort], edx          ; I/O port number that failed
```

The **Install_Mult_IO_Handlers** service installs I/O callback procedures for one or more I/O ports.

This service is only available during initialization.

Parameters

IOTable

Points to an I/O table created using the **Begin_Vxd_IO_Table**, **End_Vxd_IO_Table**, and **Vxd_IO** macros. See the "Comments" section for more information about the table.

Return Value

The carry flag is clear if all callback procedures are installed for the specified ports. If the carry flag is set, the EDX register contains the number of the I/O port for which the procedure could not be installed.

Comments

This service repeatedly calls the **Install_IO_Handler** service until all entries in the specified I/O table have been installed.

A virtual device can create an I/O table using the **Begin_Vxd_IO_Table**, **End_Vxd_IO_Table**, and **Vxd_IO** macros. The following example shows a table containing three entries for ports 30, 31, and 32:

```
Begin_Vxd_IO_Table  My_IO_Table
   Vxd_IO                30,IO_Handler_1
   Vxd_IO                31,IO_Handler_2
   Vxd_IO                32,IO_Handler_1
End_Vxd_IO_Table    My_IO_Table
```

Uses

Flags

See Also

Begin_Vxd_IO_Table, **End_Vxd_IO_Table**, **Install_IO_Handler**, **Vxd_IO**

Install_V86_Break_Point

```
include vmm.inc

mov       eax, BreakAddr              ; break point address
mov       edx, OFFSET32 RefData       ; points to reference data
mov       esi, OFFSET32 Callback      ; points to callback
                                      ;     procedure to install
VMMcall Install_V86_Break_Point

jc        not_installed
```

The **Install_V86_Break_Point** service inserts a break point in V86 memory of the current virtual machine and installs a break-point callback procedure to receive control when the break point occurs. A virtual device, such as the virtual MS-DOS manager, can use this service to place patches in the BIOS.

Parameters

BreakAddr

Specifies the V86 address to place the break point. The address must be specified as a segment:offset pair and must specify RAM. Once installed, the break point must not be moved.

RefData

Points to reference data to be passed to the callback procedure.

Callback

Points to the callback procedure to install. See the "Comments" section for more information about this procedure.

Return Value

The carry flag is clear if the service is successful. Otherwise, the carry flag is set to indicate an error.

Comments

Virtual devices typically place V86 break points in global virtual device memory during device initialization. For example, the XMS driver in the virtual V86MMGR device inserts a breakpoint in the real-mode XMS driver during device initialization. Thereafter, all calls to the real-mode XMS driver are intercepted by the virtual XMS driver.

The segment address specified when installing a V86 break point must be the segment address in the CS register when the virtual machine executes the break point. For example, if the break point is placed at 0100:0000 but the virtual machine executes the break point at the address 00FF:0010h, an error occurs even though the virtual machine executed a valid break point.

When the virtual machine executes the break point, the system calls the callback procedure as follows:

```
mov     eax, BreakAddr        ; address of breakpoint
mov     ebx, VM               ; current VM handle
mov     edx, OFFSET32 RefData ; points to reference data
mov     esi, BreakLinAddr     ; linear address of break point
mov     ebp, OFFSET32 crs     ; points to a Client_Reg_Struc
```

The *BreakAddr* parameter is the V86 address of the break point. *VM* is a handle identifying the current virtual machine and *RefData* points to the reference data specified when the callback procedure was installed. The *BreakLinAddr* parameter specified the linear address of the break point and *crs* points to a **Client_Reg_Struc** structure containing the register values for the specified virtual machine.

The **Client_CS** and **Client_IP** registers contain the address of the break point. The virtual device must change these registers to prevent the break point from being executed again when the virtual machine resumes. A virtual device can change the register by simulating the instruction that was patched, incrementing the **Client_IP** register past the patch, jumping to another address using the **Simulate_Far_Jmp** service, or returning from an interrupt handler using the **Simulate_Iret** service.

When the virtual device receives the System_Exit message, it must remove any break point that it placed in global V86 code, that is, code loaded before Windows was loaded. The virtual device can remove a V86 break point using the **Remove_V86_Break_Point** service.

Uses

Flags

See Also

Remove_V86_Break_Point

Is_Debug_Chr

```
include vmm.inc

VMMcall Is_Debug_Chr
jz      no_character         ; Z set if no character available

mov     byte ptr [Char], al ; character from debugging device
```

The **Is_Debug_Chr** service checks for a character from the debugging device.

Parameters

This service has no parameters.

Return Value

If the zero flag is clear, the AL register contains the character from the debugging device. The zero flag is set if no character is available.

Comments

This service has no effect in the retail version of Windows. It is intended to be used with the debugging version.

Uses

EAX, Flags

See Also

In_Debug_Chr

_LinMapIntoV86

```
include vmm.inc

VMMcall _LinMapIntoV86, <HLinPgNum, VM, VMLinPgNum,\
                        nPages, flags>

or      eax, eax             ; zero if error
jz      not_mapped
mov     [V86Address], eax    ; V86 address for mapped pages
```

The **_LinMapIntoV86** service maps one or more pages into the V86 address space of the specified virtual machine. This service is similar to the **_MapIntoV86** service but uses linear page numbers instead of memory handles. Virtual devices that have access to memory handles should use the **MapIntoV86** instead of this service.

Parameters

HLinPgNum

Specifies the linear page number of the first page to map. A linear page number is a ring-0 linear address shifted right by 12 bits.

VM

Specifies a handle identifying the virtual machine for which memory is mapped.

VMLinPgNum

Specifies the linear page number of an address in the V86 address space. The service maps the specified pages to this address if the *HLinPgNum* parameter does not already specify a valid V86 address. This parameter must be a page number in the range 10h through 10Fh.

nPages

Specifies the number of pages to map.

flags

Specifies the operation flags. This parameter must be set to zero.

Return Value

If the EAX register contains a nonzero value, the EDX register contains the V86 address to which the specified pages are mapped. Otherwise, EAX contains zero to indicate an error such as an invalid address range, an invalid virtual machine handle, an illegal map range, a size discrepancy, or insufficient memory locking. The EDX register contents are valid only if the EAX register contains a nonzero value.

Comments

A virtual device typically uses this service to map buffers having protected-mode addresses into the V86 address space. This gives software running in the virtual machine a means of passing data to and receiving data from the virtual device.

If *HLinPgNum* is a V86 page number (that is less than or equal to 100h), this service returns *HLinPgNum* immediately and does nothing else. Otherwise, the service returns *VMLinPgNum*.

If the specified linear pages belong to a free physical region, this service calls the **_PhysIntoV86** service to carry out the request.

If the specified linear pages belong to the high addressing region for a virtual machine, this service maps the memory from that virtual machine into the virtual machine specified by the VM parameter. The V86MMGR device uses this capability to map a region of V86 address space which is currently local to one VM into a global region that is addressable by all virtual machines. Virtual devices must not use this capability directly; they should always use the V86MMGR services to map local memory into global memory.

Although a virtual device can map the same page into multiple addresses in the V86 address space, this is not recommended.

For each mapped page, this service sets the P_USER, P_PRES, and P_WRITE bits, but clears the P_DIRTY and P_ACC bits. The service sets the page type to be identical to the page type for the pages at the specified protected-mode linear address.

If the virtual pageswap device uses MS-DOS or BIOS functions to write to the device, this service automatically locks all mapped pages and unlocks any previously mapped pages.

If a virtual device no longer needs the mapped region, it should map the system nul page into the V86 address space using the **_MapIntoV86** service. A virtual device can retrieve the handle for the system nul page using the **_GetNulPageHandle** service.

This service accepts V86 page numbers between 10h and the page number returned by the **_GetFirstV86Page** service. This supports virtual devices that use the **_Allocate_Global_V86_Data_Area** service. Mapping a region which spans across the first V86 page is not allowed. Mapping pages in this region to other addresses can easily crash the system, and should be avoided.

Uses

EAX, EDX

See Also

_Allocate_Global_V86_Data_Area, **_GetFirstV86Page**, **_GetNulPageHandle**, **_MapIntoV86**, **_PageLock**, **_PhysIntoV86**

_LinPageLock

```
include vmm.inc

VMMcall _LinPageLock, <HLinPgNum, nPages, flags>

or      eax, eax            ; nonzero if locked, zero if error
jz      not_locked
```

The **_LinPageLock** service unlocks one or more pages starting at the specified linear page number. This service is similar to the **_PageLock** service, but uses linear page numbers instead of memory handles.

Parameters

HLinPgNum

Specifies the linear page number of the first page to lock. A linear page number is a ring-0 linear address shifted right by 12 bits.

nPages

Specifies the number of pages to lock.

flags

Specifies the operation flags. This parameter can be the following value:

Value	Meaning
PageLockedIfDP	Locks pages only if the virtual pageswap device use MS-DOS or BIOS functions to write pages to the hardware. If the virtual pageswap device writes directly to hardware, this service returns immediately without locking the pages.

All other values are reserved.

Return Value

The EAX register contains a nonzero value if the lock is successful. Otherwise, EAX contains zero to indicate an error such as an invalid address range or insufficient memory for locking.

See Also

_LinMapIntoV86, **_LinPageUnLock**, **_PageLock**

_LinPageUnLock

```
include vmm.inc

VMMcall _LinPageUnLock, <HLinPgNum, nPages, flags>

or      eax, eax          ; nonzero if unlocked, zero if error
jz      not_unlocked
```

The **_LinPageUnLock** service unlocks one or more pages starting at the specified linear page number. This service is similar to the **_PageUnLock** service, but uses linear page numbers instead of memory handles.

Parameters

HLinPgNum

Specifies the linear page number of the first page to unlock. A linear page number is a ring-0 linear address shifted right by 12 bits.

nPages

Specifies the number of pages to unlock.

flags

Specifies the operation flags. This parameter can be a combination of the following values:

Value	Meaning
PageLockedIfDP	Unlocks pages only if the virtual pageswap device use MS-DOS or BIOS functions to write to the hardware. If the virtual pageswap device writes directly to the hardware, this service returns immediately without unlocking the pages.
PageMarkPageOut	Marks pages for immediate swapping if this service sets the lock count for the pages to zero. This service marks the pages by clearing the P_ACC bit for each page. The PageMarkPageOut value should only be used if the pages are unlikely to be accessed for some time.

All other values are reserved.

Return Value

The EAX register contains a nonzero value if the unlock is successful. Otherwise, EAX contains zero to indicate an error, such as an invalid address range.

Uses

EAX

See Also

_LinMapIntoV86, **_LinPageLock**, **_PageUnLock**

List_Allocate

```
include vmm.inc

mov     esi, List        ; list handle
VMMcall List_Allocate

jc      not_allocated    ; carry set if error
mov     [Node], eax      ; address of new node
```

The **List_Allocate** service allocates a new node for the specified list. A virtual device can attach the new node to the list using the **List_Attach** or **List_Insert** service. The contents of the new node are undefined.

Parameters

List

Specifies the handle for the list.

Return Value

The EAX register contains the address of the new node if this service is successful. For lists created using the LF_Alloc_Error value, the carry flag is clear if the service is successful. For other lists, this service never returns if the new node cannot be allocated.

Comments

This service normally allocates nodes from a pool of free nodes. This prevents the overhead of calling the **_HeapAlloc** service for every node allocation. If the list is created using the LF_Use_Heap value, this service calls the **_HeapAlloc** service for each node.

Uses

EAX, Flags

See Also

List_Attach, **List_Create**, **List_Deallocate**, **List_Insert**

List_Attach

```
include vmm.inc

mov     esi, List        ; list handle
mov     eax, Node        ; address of node to attach
VMMcall List_Attach
```

The **List_Attach** service attaches a list node to the head (front) of a list. A virtual device can attach a node to any list that has a matching node size. This service can be used, for example, to move a node from one list to another.

Parameters

List

Specifies the handle identifying a list. The handle must have been previously created using the **List_Create** service.

Node

Specifies the address of the node to attach. The node must have been previously created using the **List_Allocate** service.

Return Value

This service has no return value.

Comments

The service attaches the node to the head of the list. Subsequent calls to the **List_Get_First** service return the address of this node. The address of the previous head of the list can be retrieved using the **List_Get_Next** service.

Uses

Flags

See Also

List_Allocate,   List_Create,   List_Get_First,   List_Get_Next,   List_Remove, List_Remove_First

List_Attach_Tail

```
include vmm.inc

mov     esi, List        ; list handle
mov     eax, Node        ; address of node to attach
VMMcall List_Attach_Tail
```

The **List_Attach_Tail** service attaches a list node to the tail (end) of a list. A virtual device can attach a node to any list that has a matching node size. This service can be used, for example, to move a node from one list to another.

Parameters

List

Specifies the handle identifying a list. The handle must have been previously created using the **List_Create** service.

Node

Specifies the address of the node to attach. The node must have been previously created using the **List_Allocate** service.

Return Value

This service has no return value.

Comments

The service attaches the node to the end of the list. A virtual device can retrieve the address of the node by calling the **List_Get_Next** service and specifying the address of the previous end of the list.

Uses

Flags

See Also

List_Allocate, **List_Create**, **List_Get_Next**, **List_Remove**

List_Create

```
include vmm.inc

mov      eax, Flags       ; creation flags
mov      ecx, NodeSize    ; size in bytes of each node in list
VMMcall List_Create
jc       error            ; carry set if error
mov      [List], esi      ; list handle
```

The **List_Create** service creates a new list structure and returns a list handle that virtual devices use in subsequent calls to other list services.

Parameters

Flags

Specifies the creation flags. This parameter can be a combination of the following values:

Value	Meaning
LF_Use_Heap	Allocates nodes on the system heap. This value must not be used in combination with the LF_Async value.
LF_Async	Creates an asynchronous list that can be used while processing interrupts.
LF_Alloc_Error	Directs the **List_Allocate** service to returns with carry flag set if new node could not be allocated.

NodeSize

Specifies the size in bytes of each node in the list.

Return Value

If carry flag is clear, the ESI register contains the list handle. The carry flag is set to indicate an error.

Comments

If a virtual device requires large nodes, it should specify the LF_Use_Heap value to force the nodes to be allocated from the system heap. All allocate and deallocate calls for lists created in this way use the **_HeapAlloc** and **_HeapFree** services to create and destroy nodes.

To access a list during hardware interrupts, a virtual device must set the LF_Async value when creating the list. This forces list operations to be atomic operations which cannot be re-entered. When using an asynchronous list, the virtual device must disable interrupts before calling the list services. The virtual device must disable interrupts even if when not calling during an interrupt. The virtual device must use the pushf, cli, and popf instructions to disable and re-enable interrupts. It must not use the sti instruction to enable interrupts unless other documentation states that this is permitted.

If the LF_Alloc_Error value is not specified, the system crashes the current virtual machine if the **List_Allocate** service fails. If this value is specified, **List_Allocate** returns with the carry flag set when an allocation fails.

Uses

ESI, Flags

See Also

List_Allocate, **List_Deallocate**, **List_Destroy**

List_Deallocate

```
include vmm.inc

mov      esi, List        ; list handle
mov      eax, Node        ; address of node to deallocate
VMMcall List_Deallocate
```

The **List_Deallocate** service deallocates the specified node. Once a virtual device deallocates a node, it must not attempt to use the node.

Parameters

List

Specifies the handle identifying a list. The handle must have been previously created using the List_Create service.

Node

Specifies the address of the node to attach. The node must have been previously created using the List_Allocate service.

Return Value

This service has no return value.

Comments

This service normally never destroys a node. Instead, the service places the node back in the free pool. The node can then quickly be reclaimed when the **List_Allocate** service is called. If the list is created using the LF_Use_Heap value, this service calls the **_HeapFree** service for each node.

Uses

EAX, Flags

See Also

_HeapFree, List_Allocate, List_Create

List_Destroy

```
include vmm.inc

mov      esi, List        ; list handle
VMMcall List_Destroy
```

The **List_Destroy** service deallocates all nodes in a list and destroys the list handle. Once a virtual device destroys a list, it must not attempt to use the list handle.

Parameters

List

Specifies the handle identifying a list. The handle must have been previously created using the **List_Create** service.

Return Value

This service has no return value.

Uses

ESI, Flags

See Also

List_Create

List_Get_Next

```
include vmm.inc

mov      esi, List    ; list handle
mov      eax, Node    ; address of node
VMMcall List_Get_Next

jz       empty_list   ; zero flag set if not other nodes in list
mov      [Node], eax ; address of next node
```

The **List_Get_Next** service return the next node in a list. It is used to search a list for a specific element. When the service reaches the end of the list, it returns zero and sets the zero flag.

This service is typically used in conjunction with the **List_Get_First** service to scan an entire list.

Parameters

List

Specifies the handle identifying a list. The handle must have been previously created using the **List_Create** service.

Node

Specifies the address of a node in the list. The address must have been previously retrieved using the **List_Get_First** or **List_Get_Next** service.

Return Value

If the zero flag is clear, the EAX register contains the address of the next node in the list. If there are no other nodes in the list, the zero flag is set and EAX is zero.

Uses

EAX, Flags

See Also

List_Create, **List_Get_First**

List_Remove

```
include vmm.inc

mov     esi, List       ; list handle
mov     eax, Node       ; address of node to remove
VMMcall List_Remove_First

jc      not_removed     ; carry flag set if error
```

The **List_Remove** service removes the specified node from the list.

Parameters

List

Specifies the handle identifying a list. The handle must have been previously created using the **List_Create** service.

Node

Specifies the address of the node to remove. The node must have been previously retrieved using the **List_Get_First** or **List_Get_Next** service.

Return Value

The carry flag is clear if the service is successful. Otherwise, the carry flag is set to indicate an error.

Comments

This service does not deallocate the node. It is up to the virtual device to deallocate the node or attach it to another list.

Uses

EAX, Flags

See Also

List_Create, List_Remove_First

List_Remove_First

```
include vmm.inc

mov     esi, List        ; list handle
VMMcall List_Remove_First

jz      list_empty       ; zero flag set if list is empty
mov     [Node], eax      ; address of node removed
```

The **List_Remove_First** service removes the first node from a list.

Parameters

List

Specifies the handle identifying a list. The handle must have been previously created using the **List_Create** service.

Return Value

If the zero flag is clear, the EAX register contains the address of the node that was removed. If the list is empty, the zero flag is set and EAX contains zero.

Comments

This service does not deallocate the node. It is up to the virtual device to deallocate the node or attach it to another list.

Uses

EAX, Flags

See Also

List_Create, List_Remove

Locate_Byte_In_ROM

```
include vmm.inc

mov     al, Byte               ; byte to locate
VMMcall Locate_Byte_In_ROM

jc      not_found              ; carry set if byte not found
mov     [Location], eax        ; linear address of byte
```

The **Locate_Byte_In_ROM** service scans the system ROM for a specified byte. Virtual devices use this service to locate single byte instructions, such as the iret instruction, that must be protected from modification by programs running in a virtual machine.

Parameters

Byte

    Specifies the value of the byte to search for.

Return Value

If the carry flag is clear, the EAX register contains the linear address of the byte. This address will be less than 1 megabyte. If the carry flag is set, the byte was not found or the user has disabled the service.

Comments

Users can disable this service by setting to false the SystemROMBreakpoint setting in the [386Enh] section of the SYSTEM.INI file.

Uses

EAX, Flags

Map_Flat

```
include vmm.inc

mov     ah, SegOffset     ; offset in Client_Reg_Struc
                          ;    to segment reg
mov     al, OffOffset     ; offset in Client_Reg_Struc
                          ;    to offset reg
VMMcall Map_Flat

cmp     eax, -1           ; -1 if error

je      error
mov     [LinAddr], eax    ; ring-0 linear address
```

The **Map_Flat** service converts a segment:offset or selector:offset pair into a linear address. This service works only for the current virtual machine. It determines whether the value passed to it is a V86 segment or a protected-mode selector by the execution mode of the current virtual machine.

Parameters

SegOffset

Specifies the offset in bytes from the start of the **Client_Reg_Struc** structure to the segment register that contains the segment address or selector to convert.

OffOffset

Specifies the offset in bytes from the start of the **Client_Reg_Struc** structure to the register that contains the address offset to convert. If this parameter is -1, this service uses 0 as the address offset to convert.

Return Value

The EAX register contains the ring-0 linear address that corresponds to the specified V86 or protected-mode address. The EAX register contains -1 if if the specified selector is invalid.

Comments

Before converting an address, **Map_Flat** checks the current execution mode and, for protected-mode applications, the segment granularity (16- or 32-bit offsets). If the virtual machine is running a 32-bit protected mode application, it uses 32-bit address offsets. For V86 and 16-bit protected-mode applications, it uses 16-bit address offsets and ignores the high word if the OffOffset parameter specifies a 32-bit register.

Example

The following example converts the address Client_DS:Client_DX and returns the linear address in EAX:

```
mov     ax, (Client_DS SHL 8) + Client_DX
VMMcall Map_Flat
```

Uses

EAX, Flags

See Also

Client_Ptr_Flat

_MapFreePhysReg

```
include vmm.inc

VMMcall _MapFreePhysReg, <LinPgNum, nPages, flags>

or      eax,eax         ; nonzero if mapped, zero if error
je      not_mapped
```

The **_MapFreePhysReg** service maps one or more physical pages into a free physical region. The service maps physical pages currently in the free list to the specified pages in the region.

Parameters

LinPgNum

Specifies the linear page number of the first page to map. The page must be in a free physical region previously created using the **_PageAllocate** service. A linear page number is a linear address shifted right by 12 bits right.

nPages

Specifies number of pages to map. All pages must be within the free physical region.

flags

Specifies the operation flags. This parameter can be the following value:

Value	Meaning
PageFixed	Maps the specified pages as fixed pages, permanently locking the pages at the specified address. If this value is not given, the pages are not fixed. Virtual devices never return fixed pages to the system.

All other values are reserved.

Return Value

The EAX register contains a nonzero value if the service is successful. Otherwise, EAX contains returns zero specifying an invalid linear page number, an invalid range of pages, part of the page range already present, insufficient number of pages on free list, or an invalid use of the PageFixed value.

Comments

This service is intended to be used in a free-physical-region callback procedure installed using the **_SetFreePhysRegCalBk** service. Virtual devices should not call this service until after the Sys_VM_Init message or the Init_Complete message has been received.

The PageFixed value allows a virtual device to maintain a cache of memory which has a minimum size. The virtual device maps a predetermined number of pages using the PageFixed value to ensure that this cache has its minimum size. The virtual device never unmaps these pages. The virtual device maps any additional pages without using the PageFixed value. This allows these pages to be unmapped later. Occasionally, there may be too few physical pages to attain the minimum cache size. The virtual device must be prepared to handle this condition.

Uses

EAX

See Also

_SetFreePhysRegCalBk, _UnmapFreePhysReg

_MapIntoV86

```
include vmm.inc

VMMcall _MapIntoV86, <hMem, VM, VMLinPgNum,\
                     nPages, PageOff, flags>

or      eax, eax     ; nonzero if pages mapped, zero if error
jz      not_mapped
```

The **_MapIntoV86** service maps one or more pages of a memory block into the V86 address space of the specified virtual machine.

Parameters

hMem

Specifies the handle identifying the memory block to map. This handle must have been previously created using the PageAllocate or PageReAllocate service.

VM

Specifies a handle identifying the virtual machine for which to map the memory.

VMLinPgNum

Specifies the linear page number of a V86 address. The service maps the specified pages to this address. This parameter must be a page number in the range 10h through 10Fh.

nPages

Specifies the number of pages to map.

PageOff

Specifies the offset in pages from the beginning of the memory block to the first page to map.

flags

Specifies the operation flags. This parameter can be the following value:

Value	Meaning
PageDEBUGNulFault	Enables page faults for system nul pages. If the memory block contains system nul pages, a page fault occurs whenever a nul page is accessed. This value only applies when running the debugging version of the Windows virtual machine manager. If this value is not given or the debugging version is not running, no page faults occur.

All other values are reserved.

Return Value

The EAX register contains a nonzero value if the map is successful. Otherwise, EAX contains zero to indicate an error such as an invalid memory handle, an invalid virtual machine handle, an illegal map range, a size discrepancy, or insufficient memory for locking.

Comments

A virtual device typically uses this service to map buffers having protected-mode addresses into the V86 address space. This gives software running in the virtual machine a means of passing data to and receiving data from the virtual device.

The service returns an error if the sum of the *PageOff* and *nPages* parameters is greater than the size of the memory block.

Although a virtual device can map the same page into multiple addresses in the V86 address space, this is not recommended.

For each mapped page, this service sets the P_USER, P_PRES, and P_WRITE bits but clears the P_DIRTY and P_ACC bits. The service sets the page type to be identical to the page type for the pages at the specified protected-mode linear address. Although the memory block to be mapped can have PG_SYS page type, it is not recommended.

If the virtual pageswap device uses MS-DOS or BIOS functions to write to the hardware, **_MapIntoV86** automatically locks the mapped pages and unlocks any previously mapped pages. If the virtual pageswap device writes directly to the hardware, this service neither lock nor unlocks the pages.

If a virtual device no longer needs the mapped region, it should map the system nul page into the V86 address space using the **_MapIntoV86** service. A virtual device can retrieve the handle for the system nul page using the **_GetNulPageHandle** service.

This service accepts V86 page numbers between 10h and the page number returned by the **_GetFirstV86Page** service. This supports virtual devices that use the **_Allocate_Global_V86_Data_Area** service. Mapping a region which spans across the first V86 page is not allowed. Mapping pages in this region to other addresses can easily crash the system and should be avoided.

Uses

EAX

See Also

_Allocate_Global_V86_Data_Area, **_GetFirstV86Page**, **_GetNulPageHandle**, **_LinMapIntoV86**

Map_Lin_To_VM_Addr

```
include vmm.inc

mov      eax, LineAddr    ; Linear address to convert
mov      ecx, Limit       ; segment limit in bytes
VMMcall Map_Lin_To_VM_Addr

jc       error            ; carry set if error
mov      [SegSel], cx      ; segment or selector
mov      [Offset], edx     ; address offset
```

The **Map_Lin_To_VM_Addr** service converts a 32-bit ring-0 linear address into an V86 or protected-mode address. This service converts the address for use with the current execution mode of the current virtual machine.

Parameters

LinAddr

Specifies the linear address to convert.

Limit

Specifies the zero-based segment limit (0 specifies a one-byte segment, 1 is a two-byte segment, and so on). This parameter is used only if the service creates an LDT selector.

Return Value

If the carry flag is clear, the CX register contains the segment address or selector, and EDX regsiter contains the address offset. This offset is always zero if the virtual machine is running a protected mode application.

The carry flag is set to indicate an error such as no LDT selectors available.

Comments

If the virtual machine is running in V86 mode, the *LinAddr* parameter must specify a linear address that is within the 1 megabyte V86 address space of the current virtual machine. The service returns a segment:offset pair.

If the virtual machine is running a protected-mode application, the service returns a selector:offset pair. This service creates a new selector in the current virtual machine's LDT if the specified base and limit values do not match a selector the service previously allocated.

A virtual device must never free a selector that is returned by this service. For this reason, this service should be used sparingly.

Uses

ECX, EDX, Flags

See Also

Map_Flat

_MapPhysToLinear

```
include vmm.inc

VMMcall _MapPhysToLinear, <PhysAddr, nBytes, flags>

cmp     eax, 0FFFFFFFFh     ; 0FFFFFFFFh if not addressable
je      not_addressable
mov     [Address], eax      ; address of first byte
```

The **_MapPhysToLinear** service returns the linear address of the first byte in the specified range of physical addresses.

Parameters

PhysAddr

Specifies the 32-bit physical address of the start of the region to examine. Physical addresses start at 0, thus the address of physical page 0A0h is 0A0000h.

nBytes

Specifies the length in bytes of the physical region. The service uses this parameter to verify that the entire range is addressable.

flags

> Specifies the operation flags. This parameter must be set to 0.

Return Value

The EAX register contains the ring-0 linear address of the first byte of the physical region if this service is successful. Otherwise, EAX contains 0FFFFFFFFh if the specified range is not addressable.

Comments

This service is intended to be used to examine device-specific physical memory. Virtual devices must not use this service for any other purpose.

Since physical addresses do not move, the linear address returned by this service remains valid even after the virtual device returns from the Device_Init message.

Example

The following example returns a linear address for the physical page A0h:

```
VMMcall _MapPhysToLinear,<0A0000h,10000h,0>
```

Since physical memory is mapped contiguously, the linear address for page 0A1h is 4096 bytes beyond the return linear address.

Uses

EAX

MMGR_SetNULPageAddr

```
include vmm.inc

mov      eax, PhysAddr       ; physical address for
                             ;    system nul page
VMMcall MMGR_SetNULPageAddr
```

The **MMGR_SetNULPageAddr** service sets the physical address of the system nul page.

This service is for the exclusive use of the virtual V86MMGR device. The virtual device calls this service, while processing the Init_Complete message, to set the address of a known nonexistent page in the system.

Parameters

PhysAddr

> Specifies the physical address of the system nul page. This parameter is the page number for the nul page shifted left by 12 bits.

Return Value

This service has no return value.

Uses

Flags

See Also

_GetNULPageHandle

_MMGR_Toggle_HMA

```
include vmm.inc

VMMcall _MMGR_Toggle_HMA, <VM, flags>

cmp     flags, MMGRHMAQuerry
jne     did_toggle
mov     [HMAState], eax      ; 0 if disabled, 1 if enabled

did_toggle:
or      eax, eax             ; nonzero if enabled/disabled,
                             ;    zero if error
jz      error
```

The _MMGR_Toggle_HMA service enables or disables the high memory area (HMA).
The V86MMGR XMS device uses this service to control the state of the HMA for a
specified virtual machine and to notify the instance data manager that the state is
changing.

This service is for exclusive use by the V86MMGR XMS device.

Parameters

VM

Specifies a handle identifying the virtual machine.

flags

Specifies the operation flags. It can be one of the following values:

Value	Meaning
MMGRHMAPhysical	Specifies whether the service maps physical pages 100h through 10Fh into the HMA or expects the virtual device to map some other physical pages into

	the area. The value is used only if the MMGRHMAEnable value is also given.
MMGRHMAEnable	Enables the HMA, allowing addresses greater than 1 megabyte to access pages 100h through 10Fh. If the MMGRHMAPhysical value is given, the service maps physical pages 100h through 10Fh into the linear pages 100h through 10Fh for the virtual machine, enabling the global HMA for this virtual machine and which all virtual machines share.
	If the MMGRHMAPhysical value is not given, the service marks the linear pages 100h through 10Fh as not present system pages. To prevent a system crash when these pages are accessed, the virtual device must provide its own physical pages to map into these linear pages. This effectively creates a local HMA that is specific to the given virtual machine.
MMGRHMADisable	Disables the HMA, causing addresses greater than 1 megabyte to be wrapped back to addresses in pages 0 through 0Fh.
MMGRHMAQuery	Returns the current state of the HMA for the virtual machine.

The MMGRHMAEnable, MMGRHMADisable, MMGRHMAQuerry values are mutually exclusive.

All other values are reserved.

Return Value

If MMGRHMAEnable or MMGRHMADisable are given, the EAX register contains a nonzero if the service is successful. Otherwise, EAX contains zero to indicate an error.

If the MMGRHMAQuerry value is given, the EAX register contains a nonzero value if the HMA is enabled and zero if the HMA is disabled.

Comments

This service can fail if the MMGRHMAEnable and MMGRHMAPhysical values are given but the system is already using the physical pages 100h through 10Fh for some other purpose.

A virtual device must not call this service unless it has already used the **_Assign_Device_V86_Pages** service to assign the pages 100h through 10Fh to itself. For this reason, this service is intended to be used by one and only one virtual device.

When the system creates a virtual machine, it disables the HMA and causes the virtual machine to operate like an 8086 processor. To override this default, the virtual device responsible for the HMA must enable the HMA while processing the VM_Critical_Init message.

Virtual devices must not identify instance data in the HMA.

Uses

EAX

See Also

_Assign_Device_V86_Pages, **VM_Critical_Init**

_ModifyPageBits

```
include vmm.inc

VMMcall _ModifyPageBits, <VM, VMLinPgNum, nPages, bitAND,\
                         bitOR, pType, flags>

or      eax, eax            ; nonzero if modified,
                            ;    zero if error
jz      not_modified
```

The **_ModifyPageBits** service modifies the page attribute bits associated with PG_HOOKED pages in the V86 address space of a virtual machine. Virtual devices use this service to modify the P_PRES, P_WRITE, and P_USER bits and the PG_TYPE, if appropriate.

Parameters

VM

Specifies a handle identifying the virtual machine owning the pages to modify.

VMLinPgNum

Specifies the linear page number of the first page to modify. All pages must be in the 1 megabyte V86 address space. Page numbers below the first page of the specified virtual machine or above 10Fh cause an error.

nPages

Specifies the number of pages to modify.

bitAND

Specifies the AND mask for the page attribute bits. All AND mask bits, except the P_PRES, P_WRITE, and P_USER bits, must be set to 1. The P_PRES, P_WRITE, and P_USER bits can be 0 or 1 to clear or preserve the corresponding page attributes.

bitOR

Specifies the OR mask for the page attribute bits. All bits, except the P_PRES, P_WRITE, and P_USER bits, must be set to 0. The P_PRES, P_WRITE, and P_USER bits can be 0 or 1 to preserve or set the corresponding page attributes.

pType

Specifies the page type. It can be one of the following values:

Value	Meaning
PG_HOOKED	Changes the page type to hooked. This value must be specified if the service clears any one of the P_PRES, P_WRITE and P_USER bits.
PG_IGNORE	Leaves the current page type unchanged.

All other values are reserved.

flags

Specifies the operation flags. This parameter must be set to 0.

Return Value

The EAX register contains a nonzero value if the service is successful. Otherwise, EAX contains zero to indicate an error such as an invalid virtual machine handle, invalid bits in AND and OR masks, an invalid type, or a bad page range.

Comments

This service always clears the P_DIRTY and P_ACC bits regardless of the AND and OR mask values.

If a virtual device clears the P_PRES, P_WRITE, or P_USER bits, the virtual device must set the page type for all such pages to PG_HOOKED. Also the virtual device must have previously installed a hook page fault handler for these pages.

This service cannot be used to set the P_PRES bit. Virtual devices can use the **_MapIntoV86** or **_PhysIntoV86** service to make pages present. Since the **_MapIntoV86** service resets the page type to the same page type as the memory specified by the memory handle, the virtual devices should set the page type to PG_HOOKED when it creates the memory handle using the **_PageAllocate** service. Since the **_PhysIntoV86** service sets the page type to PG_SYS, the virtual devices must use the **_ModifyPageBits** service to change the page type to PG_HOOKED if it uses **_PhysIntoV86** to map physical pages into a hooked page region.

If using the P_WRITE bit to simulate ROM in a virtual machine, a virtual device should map the pages using the **_PhysIntoV86** service and immediately call the **_ModifyPageBits** service to clear the P_WRITE bit and change the page type to PG_HOOKED.

Uses

EAX

See Also

_MapIntoV86, **_PhysIntoV86**

No_Fail_Resume_VM

```
include vmm.inc

mov     ebx, VM             ; VM handle
VMMcall No_Fail_Resume_VM
```

The **No_Fail_Resume_VM** service resumes the execution of a virtual machine previously suspended by the **Suspend_VM** service. Unlike the **Resume_VM** service, this service never returns an error.

Parameters

VM

Specifies a handle identifying the virtual machine to resume.

Return Value

This service has no return value.

Comments

This service decrements the suspend count, and places the virtual machine in the ready-processes queue if the new count is zero. The system carries out a task switch to the resumed virtual machine if the virtual machine has a higher priority than the current virtual machine.

If the virtual machine cannot be resumed for some reason, the system notifies the user of the problem and handles the error automatically, resuming the virtual machine when there is sufficient memory available.

Uses

Flags

See Also

Resume_VM, Suspend_VM

Nuke_VM

```
include vmm.inc

mov     ebx, VM          ; VM handle
VMMcall Nuke_VM
```

The **Nuke_VM** service closes a virtual machine that has not yet terminated.

Parameters

VM

Specifies the handle identifying the virtual machine to destroy. If this parameter specifies the system virtual machine, the service closes Windows and returns to MS-DOS.

Return Value

The service has no return value. If the *VM* parameter specifies the current or system virtual machine, this service never returns.

Comments

The virtual shell device typically calls this service to close a virtual machine whenever the user chooses the Terminate button from the virtual machine's Settings dialog box.

This service should be used with caution.

Uses

ECX, EDX, Flags

See Also

Close_VM, Crash_Cur_VM

OpenFile

```
include vmm.inc

mov      edx, OFFSET32 Filename   ; points to name of
                                  ;     file to open
mov      edi, OFFSET32 Buffer     ; points to buffer
                                  ;     to receive full path
VMMcall OpenFile

jc       not_found               ; carry flag is set
                                  ;     if file not found
mov      [Handle], eax           ; MS-DOS file handle
```

The **OpenFile** service opens the file having the specified name. If the *Filename* parameter specifies only a filename (no drive letter or path separators included), this service searches for the file in the directories specified by the following:

- WINDIR environment variable

- First command-line argument (argv[0]) of Windows

- Current working directory

- PATH environment variable

Otherwise, the service does not search for the file. In either case, the service attempts to opens the file for reading (in compatibility mode), and returns the MS-DOS file handle if it is successful.

This service is only available during initialization.

Parameters

Filename

Points to a null-terminated string specifying the name of the file to open.

Buffer

Points to a buffer that receives the full path of the file (if found). The buffer must be at least 128 bytes.

Return Value

If the carry flag is clear, the EAX register contains a valid MS-DOS file handle (in the low word). The handle can be used in subsequent MS-DOS functions to read from or close the file. If the carry flag is set, the file cannot be found.

Comments

If WINDIR and PATH environment variables are not well formed, this service cannot guarantee that the full path copied to the Buffer parameter will be well formed.

This service fails if the current virtual machine cannot support a call to the **Exec_Int** service, or if the virtual machine has already used the **_Allocate_Temp_V86_Data_Area** service to allocate the temporary buffer.

Uses

EAX, Flags

See Also

_Allocate_Temp_V86_Data_Area, Exec_Int

Out_Debug_Chr

```
include vmm.inc

mov     al, Char          ; character to write
VMMcall Out_Debug_Chr
```

The **Out_Debug_Chr** service writes a character to the debugging device.

Parameters

Char

Specifies the character to write to the debugging device.

Return Value

This service has no return value.

Comments

This service has no effect in the retail version of Windows. It is intended to be used with the debugging version.

Uses

EAX

See Also

Out_Debug_String

Out_Debug_String

```
include vmm.inc

pushfd                                  ; save flags on stack
pushad                                  ; save registers on stack
mov     esi, OFFSET32 String            ; points to string to write
VMMcall Out_Debug_String
popad
popfd
```

The **Out_Debug_String** service writes the specified null-terminated string to the debugging device (the COM1 serial port). If the string contains register placeholders, **Out_Debug_String** replaces these with the actual register values (in hexadecimal), or the symbolic label nearest to the specified addresses.

Parameters

String

Points to a null-terminated string specifying the message to write to the debugging device. **Out_Debug_String** uses the lods instruction to process characters in the string, so the DS register must specify the correct segment selector for the string.

The string can contain one or more placeholders having the following forms:

Placeholder	Description
#register	Displays the current value of the specified register. For example, the service replaces #AX with the value of the AX register. The register must not be the name of a segment register.
?register	Displays the label nearest the address specified by the registers. For example, the service replaces ?EAX with the VMM code segment label nearest the address in the EAX register. The register must not be the name of a segment register.
?register:register	Displays the label nearest the address specified by the registers. For example, the service replaces ?AX:EBX with the label in the segment specified by the AX register that is nearest to the address in the EBX register. The register must not be the name of a segment register.

Return Value

This service has no return value.

Comments

This service has no effect in the retail version of Windows. It is intended to be used with the debugging version. If the string contains placeholders, **Out_Debug_String** requires the caller to use the pushfd and pushad instructions before carrying out a near call to this service.

Uses

All registers and flags

See Also

Trace_Out

Out_Mono_Chr

```
include vmm.inc

mov     al, Char        ; character to write
VMMcall Out_Mono_Chr

mov     eax, 0          ; write character and attribute
mov     bl, Char        ; character to write
mov     bh, Attr        ; attribute to write
VMMcall Out_Mono_Chr
```

The **Out_Mono_Chr** service writes a character to the current position on the secondary display.

If the EAX register is not zero, the service writes the character in the AL register and applies the normal attribute. Otherwise, it writes the character and attribute pair in the BX register.

Parameters

Char

Specifies the character to write to the secondary display.

Attr

Specifies the attribute to apply to the character when written.

Return Value

This service has no return value.

Comments

If the linefeed or carriage return character is written, the service automatically adjusts the cursor position, scrolling the screen if necessary.

This service has no effect in the retail version of Windows. It is intended to be used with the debugging version.

Uses

Flags

See Also

Out_Mono_String

Out_Mono_String

```
include vmm.inc

mov     esi, OFFSET32 String      ; points to string to write
VMMcall Out_Mono_String
```

The **Out_Mono_String** service writes the specified null-terminated string to the secondary display. If the string contains register placeholders, **Out_Mono_String** replaces these with the actual register values (in hexadecimal), or the symbolic label nearest to the specified addresses.

Parameters

String

Points to a null-terminated string specifying the message to write to the debugging device. **Out_Mono_String** uses the lods instruction to process characters in the string, so the DS register must specify the correct segment selector for the string.

The string can contain one or more placeholders having the following forms:

Placeholder	Description
#register	Displays the current value of the specified register. For example, the service replaces #AX with the value of the AX register. The register must not be the name of a segment register.
?register	Displays the label nearest the address specified by the registers. For example, the service replaces ?EAX with

the VMM code segment label nearest the address in the EAX register. The register must not be the name of a segment register.

?register:register

Displays the label nearest the address specified by the registers. For example, the service replaces ?AX:EBX with the label in the segment specified by the AX register that is nearest to the address in the EBX register. The register must not be the name of a segment register.

Return Value

This service has no return value.

Comments

This service has no effect in the retail version of Windows. It is intended to be used with the debugging version.

Uses

All registers and flags

See Also

Mono_Out, **Out_Debug_String**

_PageAllocate

```
include vmm.inc

VMMcall _PageAllocate, <nPages, pType, VM, AlignMask,\
                        minPhys, maxPhys,\
                        <OFFSET32 PhysAddr>, flags>

mov     ecx, eax           ; zero in eax and edx if error
or      ecx, edx
jz      error

mov     [Handle], eax      ; memory handle
mov     [Address], edx     ; ring-0 address of memory block
```

The **_PageAllocate** service allocates a block of memory consisting of the specified number of pages. This service reserves linear address space for the memory block, and depending on the value of the flags parameter, may also map the linear addresses to physical memory, locking the pages in memory. The service returns a memory handle that can be used in subsequent memory management functions to lock, unlock, reallocate, and free the memory block.

Parameters

nPages

Specifies the number of pages to allocate for the memory block. This parameter must not be zero.

pType

Specifies the type of pages to allocate. It can be one of the following values:

Value	Meaning
PG_VM	Allocates pages that are specific to a particular virtual machine. The handle of PG_VM memory blocks will typically be placed in the virtual machine's control block.
PG_SYS	Allocates global system pages that are valid in all virtual machines.
PG_HOOKED	Allocates pages that are mapped into the virtual machine at locations for which a page-fault handler has been installed. These pages are specific to a particular virtual machine.

VM

Specifies a handle identifying the virtual machine for which to allocate the pages. This parameter applies to pages allocated using the PG_VM and PG_HOOKED values only. This parameter must be set to zero when using the PG_SYS value.

AlignMask

Specifies an alignment mask that defines acceptable starting page numbers for the memory block. This parameter can be one of the following values:

Value	Meaning
00000000h	Physical address is a multiple of 4K.
00000001h	Physical address is a multiple of 8K.
00000003h	Physical address is a multiple of 16K.
00000007h	Physical address is a multiple of 32K.
0000000Fh	Physical address is a multiple of 64K.

0000001Fh   Physical address is a multiple of 128K.

This parameter is used only if the *flags* parameter specifies the PageUseAlign value.

minPhys

Specifies the minimum acceptable physical page number in the memory block. All page numbers must be greater than or equal to this value.

This parameter is used only if the *flags* parameter specifies the PageUseAlign value.

maxPhys

Specifies the maximum acceptable physical page number in the memory block. All page numbers must be less than this value. This parameter is used only if the *flags* parameter specifies the PageUseAlign value.

PhysAddr

Points to the four-byte buffer to receive the physical address of the start of the memory block. The service uses this parameter only if the *flags* parameter specifies the PageUseAlign value.

flags

Specifies the operation flags. This parameter can be a combination of the following values:

Value	Meaning
PageZeroInit	Fills the memory block with zeros. If this value is not given, the contents of the memory block are undefined.
PageUseAlign	Allocates pages using the alignment and physical addresses specified by the *AlignMask*, *minPhys*, and *maxPhys* parameters. The PageUseAlign value is only available during initialization and can only be used in combination with the PageFixed value.
PageContig	Allocates contiguous physical pages to create the memory block. This value is ignored if the PageUseAlign value is not also specified.
PageFixed	Locks the allocated pages in memory at a fixed linear address and prevents the pages from subsequently being unlocked or moved. The service locks the memory block regardless of the type of virtual pageswap device present.

PageLocked	Locks the allocated pages in the memory. The pages can be subsequently unlocked using the **_PageUnLock** service. The service locks the memory block regardless of the type of virtual pageswap device present.
PageLockedIfDP	Locks the allocated pages in the memory only if the virtual pageswap device uses MS-DOS or BIOS functions to write to the hardware. If the pages are locked, they can be subsequently unlocked using the **_PageUnLock** service.
	A virtual device must not specify the PageLockedIfDP value until after it has received the Init_Complete message.
	The PageLocked and PageLockedIfDP values are mutually exclusive.
PageMapFreePhysReg	Allocates a free physical region which a virtual device may use to map physical pages that otherwise are placed in the system's free memory pool. The *nPages* parameter specifies the number of pages in the region. The *pType* parameter must be set to PG_SYS and the *VM*, *AlignMask*, *minPhys*, *maxPhys*, and *PhysAddrPTR* parameters must be set to zero. A free physical region cannot be reallocated or freed; these regions exist for the duration of the Windows session.
	This value is only available during initialization, and only in Windows version 3.1 or later.

All other values are reserved.

Return Value

The EAX register contains the memory handle of the block, and the EDX register contains the ring-0 linear address of the memory block. Otherwise, the EAX and EDX registers both contain zero to indicate an error such insufficient memory to satisfy the request.

Comments

Unless PageLocked, PageLockedIfDP, or PageFixed is specified, this service allocates linear address space without mapping the addresses to physical memory. In this case, the system maps the physical page when the virtual device attempts to access an address in the address space. A virtual device can also use the **_PageLock** service to force this mapping.

Virtual devices use the PageUseAlign value to allocate buffers for use by the device which have additional alignment restrictions enforced by the hardware. For example, a DMA may require buffers to start at addresses that are a multiple of 64K or 128K. When allocating such buffers, the PageContig value is often used in combination with PageUseAlign.

The action specified by the PageLockedIfDP value is available only after the virtual pageswap device has been initialized.

Virtual devices must never rely on apparent relationships between the memory handle and the ring-0, or physical address of a memory block.

All pages in the free physical region are initially not present. Virtual devices use the **MapFreePhysReg** service to map physical pages into the region and use the **UnmapFreePhysReg** service to remove pages from the region. Since the system does not provide a backing store for a free physical region, unmapping a page makes the previous contents unrecoverable. The **MapFreePhysReg** and **UnmapFreePhysReg** services can only be be used within a free-physical-region callback procedure installed using the **_SetFreePhysRegCalBk** service.

Uses

EAX, EDX

See Also

_PageFree, **_PageLock**, **_PageReAllocate**, **_PageUnLock**

_PageFree

```
include vmm.inc

VMMcall _PageFree, <hMem, flags>

or      eax, eax        ; nonzero if freed, zero if error
jz      not_freed
```

The **_PageFree** service frees the specified memory block.

Parameters

hMem

Specifies a handle identifying the memory block to free. This handle must have been previously created using the **_PageAllocate** or **_PageReAllocate** service.

flags

> Specifies the operation flags. This parameter must be set to zero.

Return Value

The EAX register contains a nonzero value if the service is successful. Otherwise, EAX contains zero to indicate an error, such as an invalid memory handle.

Comments

Virtual devices that allocate PG_VM or PG_HOOKED pages must free these pages when the associated virtual machine is destroyed. PG_SYS pages do not need to be freed when Windows exits.

If a virtual device maps a memory block into the V86 address space (using the **_MapIntoV86** service), it should unmap the memory block before attempting to free it.

It is not an error to free memory which is all or partially locked.

Uses

EAX

See Also

_PageAllocate, **_PageReAllocate**

_PageGetAllocInfo

```
include vmm.inc

VMMcall _PageGetAllocInfo, <flags>

mov     [Free], eax          ; count of free pages
mov     [Lockable], edx      ; count of lockable pages
```

The **_PageGetAllocInfo** service returns the size in pages of the largest block of linear address space that can be allocated. It also returns the number of pages that can be allocated as locked or fixed memory.

Parameters

flags

> Specifies the operation flags. This parameter must be set to 0.

Return Value

The EAX register contains a count of free pages available, and the EDX register contains a count of pages available for allocating as locked pages.

Comments

Virtual devices must not rely on being able to allocate all pages specified by this service. In general, virtual devices should allocate memory as needed, and not attempt to allocate all available memory.

Virtual devices must not rely on the count of free pages being greater than or equal to the count of pages available for locking.

Uses

EAX, EDX

See Also

_PageAllocate

_PageCheckLinRange

```
include vmm.inc

VMMcall _PageCheckLinRange, <HLinPgNum, nPages, flags>

cmp     eax, 0          ; zero if not valid
je      not_valid
mov     [Pages], eax    ; actual number of pages in valid range
```

The **_PageCheckLinRange** service determines whether all bytes in the specified range of linear addresses are valid. Virtual devices typically use this service to validate an address range before specifying the range in a call to the **_LinPageLock** or **_LinMapIntoV86** service.

Parameters

HLinPgNum

Specifies the linear page number of the first page to check. A linear page number is a ring-0 linear address shifted right by 12 bits.

nPages

Specifies the number of pages to check.

flags

Specifies the operation flags. This parameter must be zero.

Return Value

The EAX register contains the actual number of pages which contain valid addresses. This value is zero if the entire range is invalid.

Uses

EAX

See Also

_LinMapIntoV86, **_LinPageLock**

_PageDiscardPages

```
include vmm.inc

VMMcall _PageDiscardPages, <LinPgNum, VM, nPages, flags>

or      eax, eax        ; nonzero if discarded, zero if error
jz      not_discarded
```

The **_PageDiscardPages** service marks pages as no longer in use, allowing the system to discard the pages. Subsequent attempts to access the page do not cause the system to read the previous contents of the page from disk.

Parameters

LinPgNum

Specifies linear page number of the first page to discard. If this parameter is less than 110h or corresponds to a virtual machine high linear address, the VM parameter must specify a valid virtual machine handle. All pages of the specified range must be marked V86Pageable.

VM

Specifies a handle identifying the virtual machine containing the pages to discard.

nPages

Specifies the number of pages to discard.

flags

Specifies the operation flags. This parameter can be a combination of the following values:

Value	Meaning
PageZeroInit	Fills the specified pages with zeros when a subsequent attempt to page in the pages is made. This value only applies when the PageDiscard value is also given. If this value is not given, the content of the pages is undefined.
PageDiscard	Marks pages for a full discard by clearing both the P_ACC and P_DIRTY bits in the page table entries. If this value is not given, this service only clears the P_ACC bit in the page table entries.

All other values are reserved.

Return Value

The EAX register contains a nonzero value if the service is successful. Otherwise EAX contains zero indicating an error, such as an invalid range or an invalid virtual machine handle.

Comments

This service ignores pages in the range which are not present or are locked. This service affects only pages that are subject to demand paging.

Uses

EAX

_PageGetSizeAddr

```
include vmm.inc

VMMcall _PageGetSizeAddr, <hMem, flags>

mov     ecx, eax        ; zero in eax and edx if error
or      ecx, edx
jz      error

mov     [Pages], eax    ; number of pages in memory block
mov     [Address], edx  ; ring-0 linear address of memory block
```

The **_PageGetSizeAddr** service returns the size and linear address of an existing block of memory.

Parameters

hMem

Specifies a handle identifying the memory block for which to return information. This handle must have been previously created using the **_PageAllocate** or **_PageReAllocate** service.

flags

Specifies the operation flags. This parameter must be set to zero.

Return Value

The EAX register contains the number of pages in the memory block, and EDX register contains the ring-0 linear address of the memory block. The EAX and EDX registers both contain zero to indicate an error, such as an invalid memory handle.

Comments

The returned number of pages specifies the total size of the block, not just the number of pages currently present.

Uses

EAX, EDX

See Also

_PageAllocate, **_PageReAllocate**

_PageLock

```
include vmm.inc

VMMcall _PageLock, <hMem, nPages, PageOff, flags>

or      eax, eax        ; nonzero if locked, zero if error
jz      not_locked
```

The **_PageLock** service locks one or more pages in the specified memory block.

Parameters

hMem

Specifies a handle identifying the memory block to lock. This handle must have been previously created using the **_PageAllocate** or **_PageReAllocate** service.

nPages

Specifies the number of pages to lock.

PageOff

Specifies the offset in pages from the start of the memory block to the first page to lock.

flags

Specifies the operation flags. This parameter can be the following value:

Value	Meaning
PageLockedIfDP	Lock pages only if the virtual pageswap device uses MS-DOS or BIOS function to write pages to the hardware. If the virtual pageswap device writes directly to the hardware, this service returns immediately without locking the pages.
	The PageLockedIfDP value cannot be used until after the Init_Complete message has been processed.

All other values are reserved.

Return Value

The EAX register contains a nonzero value if the service is successful. Otherwise, EAX contains zero to indicate an error, such as invalid memory handle or insufficient memory.

Comments

This service returns an error if the sum of the *PageOff* and *nPages* parameters is greater than the number of pages in the memory block.

This service has no affect on memory blocks allocated using the PageFixed value; such memory is always locked.

Virtual devices must not assume that the requested number of pages can always be locked.

Each page in a memory block has an individual lock count. This service increments the lock count each time the page is locked, and decrements the count each time the page is unlocked. The lock count must be zero for the page to be unlocked. This means that if the handle is locked 5 times, it has to be unlocked 5 times. Virtual devices must not leave handles locked when not needed.

Uses

EAX

See Also

_PageAllocate, _PageUnlock

_PageOutDirtyPages

```
include vmm.inc

VMMcall _PageOutDirtyPages, <nPages, flags>

mov     [DirtyPages], eax       ; count of dirty pages flushed
```

The **_PageOutDirtyPages** service flushes dirty pages. The virtual pageswap device uses this service to prevent a large number of dirty pages from accumulating in the system.

This service is intended for exclusive use by the virtual pageswap device.

Parameters

nPages

Specifies the maximum number of dirty pages to flush.

flags

Specifies the operation flags. This parameter can be a combination of the following values:

Value	Meaning
PagePDPSetBase	Sets the base page number to the current starting point of the dirty-page scan.
PagePDPClearBase	Clears the base page number.
PagePDPQueryDirty	Returns a count of dirty pages without flushing the pages. The service ignores the nPages parameter and all other flags if this value is given.

All other values are reserved.

Return Value

The EAX register contains the actual count of dirty pages flushed by the service.

Comments

The virtual pageswap device typically flushes dirty pages in the system as part of a background activity. It uses this service to scan for and flush current page-out candidates.

The virtual pageswap device can flush all the dirty pages by specifying a large value for the nPages parameter. The PagePDPSetBase and PagePDPClearBase values let the virtual pageswap device set and clear a variable that causes the scan for page-out candidates tostop at the given point, and return zero to indicate that the entire address space has been scanned.

Uses

EAX

See Also

_PageDiscardPages

_PageReAllocate

```
include vmm.inc

VMMcall _PageReAllocate, <hMem, nPages, flags>

mov     ecx, eax              ; zero in eax and edx if error
or      ecx, edx
jz      error

mov     [Handle], eax         ; memory handle
mov     [Address], edx        ; physical address of start
                              ;    of memory block
```

The **_PageReAllocate** service reallocates and optionally reinitializes an existing memory block. The service can increase or decrease the number of pages in the memory block.

Parameters

hMem

Specifies a handle identifying the memory block to reallocate. This handle must have been previously created using the **_PageAllocate** or **_PageReAllocate** service.

nPages

Specifies the number of pages in the reallocated memory block. This parameter must not be set to zero. To free a memory block, use the **_PageFree** service.

flags

Specifies the operation flags. This parameter can be a combination of the following values:

Value	Meaning
PageZeroInit	Fills any new pages with zeros. All existing pages remain unchanged.

PageZeroReInit	Fills all pages, new and existing, with zeros.
PageNoCopy	Does not preserve contents of existing pages. If this value is not given, the service preserves the contents of each existing page by copying the contents of the old memory block into the corresponding pages of the new block.
PageLocked	Locks the allocated pages in the memory. The pages can be subsequently unlocked using the **_PageUnLock** service. The service locks the memory block regardless of the type of virtual pageswap device present.
PageLockedIfDP	Locks the allocated pages in the memory only if the virtual pageswap device uses MS-DOS or BIOS functions to write to the hardware. If the pages are locked, they can be subsequently unlocked using the **_PageUnLock** service.
	A virtual device must not specify the PageLockedIfDP value until after the **Init_Complete** message has been processed by all virtual devices.

All other values are reserved.

Return Value

The EAX register contains the memory handle of the new memory block, and the EDX register contains the ring-0 linear address of the block. Otherwise, the EAX and EDX registers both contain zero to indicate an error such as insufficient memory, an invalid memory handle, or wrong memory type.

Comments

If successful, this service frees the old memory block, making the old memory handle and starting address invalid. If this service returns an error, the old memory handle and starting address remain valid.

If the specified memory handle identifies a fixed memory block (allocated using the PageFixed value), this service implicitly allocates fixed pages for the new memory block.

If the specified handle identifies an aligned memory block (allocated using the PageUseAlign value), this service returns an error.

Virtual devices must never rely on the new and old memory handles being the same, or the new and old starting addresses being equal.

The action specified by the PageLockedIfDP value is available only after the virtual pageswap device has been initialized.

Uses

EAX, EDX

See Also

_PageAllocate, **_PageFree**, **_PageLock**, **_PageUnLock**

_PageResetHandlePAddr

```
include vmm.inc

VMMcall _PageResetHandlePAddr, <hMem, PgOff, nPages,\
                               PhysPgNum, flags>

or       eax, eax      ; nonzero if substituted, zero if error
jz       not_substituted
```

The **_PageResetHandlePAddr** service substitutes one or more pages in a memory block with physical pages not previously available to the system. This service is similar to the **_AddFreePhysPage** service, but allows memory to be used in a slightly different way.

This service is only available for Windows version 3.1 and later.

Parameters

hMem

Specifies a handle identifying a memory block. This handle must have been previously created using the **_PageAllocate** or **_PageReAllocate** service.

PgOff

Specifies the offset in pages from the start of the memory block to the first page to be substituted.

nPages

Specifies the number of pages to substitute.

PhysPgNum

Specifies the number of the first physical page to substitute into the memory block. The page number must be greater than or equal to 110h; only extended memory pages may be added to the block. The specified pages must be read/write physical memory pages, and must be available for use at any time.

flags

> Specifies the operation flags. This parameter must be set to 0.

Return Value

The EAX register contains a nonzero if the service is successful. Otherwise, EAX contains zero to indicate an error, such as an invalid memory handle, an invalid range of pages, or an invalid physical page number.

Comments

This service returns an error if the sum of the *PgOff* and *nPages* is greater than the size of the memory block. A virtual device must not attempt to use pages once it has added them to the free pool, or attempt to add pages that are already available to the system.

This service returns an error if the number of pages to add exceeds the limit of the internal data structure the system uses the manage the free pool. The internal data structure is allocated during initialization and cannot be modified.

This service converts pages that are substituted into the block to fixed pages. These pages are always locked, and cannot be unlocked.

This service maps a new physical page in at the specified locations andputs the existing physical memory in the free list. The contents of the freed pages are not preserved.

Uses

EAX

See Also

_AddFreePhysPage

_PageUnLock

```
include vmm.inc

VMMcall _PageUnLock, <hMem, nPages, PageOff, flags>

or      eax, eax           ; nonzero if unlocked, zero if error
jz      not_unlocked
```

The **_PageUnLock** service unlocks one or more pages in the specified memory block.

Parameters

hMem

Specifies a handle identifying the memory block to unlock. This handle must have been previously created using the **PageAllocate** or **PageReAllocate** service.

nPages

Specifies the number of pages to unlock.

PageOff

Specifies the offset in pages from the start of the block to the first page to unlock.

flags

Specifies the operation flags. This parameter can be a combination of the following values:

Value	Meaning
PageLockedIfDP	Unlock pages only if the virtual pageswap device use MS-DOS or BIOS functions to write to the hardware. If the virtual pageswap device writes directly to the hardware, this service returns immediately without unlocking the pages.
	The PageLockedIfDP value cannot be used until after the **Init_Complete** message has been processed.
PageMarkPageOut	Marks pages for immediate swapping if this service sets the lock count for the pages to zero. This service marks the pages by clearing the P_ACC bit for each page. The PageMarkPageOut value should only be used if the pages are unlikely to be accessed for some time.

All other values are reserved.

Return Value

The EAX register contains a nonzero value if the service is successful. Otherwise, EAX contains zero to indicate an error, such as an invalid memory handle.

Comments

This service returns an error if the sum of the *PageOff* and *nPages* parameters is greater than the number of pages in the memory block. It also returns an error if the specified pages are not already locked.

Each page in a memory block has an individual lock count. This service increments the lock count each time the page is locked, and decrements the count each time the page is unlocked. The lock count must be zero for the page to be unlocked. This means that if the handle is locked 5 times, it has to be unlocked 5 times. Virtual devices must not leave handles locked when not needed.

Uses

EAX

See Also

_PageLock

_PhysIntoV86

```
include vmm.inc

VMMcall _PhysIntoV86, <PhysPage, VM, VMLinPgNum,\
                       nPages, flags>

or      eax, eax        ; nonzero if mapped, zero if an error
jz      not_mapped
```

The **_PhysIntoV86** service maps the specified physical pages in the V86 address space. This service is similar to the **_MapIntoV86** service, but takes physical page numbers instead of memory handles. Virtual devices use this service to associate physical device memory (such as the video memory) with a particular virtual machine.

Parameters

PhysPage

Specifies the physical page number of the start of the region to map. A physical page number is a physical address shifted right by 12 bits.

VM

Specifies a handle identifying the virtual machine for which the memory is mapped.

VMLinPgNum

Specifies the linear page number of a page in the 1 megabyte V86 address space. This service maps the physical pages starting at the associated given V86 address. This parameter must not specify page number below 10h or above 10Fh.

nPages

Specifies the number of pages to map.

flags

Specifies the operation flags. This parameter must be set to 0.

Return Value

The EAX register contains a nonzero value if the service is successful. Otherwise, EAX contains zero to indicate an error, such as an invalid virtual machine handle or an illegal map range.

Comments

If more than one physical page is specified, this service maps the pages contiguously. If the physical memory is not contiguous, the virtual device must make individual calls for each page.

Virtual devices must not map physical pages that do not contain actual memory, or that belong to some other device.

For each mapped page, this service sets the P_USER, P_PRES, and P_WRITE bits, but clears the P_DIRTY and P_ACC bits. The service sets the page type to be identical to the type for the specified protected-mode linear address. This service sets the page type to PG_SYS.

Uses

EAX

See Also

_MapIntoV86

Queue_Debug_String

```
include vmm.inc

mov     eax, Value1             ; value for string
push    eax
mov     eax, Value2             ; value for string
push    eax
mov     esi, OFFSET32 String    ; points to string to queue
VMMcall Queue_Debug_String
```

The **Queue_Debug_String** service queues a string and corresponding values for display at a later time. The message remains queued until the user enters the .LQ command using the debugger.

Parameters

Value1

Specifies a value to queue with the string. If the string contains the #EAX or ?EAX placeholder, this value is used when the string is displayed.

Value2

Specifies a value to queue with the string. If the string contains the #EBX or ?EBX placeholder, this value is used when the string is displayed.

String

Points to a null-terminated string to queue. It can contain one or more of the following register placeholders: #AX, #EAX, ?EAX, #BX, #EBX, ?EBX, ?AX:EBX, ?BX:EAX.

Return Value

This service has no return value.

Comments

This service has no effect in the retail version of Windows. It is intended to be used with the debugging version.

Uses

Flags

See Also

Out_Debug_String

Release_Critical_Section

```
include vmm.inc

mov     ecx, Claims            ; number of times to
                               ;     release critical section
VMMcall Release_Critical_Section
```

The **Release_Critical_Section** service decrements the claim count by the specified value. It has the same effect as calling the **End_Critical_Section** section repeatedly.

Parameters

Claims

Specifies the number of times to release ownership of critical section. Zero is a valid number, but is ignored.

Return Value

This service has no return value.

Uses

Flags

See Also

Claim_Critical_Section, **End_Critical_Section**

Release_Time_Slice

```
include vmm.inc

VMMcall Release_Time_Slice
```

The **Release_Time_Slice** service discards any remaining time in the current time slice and immediately starts a new time slice for the next virtual machine in the time-slice queue.

This service effectively suspends the current virtual machine. The virtual machine remains suspended until another virtual machine or a hardware interrupt calls the **Wake_Up_VM** service for this virtual machine.

Parameters

This service has no parameters.

Return Value

This service has no return value.

Comments

This service returns immediately (does nothing) if the current virtual machine is the only one in the time-slice queue.

Virtual devices should use this service whenever the virtual machine is idle. If the current virtual machine is a background virtual machine, this service releases the time slice and decreases the execution time by -500 milliseconds. If the current virtual machine has the execution focus or is a high-priority background virtual machine, this service releases the time slice but does not adjust the execution time.

Uses

Flags

See Also

Adjust_Execution_Time, **Get_Execution_Focus**, **Wake_Up_VM**

Remove_V86_Break_Point

```
include vmm.inc

mov     eax, BreakAddr        ; V86 address of break point
VMMcall Remove_V86_Break_Point
```

The **Remove_V86_Break_Point** service removes a V86 break point that was installed using the **Install_V86_Break_Point** service. It restores the original contents of the memory automatically.

Parameters

BreakAddr

Specifies the address of the break point to remove. The address must be a segment:offset pair.

Return Value

The carry flag is clear if the service is successful. Otherwise, the carry flag is set to indicate an error such as an invalid break point address.

Uses

Flags

See Also

Install_V86_Break_Point

Restore_Client_State

```
include vmm.inc

mov     esi, Buffer           ; points saved state
VMMcall Restore_Client_State
```

The **Restore_Client_State** service restores a virtual machine execution state that was saved using the **Save_Client_State** service.

Parameters

Buffer

Points to the buffer containing the client state previously saved using the **Save_Client_State** service.

Return Value

This service has no return value.

Comments

This service can have the following side effects:

- Changes the execution mode if the state being restored is in a different execution mode from the current one.

- May change the state of the current virtual machine's interrupt flag and cause the system to call event callback procedures that were previously scheduled using the **Call_When_VM_Ints_Enabled** and **Call_Priority_VM_Event** services.

Uses

Flags

See Also

Call_When_VM_Ints_Enabled, **Call_Priority_VM_Event**, **Save_Client_State**

Resume_Exec

```
include vmm.inc

VMMcall Resume_Exec
```

The **Resume_Exec** service immediately executes the current virtual machine. This service may only be called in a nested execution block created using the **Begin_Nest_Exec** or **Begin_Nest_V86_Exec** service.

Parameters

This service has no parameters.

Return Value

This service has no return value.

Comments

This service can be use any number of times in a nested execution block. This service returns when the virtual machine returns to the same point it was at when **Begin_Nest_Exec** was called.

Uses

Flags

See Also

Begin_Nest_Exec, **Begin_Nest_V86_Exec**

No_Fail_Resume_VM

```
include vmm.inc

mov     ebx, VM              ; VM handle
VMMcall No_Fail_Resume_VM
```

The **No_Fail_Resume_VM** service resumes the execution of a virtual machine previously suspended by the Suspend_VM service. Unlike the Resume_VM service, this service never returns an error.

Parameters

VM

Specifies a handle identifying the virtual machine to resume.

Return Value

This service has no return value.

Comments

This service decrements the suspend count, and places the virtual machine in the ready-processes queue if the new count is zero. The system carries out a task switch to the resumed virtual machine if the virtual machine has a higher priority than the current virtual machine.

If the virtual machine cannot be resumed for some reason, the system notifies the user of the problem and handles the error automatically, resuming the virtual machine when there is sufficient memory available.

Uses

Flags

See Also

Resume_VM, **Suspend_VM**

Save_Client_State

```
include vmm.inc

mov     edi, Buffer         ; points to the buffer
                            ;    to receive client state
VMMcall Save_Client_State
```

The **Save_Client_State** service copies the contents of the current virtual machine's **Client_Reg_Struc** structure to the specified buffer. The saved state can later be restored by calling the **Restore_Client_State** service.

Parameters

Buffer

Points to the buffer to receive the client state. The buffer must have the same size as a Client_Reg_Struc structure.

Return Value

This service has no return value.

Comments

Virtual devices typically use this service to save client registers prior to creating a nested execution block with the **Begin_Nest_Exec** or **Begin_Nest_V86_Exec** service.

Never attempt to restore the client state by directly copying saved register values back to the **Client_Reg_Struc** structure; this will almost certainly cause the virtual machine manager to crash.

Uses

Flags

See Also

Restore_Client_State

Schedule_Global_Event

```
include vmm.inc

mov     esi, OFFSET32 EventCallback ; points to
                                     ;      callback procedure
mov     edx, OFFSET32 RefData        ; points to
                                     ;      reference data
VMMcall Schedule_Global_Event

mov     [Event], esi                 ; event handle
```

The **Schedule_Global_Event** service schedules a global event, which is an event that does not require a specific virtual machine to process it. The system calls the event callback procedure immediately before the returning from the current interrupt. Since any virtual machine can process the event, the system does not switch tasks before calling the procedure.

This is an asynchronous service.

Parameters

EventCallback

Points to the callback procedure. See the Comments section for more information about the procedure.

RefData

Points to reference data to be passed to the event callback procedure.

Return Value

The ESI register contains the event handle. The handle can be used in a subsequent call to the **Cancel_Global_Event** service to cancel the event.

Comments

The callback procedure can carry out any actions and use any VMM services. The system calls the event callback procedure as follows:

```
mov     ebx, VM                 ; current VM handle
mov     edx, OFFSET32 RefData   ; points to reference data
mov     ebp, OFFSET32 crs       ; points to a Client_Reg_Struc
call    [EventCallback]
```

The *VM* parameter is a handle identifying the current virtual machine, *RefData* points to reference data supplied by the virtual machine that scheduled the event, and *crs* points to a **Client_Reg_Struc** structure containing the contents of the virtual machine's registers.

The callback procedure can modify EAX, EBX, ECX, EDX, ESI, and EDI.

See Also

Call_Global_Event, **Cancel_Global_Event**

Schedule_VM_Event

```
include vmm.inc

mov     ebx, VM                    ; VM handle
mov     esi, OFFSET32 EventCallback ; callback procedure
mov     edx, OFFSET32 RefData       ; reference data
VMMcall Schedule_VM_Event

mov     [Event], esi               ; event handle
```

The **Schedule_VM_Event** service schedules an event for the specified virtual machine. Since the event must be processed by the specified virtual machine, the system carries out a task switch to the virtual machine (if necessary) before calling the event callback procedure. The system completes the event processing before the VMM returns from the current interrupt.

This is an asynchronous service.

Parameters

VM

Specifies a handle identifying the virtual machine to process the event.

EventCallback

Points to the callback procedure. See the Comments section for more information about the procedure.

RefData

Points to reference data to be passed to the event callback procedure.

Return Value

The ESI register contains the event handle. The event handle can be used in subsequent calls to the **Cancel_VM_Event** service to cancel the event.

Comments

Since the specified virtual machine must process the event, the system carries out a task switch if necessary before calling the procedure. The callback procedure can carry out any actions and use any VMM services. The system calls the event callback procedure as follows:

```
mov     ebx, VM                 ; current VM handle
mov     edx, OFFSET32 RefData    ; points to reference data
```

```
mov     ebp, OFFSET32 crs     ; points to a Client_Reg_Struc
call    [EventCallback]
```

The *VM* parameter is a handle identifying the current virtual machine, *RefData* points to reference data supplied by the virtual machine that scheduled the event, and *crs* points to a **Client_Reg_Struc** structure containing the contents of the virtual machine's registers.

The callback procedure can modify EAX, EBX, ECX, EDX, ESI, and EDI.

See Also

Call_VM_Event, **Cancel_VM_Event**

_SetDescriptor

```
include vmm.inc

VMMcall _SetDescriptor, <Selector, VM, DescDWORD1,
                         DescDWORD2, flags>
or      eax, eax         ; nonzero if set, zero if error
jz      not_set
```

The **_SetDescriptor** service sets (changes) the descriptor of the given selector.

Parameters

Selector

Specifies the GDT or LDT selector to set.

VM

Specifies a handle identifying the virtual machine to which the specified LDT selector belongs. The service ignores this parameter if Selector is a GDT selector. Otherwise, the handle must be valid for LDT selectors.

DescDWORD1

Specifies the high doubleword of the descriptor for the selector. This parameter contains the high 16 bits of the base address, the high 4 bits of the limit, and the status and type bits.

DescDWORD2

Specifies the low doubleword of the descriptor for the selector. This parameter contains the low 16 bits of the base address and limit.

flags

> Specifies the operation flags. This parameter must be set to 0.

Return Value

The EAX register contains a nonzero value if the service is successful. Otherwise, EAX contains zero to indicate an error, such as an invalid selector or an invalid virtual machine handle.

Comments

This service ignores the high 16-bits of the *Selector* parameter; the 80386 CPU often sets these bits to random values when doubleword operations are performed on segment registers.

The service ignores the RPL bits of the selector.

Uses

EAX

See Also

_GetDescriptor

_SelectorMapFlat

```
include vmm.inc

VMMcall _SelectorMapFlat, <VM, Selector, flags>

cmp     eax, 0FFFFFFFFh          ; 0FFFFFFFFh if error
je      error
mov     [Address], eax          ; base address of selector
```

The **_SelectorMapFlat** service returns the base address of the specified GDT or LDT selector. The address mapper uses this service to convert pointers, consisting of selector and offset pairs, to flat-model linear addresses suitable for use as parameters for the **_LinMapIntoV86** service.

Parameters

VM

> Specifies a handle identifying the virtual machine to which the specified selector belongs. This parameter is not used if Selector is a GDT selector. This parameter must be valid for LDT selectors.

Selector

Specifies a GDT or LDT selector.

flags

Specifies the operation flags. This parameter must be set to 0.

Return Value

The EAX register contains the linear address of the base of the selector if the service is successful. Otherwise, EAX contains 0FFFFFFFFh to indicate an error, such as an invalid selector.

Comments

This service ignores the high 16 bits of the *Selector* parameter; the 80386 CPU often sets these bits to somewhat random values when doubleword operations are performed on segment registers.

Uses

EAX

See Also

_LinMapIntoV86

Set_Execution_Focus

```
include vmm.inc

mov      ebx, VM           ; VM handle
VMMcall Set_Execution_Focus

jc       focus_not_set    ; carry set if the focus cannot be set
```

The **Set_Execution_Focus** service assigns the execution focus to the specified virtual machine.

Parameters

VM

Specifies a handle identifying the virtual machine to receive the execution focus.

Return Value

The carry flag is clear if the execution focus was set to the specified virtual machine. Otherwise, the carry flag is set.

Comments

When a virtual machine has the execution focus, it executes using its foreground priority. If the specified virtual machine has exclusive execution priority, it is the only virtual machine to receive time slices. If the specified virtual machine does not have exclusive execution priority, the system schedules background virtual machines as well.

When a virtual machine receives the execution focus, the system suspends all other virtual machines except the system virtual machine and background virtual machines.

Only the system virtual machine can assign the execution focus to other virtual machines; a nonsystem virtual machine can only assign the execution focus to itself.

Uses

Flags

See Also

Get_Execution_Focus, **Set_Time_Slice_Granularity**, **Set_Time_Slice_Priority**

_SetFreePhysRegCalBk

```
include vmm.inc

VMMcall _SetFreePhysRegCalBk, <Callback, flags>

or      eax, eax        ; nonzero if installed, zero if error
jz      not_installed
```

The **_SetFreePhysRegCalBk** service installs a callback procedure for managing the free list for a free physical region. The system calls the callback procedure whenever the memory manager puts a page on the free list or wants to obtain a physical page.

Any number of callback procedures can be installed.

This service is only available during initialization.

Parameters

Callback

Points to the callback procedure to install. See the Comments section for more information about this procedure.

flags

Specifies the operation flags. This parameter must be set to 0.

Return Value

The EAX register contains a nonzero value if the service is successful. Otherwise, EAX contains zero to indicate an error such as insufficient memory to define the callback procedure.

Comments

When the system places a page on the free list, the system gives a callback procedure the option to take the page and map it in a free physical region using the **_MapFreePhysReg** service. When the system needs a page, the system requests pages from the callback procedures. They provide pages by using the **_UnmapFreePhysReg** service to unmap the pages from the free physical region and put it back on the free list.

The system calls the callback procedure as follows:

```
mov     eax, Request    ; 0 for pages available,
                        ;   1 for pages needed
mov     ecx, Pages      ; count of pages available or needed
call    [Callback]

jc      dont_chain      ; carry set if request satisfied
```

The *Request* parameter specifies whether the call is a notification of free pages or a request for free pages. This parameter is 0 if the pages are available and 1 if the pages are needed. All other values are reserved.

The *Pages* parameter specifies the count of page either currently available in the free list, or requested by the memory manager to be placed on the free list.

The callback procedure sets the carry flag to indicate that it carried out the request, and to prevent the system from calling the next callback procedure in the chain. If the callback procedure cannot complete the entire request, it must clear the carry flag.

The callback procedure can modify all registers except the segment registers and EBP.

If more than one callback procedure is installed, the system calls each procedure in the chain unless a procedure returns with the carry flag set. The system varies the order in which it calls the procedures, ensuring that every procedure is periodically the first to be called.

When Request is 1, the callback procedure must release pages for regions which were mapped without the PageFixed value.

The callback procedure must release all free physical region pages which were mapped without the PageFixed value.

The callback procedure can release more pages than requested. The extra pages remain on the free list until the next operation places pages on the free list. At this point, the system sends a notification (Request is 0) to the callback procedure for all of the pages currently on the free list.

In general, a callback procedure should not call any services other than the **_MapFreePhysReg** and **_UnmapFreePhysReg** services. Calling other services, particularly nonasynchronous services, may cause the system to be re-entered.

The system does not begin calling the free-physical-region callback procedures until after the **Init_Complete** message has been processed by all virtual devices.

Uses

EAX

See Also

_MapFreePhysReg, **_PageAllocate**

Set_Global_Time_Out

```
include vmm.inc

mov     eax, Time                       ; milliseconds
                                        ;    to time-out
mov     edx, OFFSET32 RefData           ; points to
                                        ;    reference data
mov     esi, OFFSET32 TimeOutCallback   ; points to
                                        ;    callback procedure
VMMcall Set_Global_Time_Out

mov     [TimeOut], esi                  ; time-out handle
```

The **Set_Global_Time_Out** service schedules a time-out to occur after the specified number of milliseconds have elapsed.

Parameters

Time

Specifies the number of milliseconds to wait until calling the time-out callback procedure.

RefData

Points to reference data to be passed to the callback procedure.

TimeOutCallback

Points to the callback procedure. See the Comments section for more information about the procedure.

Return Value

The ESI register contains the handle of the time-out if the service is successful. Otherwise, the ESI is zero indicating that the time-out is not scheduled.

Comments

The system calls the time-out callback procedure when the specified number of milliseconds elapse. The system calls the procedure as follows:

```
mov      ebx, VM                    ; current VM handle
mov      ecx, Extra                 ; number of milliseconds
                                    ;     since time-out
mov      edx, OFFSET32 RefData      ; points to reference data
mov      ebp, OFFSET32 crs          ; points to Client_Reg_Struc
call     [TimeOutCallback]
```

The *VM* parameter is a handle specifying the current virtual machine. The *RefData* parameter points to the reference data for the callback procedure, and the *crs* parameter points to a **Client_Reg_Struc** structure that contains the register values for the current virtual machine.

The *Extra* parameter specifies the number of milliseconds that have elapsed since the actual time-out occurred. Time-outs are often delayed by 10 milliseconds or more because the normal system timer runs at 20 milliseconds or slower.

If a virtual device needs more accurate time-outs, it must increase the timer interrupt frequency using virtual timer device (VTD) services.

Uses

ESI, Flags

See Also

Set_VM_Time_Out

_SetLastV86Page

```
include vmm.inc

VMMcall _SetLastV86Page, <PgNum, flags>

or       eax, eax               ; nonzero if set, zero if error
jz       not_set
```

The **_SetLastV86Page** service sets the page number of the last page in V86 memory for the current virtual machine.

This service is intended for exclusive use by the virtual V86 memory manager device, and is only available for Windows version 3.1 or later.

Parameters

PgNum

Specifies the linear page number to set the last V86 page.

flags

Specifies the operation flags. This parameter must be set to 0.

Return Value

The EAX register contains a nonzero value if the new last page is set. Otherwise, EAX contains zero to indicate an error, such as an invalid page number.

Comments

This service is intended to help the V86MMGR support backfill machines. These machines have unused, unoccupied memory from the end of MS-DOS memory (typically at 512k) up to 640k (page 0A0h). On such machines, it is desirable to fill out (backfill) this unoccupied space so that virtual machines provide memory up to 640k.

Uses

EAX

See Also

_GetLastV86Page

Set_Mono_Cur_Pos

```
include vmm.inc

mov     dl, Column      ; current column position
mov     dh, Row         ; current row position
VMMcall Set_Mono_Cur_Pos
```

The Set_Mono_Cur_Pos service sets the current cursor position for the secondary display.

Parameters

Column

Specifies the column position.

Row

Specifies the row position.

Return Value

This service has no return value.

Comments

This service has no effect in the retail version of Windows. It is intended to be used with the debugging version.

Uses

Flags

See Also

Get_Mono_Cur_Pos

Set_NMI_Handler_Addr

```
include vmm.inc

mov     esi, OFFSET32 nmi       ; points to new NMI handler
VMMcall Set_NMI_Handler_Addr
```

The **Set_NMI_Handler_Addr** service sets the Non-Maskable Interrupt (NMI) vector to the address of the specified NMI handler.

Parameters

nmi

Points to the new NMI handler.

Return Value

This service has no return value.

Comments

To install an NMI handler, a virtual device must retrieve and save the current NMI handler address using the **Get_NMI_Handler_Addr** service, and set the new address using **Set_NMI_Handler_Addr**.

The NMI handler must not call VMM or virtual device services. This restriction includes calls to asynchronous VMM services. The NMI handler can examine and modify local data in the **VxD_LOCKED_DATA_SEG** segment, but it must not attempt to access any other memory, including virtual machine and V86 memory. If a virtual device needs to use VMM services in response to an NMI, it should install an NMI event handler using the **Hook_NMI_Event** service.

The NMI handler must not execute the iret instruction. Instead, it must jump to the address of the previous NMI handler (retrieved using the **Get_NMI_Handler_Addr** service). The CPU ignores additional NMIs until it executes the iret instruction. Because no NMI handlers in the chain execute this instruction, the handlers are guaranteed not to be re-entered.

Some computers require the latch at port 70h be reset to enable further NMIs. To simplify NMI processing for other NMI handlers, the virtual parity device (PARITY) automatically resets this latch.

Uses

Flags

See Also

Get_NMI_Handler_Addr, **Hook_NMI_Event**

Set_Physical_HMA_Alias

```
include vmm.inc

mov     esi, Entries         ; points to PTEs for
                             ;    physical HMA alias
VMMcall Set_Physical_HMA_Alias
```

The **Set_Physical_HMA_Alias** service defines an HMA alias for pages 100h through 10Fh. This service is for the exclusive use of the XMS driver, a part of the virtual V86MMGR device, and is only available during initialization.

Parameters

Entries

Points to an array of 16 page table entries which define the physical HMA alias.

Return Value

This service has no return value.

Comments

This service does not map new pages into the HMA. Instead, the virtual device must call the **_MMGR_Toggle_HMA** service with the MMGRHMAPhysical value after the calling this service. This service specifies which pages are mapped when the MMGRHMAPhysical value is specified in a call to the **_MMGR_Toggle_HMA** service.

Uses

EDI, ESI, EAX, ECX, Flags

See Also

_MMGR_Toggle_HMA

Set_PM_Exec_Mode

```
include vmm.inc

VMMcall Set_PM_Exec_Mode
```

The **Set_PM_Exec_Mode** service forces the current virtual machine into protected mode. If the current virtual machine is already in protected mode, this service has no effect.

Parameters

This service has no parameters.

Return Value

This service has no return value.

Comments

Whenever possible, a virtual device should use the **Begin_Nest_Exec** service instead of this service.

Changing the execution mode of a virtual machine does not change the virtual machine's EAX, EBX, ECX, EDX, ESI, EDI, and EBP registers or most flags. The VM flag and IOPL flags change. The DS, ES, FS, GS, SS, ESP, CS, and EIP register are restored to the previous values for V86 mode.

Uses

Flags

See Also

Begin_Nest_Exec, **Set_V86_Exec_Mode**

Set_PM_Int_Type

```
include vmm.inc

mov     eax, Interrupt      ; interrupt number
mov     edx, Type           ; zero for trap gate,
                            ;     nonzero for interrupt gate
VMMcall Set_PM_Int_Type
```

The **Set_PM_Int_Type** service sets the gate type for a protected-mode interrupt vector.

Parameters

Interrupt

Specifies the number of the interrupt to set.

Type

Specifies the type of gate to set. If this parameter is zero, the service sets a trap gate; if nonzero, it sets an interrupt gate.

Return Value

This service has no return value.

Comments

An interrupt through an interrupt gate automatically clears the interrupt flag bit to disable interrupts. Interrupts through trap gate do not modify the interrupt bit. All protected-mode interrupts default to the trap gate type, but virtual devices such as the virtual PIC device, may change some trap gates to interrupt gates so that hardware interrupts disable interrupts. The virtual PIC device leaves software interrupts, such as Interrupt 21h, unchanged. This avoids an unnecessary ring transition by eliminating the need for the software interrupt handlers to execute an sti instruction.

Uses

Flags

See Also

Get_PM_Int_Type, Set_PM_Int_Vector

Set_PM_Int_Vector

```
include vmm.inc

mov     eax, Interrupt      ; interrupt number
mov     cx, Segment         ; segment selector for
                            ;     interrupt routine
```

```
       mov     edx, Offset         ; offset to interrupt routine
       VMMcall Set_PM_Int_Vector
```

The **Set_PM_Int_Vector** service sets the specified protected-mode interrupt vector to the address of the given interrupt routine.

Parameters

Interrupt

Specifies the number of the interrupt to set.

Segment

Specifies the selector of the code segment containing the interrupt routine.

Offset

Specifies the offset to the interrupt routine. If the code segment containing the routine is a 16-bit segment, the high word of this parameter must be zero.

Return Value

This service has no return value.

Comments

If the Set_PM_Int_Vector service is called before the Sys_VM_Init control call, the installed interrupt routine becomes part of the default interrupt vector table for every virtual machine. Otherwise, this service affects the interrupt vector table for the current virtual machine only. By default, each table entry points to a protected-mode breakpoint procedure that reflects the interrupt to V86 mode.

Uses

Flags

See Also

Get_PM_Int_Vector, **Set_PM_Int_Type**, **Set_V86_Int_Vector**

_SetResetV86Pageable

```
       include vmm.inc

       VMMcall _SetResetV86Pageable, <VM, VMLinPgNum, nPages, flags>

       or      eax, eax    ; nonzero if set or reset, zero if error
       jz      error
```

This service returns
is inconsistent w
PageSetV86IntsLock

This service returns
values are given, but

The V86MMGR dev
are created with thei

Virtual devices shou
above page 0A0h. A
or local region set by

If the PageSetV86I
applies the modific
HLinPgNum and nP

By default, the _Ma
running a protected-

Uses

EAX

See Also

_Assign_Device_V8

Set_System_Exit_

```
       include vmm.inc

       mov     al, ExitCo
       VMMcall Set_System
```

The **Set_System_Ex**
DOS when Window
executes the MS-DO

This service is inten

Parameters

ExitCode

Specifies the ex

The **_SetRes**
associated wit

Parameters

VM

Specifies

VMLinPgNum

Specifies
modify. T
above 10(

nPages

Specifies

flags

Specifies

Value

PageSetV

PageClea

PageSetV

PageClea

All other

Return Value

The EAX regi
contains zero t
address range.

Comments

This service is
virtual machin

Parameters

This service has no parameters.

Return Value

This service has no return value.

Comments

This services pops two word values from the stack if the segment containing the address is a 16-bit segment. Otherwise, this service pops two double-word values.

Uses

Flags

See Also

Simulate_Far_Call, **Simulate_Far_Ret_N**

Simulate_Far_Ret_N

```
include vmm.inc

mov     eax, Bytes        ; number of bytes to pop from stack
VMMcall Simulate_Far_Ret_N
```

The **Simulate_Far_Ret_N** service simulates a far return in the current virtual machine. This service pops the top two words (or double words) from the stack of the current virtual machine, and places the values in the Client_CS and Client_EIP or Client_IP registers. It then subtracts the **Bytes** parameter from the Client_ESP or Client_ESP register, effectively popping any pushed parameters from the stack.

Parameters

Bytes

Specifies the number of bytes to pop from the stack.

Return Value

This service has no return value.

Uses

Client_CS, Client_EIP, Client_ESP, Flags

See Also

Simulate_Far_Call, **Simulate_Far_Ret**

Simulate_Int

```
include vmm.inc

mov      eax, Interrupt      ; interrupt number
VMMcall  Simulate_Int
```

The **Simulate_Int** service simulates an interrupt in the current virtual machine. The service first calls any hook procedures set by the **Hook_V86_Int_Chain** service. If no hook procedure services the interrupt, this service pushes the Client_Flags, Client_CS, and Client_IP registers on the stack of the current virtual machine. When the virtual machine resumes execution (such as when an **Resume_Exec** service is called), the system carries out the simulated interrupt and executes the corresponding V86 mode interrupt routine.

The virtual PIC device uses this service to simulate hardware interrupts.

Other virtual devices use the **Exec_Int** service to simulate interrupts.

Parameters

Interrupt

Specifies the number of the interrupt to simulate.

Return Value

This service has no return value.

Comments

If the virtual machine is currently in V86 mode, this service simulates a V86 interrupt. Otherwise, the service simulates a protected-mode interrupt.

Simulating an interrupt in a virtual machine running a protected-mode application can have undesirable effects if the corresponding interrupt attempts to reflect the interrupt to V86 mode.

Virtual devices that need immediate execution of an interrupt should use the **Exec_Int** service in a nested execution block.

Uses

Client_CS, Client_EIP, Client_Flags, Flags

See Also

Exec_Int

Simulate_IO

```
include vmm.inc

mov      eax, Data              ; data for output operations
mov      ebx, VM                ; current VM handle
mov      ecx, IOType            ; type of I/O (as passed
                                ;    to I/O trap routine)
mov      edx, Port              ; I/O port number
mov      ebp, OFFSET32 crs      ; points to a Client_Reg_Struc
VMMjmp   Simulate_IO

mov      [Data], eax            ; data for input operation
```

The **Simulate_IO** service reduces complex I/O instructions to simpler I/O operations. An I/O callback procedure typically jumps to this service whenever the procedure receives a type of I/O that it does not directly support.

Parameters

Data

> Specifies the data for an output operation. This parameter is used only if the *IOType* parameter specifies an output operation.

VM

> Specifies a handle identifying the current virtual machine.

IOType

> Specifies the type of I/O operation. This parameter can be a combination of the following values:

Value	Meaning
Byte_Input	Input a single byte; place in AL if String_IO not given.
Byte_Output	Output a single byte from AL if String_IO not given.
Word_Input	Input a word; place in AX if String_IO not given.
Word_Output	Output a word from AX if String_IO not given.
Dword_Input	Input a double word; place in EAX if String_IO not given.
Dword_Output	Output a double word from EAX if String_IO not given.
String_IO	Input or output a string. The high 16-bits specifies segment address of buffer containing the string to output or to receive the string input.

Rep_IO	Repeat the input or output string operation the number of times specified by the Client_CX field in the **Client_Reg_Struc** structure.
Addr_32_IO	Use 32-bit address offsets for input or output string operations. If this value is not given, the 16-bit offsets are used.
Reverse_IO	Decrement string address on each input or output operation. If this value is not given, the string address is incremented on each operation.

Port

Specifies the number of the I/O port through which to carry out the operation.

crs

Points to a **Client_Reg_Struc** structure containing the register contents for the current virtual machine.

Return Value

The EAX register contains input data if the *IOType* parameter specifies an input operation. *IOType* also specifies the size of the data in EAX.

Comments

The parameters to this service are identical to the parameters passed to an I/O callback procedure. A callback procedure should jump to this service using the VMMjmp macro with all of the registers in the same state as when the procedure was called. The procedure may modify the ESI and EDI register before jumping, if necessary.

Uses

EAX, EBX, ECX, EDX, ESI, EDI, Flags

See Also

Dispatch_Byte_IO, **Emulate_Non_Byte_IO**

Simulate_Iret

```
include vmm.inc

VMMcall Simulate_Iret
```

The **Simulate_Iret** service simulates a return from an interrupt. This service pops the top three word or double-word values from the stack of the current virtual machine, and places the values in the Client_Flags, Client_CS, and Client_EIP or Client_IP registers.

Parameters

This service has no parameters.

Return Value

This service has no return value.

Comments

This service pops three word values from the stack if the segment corresponding to the return address is a 16-bit segment. Otherwise, the service pops three double-word values.

Uses

Client_CS, Client_EIP, Client_ESP, Client_Flags, Flags

See Also

Simulate_Int

Simulate_Pop

```
include vmm.inc

VMMcall Simulate_Pop

mov     [Value], eax        ; value popped from stack
```

The **Simulate_Pop** service returns the word or double-word value at the top of the stack of the current virtual machine, and adds two or four to the Client_ESP register.

Parameters

This service has no parameters.

Return Value

The EAX register contains the value popped from virtual machine stack. The high word is zero if in V86 mode or the virtual machine is running a 16-bit program.

Uses

EAX, Client_ESP, Flags

See Also

Simulate_Push

Simulate_Push

```
include vmm.inc

mov     eax, Value           ; value to push
VMMcall Simulate_Push
```

The **Simulate_Push** service pushes a word or double-word value on the stack of the current virtual machine and subtracts two or four from the Client_ESP register.

Parameters

Value

Specifies the value to push on the stack. In V86 mode or when the virtual machine is running a 16-bit program, only the low word is pushed.

Return Value

This service has no return value.

Uses

Client_ESP, Flags

See Also

Simulate_Pop

Suspend_VM

```
include vmm.inc

mov     ebx, VM          ; VM handle
VMMcall Suspend_VM

jc      not_suspended    ; carry set if virtual machine
                         ;    not suspended
```

The **Suspend_VM** service suspends the execution of a specified virtual machine. This service fails if the specified virtual machine either owns the critical section, or is the system virtual machine.

Parameters

VM

Specifies a handle identifying the virtual machine to suspend.

Return Value

The carry flag is clear if the virtual machine is suspended. The carry flag is set to indicate an error.

Comments

An error occurs if the virtual machine is in a critical section or is the VM parameter specifies the system virtual machine.

This service increments the suspend count for the virtual machine. If the virtual machine was not already suspended, the system notifies virtual devices of the suspension by sending a **VM_Suspend** command to the control procedure for each virtual device. A virtual device must not refuse to suspend a virtual machine. If a virtual machine remains suspended, subsequent calls to **Suspend_VM** do not cause the **VM_Suspend** notification.

When a virtual machine is suspended, the system sets the VMStat_Suspended bit in the CB_VM_Status field of the virtual machine's control block. Although virtual devices may examine and modify the contents of the control block of a virtual machine, the virtual devices must not examine or modify any memory owned by a suspended virtual machine unless the virtual device previously locked that memory.

Uses

Flags

See Also

No_Fail_Resume_VM, Resume_VM

System_Control

```
include vmm.inc

mov      eax, Message      ; system control message
mov      ebx, VM           ; VM handle (if needed by message)
mov      esi, Param1       ; message-specific parameter
mov      edi, Param2       ; message-specific parameter
mov      edx, Param3       ; message-specific parameter
VMMcall  System_Control
jc       error             ; carry set if error
```

The **System_Control** service sends system control messages to all the virtual devices and, depending on the message, to the VMM.

Parameters

Message

Specifies the system control message. This parameter can be one of the following values:

Value	Meaning
Begin_PM_App	A protected-mode application is starting
Close_VM_Notify	A virtual machine is closing
Create_VM	A virtual machine is being created
Critical_Reboot_Notify	System is rebooting (interrupt disabled)
Debug_Query	Requests for virtual device's debugging interface
Destroy_VM	A virtual machine is being destroyed
Device_Init	Virtual devices initializing (interrupts enabled)
Device_Reboot_Notify	System is rebooting (interrupts enabled)
End_PM_App	A protected-mode application is ending
Init_Complete	All virtual devices have initialized
Power_Event	Power is being suspended or resumed
Reboot_Processor	Virtual device must reboot system if it can
Set_Device_Focus	A virtual device is taking the focus
Sys_Critical_Exit	System is terminating (interrupt disabled)
Sys_Critical_Init	Virtual devices initializing (interrupts disabled)
Sys_VM_Init	System VM is being created
Sys_VM_Terminate	System VM is being destroyed
System_Exit	System is terminating (interrupts enabled)
VM_Critical_Init	Virtual machine being created (interrupts disabled)
VM_Init	Virtual machine being created (interrupts enabled)
VM_Not_Executeable	Virtual machine being destroyed
VM_Resume	Virtual machine execution resumed
VM_Suspend	Virtual machine execution suspended
VM_Terminate	Virtual machine begin destroyed

For more information about these messages, see the individual message descriptions.

VM

Specifies a handle identifying a virtual machine. This parameter is not required by every system control message.

Param1

Specifies a message-specific parameter.

Param2

Specifies a message-specific parameter.

Param3

Specifies a message-specific parameter.

Return Value

The carry flag is clear if the service is successful. Otherwise, the carry flag is set to indicate an error.

If the Create_VM message is successful, the EBX register contains the new virtual machine handle.

Comments

Although virtual devices may receive many of the system control messages, they may send only the following messages:

Message	Restrictions
Create_VM	May only be sent by the virtual shell device.
Destroy_VM	May only be sent by the virtual shell device.
Set_Device_Focus	May be sent by any virtual device. If the device ID is zero, all devices with settable focus must set their focus to the specified virtual machine.
End_PM_App	May only be sent by the virtual MS-DOS manager.

Virtual devices must send and reply to messages correctly to prevent erratic system behavior.

This service uses the ECX register, therefore the register cannot be used to pass data through to the virtual device receiving the control message.

Uses

Flags, EBX if Create_VM

Test_Cur_VM_Handle

```
include vmm.inc

mov     ebx, VM          ; VM handle to test
VMMcall Test_Cur_VM_Handle

je      is_current       ; zero flag set if current VM handle
```

The **Test_Cur_VM_Handle** service tests whether the given virtual machine handle is the handle of the currently running virtual machine.

This is an asynchronous service.

Parameters

VM

   Specifies a handle identifying the virtual machine to test.

Return Value

The zero flag is set if the handle is for the currently running virtual machine.

Uses

Flags

See Also

Get_Cur_VM_Handle, **Test_Sys_VM_Handle**

Test_DBCS_Lead_Byte

```
include vmm.inc

mov     eax, Value       ; value to test
VMMcall Test_DBCS_Lead_Byte

jc      not_valid        ; carry set if value not
                         ;    legal DBCS lead byte
```

The **Test_DBCS_Lead_Byte** tests whether the given value is in the legal range for a DBCS lead byte.

Parameters

Value

   Specifies the value to test.

Return Value

The carry flag is clear if the specified value is in the legal range for DBCS lead bytes. Otherwise, the carry flag is set.

Comments

For non-DBCS versions of Windows, this service always sets the carry flag.

Uses

Flags

Test_Debug_Installed

```
include vmm.inc

VMMcall Test_Debug_Installed

je      not_installed        ; zero flag set if not installed
```

The **Test_Debug_Installed** service tests whether whether the debugging version of the Windows VMM is running.

Parameters

This service has no parameters.

Return Value

The zero flag is set if the debugging version is not installed.

Uses

Flags

_TestGlobalV86Mem

```
include vmm.inc

VMMcall _TestGlobalV86Mem, <VMLinAddr, nBytes, flags>

mov     [Result], eax    ; 0 if local, 1 if global, 2 if mixed,
                         ; 3 if includes instance data region
```

The **_TestGlobalV86Mem** service tests whether a V86 address range is global, local, or instanced.

Parameters

VMLinAddr

Specifies the ring-0 linear address of the first byte of the V86 address range. For example, the linear address of the V86 address 02C1h:0FC5h is 3BD5h (02C10h + 0FC5h).

nBytes

Specifies the size in bytes of the V86 address range.

flags

Specifies the operation flags. This parameter must be set to 0.

Return Value

The EAX register contains one of the following values:

Value	Meaning
0	Address range either contains local memory, or is not a valid V86 address range.
1	Address range contains global memory.
2	Address range contains both local and global memory.
3	Address range contains global memory, but also includes an instance data region.

Comments

Global V86 memory has addresses that are valid and identical in all virtual machines. Local memory has addresses that are only valid in one virtual machine. Instanced memory has addresses that are valid in all virtual machines, but the content of the memory varies with each virtual machine.

This service may incorrectly report the type of memory in addresses above page 0A0h (in the device adapter area). If this service returns global for memory in this area, it is global. If the service returns local, however, the memory may actually be global. Generally, this region is local.

Operations involving global address ranges typically do not need to be virtualized since the range is valid and addressable in all virtual machines. Operations involving local address ranges may have to be virtualized since it is possible for software, such as an interrupt handler, to use a local address in the wrong virtual machine.

Uses

EAX

Test_Sys_VM_Handle

```
include vmm.inc

mov     ebx, VM             ; VM handle to test
VMMcall Test_Sys_VM_Handle

je      is_system           ; zero flag set if system VM handle
```

The **Test_Sys_VM_Handle** service tests whether the given virtual machine handle is the handle of the system virtual machine.

This is an asynchronous service.

Parameters

VM

Specifies the virtual machine handle to test.

Return Value

The zero flag is set if the handle identifies the system virtual machine.

Uses

Flags

See Also

Get_Sys_VM_Handle, **Test_Cur_VM_Handle**

Unhook_Invalid_Page_Fault

```
include vmm.inc

mov     esi, OFFSET32 HookProc     ; points to hook procedure
                                   ;     to remove
VMMcall Unhook_Invalid_Page_Fault
```

The **Unhook_Invalid_Page_Fault** service removes the specified hook procedure from the invalid-page-fault chain.

Parameters

HookProc

Points to the hook procedure to remove. This procedure must have been previously installed using the **Hook_Invalid_Page_Fault** service.

Return Value

If the carry flag is clear, the hook procedure was removed. Otherwise, the carry flag is set to indicate an error such as the specified procedure was not in the chain.

Uses

Flags

See Also

Hook_Invalid_Page_Fault

_UnmapFreePhysReg

```
include vmm.inc

VMMcall _UnmapFreePhysReg, <LinPgNum, nPages, flags>

or      eax, eax        ; nonzero if unmapped, zero if error
jz      not_unmapped
```

The **_UnmapFreePhysReg** service unmaps a page in a free physical region and places the physical memory back on the free list.

Parameters

LinPgNum

Specifies the linear page number of the first page to unmap. A linear page number is a linear address shifted right by 12 bits.

nPages

Specifies the number of pages in the region to unmap. This region must lie within the boundaries of a free physical region previously allocated using the **_PageAllocate** service.

flags

Specifies the operation flags. This parameter must be set to 0.

Return Value

The EAX register contains a nonzero value if the service is successful. Otherwise, EAX contains zero to indicate an error, such as an invalid linear page number, an invalid range of pages, or part of the range already not present.

Comments

This service is intended to be used in a free-physical-region callback procedure installed using the **_SetFreePhysRegCalBk** service. Virtual devices should not call this service until after the Sys_VM_Init message or the Init_Complete message has been received.

If a virtual device maps pages using the PageFixed value with the **_MapFreePhysReg** service, it must not attempt to unmap the pages using the **_UnmapFreePhysReg** service.

Uses

EAX

See Also

_MapFreePhysReg, **_PageAllocate**

Update_System_Clock

```
include vmm.inc

mov     ecx, Time            ; elapsed time in milliseconds
VMMcall Update_System_Clock
```

The **Update_System_Clock** service updates the current system time and the current virtual machine's execution time.

This service is reserved for exclusive use by the virtual timer device. If other virtual devices call this service, the VMM timing services will behave incorrectly.

Parameters

Time

Specifies the number of milliseconds that have elapsed since the last call to this service. The service adds this amount to the system time maintained by the VMM.

Return Value

This service has no return value.

Comments

The virtual timer device must disabled interrupts before calling this service.

Uses

Flags

Validate_VM_Handle

```
include vmm.inc

mov     ebx, VM              ; VM handle to test
VMMcall Validate_VM_Handle
jc      not_valid            ; carry flag set if
                             ;    VM handle not valid
```

The **Validate_VM_Handle** service tests whether the specified virtual machine handle is valid.

This is an asynchronous service.

Parameters

VM

Specifies the virtual machine handle to test.

Return Value

The carry flag is set if the handle is not valid.

Uses

Flags

See Also

Test_Cur_VM_Handle, **Test_Sys_VM_Handle**

Wake_Up_VM

```
include vmm.inc

mov     ebx, VM          ; VM handle
VMMcall Wake_Up_VM
```

The **Wake_Up_VM** service restores an idle virtual machine, allowing the system to schedule the virtual machine for subsequent time slices. A virtual machine is idle if it has called the **Release_Time_Slice** service or has set the VMStat_Idle flag in the CB_VM_Status field of its control block.

Parameters

VM

Specifies a handle identifying the virtual machine to restore.

Return Value

This service has no return value.

Comments

If the specified virtual machine is not idle, this service returns immediately (does nothing).

Uses

Flags

See Also

Release_Time_Slice

Wait_Semaphore

```
include vmm.inc

mov      eax, Semaphore      ; semaphore handle
mov      ecx, Flags          ; flags for servicing interrupts
VMMcall Wait_Semaphore
```

The **Wait_Semaphore** service blocks the current virtual machine until the semaphore is signaled using the **Signal_Semaphore** service.

Parameters

Semaphore

Specifies a handle identifying the semaphore on which to wait.

Flags

Specifies actions to take when interrupts occur while the virtual machine is blocked waiting for the semaphore. This parameter can be a combination of the following values:

Value	Meaning
Block_Svc_Ints	Service interrupts in the virtual machine even if the virtual machine is blocked.

Block_Svc_If_Ints_Locked   Service interrupts in the virtual machine even if the virtual machine is blocked and the VMStat_V86IntsLocked flag is set.

Block_Enable_Ints   Service interrupts in the virtual machine even if the virtual machine does not currently have interrupts enabled. This forces interrupts to be enabled. This value is only relevant if either Block_Svc_Ints or Block_Svc_If_Ints_Locked is set.

Block_Poll   Do not switch away from the blocked virtual machine unless another virtual machine has higher priority.

Return Value

This service has no return value.

Comments

This service blocks if the semaphore's unblock count is zero and the token count is zero or less. Otherwise, it decrements the token count and returns immediately. If the unblock count is not zero (meaning the **Signal_Semaphore** service has been called), **Wait_Semaphore** decrements the unblock count and returns immediately.

Uses

Flags

See Also

Create_Semaphore, **Signal_Semaphore**

_XchgFreePhysReg

```
include vmm.inc

VMMcall _XchgFreePhysReg, <LinPgNum, PhysAddr, flags>

cmp     eax, 0FFFFFFFFh         ; 0FFFFFFFFh if error
je      not_exchanged
mov     [PageTable], eax        ; previous page table entry
```

The **_XchgFreePhysReg** service replaces the current physical address in a page table entry with a new physical address. A virtual device typically uses this service to compact a free physical region by assigning pages that are present to adjacent linear addresses (that is, by removing not-present pages from between present pages).

This is an asynchronous service.

Parameters

LinPgNum

Specifies the linear page number of the first page in the region to exchange. A linear page number is a linear address shifted right by 12 bits. The specified page must be within a free physical region previously allocated using the **_PageAllocate** service.

PhysAddr

Specifies the physical address to insert into the page table entry specified by LinPgNum. This parameter must be a 32-bit physical address.

If this parameter is zero, the service makes the page not present.

flags

Specifies the operation flags. This parameter must be set to 0.

Return Value

The EAX register contains the previous physical address for the specified page if the service is successful. If the specified page is not present, EAX contains zero. Otherwise, EAX contains 0FFFFFFFFh to indicate an error, such as an invalid linear page number.

Comments

A virtual device typically makes a series of calls to **_XchgFreePhysReg**, using the physical address return by one call as the parameter in the next call. To start the series, the virtual device sets the *PhysAddr* parameter to zero, and specifies a page known to be present. This forces the present page to be not present. The virtual device continues calling the service, specifying different page numbers, until the service returns 0.

This service cannot be used to change the number of pages which were mapped using the PageFixed value with the **_MapFreePhysReg** service.

The virtual pageswap device uses this service to read ahead and write behind without having to copy data. Using the **_XchgFreePhysReg** service in this way is restricted to the virtual pageswap device.

Failure to use this service properly can result in invalid page faults and loss of pages.

Uses

EAX

See Also

_MapFreePhysReg, **_PageAllocate**

VMM Structure Reference

Application_Control_Block

```
include vmm.inc

mov     esi, OFFSET32 acb
mov     eax, [esi+PMCB_Flags]        ; application flags
mov     eax, [esi+PMCB_Parent]       ; application parent
```

The application control block contains information about a protected-mode application. Virtual devices can use the following offsets to access information in the control block:

Offset	Description
PMCB_Flags	Specifies the control block flags.
PMCB_Parent	Specifies the parent of the protected-mode application.

See Also

Get_Cur_PM_App_CB

Client_Reg_Struc

```
include vmm.inc

Client_Reg_Struc    struc
Client_EDI      dd      ?       ; Client's EDI
Client_ESI      dd      ?       ; Client's ESI
Client_EBP      dd      ?       ; Client's EBP

                dd      ?       ; ESP at pushall
Client_EBX      dd      ?       ; Client's EBX
Client_EDX      dd      ?       ; Client's EDX
Client_ECX      dd      ?       ; Client's ECX
Client_EAX      dd      ?       ; Client's EAX
Client_Error    dd      ?       ; Doubleword error code
Client_EIP      dd      ?       ; EIP
Client_CS       dw      ?       ; CS
                dw      ?       ;     (padding)
Client_EFlags   dd      ?       ; EFLAGS
Client_ESP      dd      ?       ; ESP
Client_SS       dw      ?       ; SS
                dw      ?       ;     (padding)
Client_ES       dw      ?       ; ES
                dw      ?       ;     (padding)
Client_DS       dw      ?       ; DS
                dw      ?       ;     (padding)
Client_FS       dw      ?       ; FS
```

```
                          dw       ?          ;     (padding)
Client_GS         dw       ?          ; GS
                          dw       ?          ;     (padding)
Client_Alt_EIP   dd       ?
Client_Alt_CS    dw       ?
                          dw       ?
Client_Alt_EFlags   dd    ?
Client_Alt_ESP   dd       ?
Client_Alt_SS    dw       ?
                          dw       ?
Client_Alt_ES    dw       ?
                          dw       ?
Client_Alt_DS    dw       ?
                          dw       ?
Client_Alt_FS    dw       ?
                          dw       ?
Client_Alt_GS    dw       ?
                          dw       ?
Client_Reg_Struc    ends
```

The **Client_Reg_Struc** structure contains the CPU register values of the virtual device or other program calling a service.

Control_Block

```
include vmm.inc

mov     esi, VM                        ; VM handle
mov     eax, [esi + CB_VM_Status]      ; virtual machine status
mov     eax, [esi + CB_High_Linear]    ; high linear address
mov     eax, [esi + CB_Client_Pointer]; -> Client_Reg_Struc
mov     eax, [esi + CB_VMID]           ; virtual machine ID
```

The control block for a virtual machine contains information and status for the virtual machine. Virtual devices can use the following symbols to access useful fields in the control block:

Offset	Description
CB_VM_Status	Specifies the status for the virtual machine. It can be a combination of the following values:

Value	Meaning
VMStat_Exclusive	Virtual machine is in exclusive mode.
VMStat_Background	Virtual machine runs in the background.
VMStat_Creating	Virtual machine is being created.
VMStat_Suspended	Virtual machine is not scheduled.
VMStat_Not_Executeable	Virtual machine is partially destroyed.

VMStat_PM_Exec	Virtual machine execution currently in a protected-mode application.
VMStat_PM_App	Virtual machine contains a protected-mode application.
VMStat_PM_Use32	Virtual machine contains a 32-bit protected-mode application.
VMStat_VxD_Exec	Virtual machine has received a call from a virtual device.
VMStat_High_Pri_Back	Virtual machine has high priority background execution.
VMStat_Blocked	Virtual machine is blocked on a semaphore.
VMStat_Awakening	Virtual machine is waking up after being blocked on a semaphore.
VMStat_PageableV86	Virtual machine has pageable V86 memory (protected-mode application). The default behavior for one or more pages in V86 memory has been modified and the _GetV86PageableArray service returns at least one nonzero bit in the array.
VMStat_V86IntsLocked	Virtual machine locks any V86 memory that is not pageable. Locking regardless of the pager type has been enabled for the virtual machine.
VMStat_TS_Sched	Virtual machine is scheduled by the time slicer.
VMStat_Idle	Virtual machine has released its time slice.
VMStat_Closing	Virtual machine has received a Close_VM message.

CB_High_Linear   Specifies the liner address in the VMM linear address space of the virtual machine memory. Virtual devices can add a V86 linear address to this value calculate the location of a virtual machine memory in the VMM address space.

CB_Client_Pointer   Specifies the address of a Client_Reg_Struc structure containing the register values for the virtual machine.

CB_VMID   Specifies the virtual machine identifier.

See Also

    Close_VM

DemandInfoStruc

```
include vmm.inc

DemandInfoStruc struc
  DILin_Total_Count  dd  ?  ; size of linear address space
                            ;    in pages
  DIPhys_Count       dd  ?  ; count of phys pages
  DIFree_Count       dd  ?  ; count of free phys pages
  DIUnlock_Count     dd  ?  ; count of unlocked Phys Pages
  DILinear_Base_Addr dd  ?  ; case of pageable address space
  DILin_Total_Free   dd  ?  ; total free linear pages
  DIReserved         dd  10 DUP(?)  ; reserved
DemandInfoStruc ends
```

The **DemandInfoStruc** structure contains information about pages that are subject to demand paging.

Members

DILin_Total_Count

    Specifies the total number of pages subject to demand paging.

DIPhys_Count

    Specifies the total number of physical pages managed by the memory manager.

DIFree_Count

    Specifies the number of pages currently in the free pool.

DIUnlock_Count

    Specifies the number of pages that are currently unlocked. Free pages are always unlocked.

DILinear_Base_Addr

    Specifies the linear address of the first page subject to demand paging. If DILinear_Base_Addr is zero, the pages subject to demand paging are not contiguous.

DILin_Total_Free

    Specifies the number of the pages that are currently free as well as subject to demand paging. There is no guarantee that these free pages are contiguous.

DIReserved

> Specifies a reserved field. Virtual devices must make no assumptions about the content or purpose of this field.

See Also

_GetDemandPageInfo

InstDataStruc

```
include vmm.inc

InstDataStruc struc
  InstLinkF      dd      ?   ; RESERVED SET TO 0
  InstLinkB      dd      ?   ; RESERVED SET TO 0
  InstLinAddr    dd      ?   ; Linear address of start of block
  InstSize       dd      ?   ; Size of block in bytes
  InstType       dd      ?   ; Type of the block
InstDataStruc ends
```

The **InstDataStruc** structure contain information about an instance data block.

Members

InstLinkF

> Reserved. This field is filled in by the instance data manager and must not be used.

InstLinkB

> Reserved. This field is filled in by the instance data manager and must not be used.

InstLinAddr

> Specifies the linear address of the start of the block of instance data. Thus the correct value for 40:2F would be 42F.

InstSize

> Specifies the size in bytes of the instance data block.

InstType

> Specifies the instance data type. It can be one of the following values:

Value	Meaning
INDOS_Field	Reserved for special types of MS-DOS internal data which only need to be switched with the virtual machine if the virtual machine is currently INDOS.
ALWAYS_Field	Indicates that the field must always be switched when a virtual machine is switched. All instance data specified by devices should be of this type.

See Also

_AddInstanceItem

IPF_Data

```
include vmm.inc

IPF_Data      struc
    IPF_LinAddr      dd   ?    ; CR2 address of fault
    IPF_MapPageNum   dd   ?    ; Possible converted page
                              ;     number of fault
    IPF_PTEEntry     dd   ?    ; Contents of PTE that faulted
    IPF_FaultingVM   dd   ?    ; May not = current VM
                              ;     (IPF_V86PgH set)
    IPF_Flags        dd   ?    ; Flags
IPF_Data      ends
```

The **IPF_Data** structure contains information about the current invalid page fault.

Members

IPF_LinAddr

Specifies the CR2 address of the page fault.

IPF_MapPageNum

Specifies the possible converted page number of the fault.

IPF_PTEEntry

Specifies the contents of the page-table entry that caused the fault.

IPF_FaultingVM

Specifies the handle identifying the virtual machine that caused the fault. This is not necessarily the current virtual machine.

IPF_Flags

Specifies the invalid-page-fault flags. It can be a combination of the following values:

Value	Meaning
IPF_PgDir	Page directory entry not present (not-present page table).
IPF_V86Pg	Unexpected not-present page in V86.
IPF_V86PgH	Unexpected not-present page in V86 at high linear address.
IPF_InvTyp	Page has invalid not-present type.
IPF_PgErr	Pageswap device could not page for some reason.
IPF_ReFlt	Re-entrant page fault.
IPF_VMM	Page fault caused by a virtual device.
IPF_PM	Page fault caused by virtual machine running in protected mode.
IPF_V86	Page fault caused by virtual machine running in V86 mode.

Comments

Invalid page faults occur in a virtual machine other than the current virtual machine if the high linear address of the virtual machine is accessed. In this case, the IPF_FaultingVM field is set to the handle of the virtual machine that owns the high linear address.

See Also

Hook_Invalid_Page_Fault

VMM Message Reference

Begin_Message_Mode

```
include vmm.inc

mov     ebx, VM                 ; VM handle
mov     eax, Begin_Message_Mode
VMMcall System_Control
```

The **Begin_Message_Mode** message notifies the virtual display, keyboard, and mouse devices to prepare to display messages and read input from the keyboard. The system sends this message if Windows cannot display the requested warning or error message.

Parameters

VM

Specifies a handle identifying the virtual machine entering message mode.

Return Value

The carry flag must be clear.

Comments

This message is usually processed only by the virtual keyboard, mouse, and display devices.

Uses

Flags

See Also

End_Message_Mode

Begin_PM_App

```
include vmm.inc

mov     ebx, VM                 ; current VM handle
mov     edx, Flags              ; flags
mov     edi, OFFSET32 acb       ; -> Application Control Block
mov     eax, Begin_PM_App
VMMcall System_Control
```

The **Begin_PM_App** message notifies the virtual device that the system is starting a protected-mode application.

Parameters

VM

Specifies a handle identifying the current virtual machine.

Flags

Specifies the operation flags. It can be the following value:

Value	Meaning
BPA_32_Bit	Application has 32-bit segments. If this value is not given, the application has 16-bit segments.

All other values are reserved.

acb

Points to an application control block.

Return Value

The carry flag is clear if the virtual device can support the protected-mode application. Otherwise, the carry flag is set to indicate an error.

Uses

Flags

See Also

End_PM_App

Close_VM_Notify

```
include vmm.inc

mov      ebx, VM              ; current VM handle
mov      edx, Flags           ; flags
mov      eax, Close_VM_Notify
VMMcall System_Control
```

The **Close_VM_Notify** message notifies a virtual device that the **Close_VM** service has been called and the specified virtual machine is terminating.

Parameters

VM

Specifies a handle identifying the virtual machine to close.

Flags

Specifies the operation flags. This parameter can be the following value:

Value	Meaning
CVNF_Crit_Close	The virtual machine has not released the critical section.

All other values are reserved.

Return Value

The carry flag is set if the virtual device supports termination of the virtual machine. Otherwise, the carry flag is set to indicate an error.

Uses

Flags

See Also

Close_VM

Create_VM

```
include vmm.inc
mov     ebx, VM          ; new VM handle
mov     eax, Create_VM
VMMcall System_Control
```

The **Create_VM** message notifies a virtual machine that the system is creating a new virtual machine. Virtual devices typically initialize data associated with the virtual machine, such as data in the control block for the virtual machine.

Parameters

VM

Specifies a handle identifying the new virtual machine.

Return Value

The carry flag is clear if the virtual device can support the new virtual machine. Otherwise, the carry flag is set to indicate an error and prevent the system from creating the virtual machine.

Uses

Flags

See Also

Destroy_VM

Crit_Reboot_Notify

```
include vmm.inc

mov     eax, Crit_Reboot_Notify
VMMcall System_Control
```

The **Crit_Reboot_Notify** message notifies a virtual device that the system is about to restart. Virtual devices typically prepare for restarting by cleaning up data or resetting devices. The system disables interrupts before it sends this message.

Parameters

This message has no parameters.

Return Value

The carry flag must be clear.

Uses

Flags

See Also

Device_Reboot_Notify

Debug_Query

```
include vmm.inc

mov     eax, Debug_Query
VMMcall System_Control
```

The **Debug_Query** message directs the virtual device to enable its debugging commands (if any). The virtual device should display a list of debugging commands, then read the debugging device for command input from the user.

The system sends this message when the user enters a virtual-device command (a period followed by the name of the virtual device) at the WDEB386 prompt.

Parameters

This message has no parameters.

Return Value

The carry flag must be clear.

Comments

This message is intended to be used only in debugging versions of the virtual device. Support for this message should be removed from the final virtual device.

Uses

Flags

Destroy_VM

```
include vmm.inc

mov     ebx, VM           ; VM handle
mov     eax, Destroy_VM
VMMcall System_Control
```

The **Destroy_VM** message notifies the virtual device that the system has destroyed the virtual machine. Virtual devices typically remove any data associated with the specified virtual machine.

Parameters

VM

Specifies a handle identifying the virtual machine to destroy.

Return Value

The carry flag must be clear.

Comments

The virtual device must not call the Simulate_Int or Exec_Int service in the specified virtual machine.

Considerable time can elapse between receipt of the **VM_Not_Executeable** message and this message.

Uses

Flags

See Also

Create_VM, VM_Not_Executeable

Device_Init

```
include vmm.inc

mov       ebx, SysVM                    ; system VM handle
mov       esi, OFFSET32 CommandTail     ; points to WIN386
                                        ;       command tail
mov       eax, Device_Init
VMMcall System_Control
```

The **Device_Init** message directs the virtual device to initialize itself. The virtual device typically allocates memory for a device-specific section in the control block, allocates other memory areas, hooks interrupts and I/O ports, and specifies instance data.

Parameters

SysVM

Specifies a handle identifying the system virtual machine.

CommandTail

Points to the command tail retrieved from the program segment prefix (PSP) of WIN386.EXE. The first byte in the command tail specifies the length in bytes of the tail.

Return Value

The carry flag is clear if the virtual device is initialized successfully. Otherwise, the carry flag is set to indicate an error and prevent the system from loading the virtual device.

Comments

The virtual device should allocate a device-specific section in the control block of the system virtual machine and initialize the section.

The virtual device can call the **Simulate_Int** and **Exec_Int** services in the system virtual machine.

Uses

Flags

See Also

> **Init_Complete**, **Sys_Critical_Init**

Device_Reboot_Notify

```
include vmm.inc

mov     eax, Device_Reboot_Notify
VMMcall System_Control
```

The **Device_Reboot_Notify** message notifies the virtual device that the system is about to restart. Interrupts remain enabled while virtual devices process this message.

Parameters

> This message has no parameters.

Return Value

> The carry flag must be clear.

Uses

> Flags

See Also

> **Crit_Reboot_Notify**

End_Message_Mode

```
include vmm.inc

mov     ebx, VM            ; VM handle
mov     eax, End_Message_Mode
VMMcall System_Control
```

The **End_Message_Mode** message directs the virtual device to end message mode processing.

Parameters

> *VM*

> > Specifies a handle identifying the virtual machine leaving message mode.

Return Value

> The carry flag must be clear.

Uses

Flags

See Also

Begin_Message_Mode

End_PM_App

```
include vmm.inc

mov      ebx, VM              ; current VM handle
mov      edi, OFFSET32 acb    ; -> Application Control Block
mov      eax, End_PM_App
VMMcall System_Control
```

The **End_PM_App** message notifies the virtual device that the system is terminating a protected-mode application.

Parameters

VM

Specifies a handle identifying the current virtual machine.

acb

Points to an application control block.

Return Value

The carry flag must be clear.

Uses

Flags

See Also

Begin_PM_App

Init_Complete

```
include vmm.inc

mov      ebx, SysVM                      ; system VM handle
mov      esi, OFFSET32 CommandTail       ; points to WIN386
                                         ;      command tail
```

```
mov      eax, Init_Complete
VMMcall System_Control
```

The **Init_Complete** message notifies the virtual device that the system and virtual devices have initialized successfully. Virtual devices that use V86 memory typically search for available pages, in the range 0A0h through 100h, when processing this message.

Parameters

SysVM

Specifies a handle identifying the system virtual machine.

CommandTail

Points to the command tail retrieved from the program segment prefix (PSP) of WIN386.EXE. The first byte in the command tail specifies the length in bytes of the tail.

Return Value

The carry flag is clear if the virtual device successfully completes its initialization. Otherwise, the carry flag is set to prevent the system from loading the virtual device.

Comments

The system sends this message just before it releases its INIT pages and takes the instance snapshot.

Virtual devices can use the **Simulate_Int** and **Exec_Int** services to execute code in the system virtual machine.

Uses

Flags

See Also

Device_Init

Power_Event

```
include vmm.inc
include power.inc

mov      ebx, 0
mov      esi, Event             ; event notification message
mov      edi, OFFSET32 Return   ; points 4-byte return value
mov      eax, Power_Event
VMMcall System_Control
```

The **Power_Event** message notifies the virtual device that a power event has just occurred.

Parameters

Event

Specifies the type of power event. This parameter can be one of the following values:

Value	Meaning
PWR_SUSPENDREQUEST	Suspend operation.
PWR_SUSPENDRESUME	Resume operation after suspension.
PWR_CRITICALRESUME	Resume critical operations after suspension.

Return

Points to the doubleword to receive the return value. The return value can be one of the following values:

Value	Meaning
PWR_OK	Virtual device processed the event successfully.
PWR_FAIL	Virtual device failed to process the event.

All other values are reserved.

Return Value

The carry flag is clear and the doubleword pointed to by *Return* contains the return value.

Comments

The EBX register must be zero on entry. The EDX register is reserved; its value must be preserved.

Uses

Flags

Query_Destroy

```
include vmm.inc

mov     ebx, VM          ; VM handle
```

```
mov     eax, Query_Destroy
VMMcall System_Control
```

The **Query_Destroy** message directs the virtual device to display a warning message if the destruction of the specified virtual machine will disrupt the operation of the virtual device. The virtual shell device sends this message before attempting to destroy a virtual machine that has not terminated normally.

Parameters

VM

Specifies a handle identifying the virtual machine to destroy.

Return Value

The carry flag is set if the destruction of the virtual machine will disrupt the virtual device. Otherwise, the carry flag is clear.

Comments

Virtual devices that set the carry flag must also display a message box, using the **SHELL_Message** service to inform the user of the potential problem. The user can then decide whether to continue destroying the virtual machine.

Uses

Flags

See Also

Destroy_VM, **SHELL_Message**

Reboot_Processor

```
include vmm.inc

mov     eax, Reboot_Processor
VMMcall System_Control
```

The **Reboot_Processor** message directs the virtual device to restart the computer. The system continues to call the virtual devices until one that can restart the computer (usually the virtual keyboard device) does so.

Parameters

This message has no parameters.

Return Value

The carry flag is clear.

Uses

Flags

See Also

Crit_Reboot_Notify

Set_Device_Focus

```
include vmm.inc

mov      ebx, VM          ; VM handle
mov      edx, VID         ; ID of virtual device to receive focus
mov      esi, Flags       ; flags for device-critical focus
mov      edi, AssocVM     ; handle of associated VM
mov      eax, Set_Device_Focus
VMMcall System_Control
```

The **Set_Device_Focus** message sets the focus of the specified virtual device to the specified virtual machine.

Parameters

VM

Specifies a handle identifying the virtual machine.

VID

Specifies the identifier for the virtual device to receive the focus. If this parameter is zero, all virtual devices receive the focus.

Flags

Specifies how to set the focus if the VID parameter is zero. This parameter can have the following value:

Value	Meaning
1	Used by the virtual shell device to determine which virtual machine to set focus for. If this value is given, the AssocVM parameter may specify a virtual machine.

All other values are reserved.

AssocVM

Specifies a handle identifying a virtual machine associated with a problem. This parameter is zero if there is no such virtual machine. This parameter is used only if the Flags parameter is set to 1.

Return Value

The carry flag must be clear.

Comments

A virtual device that receives the focus should take steps, such as disabling I/O trapping, to allow the virtual machine to run as fast as possible.

Uses

Flags

Sys_Critical_Exit

```
include vmm.inc

mov     eax, Sys_Critical_Exit
VMMcall System_Control
```

The **Sys_Critical_Exit** message notifies the virtual device that the system is exiting either normally or as a result of a crash. Virtual devices should reset their associated hardware to allow for a return to the state before Windows was started.

The system disables interrupts before sending this message.

Parameters

This message has no parameters.

Return Value

The carry flag must be clear.

Comments

The virtual device must not call the **Simulate_Int** or **Exec_Int** service.

Uses

Flags

See Also

Sys_Critical_Init, Sys_VM_Terminate

Sys_Critical_Init

```
include vmm.inc

mov      ebx, SysVM                   ; system VM handle
mov      esi, OFFSET32 CommandTail    ; points to WIN386
                                      ;      command tail
mov      eax, Sys_Critical_Init
VMMcall System_Control
```

The **Sys_Critical_Init** message notifies the virtual device that Windows is starting. The system sends this message to direct virtual devices to carry out, as quickly as possible, the minimum number of tasks needed to prepare the device for enabled interrupts. While virtual devices process this message, interrupts are disabled.

Parameters

SysVM

Specifies a handle identifying the system virtual machine.

CommandTail

Points to the command tail retrieved from the program segment prefix (PSP) of WIN386.EXE. The first byte in the command tail specifies the length in bytes of the tail.

Return Value

The carry flag is clear if the virtual device initialized successfully. Otherwise, the carry flag is set to prevent the system from loading the virtual device.

Comments

While processing this message, virtual devices typically initialize any critical functions needed to support interrupts and claim any V86 pages required to support the device. For example, the virtual display device claims the video memory. If a virtual device provides services, it should initialize any data associated with those services.

The virtual device must not use the Simulate_Int or Exec_Int services.

Uses

Flags

See Also

Device_Init, **Sys_Critical_Exit**

Sys_VM_Init

```
include vmm.inc

mov      ebx, SysVM        ; system VM handle
mov      eax, Sys_VM_Init
VMMcall System_Control
```

The **Sys_VM_Init** message directs the virtual device to initialize the state of the software in the system virtual machine. For example, the virtual display device issues an Interrupt 10h function to set the initial display mode.

Parameters

SysVM

Specifies a handle identifying the system virtual machine.

Return Value

The carry flag is clear if the virtual device initializes the system virtual machine successfully. Otherwise, the carry flag is set to direct Windows to exit immediately.

Uses

Flags

See Also

VM_Init

Sys_VM_Terminate

```
include vmm.inc

mov      ebx, SysVM                   ; system VM handle
mov      eax, Sys_VM_Terminate
VMMcall System_Control
```

The **Sys_VM_Terminate** message notifies the virtual device that the system virtual machine is terminating. The system sends this message only after all other virtual machines have terminated, and only when the system is terminating normally.

Parameters

SysVM

Specifies a handle identifying the system virtual machine.

Return Value

The carry flag must be clear.

Comments

The virtual device can use the **Simulate_Int** and **Exec_Int** services in the system virtual machine.

Uses

Flags

See Also

VM_Terminate

System_Exit

```
include vmm.inc

mov      ebx, SysVM        ; system VM handle
mov      eax, System_Exit
VMMcall System_Control
```

The **System_Exit** message notifies the virtual device that the system is terminating either normally or as a result of a crash. Interrupts remain enabled while virtual devices process this message.

Parameters

SysVM

Specifies a handle identifying the system virtual machine.

Return Value

The carry flag must be clear.

Comments

The virtual device must not call the **Simulate_Int** or **Exec_Int** service, but the virtual device may modify the system virtual machine memory to restore the system state to allow Windows to exit without complication.

The system restores the instance snapshot before sending this message.

Uses

Flags

See Also

Sys_Critical_Exit

VM_Critical_Init

```
include vmm.inc

mov     ebx, VM                    ; new VM handle
mov     eax, VM_Critical_Init
VMMcall System_Control
```

The **VM_Critical_Init** message directs the virtual device to initialize itself for the new virtual machine. The system disables interrupts before sending this message.

Parameters

VM

Specifies a handle identifying the virtual machine to create.

Return Value

The carry flag is clear if the virtual device initialized successfully. Otherwise, the carry flag is set to prevent the virtual machine from being created.

Comments

The virtual device must not use the **Simulate_Int** or **Exec_Int** services in the specified virtual machine.

Uses

Flags

See Also

Create_VM, VM_Init

VM_Init

```
include vmm.inc

mov     ebx, VM          ; new VM handle
mov     eax, VM_Init
VMMcall System_Control
```

The **VM_Init** message directs the virtual device to initialize the state of the software in the new virtual machine. For example, the virtual display device issues Interrupt 10h to set the initial display mode. The system enables interrupts before sending this message.

Parameters

VM

Specifies a handle identifying the virtual machine to create.

Return Value

The carry flag is clear if the virtual device initialized the virtual machine successfully. Otherwise, the carry flag is set to prevent the system from creating the virtual machine.

Comments

The virtual device can use the **Simulate_Int** and **Exec_Int** services in the specified virtual machine.

Uses

Flags

See Also

Create_VM, **VM_Critical_Init**

VM_Not_Executeable

```
include vmm.inc

mov     ebx, VM            ; VM handle
mov     edx, Flags         ; flags
mov     eax, VM_Not_Executeable
VMMcall System_Control
```

The **VM_Not_Executeable** message notifies the virtual device that the virtual machine is no longer capable of executing. The system sends this message as the first phase of terminating the virtual machine.

Parameters

VM

Specifies a handle identifying the virtual machine.

Flags

Specifies the reason the virtual machine is no longer executable. This parameter can be one of the following values:

Value	Meaning
VNE_Crashed	Virtual machine has crashed.
VNE_Nuked	Virtual machine was destroyed while active.
VNE_CreateFail	Some device failed Create_VM.

VNE_CrInitFail   Some device failed VM_Critical_Init.

VNE_InitFail   Some device failed VM_Init.

Return Value

The carry flag must be clear.

Comments

When destroying a running virtual machine, the system sends this message first and never sends the **VM_Terminate** message.

The virtual device must not call the **Simulate_Int** or **Exec_Int** service in the specified virtual machine.

Uses

Flags

See Also

VM_Terminate

VM_Resume

```
include vmm.inc

mov      ebx, VM          ; VM handle
mov      eax, VM_Resume
VMMcall System_Control
```

The **VM_Resume** message notifies the virtual device that the virtual machine is resuming after having been suspended. The virtual device should lock any resources, and prepare internal data structures for the virtual machine to start running again.

Parameters

VM

Specifies a handle identifying the virtual machine to resume.

Return Value

The carry flag is clear if the virtual device can support resumption of the virtual machine. Otherwise, the carry flag is set to prevent the system from resuming the virtual machine.

Comments

The system never sends the **VM_Resume** message without having first sent a **VM_Suspend** message.

Uses

Flags

See Also

VM_Suspend

VM_Suspend

```
include vmm.inc

mov     ebx, VM          ; VM handle
mov     eax, VM_Suspend
VMMcall System_Control
```

The **VM_Suspend** message notifies the virtual device that the system is suspending execution of the virtual machine. The virtual device should unlock any resources associated with the virtual machine.

Parameters

VM

Specifies a handle identifying the virtual machine to suspend.

Return Value

The carry flag must be clear.

Comments

The virtual machine remains suspended until explicitly resumed. The system sends the **VM_Suspend** message each time the virtual machine is suspended. It sends a **VM_Resume** message when the virtual machine is resumed.

The CB_VM_Status field in the control block for the virtual machine specifies whether the virtual machine is suspended.

Uses

Flags

See Also

VM_Resume

VM_Terminate

```
include vmm.inc

mov     ebx, VM              ; VM handle
mov     eax, VM_Terminate
VMMcall System_Control
```

The **VM_Terminate** message notifies the virtual device that system is terminating the specified virtual machine. The system sends this message when a virtual machine terminates normally.

Parameters

VM

Specifies a handle identifying the virtual machine to terminate.

Return Value

The carry flag must be clear.

Comments

The virtual machine can call the **Simulate_Int** and **Exec_Int** services in the specified virtual machine.

Uses

Flags

See Also

System_Exit, **VM_Not_Executeable**

VMM Macro Reference

Begin_Control_Dispatch

```
include vmm.inc

Begin_Control_Dispatch DeviceName
```

The **Begin_Control_Dispatch** macro builds a table for dispatching messages passed to the control procedure for the specified virtual device. This macro is used in conjunction with the **Control_Dispatch** and **End_Control_Dispatch** macros.

Parameters

DeviceName

Specifies the name of the virtual device. The macro uses this parameter to construct the label for the control procedure (appends _Control to the end of this name). This control procedure label must also be specified in the **Declare_Virtual_Device** macro

Return Value

This macro has no return value.

Comments

The **Control_Dispatch** macro can be used without **Begin_Control_Dispatch**, but then it the programmer's responsibility to declare a procedure in locked code (**VxD_LOCKED_CODE_SEG**) and clear the carry flag for any messages not processed. The advantage in using **Begin_Control_Dispatch** macro is when a large number of messages are processed by a device. The macro builds a jump table which usually requires less code then the sequence of compare and jump instructions that are generated when Control_Dispatch is used alone.

Example

The following example builds a complete dispatch table for the virtual device named MyDevice:

```
Begin_Control_Dispatch MyDevice
   Control_Dispatch   Device_Init,  MyDeviceInitProcedure
   Control_Dispatch   Sys_VM_Init,  MyDeviceSysInitProcedure
   Control_Dispatch   Create_VM,    MyDeviceCreateVMProcedure
End_Control_Dispatch MyDevice
```

See Also

Control_Dispatch, Declare_Virtual_Device, End_Control_Dispatch

___

BeginProc

```
include vmm.inc

BeginProc ProcName, Attributes
```

The **BeginProc** macros marks the start of a procedure having the specified attributes.

Parameters

ProcName

Specifies the name of the procedure to create.

Attributes

Specifies one or more procedure attributes. This parameter can be a combination of the following attributes:

Attribute	Description
ASYNC_SERVICE	Creates an asynchronous service that can be called by other virtual devices. The procedure must be reentrant, must not call synchronous services, and must be defined in a locked segment. Asynchronous services are intended to be called by interrupt handling routines when processing interrupts.
HIGH_FREQ	Specifies a frequently called procedure. The macro aligns the start of the procedure on a doubleword boundary to optimize calls to the procedure.
NO_LOG	Prevents a call to the Log_Call_Proc service from being inserted at the beginning of the procedure. The macro inserts the Log_Call_Proc service only if the DEBUG symbol is defined.
PUBLIC	Creates a global procedure that other procedures in the virtual device can call.
SERVICE	Creates a service that other virtual devices can call. If the DEBUG symbol is defined, the macro inserts a call to the Test_Reenter service at the beginning of the procedure.

If more than one attribute is given, they must be separated by commas.

Return Value

This macro has no return value.

See Also

EndProc

Begin_Service_Table

```
include vmm.inc

Begin_Service_Table DeviceName, DefSegment
```

The **Begin_Service_Table** macro marks the start of the service table for a virtual device. A virtual device uses the service table to export the names and addresses of its services. Other virtual devices can use the **VxDcall** macro to call these services.

Parameters

DeviceName

Specifies the name of the virtual device. This name is used to create a macro, named *DeviceName*_**Service**, that is used in the table to define each exported service. See the "Comments" section for a description of the macro.

DefSegment

Specifies the name of the data segment to place the table. This parameter is optional. If given, the macro uses the *DefSegment*_**LOCKED_DATA_SEG** macro to define the segment. Otherwise, it uses the **VxD_LOCKED_DATA_SEG** macro.

Return Value

This macro has no return value.

Comments

A virtual device exports its services by defining the symbol **Create_*DeviceName*_Service_Table** before using the **Begin_Service_Table** macro. Virtual devices that call these service also use the **Begin_Service_Table** macro but must *not* define the **Create_*DeviceName*_Service_Table** symbol.

The complete service table has the following form:

```
Begin_Service_Table DeviceName, DefSegment
DeviceName_Service Procedure, LocalSeg
    .
    .
    .
End_Service_Table DeviceName, DefSegment
```

The *DeviceName*_**Service** macro, created by **Begin_Service_Table**, adds the specified service to the table. A table may have any number of these macros.

The *Procedure* parameter specifies the name of the service to add to the table. If RESERVED is given, the macro reserves an entry in the table instead adding a procedure.

The *LocalSeg* parameter specifies which segment contains the procedure. This parameter is optional.

See Also

End_Service_Table, **VxD_LOCKED_DATA_SEG**

Begin_VxD_IO_Table

```
include vmm.inc

Begin_VxD_IO_Table TableName
```

The **Begin_VxD_IO_Table** macro marks the beginning of an I/O table. Virtual devices use the macro in conjunction with the **End_VxD_IO_Table** and **VxD_IO** macros to create a table of I/O callback procedures for the **Install_Mult_IO_Handlers** service.

Parameters

TableName

Specifies the name of the table. This parameter can be used in subsequent calls to the **Install_Mult_IO_Handlers** to specify the address of the table.

See Also

Install_Mult_IO_Handlers, **End_VxD_IO_Table**, **VxD_IO**

cCall

```
include vmm.inc

cCall Procedure, Parameters
```

The **cCall** macro pushes the specified parameters on the stack and calls the specified procedure. When the procedure returns, the macro pops the parameters from the stack.

Parameters

Procedure

Specifies the name of the procedure to call. This parameter can be either a local or public procedure, but must be defined within the virtual device making the call.

Parameters

Specifies the parameters to pass to the specified procedure. If more than one parameter is given, they must be separated with commas and enclosed in angle brackets (<>). This parameter is optional.

Return Value

The return value is as specified for the given service.

Comments

This macro pushes the parameters using the C-language calling convention, in order from right to left.

See Also

VMMcall, VxDcall

Client_Ptr_Flat

```
include vmm.inc

Client_Ptr_Flat LinAddr, Segment, Offset
```

The **Client_Ptr_Flat** macro converts the specified segment:offset or selector:offset pair into a linear address.

Parameters

LinAddr

Specifies the 32-bit register to receive the linear address.

Segment

Specifies the client segment register containing the segment address or selector to convert.

Offset

> Specifies the register containing the address offset to convert. If this optional parameter is not given, the macro converts the address using address offset 0.

Return Value

The register specified by *LinAddr* contains the linear address. The register contains -1 if the specified selector is invalid.

Example

This example converts the address **Client_DS:Client_DX** and places the corresponding linear address in the EAX register.

```
Client_Ptr_Flat eax, DS, DX
```

See Also

Map_Flat

Debug_Out

```
include debug.inc

Debug_Out String
```

The **Debug_Out** macro writes the specified string to the debugging device and breaks execution by executing an int 1 instruction if the debugging version of Windows is installed.

Parameters

String

> Specifies the string to display. The string must be enclosed in double quotation marks. The string can contain register placeholders in the same forms as described for the **Out_Debug_String** service.

Return Value

This service has no return value.

Comments

The macro calls the **Test_Debug_Installed** service to determine whether to execute the int 1 instruction. If the debugging version is not installed, the instruction is skipped.

The assembler generates code for the macro only if the constant DEBUG is defined before including the DEBUG.INC file.

See Also

Out_Debug_String, Test_Debug_Installed

Declare_Virtual_Device

```
include vmm.inc

Declare_Virtual_Device Name, MajorVer, MinorVer, CtrlProc,\
                        DeviceNum, InitOrder, V86Proc, PMProc
```

The **Declare_Virtual_Device** macro defines the name, device number, control procedure, and other attributes of a virtual device. Every virtual device must use the **Declare_Virtual_Device** macro.

Parameters

Name

Specifies the name of the virtual device.

MajorVer

Specifies the major version number for the virtual device.

MinorVer

Specifies the minor version number for the virtual device.

CtrlProc

Specifies the control procedure for the virtual device. The control procedure handles all system control messages sent to the virtual device. For most virtual devices, this parameter is the name of the procedure created by the Begin_Control_Dispatch macro.

DeviceNum

Specifies the device identifier for the virtual device. If the virtual device replaces an existing virtual device, the device identifier must be one of the following:

Value	Meaning
APM_Device_ID	Power management
BiosHook_Device_ID	BIOS interrupt hook
BIOSXlat_Device_ID	BIOS translation

BlockDev_Device_ID	Block devices
Debug_Device_ID	Debug device
DOSMGR_Device_ID	MS-DOS manager
DOSNET_Device_ID	MS-DOS networks
EBIOS_Device_ID	EBIOS
Int13_Device_ID	Interrupt 13h hook
MCA_POS_Device_ID	MCA_POS device
PageFile_Device_ID	Paging file
PageSwap_Device_ID	Page swap
Parity_Device_ID	Parity
Reboot_Device_ID	Reboot
SCSI_Device_ID	SCSI device
SCSIFD_Device_ID	SCSI FastDisk device
SHELL_Device_ID	386-enhanced mode Windows shell
TSRLoad_Device_ID	TSR instance utility
Undefined_Device_ID	Reserved
V86MMGR_Device_ID	V86 mode memory manager
VCD_Device_ID	Communications ports
VDD2_Device_ID	Secondary display adapter
VDD_Device_ID	Display adapter
VDMAD_Device_ID	DMA
VFD_Device_ID	Floppy disk
VKD_Device_ID	Keyboard
VMCPD_Device_ID	Math coprocessor
VMD_Device_ID	Mouse or pointing device
VMM_Device_ID	Reserved; do not use
VMPoll_Device_ID	Virtual machine polling
VNETBIOS_Device_ID	Network BIOS
VPD_Device_ID	Printer ports

VPEND_Device_ID	Pen device
VPICD_Device_ID	Programmable interrupt controller
VPROD_Device_ID	Profiling
VSD_Device_ID	Sound adapter
VTD_Device_ID	Timer
WINDEBUG_Device_ID	Windows debugging
WINLOAD_Device_ID	Windows loader

If the type of virtual device is new, a new OEM virtual deviceidentifier must be explictly requested from Microsoft.

InitOrder

Specifies when the virtual device should be initialized relative to other virtual devices. For an existing device type, this parameter can be one of the following values:

APM_Init_Order

BiosHook_Init_Order

BIOSXlat_Init_Order

BlockDev_Init_Order

Debug_Init_Order

DOSMGR_Init_Order

DOSNET_Init_Order

EBIOS_Init_Order

Int13_Init_Order

MCA_POS_Init_Order

PageFile_Init_Order

PageSwap_Init_Order

Parity_Init_Order

Reboot_Init_Order

SCSIFD_Init_Order

SCSIMaster_Init_Order

SHELL_Init_Order

Undefined_Init_Order

V86MMGR_Init_Order

VCD_Init_Order

VDD_Init_Order

VDMAD_Init_Order

VFD_Init_Order

VKD_Init_Order

VMCPD_Init_Order

VMD_Init_Order

VMM_Init_Order

VMPoll_Init_Order

VNETBIOS_Init_Order

VPD_Init_Order

VPICD_Init_Order

VPROD_Init_Order

VSD_Init_Order

VTD_Init_Order

WINDEBUG_Init_Order

WINLOAD_Init_Order

V86Proc

Specifies the V86-mode API procedure. This procedure processes any calls to the virtual device made by V86-mode applications running in a virtual machine. This parameter is optional.

PMProc

Specifies the protected-mode API procedure. This procedure processes any calls to the virtual device made by protected-mode applications running in a virtual machine. This parameter is optional.

Return Value

This macro has no return value.

See Also

Begin_Control_Dispatch

Dispatch_Byte_IO

```
include vmm.inc

Dispatch_Byte_IO In_Proc, Out_Proc
```

The **Dispatch_Byte_IO** macro checks the size of the I/O request and dispatches the request to either the **Simulate_IO** service or to the specified single-byte input or output procedure. I/O callback procedures use this macro to simplify processing of I/O requests.

Parameters

In_Proc

Specifies the name of the procedure to carry out a single-byte input operation. If this parameter is the **Fall_Through** keyword, the macro ignores input operations.

Out_Proc

Specifies the name of the procedure to carry out a single-byte output operation. If this parameter is the **Fall_Through** keyword, the macro ignores output operations.

Return Value

This macro has no return value.

Comments

The EAX, EBX, ECX, EDX, and EBP registers must contain values specified as valid input parameters for the **Simulate_IO** service. **Dispatch_Byte_IO** checks the ECX register for the I/O type. If this type specifies an I/O request that is larger than a byte, the macro jumps to the **Simulate_IO** service.

See Also

Emulate_Non_Byte_IO, Simulate_IO

Dword_Align

```
include vmm.inc

Dword_Align SegName
```

The **Dword_Align** macro aligns the specified segment on a doubleword boundary by inserting nop instructions.

Parameters

SegName

Specifies the name of the segment to align. This parameter can be **_TEXT**, **_ITEXT**, or **_LTEXT**.

Return Value

This macro has no return value.

Emulate_Non_Byte_IO

```
include vmm.inc

Emulate_Non_Byte_IO
```

The **Emulate_Non_Byte_IO** macro checks the size of the I/O request and jumps to the **Simulate_IO** service if the request is larger than a byte. I/O callback procedures use this macro to simplify processing of I/O requests.

Parameters

This macro has no parameters.

Return Value

This macro has no return value.

Comments

The EAX, EBX, ECX, EDX, and EBP registers must contain values specified as valid input parameters for the **Simulate_IO** service. **Emulate_Non_Byte_IO** checks the ECX register for the I/O type. If this type specifies an I/O request that is larger than a byte, the macro jumps to the **Simulate_IO** service.

See Also

Dispatch_Byte_IO, **Simulate_IO**

End_Control_Dispatch

```
include vmm.inc

End_Control_Dispatch DeviceName
```

The **End_Control_Dispatch** macro marks the end of a dispatch table for a virtual device. This macro is used in conjunction with the **Control_Dispatch** and **Begin_Control_Dispatch** macros to build the table.

Parameters

DeviceName

Specifies the name of the virtual device. This name *must* have been used with the **Begin_Control_Dispatch** macro that started the table.

Return Value

This macro has no return value.

See Also

Begin_Control_Dispatch, **Control_Dispatch**

EndProc

```
include vmm.inc

EndProc ProcName
```

The **EndProc** macro marks the end of a procedure definition. This macro is used in conjunction with the **BeginProc** macro to define a procedure in a virtual device.

Parameters

ProcName

Specifies the name of the procedure. This name *must* have been used in the **BeginProc** macro that started the procedure definition.

Return Value

This macro has no return value.

See Also

BeginProc

End_Service_Table

```
include vmm.inc

End_Service_Table DeviceName, DefSegment
```

The **End_Service_Table** macro marks the end of the service table for a virtual machine. This macro is used in conjunction with the **Begin_Service_Table** macro to create a service table.

Parameters

DeviceName

Specifies the name of the virtual device. This name *must* be the same as specified by the corresponding **Begin_Service_Table** macro.

DefSegment

Specifies the name of the data segment to place the table. This parameter is optional. If given, it *must* be the same as specified by the corresponding **Begin_Service_Table** macro.

Return Value

This macro has no return value.

See Also

Begin_Service_Table

End_VxD_IO_Table

```
include vmm.inc

End_VxD_IO_Table TableName
```

The **End_VxD_IO_Table** macro marks the end of an I/O table. Virtual devices use the macro in conjunction with the **Begin_VxD_IO_Table** and **VxD_IO** macros to create a table of I/O callback procedures for the **Install_Mult_IO_Handlers** service.

Parameters

TableName

Specifies the name of the I/O table. This parameter *must* have been previously defined in a matching **Begin_VxD_IO_Table** macro.

See Also

Begin_VxD_IO_Table

Fatal_Error

```
include vmm.inc

Fatal_Error Msg_Ptr, Exit_Flags
```

The **Fatal_Error** macro calls the **Fatal_Error_Handler** service which terminates Windows. A virtual device typically calls this macro in response to an unrecoverable error. The macro passes the *Msg_Ptr* and *Exit_Flags* parameters (if given) to **Fatal_Error_Handler**.

Parameters

Msg_Ptr

Points to a zero-terminated string. This parameter is optional.

Exit_Flags

Specifies the exit flags. This optional parameter can be a combination of the following values:

Value	Meaning
EF_Hang_On_Exit	Hangs the system on a fatal exit.

Return Value

This macro never returns.

Examples

The following example exits Windows without displaying an error message:

```
Fatal_Error
```

The following example exits Windows and prints the error message pointed to by My_Err_Msg:

```
Fatal_Error OFFSET32 My_Err_Msg
```

See Also

Fatal_Error_Handler

IO_Delay

```
include vmm.inc

IO_Delay
```

The **IO_Delay** macro delays the execution of the next instruction so that an I/O device has time to carry out an I/O operation.

Parameters

This macro has no parameters.

Return Value

This macro has no return value.

Comments

This macro generates a jmp instruction to the next instruction.

Mono_Out

```
include debug.inc

Mono_Out String, nocrlf
```

The **Mono_Out** macro calls the **Out_Mono_String** service to display the given string.

Parameters

String

Specifies the string to display. The string must be enclosed in double quotation marks. The string can contain register placeholders in the same forms as described for the **Out_Mono_String** service.

nocrlf

Specifies whether the macro should not append a newline and carriage return character combination to the end of the string. If the parameter is not given, the macro appends the character combination by default.

Return Value

This macro has no return value.

Comments

The assembler generates code for the macro only if the constant DEBUG is defined before including the DEBUG.INC file.

Examples

The following example writes a string to the secondary display device:

```
Mono_Out "Element not found"
```

The following example writes a string containing the value of the AX register to the debugging device:

```
Mono_Out "AX value is #AX"
```

See Also

Out_Mono_String

Mono_Out_At

```
include debug.inc

Mono_Out_At Row, Column, String, nocrlf
```

The **Mono_Out_At** macro calls the **Set_Mono_Cur_Pos** service to position the cursor, then calls the **Out_Mono_String** service to display the given string.

Parameters

Row

Specifies the row to place the first character of the string.

Column

Specifies the column in which to place the first character of the string.

String

Specifies the string to display. The string must be enclosed in double quotation marks. The string can contain register placeholders in the same forms as described for the **Out_Mono_String** service.

nocrlf

Specifies whether the macro should not append a newline and carriage return character combination to the end of the string. If the parameter is not given, the macro appends the character combination by default.

Return Value

This macro has no return value.

Comments

The assembler generates code for the macro only if the constant DEBUG is defined before including the DEBUG.INC file.

Examples

The following example writes a string starting at the position (10,10) on the secondary display device:

```
Mono_Out_At 10,10,"Element not found"
```

See Also

Out_Mono_String, **Set_Mono_Cur_Pos**

Pop_Client_State

```
include vmm.inc

Pop_Client_State
```

The **Pop_Client_State** macro restores the client registers for the virtual machine.

Parameters

This macro has no parameters.

Return Value

This macro has no return value.

Comments

This macro must not be used unless the **Push_Client_State** macro was previously used to save the client registers.

See Also

Push_Client_State

Push_Client_State

```
include vmm.inc

Push_Client_State
```

The **Push_Client_State** macro copies the client state to the protected-mode stack.

Parameters

This macro has no parameters.

Return Value

This macro has no return value.

Comments

This macro reserves space on the stack for the client registers.

A virtual device must use the **Pop_Client_State** macro to restore the client registers, and free the reserve stack space.

See Also

Pop_Client_State

Queue_Out

```
include debug.inc

Queue_Out String, Value1, Value2
```

The **Queue_Out** macro calls the **Queue_Debug_String** service to queue the given string for display at a later time.

Parameters

String

Specifies the string to display. The string must be enclosed in double quotation marks. The string can contain register placeholders in the same forms as described for the **Queue_Debug_String** service.

Value1

Specifies a value to queue with the string. If the string contains the #EAX or ?EAX placeholder, this value is used when the string is displayed.

Value2

Specifies a value to queue with the string. If the string contains the #EBX or ?EBX placeholder, this value is used when the string is displayed.

Return Value

This macro has no return value.

Comments

The assembler generates code for the macro only if the constant DEBUG is defined before including the DEBUG.INC file.

Examples

The following example queues a string:

```
Queue_Out "Element not found"
```

The following example queues a string containing the value of the AX register to the debugging device:

```
Queue_Out "AX value is #AX", AX
```

See Also

Queue_Debug_String

ShiftState

```
include vmm.inc

ShiftState Mask, Compare
```

The **ShiftState** macro sets the EBX register with the shift state mask and shift state compare value required for a call to the **VKD_Define_Hot_Key** service.

Parameters

Mask

Specifies the shift state bits that should be excluded before the compare is done.

Compare

Specifies the value to compare

Return Value

EBX is loaded with the shift state mask and shift state compare values.

See Also

VKD_Define_Hot_Key

Trace_Out

```
include debug.inc

Trace_Out String, nocrlf
```

The **Trace_Out** macro calls the **Out_Debug_String** service to display the given string.

Parameters

String

Specifies the string to display. The string must be enclosed in double quotation marks. The string can contain register placeholders in the same forms as described for the **Out_Debug_String** service.

nocrlf

Specifies whether the macro should not append a newline and carriage return character combination to the end of the string. If the parameter is not given, the macro appends the character combination by default.

Return Value

This macro has no return value.

Comments

The assembler generates code for the macro only if the constant DEBUG is defined before including the DEBUG.INC file.

Examples

The following example writes a string to the debugging device:

```
Trace_Out "Element not found"
```

The following example writes a string containing the value of the AX register to the debugging device:

```
Trace_Out "AX value is #AX"
```

See Also

Out_Debug_String

VMMcall

```
include vmm.inc

VMMcall Service, Parameters
```

The **VMMcall** macro pushes the specified parameters on the stack, creates a dynamic link to the specified VMM service, and calls the service. When the service returns, the macro pops the parameters from the stack.

Parameters

Service

Specifies the name of the service to link to and call. This parameter can be any service that is explicitly defined in the service table for the VMM.

Parameters

Specifies the parameters to pass to the specified service. If more than one parameter is given, they must be separated with commas and enclosed in angle brackets (<>). This parameter is optional.

Return Value

The return value is as specified for the given service.

Comments

This macro pushes the parameters using the C-language calling convention, in order from right to left.

See Also

VxDcall, **VMMjmp**

VMMjmp

```
include vmm.inc

VMMjmp Service
```

The **VMMjmp** macro creates a dynamic link to the specified VMM service then jumps to the service.

Parameters

Service

Specifies the name of the service to link and jump to. This parameter can be any service that is explicitly defined in the service table for the VMM.

Return Value

This macro has no return value.

Comments

If the DEBUG symbol is defined, the macro calls the specified service then immediately returns when the service returns. This form of the macro is typically used in conjunction with the **Log_Proc_Call** service to record the path of execution through a virtual device while debugging.

See Also

VMMcall, **VxDjmp**

VxDcall

```
include vmm.inc

VxDcall Service
```

The **VxDcall** macro pushes the specified parameters on the stack, creates a dynamic link to the specified virtual device service, and calls the service. When the service returns, the macro pops the parameters from the stack.

Parameters

Service

Specifies the name of the service to link to and call. This parameter can be any service that is explicitly defined in the service table for a given virtual device.

Parameters

Specifies the parameters to pass to the specified service. If more than one parameter is given, they must be separated with commas and enclosed in angle brackets (<>). This parameter is optional.

Return Value

The return value is as specified for the given service.

Comments

This macro pushes the parameters using the C-language calling convention, in order from right to left.

See Also

VMMcall, **VxDjmp**

VxD_CODE_ENDS

```
include vmm.inc

VxD_CODE_ENDS
```

The **VxD_CODE_ENDS** macro defines the end of a code segment. Virtual devices use this macro with in conjunction with the **VxD_CODE_SEG** macro to create segments for noninitialization code.

Parameters

This macro has no parameters.

Return Value

This macro has no return value.

Comments

This macro is equal to the **VxD_LOCKED_CODE_ENDS** macro.

See Also

VxD_CODE_SEG, **VxD_LOCKED_CODE_ENDS**

VxD_CODE_SEG

```
include vmm.inc

VxD_CODE_SEG
```

The **VxD_CODE_SEG** macro defines the start of a code segment. Virtual devices use this segment for all code that is not explicitly for initialization of the device.

Comments

This macro creates a 32-bit segment named **_LTEXT**. The segment is assembled for flat model memory so segment registers CS, DS, ES, and SS are assumed to be equal.

This macro is equal to the **VxD_LOCKED_CODE_SEG** macro.

See Also

VxD_CODE_ENDS, **VxD_ICODE_SEG**, **VxD_DATA_SEG**, **VxD_LOCKED_CODE_SEG**

VxD_DATA_ENDS

```
include vmm.inc

VxD_DATA_ENDS
```

The **VxD_DATA_ENDS** macro defines the end of a data segment. Virtual devices use this macro with in conjunction with the **VxD_DATA_SEG** macro to create segments for noninitialization data.

Parameters

This macro has no parameters.

Return Value

This macro has no return value.

Comments

This macro is equal to the **VxD_LOCKED_DATA_ENDS** macro.

See Also

VxD_DATA_SEG, **VxD_LOCKED_DATA_ENDS**

VxD_DATA_SEG

```
include vmm.inc

VxD_DATA_SEG NoAlign
```

The **VxD_DATA_SEG** macro defines the start of a data segment. Virtual devices use this segment for all data that is not explicitly for initialization of the device.

Parameters

NoAlign

Specifies that data be aligned at the next byte. If this optional parameter is not given, the macro aligns data at the next available doubleword.

Comments

This macro creates a 32-bit segment named **_LDATA**.

This macro is equal to the **VxD_LOCKED_DATA_SEG** macro.

See Also

> **VxD_CODE_SEG**, **VxD_DATA_ENDS**, **VxD_IDATA_SEG**,
> **VxD_LOCKED_DATA_SEG**

VxD_ICODE_ENDS

```
include vmm.inc

VxD_ICODE_ENDS
```

The **VxD_ICODE_ENDS** macro defines the end of an initialization code segment. Virtual devices use this macro with in conjunction with the **VxD_ICODE_SEG** macro to create initialization code.

Parameters

This macro has no parameters.

Return Value

This macro has no return value.

See Also

> **VxD_ICODE_SEG**

VxD_ICODE_SEG

```
include vmm.inc

VxD_ICODE_SEG
```

The **VxD_ICODE_SEG** macro defines the start of an initialization code segment. Virtual devices typically use this segment for code that initializes the corresponding device. The system discards the segment after the initialization is complete (after the Init_Complete message has been processed by all virtual devices).

Comments

This macro creates a 32-bit segment named **_ITEXT**. The segment is assembled for flat model memory so segment registers CS, DS, ES, and SS are assumed to be equal.

See Also

> **VxD_CODE_SEG**, **VxD_ICODE_ENDS**, **VxD_IDATA_SEG**

VxD_IDATA_ENDS

```
include vmm.inc

VxD_IDATA_ENDS
```

The **VxD_IDATA_ENDS** macro defines the end of an initialization data segment. Virtual devices use this macro with in conjunction with the **VxD_IDATA_SEG** macro to create initialization data.

Parameters

This macro has no parameters.

Return Value

This macro has no return value.

See Also

VxD_IDATA_SEG

VxD_IDATA_SEG

```
include vmm.inc

VxD_IDATA_SEG
```

The **VxD_IDATA_SEG** macro defines the start of an initialization data segment. Virtual devices typically use this segment for data used to initialize the corresponding device. The system discards the segment after the initialization is complete (after the Init_Complete message has been processed by all virtual devices).

Comments

This macro creates a 32-bit segment named **_IDATA**.

See Also

VxD_DATA_SEG, VxD_IDATA_ENDS, VxD_ICODE_SEG

VxDint

```
include vmm.inc

VxDint Int_Number
```

The **VxDint** macro executes the specified software interrupt. This macro pushes the interrupt number on the stack and calls the **Exec_VxD_Int** service.

Parameters

Int_Number

Specifies the number of the software interrupt to execute.

Return Value

One or more registers may contain return values depending the function of the specified interrupt.

See Also

Exec_VxD_Int

VxD_IO

```
include vmm.inc

VxD_IO  Port, IOCallback
```

The **VxD_IO** macro adds an I/O callback procedure and I/O port number to an I/O table. Virtual devices use the macro in conjunction with the **Begin_VxD_IO_Table** and **End_VxD_IO_Table** macros to create a table of I/O callback procedures for the **Install_Mult_IO_Handlers** service.

Parameters

Port

Specifies the number of the I/O port to be trapped.

IOCallback

Specifies the name of the I/O callback procedure. See the "Comments" section for information about this procedure.

Return Value

This service has no return value.

Comments

The I/O table can contain any number of **VxD_IO** macros. Each macro must specify an unique I/O port number, but the same I/O callback procedure can be assigned to more than one port.

After a virtual device installs the callback procedures, the system calls a procedure whenever a program in the virtual machine attempts to access the corresponding port. The system calls the procedure as follows:

```
mov      ebx, VM             ; current VM handle
mov      ecx, IOType         ; type of I/O
mov      edx, Port           ; port number
mov      ebp, OFFSET32 crs   ; points to a Client_Reg_Struc
mov      eax, Data           ; output data
                             ;    (if I/O type is output)
call     [IOCallback]

mov      [Data], eax         ; input data
                             ;    (if I/O type is input)
```

The *VM* parameter specifies the current virtual machine, *Port* specifies the I/O port, and *crs* points to a **Client_Reg_Struc** structure containing the register contents for the current virtual machine.

The *IOType* parameter specifies the type of input or output operation requested and determines whether the callback procedure receives data in the EAX register or must return data in the EAX register. The *IOType* parameter can be a combination of the following values:

Value	Meaning
Byte_Input	Input a single byte; place in AL if String_IO not given.
Byte_Output	Output a single byte from AL if String_IO not given.
Word_Input	Input a word; place in AX if String_IO not given.
Word_Output	Output a word from AX if String_IO not given.
Dword_Input	Input a double word; place in EAX if String_IO not given.
Dword_Output	Output a double word from EAX if String_IO not given.
String_IO	Input or output a string. The high 16-bits specifies segment address of buffer containing the string to output or to receive the string input.
Rep_IO	Repeat the input or output string operation the number of times specified by the Client_CX field in the Client_Reg_Struc structure.

Addr_32_IO   Use 32-bit address offsets for input or output string operations. If this value is not given, the 16-bit offsets are used.

Reverse_IO   Decrement string address on each input or output operation. If this value is not given, the string address is incremented on each operation.

In memory, an I/O table consists of a **VxD_IOT_Hdr** structure followed by one or more **VxD_IO_Struc** structures. The first word in the table specified the number of entries. Each entry consists of a word specifying the port number and a double word specifying the 32-bit offset of the callback procedure.

See Also

Begin_VxD_IO_Table, **End_VxD_IO_Table**, **Install_Mult_IO_Handlers**

VxDjmp

```
include vmm.inc

VxDjmp Service
```

The **VMMjmp** macro creates a dynamic link to the specified virtual device service then jumps to the service.

Parameters

Service

Specifies the name of the service to link and jump to. This parameter can be any service that is explicitly defined in the service table for a virtual device.

Return Value

This macro has no return value.

Comments

If the DEBUG symbol is defined, the macro calls the specified service then immediately returns when the service returns. This form of the macro is typically used in conjunction with the **Log_Proc_Call** service to record the path of execution through a virtual device while debugging.

See Also

VMMjmp, **VxDcall**

VxD_LOCKED_CODE_ENDS

```
include vmm.inc

VxD_LOCKED_CODE_ENDS
```

The **VxD_LOCKED_CODE_ENDS** macro defines the end of a code segment. Virtual devices use this macro with in conjunction with the **VxD_LOCKED_CODE_SEG** macro to create segments for noninitialization code.

Parameters

This macro has no parameters.

Return Value

This macro has no return value.

Comments

This macro is equal to the **VxD_CODE_ENDS** macro.

See Also

VxD_LOCKED_CODE_SEG, **VxD_CODE_ENDS**

VxD_LOCKED_CODE_SEG

```
include vmm.inc

VxD_LOCKED_CODE_SEG
```

The **VxD_LOCKED_CODE_SEG** macro defines the start of a code segment. Virtual devices use this segment for all code that is not explicitly for initialization of the device.

Comments

This macro creates a 32-bit segment named **_LTEXT**. The segment is assembled for flat model memory so segment registers CS, DS, ES, and SS are assumed to be equal.

This macro is equal to the **VxD_CODE_SEG** macro.

See Also

VxD_CODE_SEG, **VxD_LOCKED_CODE_ENDS**

VxD_LOCKED_DATA_ENDS

```
include vmm.inc

VxD_LOCKED_DATA_ENDS
```

The **VxD_LOCKED_DATA_ENDS** macro defines the end of a data segment. Virtual devices use this macro with in conjunction with the **VxD_LOCKED_DATA_SEG** macro to create segments for noninitialization data.

Parameters

This macro has no parameters.

Return Value

This macro has no return value.

Comments

This macro is equal to the **VxD_DATA_ENDS** macro.

See Also

VxD_DATA_ENDS, VxD_LOCKED_DATA_SEG

VxD_LOCKED_DATA_SEG

```
include vmm.inc

VxD_LOCKED_DATA_SEG NoAlign
```

The **VxD_LOCKED_DATA_SEG** macro defines the start of a data segment. Virtual devices use this segment for all data that is not explicitly for initialization of the device.

Parameters

NoAlign

Specifies that data be aligned at the next byte. If this optional parameter is not given, the macro aligns data at the next available doubleword.

Comments

This macro creates a 32-bit segment named **_LDATA**.

This macro is equal to the **VxD_DATA_SEG** macro.

See Also

VxD_DATA_SEG, VxD_LOCKED_DATA_ENDS

VxD_REAL_INIT_ENDS

```
include vmm.inc

VxD_REAL_INIT_ENDS
```

The **VxD_REAL_INIT_ENDS** macro defines the end of a real-mode initialization segment. Virtual devices use this macro with in conjunction with the **VxD_REAL_INIT_SEG** macro to create initialization code for real-mode execution.

Parameters

This macro has no parameters.

Return Value

This macro has no parameters.

See Also

VxD_REAL_INIT_SEG

VxD_REAL_INIT_SEG

```
include vmm.inc

VxD_REAL_INIT_SEG
```

The **VxD_REAL_INIT_SEG** macro defines the start of a real-mode initialization segment. Virtual devices typically use this segment for code that initializes the corresponding device before Windows changes to protected-mode execution. The system discards the segment after the initialization is complete.

Comments

This macro creates a 16-bit segment named **_RCODE**. The segment is assembled for the real-mode tiny model memory so segment registers CS, DS, ES, and SS are assumed to be equal.

See Also

VxD_ICODE_SEG, **VxD_REAL_INIT_ENDS**

Block Device Reference

BlockDev_API_Hw_Detect_End

```
include vmm.inc
include blockdev.inc

mov     ax, 1607h                ; Device callout
mov     bx, BlockDev_Device_ID   ; Block device ID
mov     cx, BlockDev_API_Hw_Detect_End
int     2Fh
```

The **BlockDev_API_Hw_Detect_End** function notifies TSRs and MS-DOS device drivers that a virtual block device has completed hardware detection.

See Also

BlockDev_API_Hw_Detect_Start

BlockDev_API_Hw_Detect_Start

```
include vmm.inc
include blockdev.inc

mov     ax, 1607h                ; Device callout
mov     bx, BlockDev_Device_ID   ; Block device ID
mov     cx, BlockDev_API_Hw_Detect_Start
int     2Fh
```

The **BlockDev_API_Hw_Detect_Start** function notifies TSRs and MS-DOS device drivers that a virtual block device is performing hardware detection. This may, for example, disable a write-behind cache.

See Also

BlockDev_API_Hw_Detect_End

BlockDev_API_Int13_Chain_Check

```
include vmm.inc
include blockdev.inc

mov     ax, 1607h                ; Device callout
mov     bx, BlockDev_Device_ID   ; Block device ID
mov     cx, BlockDev_API_Int13_Chain_Check
int     2Fh
```

```
jcxz    okay                             ; zero if okay to
                                         ;    load block device
```

The **BlockDev_API_Int13_Chain_Check** function notifies TSRs and MS-DOS device drivers that have hooked the ROM BIOS Interrupt 13h address that a block device is about to load. This notification gives the TSR or device driver a chance to cancel the loading.

Return Value

The TSR or device driver sets the CX register to zero if it is permissible for block devices, such as **WDCTRL**, to load even though the MS-DOS Interrupt 13h chain has been modified.

BlockDev_Command_Block

```
include blockdev.inc

BlockDev_Command_Block    STRUC
    BD_CB_Next                dd       ?
    BD_CB_Command             dw       ?
    BD_CB_Cmd_Status          dw       ?
    BD_CB_Flags               dd       ?
    BD_CB_Cmd_Cplt_Proc       dd       ?
    BD_CB_Sector              dq       ?
    BD_CB_Count               dd       ?
    BD_CB_Buffer_Ptr          dd       ?
    BD_CB_Reserved_Client     dd       ?
    BD_CB_Reserved_BlockDev   dd       ?
    BD_CB_Reserved_FastDisk   dd       ?
BlockDev_Command_Block    ENDS
```

The **BlockDev_Command_Block** structure contains information about a block device command.

Members

BD_CB_Next

Points to the next command in the command list.

BD_CB_Command

Specifies the command to carry out. It can be one of the following values:

Value	Meaning
BDC_Read	Read from device
BDC_Write	Write to device
BDC_Verify	Verify read or write

BDC_Cancel   Cancel command

Command values in the range 8000h through 0FFFFh are reserved for device-specific commands.

BD_CB_Cmd_Status

Specifies the status of the command. It can be one of the following values:

Value	Meaning
BDS_Success	Command completed successfully
BDS_Success_With_Retries	Command completed successfully after repetition
BDS_Success_With_ECC	Command completed successfully after error correction
BDS_Invalid_Sector_Number	Invalid sector number
BDS_Canceled	Command was canceled
BDS_Cmd_In_Progress	Can't cancel command in progress
BDS_Invalid_Cmd_Ptr	Cancel of invalid command pointer
BDS_Media_Error	Read or write failed
BDS_Device_Error	Device or adapter failed
BDS_Invalid_Command	Invalid command

All values below BDS_First_Error_Code (10h) imply successful completion; error values are greater than or equal to BDS_First_Error_Code.

BD_CB_Flags

Specifies additional actions to take when carrying out the command. This field can be a combination of the following values:

Value	Meaning
BDCF_High_Priority	High priority
BDCF_Scatter_Gather	Scatter or gather
BDCF_Dont_Cache	Noncached command

BD_CB_Cmd_Cplt_Proc

Points to the command-completion callback procedure.

BD_CB_Sector

Specifies the count of sectors for the block device.

BD_CB_Count

Specifies the count.

BD_CB_Buffer_Ptr

Points to the buffer.

BD_CB_Reserved_Client

Reserved.

BD_CB_Reserved_BlockDev

Reserved.

BD_CB_Reserved_FastDisk

Reserved.

BlockDev_Command_Complete

```
include blockdev.inc

mov     edi, OFFSET32 bdd   ; points to a
                            ;      BlockDev_Device_Descriptor
mov     esi, OFFSET32 bcb   ; points to BlockDev_Command_Block
VXDcall BlockDev_Command_Complete
```

The **BlockDev_Command_Complete** service calls the callback procedure specified in the **BlockDev_Device_Descriptor** structure. After the callback procedure returns, **BlockDev_Command_Complete** sends the pending command (if any) to the block device's command procedure. The service sends pending commands only if the BDF_Serial_Cmd flag is set in the BDD_Flags field in the device's **BlockDev_Device_Descriptor** structure.

A block device driver should call this service whenever it completes a command.

Parameters

bdd

Points to **BlockDev_Device_Descriptor** structure containing information about the block device.

bcb

> Points to a **BlockDev_Command_Block** structure containing information about the command just completed.

Return Value

This service has no return value.

Comments

The callback procedure preserves all registers and **BlockDev_Command_Complete** preserves the ESI and EDI registers.

This service enables interrupts.

Uses

EAX, EBX, EDX returned from client, Flags

BlockDev_Device_Descriptor

```
include blockdev.inc

BlockDev_Device_Descriptor STRUC
BDD_Next                 dd        ?
BDD_BD_Major_Ver         db        BD_Major_Version
BDD_BD_Minor_Ver         db        BD_Minor_Version
BDD_Device_Type          db        ?
BDD_Int_13h_Number       db        ?
BDD_Flags                dd        ?
BDD_Name_Ptr             dd        ?
BDD_Max_Sector           dq        ?
BDD_Sector_Size          dd        ?
BDD_Num_Heads            dd        ?
BDD_Num_Cylinders        dd        ?
BDD_Num_Sec_Per_Track    dd        ?
BDD_Sync_Cmd_Proc        dd        ?
BDD_Command_Proc         dd        ?
BDD_Hw_Int_Proc          dd        0
BDD_Reserved_BlockDev    db        BD_Priv_Data_Size dup (?)
BlockDev_Device_Descriptor ENDS
```

The **BlockDev_Device_Descriptor** structure contains information about the block device.

Members

BDD_Next

> Points to the next **BlockDev_Device_Descriptor** structure in the list.

BDD_BD_Major_Ver

> Specifies the major version number. It is 03h for version 3.1.

BDD_BD_Minor_Ver

Specifies the minor version number. It is 0Ah for version 3.1.

BDD_Device_Type

Specifies the type of hardware device. It can be one of the following values:

Value	Meaning
BDT_360K_5_Inch_Floppy	5.25 inch, 360 kilobyte floppy drive
BDT_1200K_5_Inch_Floppy	5.25 inch, 1.2 megabyte floppy drive
BDT_720K_3_Inch_Floppy	3.5 inch, 720 kilobyte floppy drive
BDT_Single_Dens_8_Inch	8 inch, single density floppy drive
BDT_Double_Dens_8_Inch	8 inch, double density floppy drive
BDT_Fixed_Disk	Hard disk drive
BDT_Tape_Drive	Tape drive
BDT_Other	Other storage media

BDD_Int_13h_Number

Specifies the Interrupt 13h number.

BDD_Flags

Specifies the device flags. It can be one or more of the following values:

Value	Meaning
BDF_Int13_Drive	Interrupt 13h drive
BDF_Writeable	Writable media
BDF_Removable	Removable media
BDF_Remote	Remote device
BDF_Serial_Cmd	Serial commands
BDF_Cache	Cached device

BDD_Name_Ptr

Points to a null-terminated string specifying the name of the block device.

BDD_Max_Sector

Specifies the maximum number of sectors for the block device.

BDD_Sector_Size

Specifies the size (in bytes) of each sector.

BDD_Num_Heads

Specifies the number of head for the block device.

BDD_Num_Cylinders

Specifies the number of cylinders for the block device.

BDD_Num_Sec_Per_Track

Specifies the number of sectors in each track of the block device.

BDD_Sync_Cmd_Proc

Points to the synchronous command procedure for the block device.

BDD_Command_Proc

Points to the command procedure for the block device.

BDD_Hw_Int_Proc

Points to the hardware interrupt handler for the block device.

BDD_Reserved_BlockDev

Reserved.

See Also

BlockDev_Command_Complete

BlockDev_Find_Int13_Drive

```
include blockdev.inc

mov     al, DriveNum              ; Interrupt 13h drive number
VXDcall BlockDev_Find_Int13_Drive

jc      Error                     ; error if carry set
mov     dword ptr [bdd], edi      ; points to
                                  ;     BlockDev_Device_Descriptor
```

The **BlockDev_Find_Int13_Drive** service returns a pointer to the **BlockDev_Device_Descriptor** structure for a specified Interrupt 13h drive.

This service is available during initialization only.

Parameters

DriveNum

Specifies an Interrupt 13h drive number.

Return Value

If the carry flag is clear, the EDI register contains the address of the **BlockDev_Device_Descriptor** structure for the specified drive. Otherwise, the carry flag is set to indicate an error.

Comments

The service sets the carry flag if the specified Interrupt 13h block device driver is not installed.

Uses

EDI, Flags

BlockDev_Get_Device_List

```
include blockdev.inc

VXDcall BlockDev_Get_Device_List

mov     dword ptr [bdd], edi   ; points to first
                               ;     BlockDev_Device_Descriptor
```

The **BlockDev_Get_Device_List** service returns a pointer to the first **BlockDev_Device_Descriptor** structure in the list of such structures maintained by the virtual device.

Parameters

This service has no entry parameters.

Return Value

The EDI register points to the first **BlockDev_Device_Descriptor** structure in the block device list. The register is 0 if no list exists.

Comments

Other virtual devices typically call this service to retrieve the information they need to send commands to the block device. The other virtual devices send commands to the block device using the **BlockDev_Send_Command** service.

Uses

ECX

See Also

BlockDev_Send_Command

BlockDev_Get_Version

```
include blockdev.inc

VXDcall BlockDev_Get_Version

mov     dword ptr [version], eax    ; block device version
mov     dword ptr [flags], ecx      ; block device flags
```

The **BlockDev_Get_Version** service returns the version number and flags for the virtual block device.

Parameters

This service has no entry parameters.

Return Value

The service returns values in the following registers:

Register	Value
EAX	Specifies the version number for the virtual block device.
ECX	Specifies the flags for the virtual block device. Bit 0 must be set to 0 for compatibility with Windows 3.0. All other bits currently reserved and must be 0.

Uses

EAX, ECX

BlockDev_Register_Device

```
include blockdev.inc

mov     edi, OFFSET32 bdd        ; points to a
                                 ;        BlockDev_Device_Descriptor
VXDcall BlockDev_Register_Device

jc      error                    ; error if carry set
```

The **BlockDev_Register_Device** service registers the specified Interrupt 13h device.

This service is available during initialization only.

Parameters

bdd

> Points to a **BlockDev_Device_Descriptor** structure containing information about the block device to be registered.

Exit

If the carry flag is clear, the block device is registered. Otherwise, the carry flag is set to indicate an error.

Comments

Virtual devices supporting block devices usually call this service to register their devices during the Sys_Critical_Init phase of device initialization.

This service returns an error if the Interrupt 13h device has already been registered by a virtual device or the Interrupt 13h drive has not been installed.

BlockDev_Send_Command

```
include blockdev.inc

mov      edi, OFFSET32 bdd     ; points to a
                               ;     BlockDev_Device_Descriptor
mov      esi, OFFSET32 bcb     ; points to first
                               ;     BlockDev_Command_Block
VXDcall BlockDev_Send_Command
```

The **BlockDev_Send_Command** service sends one or more commands to the specified block device driver.

This service may be called at interrupt time.

Parameters

bdd

> Points to a **BlockDev_Device_Descriptor** structure containing information about the block device to receive the commands.

bcb

> Points to the first **BlockDev_Command_Block** structure in a null-terminated list of commands to send to the block device.

Return Value

This service has no return value.

Comments

The command status is returned to the callback procedure specified by the **BD_CB_Cmd_Cplt_Proc** field in the **BlockDev_Command_Block** structure.

This service enables interrupts.

Uses

Flags

BlockDev_Synchronous_Command

```
include blockdev.inc

mov      ax,  CmdNum           ; command number
mov      edi, OFFSET32 bdd     ; points to a
                               ;       BlockDev_Device_Descriptor
VXDcall BlockDev_Synchronous_Command
```

The **BlockDev_Synchronous_Command** service sends a synchronous command to a specified block device.

Parameters

CmdNum

Specifies a command number. It can be one of the following:

Value	Meaning
BD_SC_Get_Version	Retrieves the version number for the block device.

bdd

Points to a **BlockDev_Device_Descriptor** structure.

Return Value

If the carry flag is clear, the EAX, EBX, ECX, EDX, ESI, EDI, and flags are modified as defined by the command. Otherwise, the carry flag is set and the AX register contains the following error value:

Value	Meaning
BD_SC_Err_Invalid_Cmd	Invalid synchronous command

Comments

Registers in addition to AX and EDI may be used as parameters for specific commands.

Uses

Registers defined by command and flags

MS-DOS Manager Reference

DOSMGR_Add_Device

```
include dosmgr.inc

VxDcall DOSMGR_Add_Device
```

The **DOSMGR_Add_Device** service adds a device to the device list.

Parameters

EBX

Specifies the handle of the virtual machine to add device to. If this parameter is zero, the device is added to all virtual machines.

EAX

Specifies the address of device header. This address must be in low memory (less than 100000h).

Return Value

The carry flag is clear if the service is successful. Otherwise, the carry flag is set if the device could not be added to device list.

Comments

The address of this device for the chain is computed as: (eax >> 4) & 0FFFFh : (eax & 000Fh)

This service links the device into the list but does not call it. If the device needs to be initialized, the caller must do it. This service adds the device to the end of the device chain. Therefore, this service cannot be used to replace an existing device. This service applies to character devices only. Block devices cannot be added with this service.

All devices put on the list this way are removed when Windows exits, including any devices added by virtual mode code.

The only supported method to add a device globally is to use the **_Allocate_Global_V86_Data_Area** service to allocate memory to contain the device header, initialize it, then call this routine to add it to the list.

Global devices must be added during the **Device_Init** message. They cannot be added later. Local devices must be added at the **VM_Init**, **VM_Critical_Init** or **Sys_VM_Init** message or they will be global because they will be part of the initial VM state.

If this device hooks an interrupt and it is a local device, the vector must be set in the appropriate virtual machine during the **VM_Init**, **VM_Critical_Init** or **Sys_VM_Init** message.

A global device can also work this way, hooking the vector in every virtual machine. This allows the global device to be removed before Windows exits. The other method for a global device is to hook the vector during the **Device_Ini**t message which makes the hook part of the initial virtual machine state. Such a hook must be removed during the **Sys_Critical_Exit** message or the vector will point to a nonexistent device after Windows exits.

Uses

Flags

DOSMGR_BackFill_Allowed

```
include dosmgr.inc

VxDcall DOSMGR_BackFill_Allowed
```

The **DOSMGR_BackFill_Allowed** service specifies whether the MS-DOS configuration allows for low-memory backfills.

The **V86MMGR** device calls this service.

Parameters

This service has no parameters.

Return Value

The carry flag is clear if backfilling is allowed. Otherwise, the carry flag is set.

Comments

This service depends on the high MS-DOS state. Certain high MS-DOS configurations prevent low memory 640k backfill from being possible.

Uses

Flags

DOSMGR_Copy_VM_Drive_State

```
include dosmgr.inc

VxDcall DOSMGR_Copy_VM_Drive_State
```

The **DOSMGR_Copy_VM_Drive_State** service copies the drive and current directory state of all drives from one virtual machine into another virtual machine.

This service can be called during a **Create_VM** message since it does not simulate calls or interrupts in either virtual machine; it just copies instance data from one to the other.

Parameters

EBX

Specifies the handle of the virtual machine to receive a copy of thedrive state.

ESI

Specifies handle of the virtual machine from which to copy the drive state.

Return Value

This service has no return value.

Comments

This service does not change the current drive of the destination virtual machine.

This service does not disturb the InitDrvDir value set using the **_DOSMGR_Set_Exec_VM_Data** service if it is called before the **_DOSMGR_Exec_VM service**. The processing of InitDrvDir occurs during calls to the **_DOSMGR_Exec_VM** service.

Uses

Flags

DOSMGR_Enable_Indos_Polling

```
include dosmgr.inc

VxDcall DOSMGR_Enable_Indos_Polling
```

The **DOSMGR_Enable_Indos_Polling** service enables the INDOS polling for the the Windows session. This allows TSR drivers that hook Interrupt 21h and claim the critical section by setting the internal MS-DOS INDOS flag to continue to operate normally.

This service is intended for use by the virtual DOSNET device so that it can enable polling if the installed network requires it. The virtual device must not call this service during a **Sys_Critical_Init** message.

Parameters

This service has no parameters.

Return Value

The carry flag is clear if INDOS polling is enabled. Otherwise, the carry flag is set to indicate polling was already enabled.

Comments

Enabling INDOS polling has a severe impact on overall system performance.

This service overrides the INDOSPOLLING value specified in the SYSTEM.INI file. Since the virtual MS-DOS manager evaluates the SYSTEM.INI file during the **Init_Complete** message, a virtual device must call this service during the **Device_Init** message.

Uses

Flags

_DOSMGR_Exec_VM

```
include dosmgr.inc

VxDcall _DOSMGR_Exec_VM <VM, V86Size, CallBack, RefData>
```

The **_DOSMGR_Exec_VM** service schedules the execution specified by previous call to the **_DOSMGR_Set_Exec_VM_Data** service and sets other parameters of the execution.

Parameters

VM

Specifies the handle of the current virtual machine.

V86Size

Specifies the size in pages of the virtual machine. This is equal to the number of pages mapped using the **MapIntoVM** service starting at the first page in the virtual machine. This service does not map these pages; the value is simply used to set the MS-DOS size of the virtual machine.

CallBk

Specifies the callback procedure to call when the virtual machine terminates. If this parameter is zero, no callback is called.

RefData

Specifies reference data to pass to the callback procedure.

Return Value

This service has no return value.

Comments

The system calls the callback when the virtual machine terminates. The callback receives the following input parameters:

EBP   points to a Client_Reg_Struc

EBX   virtual machine handle

EDX   oints to reference data

The callback must preserve the EBX, EBP and segment registers. After the callback returns, the system carries out the normal virtual machine termination sequence. At this time the virtual machine is still in a running state. The callback can delay termination by delaying its return. However, the callback must simulate interrupts into the virtual machine to keep the scheduler moving if it is holding termination.

DOSMGR_Get_DOS_Crit_Status

```
include dosmgr.inc
VxDcall DOSMGR_Get_DOS_Crit_Status
```

The **DOSMGR_Get_DOS_Crit_Status** service specifies whether it is possible to call MS-DOS at the current time (that is, whether MS-DOS is in a critical section).

This service is intended for use by the virtual pageswap device to determine whether MS-DOS is currently available to page. This is an asynchronous service.

Parameters

This service has no parameters.

Return Value

The zero flag is set if MS-DOS can be called. Otherwise, the zero flag is clear if MS-DOS is in a critical section and must not be called.

Uses

Flags

Comments

This service does not specify whether Windows is in a critical section nor does it specify which virtual machine has ownership of MS-DOS.

DOSMGR_Get_IndosPtr

```
include dosmgr.inc
VxDcall DOSMGR_Get_IndosPtr
```

The **DOSMGR_Get_IndosPtr** service returns the linear address of the MS-DOS Indos and Errormode variables.

Parameters

This service has no parameters.

Return Value

The EAX register contains the linear address (V86 mode address) of Indos and Errormode word. The low byte is the Errormode variable, the high byte is Indos.

Comments

This is a low linear address. To examine the value in a virtual machine which is not the current virtual machine, the virtual device must add the virtual-machine high-linear address to this value.

Uses

EAX, Flags

DOSMGR_Get_Version

```
include dosmgr.inc
VxDcall DOSMGR_Get_Version
```

The **DOSMGR_Get_Version** service returns the virtual MS-DOS manager version number.

Parameters

This service has no parameters.

Return Value

The AH register contains the major version number.

The AL register contains the minor version number.

Uses

EAX, Flags

DOSMGR_Instance_Device

```
include dosmgr.inc
VxDcall DOSMGR_Instance_Device
```

The **DOSMGR_Instance_Device** service instances the indicated installed MS-DOS character device driver.

This service is only valid during the **Init_Complete** message.

Parameters

ESI

Points to the 8-character device name. This name must exactly match the name as it found in the device header in low memory. Characters must be in uppercase; case conversion is not performed. Names shorter than 8 characters must be padded with spaces. The colon (:) must not be used.

Return Value

The carry flag is clear if the device is instanced. Otherwise, the carry flag is set to indicate one of the following errors:

- No device with this name in device list

- Device is in MS-DOS RAM BIOS (Segment of device == 70h)

- User overides with the GLOBAL setting in SYSTEM.INI

Comments

This service applies only to installed character devices (device segment not equal to 70h). It cannot instance devices that are in the MS-DOS RAM BIOS because there is no way to determine their start and end addresses. It is the job of the MS-DOS instancing to correctly instance things related to character devices in the MS-DOS RAM BIOS.

This service instances the entire device. It cannot differentiate code and data.

This service is available during the **Init_Complete** message only and cannot work until the **DOSMGR_Device_Init** service is complete. The service is in the ICODE segment so it becomes invalid after the **Init_Complete** message.

Calls to the **_AddInstanceItem** service are also invalid after **Init_Complete**.

Do not use this service to instance devices added with the **DOSMGR_Add_Device** service. To instance an added device, a virtual device must call the **_AddInstanceItem** service or use the *GVDAInstance* flag in the **_Allocate_Global_V86_Data_Area** service.

Uses

Flags

DOSMGR_LocalGlobalReg

```
include dosmgr.inc
VxDcall DOSMGR_LocalGlobalReg
```

The **DOSMGR_LocalGlobalReg** service specifies whether the indicated V86 memory region is local or global memory The VMM memory manager calls this service whenever the **TestGlobalV86Mem** service is called.

This service is only available for Windows 3.1 and later.

Parameters

EDX

Specifies the page number of the start of the region.

EDI

Specifies the page number of the end of the region.

Return Value

EAX

Value	Meaning
0	Page range is local

1	Page range is global
2	Page range is partially global and partially local
3	Page range is unknown

Comments

This service returns 3 unless the region is in a local high MS-DOS region.

This service supports high MS-DOS configurations for MS-DOS version 5.00 or later. Other load high configurations are supported only if the corresponding software hooks this service or the TestGlobalV86Mem service.

This service is page (4k) granular and not byte granular.

Uses

EAX, Flags

DOSMGR_Remove_Device

```
include dosmgr,inc
VxDcall DOSMGR_Remove_Device
```

The **DOSMGR_Remove_Device** service removes a device from the device list. The device must have been previously added using the **DOSMGR_Add_Device** service

Parameters

EBX

Specifies the handle of the virtual machine from which to remove the device. If this parameter is zero, the device is removed from all virtual machines.

EAX

Specifies the address of device header. This parameter must be a low memory linear address (less than 100000h).

Return Value

The carry flag is clear if the service is successful. Otherwise, the carry flag is set if the device could not be removed from device list.

Comments

Global calls to **DOSMGR_Add_Device** should not be mixed with local calls to **DOSMGR_Remove_Device** for the same device. All **DOSMGR_Add_Device** devices are automatically removed when Windows terminates.

This service removes the link to the device from the device list. It does not free any memory or resources that the device may have created or allocated.

Uses

Flags

_DOSMGR_Set_Exec_VM_Data

```
include dosmgr.inc
VxDcall _DOSMGR_Set_Exec_VM_Data, <VM, CommTail, PRGName,\
                                  InitDrvDir>
```

The **_DOSMGR_Set_Exec_VM_Data** service sets the data for the initial execution into a virtual machine. It is reserved for exclusive use by the virtual shell device.

This service can be called during the **Create_VM** message since it does not simulate calls or interrupts into the virtual machine; it just sets instance data.

Parameters

VM

Specifies the handle of the virtual machine_Handle to set execution data for.

CommTail

Points to the command tail for the execution. The tail can be up to 128 byte. The first byte must specify the number of bytes in the tail; the last byte must be 0Dh.

PRGName

Points to null-terminated string specifying the name of the program to execute.

InitDrvDir

Points to a null-terminated string specifying the initial directory and drive for the virtual machine. The drive letter must be a capital letter. The string must be less than or equal to 64 chars including null terminator.

If this parameter is zero, the service does not set the default directory. This form of the service is made by the DOSMGR_Exec_VM service. Other virtual devices should not use this form.

Return Value

This service has no return value.

Comments

This service must be called before calling the **_DOSMGR_Exec_VM** service.

See Also

_DOSMGR_Exec_VM

MS-DOS Network Device API Reference

DOSNET_Do_PSP_Adjust

```
include dosnet.inc
VxDcall DOSNET_Do_PSP_Adjust
```

The **DOSNET_Do_PSP_Adjust** service specifies whether the virtual device requires unique PSP addresses for each virtual machine. The virtual MS-DOS manager calls this service to determine whether it should adjust PSP addresses for the virtual machines.

Parameters

This service has no parameters.

Return Value

The carry flag is clear if the virtual MS-DOS manager should adjust the PSP. Otherwise, the carry flag is set to prevent the virtual MS-DOS manager from adjusting the PSP.

The EAX register contains zero if the virtual MS-DOS manager should check the SYSTEM.INI file to determine whether to override the action specified by the carry flag. Otherwise, the EAX register contains nonzero to prevent the virtual device from checking the file.

Comments

A network that uses the MS-DOS PSP addresses as part of an ID should clear the carry flag and return to direct the virtual MS-DOS manager to adjust PSP addresses. The manager adjusts PSP addresses by starting each virtual machine at a different paragraph address (using the virtual machine identifier as the basis of the adjustment). Even so this technique does not guaranteed unique PSP addresses. To ensure uniqueness, network software should always use **Get Current Virtual Machine ID** (Interrupt 2Fh, Function 1683h) to retrieve the virtual machine identifier and use this identifier to create an unique network ID.

Uses

EAX, Flags

DOSNET_Get_Version

```
include dosnet.inc
VxDcall DOSNET_Get_Version
```

The **DOSNET_Get_Version** service returns the virtual DOSNET device version number.

Parameters

This service has no parameters.

Return Value

The AH register contains the major version number.

The AL register contains the minor version number.

The carry flag is clear.

Uses

EAX, Flags

DOSNET_Send_FILESYSCHANGE

```
include dosnet.inc
VxDcall DOSNET_Send_FILESYSCHANGE
```

The **DOSNET_Send_FILESYSCHANGE** service specifies whether the given drive is local to the virtual machine. If the drive is local, the **WM_FILESYSCHANGE** message can be broadcast to Windows applications when changes to the drive are made by MS-DOS applications.

Parameters

AL

Specifies the drive number (0 = A, 1 = B, etc.)

EBX

Specifies the handle of the virtual machine to check.

Return Value

The carry flag is clear if the **WM_FILESYSCHANGE** message will be sent for the specified drive. Otherwise, the carry flag is set to prevent messages for the drive.

Comments

This service is designed exclusively for the virtual DOSNET device. Other virtual devices should not provide their own implementations, however, they can hook this service. Since the virtual DOSNET device does not install if there is no redirector, a virtual device which hooks this service must ship with a modified DOSNET device which always loads.

A virtual device must not send a **WM_FILESYSCHANGE** message for a drive that this service has not acknowledged. Sending a message incorrectly can result in unexpected errors in Windows applications.

Uses

Flags

Extended BIOS Device Reference

EBIOS_Get_Unused_Mem

```
include ebios.inc
VxDcall EBIOS_Get_Unused_Mem
```

The **EBIOS_Get_Unused_Mem** service returns information about any unused portion of the EBIOS region.

This service is intended for the use of the virtual MS-DOS manager.

Parameters

This service has no parameters.

Return Value

The carry flag is clear if the service is successful. The EAX register contains the segment address of start of unused EBIOS region, and the ECX register contains the size of the region in paragraphs. This size is zero if there is no unused EBIOS region. If the zero flag is set, the unused EBIOS region is global, that is, the region is in the same physical page in all virtual machines. Otherwise, the unused EBIOS region is local and is in different physical pages in each virtual machine.

The carry flag is set if the EBIOS device is not installed or all EBIOS memory is used by EBIOS.

Comments

On some machines, the size of the EBIOS region is not an even multiple of pages. Since the system requires that the EBIOS region be rounded to page boundaries, part of the EBIOS region may be unused.

If the EBIOS region is below the first V86 page, this service must set the carry flag and return.

Uses

EAX, ECX, Flags

EBIOS_Get_Version

```
include ebios.inc
VxDcall EBIOS_Get_Version
```

The **EBIOS_Get_Version** service returns the virtual EBIOS device version number and the location and size of the EBIOS pages.

Parameters

This service has no parameters.

Return Value

The carry flag is clear if the service is successful. The EAX register contains the version number, the EDX register contains number of the first page, and the ECX register contains the number of pages.

The carry flag is set if the virtual EBIOS device is not installed and EBIOS pages are not allocated.

Uses

EAX, ECX, EDX, Flags

Int 13h Device API Reference

Int13_Device_Registered

```
include int13.inc
VxDcall Int13_Device_Registered
```

The **Int13_Device_Registered** service is called by the virtual block device whenever a block device driver identifies itself as an Interrupt 13h drive.

Parameters

EDI

Points to a Block Device Descriptor.

Return Value

The carry flag is clear if the service is successful. Otherwise, the carry flag is set to indicate an error such as unable to allocate a handle or specified Interrupt 13h drive is already registered.

Uses

Flags

Int13_Hooking_BIOS_Int

```
include int13.inc
VxDcall Int13_Hooking_BIOS_Int
```

The **Int13_Hooking_BIOS_Int** service notifies the virtual device that the BIOS Interrupt 13h interrupt has been hooked. The virtual block device calls this service.

Parameters

EAX

Specifies the address (CS:IP) of the original Interrupt 13h BIOS handler.

ECX

Specifies the address (CS:IP) of the original ROM BIOS Interrupt 13h hook.

Return Value

This service has no return value.

Comments

This service is always called at least once during initialization, but it must remain resident since it can also be called at system exit time.

The virtual block device calls this service after the interrupt has been hooked. If the service needs to call the BIOS, it should use the **Build_Int_Stack_Frame** and **Resume_Exec** services instead of the **Exec_Int** service.

This service should save the value in the ECX register to let the **Int13_Translate_VM_Int** service chain to the original ROM BIOS at any point in time. Since this virtual device always replaces the ROM BIOS, the EAX value can be ignored.

Uses

EAX, EBX, ECX, EDX, ESI, EDI, and Flags

Int13_Translate_VM_Int

```
include int13.inc
VxDcall Int13_Translate_VM_Int
```

The **Int13_Translate_VM_Int** service notifies the virtual device that an Int 13h has been intercepted. The virtual block device calls this service.

Parameters

EBX

Specifies the handle of the current virtual machine.

EBP

Points to a **Client_Reg_Struc** structure containing the register values for the specified virtual machine.

Return Value

This service has no return value.

Int13_Unhooking_BIOS_Int

```
include int13.inc
VxDcall Int13_Unhooking_BIOS_Int
```

The **Int13_Unhooking_BIOS_Int** service notifies the virtual device that the Int 13h BIOS is being unhooked. The virtual block device calls this service before the Interrupt 13h chain is actually unhooked.

Parameters

EAX

Specifies the address (CS:IP) of the original MS-DOS BIOS Interrupt 13h hook.

ECX

Specifies the address (CS:IP) of the original ROM BIOS Interrupt 13h hook.

Return Value

This service has no return value.

Uses

EAX, EBX, ECX, EDX, ESI, EDI, and Flags

SHELL Device API Reference

SHELL_Event

```
include shell.inc
VxDcall SHELL_Event
```

The **SHELL_Event** service posts an event in the Windows shell to VMDOSAPP.

Parameters

EBX

Specifies the virtual machine Handle for the event.

ECX

Specifies the event number.

AX

Specifies the wParam parameter for the event. The high 16 bits specify the special boost flags.

ESI

> Points to the callback procedure for the event. If this parameter is zero, no callback procedure is called. See the Comments section for more information about this procedure.

EDX

> Points to reference data for the event callback procedure.

Return Value

The carry flag is clear if the event is placed in the queue. The EAX register contains the handle of the event but only if the ESI parameter is nonzero.

The carry flag is set to indicate an error such as the VMDOSAPP is not present or insufficient memory for placement.

Comments

The system calls the callback procedure with the following input parameters:

EDX   points to reference data

EBP   points to a VMDOSAPP Client_Reg_Struc frame

If the carry flag is clear on entry, the event was processed and the EBP register points to a **Client_Reg_Struc** structure containing the register values after the event returned. If the carry flag is set, the event could not be placed in the queue and only the EDX register contains valid data.

In both case, the EBX register does not contain a virtual machine handle.

Uses

EAX, Flags

SHELL_Get_Version

```
include shell.inc

VxDcall SHELL_Get_Version
```

The **SHELL_Get_Version** service returns the version number for the virtual shell device.

Parameters

This service has no parameters.

Return Value

The AH register contains the major version number.

The AL register contains the minor version number.

The carry flag is clear.

Uses

EAX, Flags

SHELL_GetVMInfo

```
include shell.inc

VxDcall SHELL_GetVMInfo
```

The **SHELL_GetVMInfo** service allows a virtual device to retrieve PIF information settings for a virtual machine.

This service is only available for Windows 3.1 and later.

Parameters

EBX

Specifies the handle of the virtual machine to examine.

Return Value

The EAX register contains one or more of the following flag values for the specified virtual machine:

Value	Meaning
SGVMI_Windowed	Is Windowed
SGVMI_ALTTABdis	Alt+Tab is reserved
SGVMI_ALTESCdis	Alt+Esc is reserved
SGVMI_ALTSPACEdis	Alt+Space is reserved
SGVMI_ALTENTERdis	Alt+Enter is reserved
SGVMI_ALTPRTSCdis	Alt+PrtSc is reserved
SGVMI_PRTSCdis	PrtSc is reserved
SGVMI_CTRLESCdis	Ctrl+Esc is reserved
SGVMI_HasHotKey	Has a shortcut key

SGVMI_Polling	Polling detection Enabled
SGVMI_FastPaste	Allow Fast paste Enabled
SGVMI_NoHMA	No HMA
SGVMI_XMS_Lock	XMS Hands Locked
SGVMI_EMS_Lock	EMS Hands Locked
SGVMI_V86_Lock	V86 Memory Locked
SGVMI_ClsExit	Close on Exit Enabled

The ECX, EDX, ESI, and EDI register contents are reserved.

Comments

The undefined bits in the EAX register are reserved. Do not depend on them being zero.

This service is not valid until after all virtual devices have processed the Create_VM message. This service if called during a Create_VM message will not return proper PIF information.

Uses

EAX, ECX, EDX, ESI, EDI, Flags

SHELL_Message

```
include shell.inc

VxDcall SHELL_Message
```

The **SHELL_Message** service displays a message box using the Windows shell.

Parameters

EBX

Specifies the handle of the virtual machine responsible for the message.

EAX

Specifies the message box flags. See the MB_ symbols in the SHELL.INC file.

ECX

Points to null-terminated string containing the message text.

EDI

Points to null-terminated string containing the caption text. If this parameter is zero, the service uses the standard caption. If this parameter points to an empty string, the message box has no caption.

ESI

Points to the callback procedure to call with response when the message box returns. If this parameter is zero, no callback procedure is called.

EDX

Specifies reference data to pass to the callback procedure.

Return Value

The carry flag is clear and the EAX register contains the handle for the event if the service is successful.

Otherwise, the carry flag is set to indicate an error such as insufficient memory to display the message.

Comments

The system calls the callback procedure after the message box is complete. The callback receives the following input parameters:

```
EAX     ; response code from the message box
EDX     ; points to reference data
```

The response code in the EAX register is one of the ID symbols defined in the SHELL.INC file.

The EBX register may or may not contain the current virtual machine handle when the callback is called. The callback must not rely on its value.

If this service returns an error, a virtual device can use the SHELL_Sysmodal_Message service to force the system to display a message.

Uses

EAX, Flags

SHELL_Resolve_Contention

```
include shell.inc

VxDcall SHELL_Resolve_Contention
```

The **SHELL_Resolve_Contention** service resolves contention for the MS-DOS shell.

Parameters

EAX

Specifies the virtual machine handle of the current device owner.

EBX

Specifies the handle of the contending virtual machine. This parameter must identify the current virtual machine.

ESI

Points to an 8-byte string identifying the name of the device in contention. The name must be in uppercase letters and be padded with spaces if necessary.

Return Value

The EBX register contains the virtual machine handle of contention winner. If the carry flag is set, contention could not be resolved.

Uses

EBX, Flags

SHELL_SYSMODAL_Message

```
include shell.inc

VxDcall SHELL_SYSMODAL_Message
```

The **SHELL_SYSMODAL_Message** service displays system model message box in the Windows shell.

Parameters

EBX

Specifies the handle of the virtual machine responsible for the message.

EAX

Specifies the message box flags. See the MB_ symbols in the SHELL.INC file. The MB_SYSTEMMODAL value must be given.

ECX

Points to null-terminated string containing the message text.

EDI

Points to null-terminated string containing the caption text. If this parameter is zero, the service uses the standard caption. If this parameter points to an empty string, the message box has no caption.

Return Value

The EAX register contains the response code from the message box. It is one of the ID symbols defined in the SHELL.INC file.

Uses

EAX, Flags

V86MMGR API Reference

V86MMGR_Allocate_Buffer

```
include v86mmgr.inc

VxDcall V86MMGR_Allocate_Buffer
```

The **V86MMGR_Allocate_Buffer** service allocates a portion of the current virtual machine's translation buffer and optionally copies data from the protected-mode pointer in FS:ESI registers into the allocated buffer.

Parameters

EBX

Specifies the current virtual machine handle. The current virtual machine must be in protected mode.

EBP

Points to a **Client_Reg_Struc** structure containing the register values of the current virtual machine.

ECX

Specifies the number of bytes to allocate.

FS:ESI

Specifies a pointer to the extended memory to copy. If the carry flag is set, the service copies the source buffer into a V86 buffer; otherwise, it copies the source buffer into V86 memory.

Return Value

The carry flag is clear if the service is successful. The ECX register contains the actual number of bytes allocated (less than or equal to the original ECX parameter). The high word of the EDI register contains the V86 segment for the translation buffer and the low word of the EDI register contains the offset of the allocated buffer.

If the carry flag is set, the service could not allocate buffer.

Comments

This service maps fewer bytes than the value specified in the ECX parameter if the length of the buffer would extend past the FS segment limit. Therefore, a virtual device needs to preserve the value returned in ECX from this service to use when deallocating the buffer using the **V86MMGR_Free_Buffer** service.

The buffers are maintained as a stack. Therefore, the last buffer allocated must be the first buffer freed.

Uses

ECX, EDI, Flags

V86MMGR_Allocate_V86_Pages

```
include v86mmgr.inc

VxDcall V86MMGR_Allocate_V86_Pages
```

The **V86MMGR_Allocate_V86_Pages** service allocates and maps the base V86 memory for a virtual machine.

Parameters

EBX

Specifies the virtual machine handle.

ESI

Specifies the desired size of virtual machine address space in kilobytes.

EDI

> Specifies the minimum size of virtual machine address space in kilobytes.

ECX

> Specifies the flags. See the V86MMGR.INC file for bit definitions.

Return Value

The carry flag is clear if the service allocates memory and maps it into the virtual machine. The EAX register contains the actual number of pages allocated and mapped (that is, the size of the virtual machine). This size does not include the space from 0 to the first virtual machine page.

If the carry flag is set, the service could not allocate memory.

Comments

On an error, this service calls the **GetSetDetailedVMError** service to set an error value.

The sizes specified by the ESI and EDI parameters include the region of V86 address space from 0 through the first virtual machine page.

Uses

EAX, Flags

V86MMGR_Free_Buffer

```
include v86mmgr.inc

VxDcall V86MMGR_Free_Buffer
```

The **V86MMGR_Free_Buffer** service deallocates a buffer that was allocated by the **V86MMGR_Allocate_Buffer** service. It will optionally copy data from the translation buffer to the buffer pointed to by FS:ESI.

The buffers are maintained as a stack. Therefore, the last buffer allocated must be the first buffer freed.

Parameters

EBX

> Specifies the current virtual machine handle. The current virtual machine must be in protected mode.

EBP

> Points to a **Client_Reg_Struc** structure containing the register values of the current virtual machine.

ECX

> Specifies the number of bytes to free (returned from the **V86MMGR_Allocate_Buffer** service).

FS:ESI

> Specifies a pointer to an extended memory buffer. If the carry flag is set, the service copies the buffer from V86 memory; otherwise, it does not copy the buffer.

Return Value

This service has no return value.

Uses

Flags

V86MMGR_Free_Page_Map_Region

```
include v86mmgr.inc

VxDcall V86MMGR_Free_Page_Map_Region
```

The **V86MMGR_Free_Page_Map_Region** service unmap pages that were mapped by the **V86MMGR_Map_Pages** service.

Parameters

ESI

> Specifies the map handle to free.

Return Value

This service has no return value.

Comments

After a call to this service, the old map buffer address contains null memory is invalid and the ESI register is undefined.

Uses

ESI, Flags

V86MMGR_Get_EMS_XMS_Limits

```
include v86mmgr.inc

VxDcall V86MMGR_Get_EMS_XMS_Limits
```

The **V86MMGR_Get_EMS_XMS_Limits** service returns the current EMS and XMS limits.

Parameters

EBX

Specifies the virtual machine handle to get limits of.

Return Value

The following registers contain values:

Register	Description
EAX	Minimum EMS kilobytes (multiple of 4)
EDX	Maximum EMS kilobytes (multiple of 4)
ESI	Minimum XMS kilobytes (multiple of 4)
EDI	Maximum XMS kilobytes (multiple of 4)
ECX	Access to HMA is disabled (if zero) or enabled (if 1).

Uses

All registers except EBX, EBP, and segment registers

V86MMGR_Get_Mapping_Info

```
include v86mmgr.inc

VxDcall V86MMGR_Get_Mapping_Info
```

The **V86MMGR_Get_Mapping_Info** service returns information about the current page mapping areas.

Parameters

This service has no parameters.

Return Value

The CH register contains the total number of pages reserved for global mapping and the CL register contains the number of pages available (not in use) for global mapping.

Uses

ECX, Flags

V86MMGR_Get_Version

```
include v86mmgr.inc

VxDcall V86MMGR_Get_Version
```

The **V86MMGR_Get_Version** service returns the V86MMGR version number.

Parameters

This service has no parameters.

Return Value

The AH register contains the major version number.

The AL register contains the minor version number.

The carry flag is clear.

Uses

EAX, Flags

V86MMGR_Get_VM_Flat_Sel

```
include v86mmgr.inc

VxDcall V86MMGR_Get_VM_Flat_Sel
```

The **V86MMGR_Get_VM_Flat_Sel** service returns a selector that points to the base of the specified virtual machine's V86 address space. This is useful for 32-bit applications since this selector can be used to point to any address in the virtual machine's V86 address space. The selector is writable and has a limit of 11000h bytes so that the high memory area is also addressable.

The selector returned is in the specified virtual machine's LDT. Therefore, the selector is only valid to use when the virtual machine is running (is the current virtual machine).

Parameters

EBX

Specifies a virtual machine handle (any virtual machine handle is valid).

Return Value

The EAX register contains a selector with the base at the high linear address of V86 memory (the high word is zero).

Uses

EAX, Flags

V86MMGR_Get_Xlat_Buff_State

```
include v86mmgr.inc

VxDcall V86MMGR_Get_Xlat_Buff_State
```

The **V86MMGR_Get_Xlat_Buff_State** service returns information about the current mapping buffer status.

Always call this service to find the segment of the translation buffer. Since the buffer can move at any time a virtual device should never make any assumptions about the size or location of the buffer.

Parameters

EBX

Specifies the virtual machine handle.

Return Value

The EAX register contains the V86 segment of the translation buffer; the high word is zero.

The ECX register contains the number of bytes of the buffer not in use.

The EDX register contains the total size of the buffer in bytes; the maximum size is 10000h.

Uses

EAX, ECX, EDX, Flags

V86MMGR_GetPgStatus

```
include v86mmgr.inc

VxDcall V86MMGR_GetPgStatus
```

The **V86MMGR_GetPgStatus** service returns the status of a page. This service allows the caller to discover various aspects of what a specific page is being used for. This service can be called with any page number in the 0 through 110h range, but it is intended to return useful information only for pages above the last V86 page.

This service is only available for Windows 3.1 and later.

Parameters

EBX

Specifies the virtual machine handle to get information for. If this parameter is zero, the service retrieves global information.

ECX

Specifies the V86 page number. It must be in the rage 0 through 110h.

Return Value

The EAX register contains one or more of the following information values for the page:

Value	Meaning
V86PS_MAP	Page belongs to mapper
V86PS_XMS	Page belongs to XMS driver
V86PS_EMM	Page belongs to EMM driver
V86PS_UMB	Page is part of a UMB

The V86PS_XMS value is not necessarily set.

Comments

One particular use of this service is to determine if a page is part of an imported high memory UMB.

This service will not work if called during the Sys_Critical_Init message. The service is not valid until the Device_Init message. Calls during Device_Init only return useful information if paging import from a LIMulator/UMBulator is performed. In cases where no paging import exists, the information will not be correct until after the Init_Complete message.

Uses

EAX, Flags

V86MMGR_Load_Client_Ptr

```
include v86mmgr.inc
VxDcall V86MMGR_Load_Client_Ptr
```

The **V86MMGR_Load_Client_Ptr** service loads the FS:ESI register with the specified client segment and offset values. If the virtual machine is running a 16-bit protected mode application, the high word of the offset in ESI is set to zero. Otherwise, if the virtual machine is running a 32-bit program or is in VxD_Exec_Mode, the high word of ESI is not set to zeroed.

This allows most translation procedures to operate correctly without the need to test the execution mode of the current virtual machine.

Parameters

AH

> Specifies a client segment register.

AL

> Specifies a client offset register.

EBX

> Specifies the current virtual machine handle. The virtual machine must be in protected mode.

EBP

> Points to a **Client_Reg_Struc** structure containing the register values for the virtual machine.

Return Value

The FS:ESI register pair points to the client's buffer.

Example

The value passed in AX should be formed from the **Client_Reg_Struc** structure fields. For example, to load the virtual machine's DS:(E)DX, use the following code:

```
mov ax, (Client_DS * 100h) + Client_DX
VxDcall V86MMGR_Load_Client_Ptr
```

Uses

FS, ESI, Flags

V86MMGR_LocalGlobalReg

```
include v86mmgr.inc

VxDcall V86MMGR_LocalGlobalReg
```

The **V86MMGR_LocalGlobalReg** service specifies whether the indicated V86 memory region is local or global memory. This VMM memory manager calls this service whenever the **TestGlobalV86Mem** service is called.

This service is only available for Windows 3.1 and later.

Parameters

EDX

Specifies the page number of the start of the region.

EDI

Specifies the page number of the end of the region.

Return Value

The EAX register contains one of the following values:

Value	Meaning
0	Page range is local
1	Page range is global
2	Page range is partially global and partially local
3	Page range is unknown

Comments

This service is intended to support UMBs. UMB regions are local or global depending on the free per virtual machine UMB list.

Uses

EAX, Flags

V86MMGR_Map_Pages

```
include v86mmgr.inc

VxDcall V86MMGR_Map_Pages
```

The **V86MMGR_Map_Pages** service maps the specified buffer into every virtual machine at the same address using page mapping. If the contents of memory are changed in one virtual machine the change will be reflected in the original buffer as well in all other virtual machines.

If the address specified in ESI is zero, no memory is mapped, but a global linear address range is allocated. It is then up to the caller to map appropriate pages into virtual machines. Use the linear address returned in EDI for the base page to map memory into.

Parameters

ESI

Points to the linear address to map. If this parameter is zero, the service reserves the map region without mapping memory.

ECX

Specifies the number of bytes to map.

Return Value

If the carry flag is clear, the memory is mapped. The ESI register contains the map handle (used to free the map region), and the EDI register contains the linear address of map buffer. It is less than 1 megabyte.

If the carry flag is set, the service could not map the memory.

Uses

ESI, EDI, Flags

V86MMGR_NoUMBInitCalls

```
include v86mmgr.inc

VxDcall V86MMGR_NoUMBInitCalls
```

The **V86MMGR_NoUMBInitCalls** service supports QEMM version 5.x. This service is called by the VMM before the SyS_Critical_Init message is done, and allows the XMSUMBINITCALLS=FALSE setting in the SYSTEM.INI file.

This service is only available for Windows 3.1 and later.

Parameters

This service has no parameters.

Return Value

This service has no return value.

V86MMGR_ResetBasePages

```
include v86mmgr.inc

VxDcall V86MMGR_ResetBasePages
```

The **V86MMGR_ResetBasePages** service is used by the virtual MS-DOS manager to manipulate MS-DOS related memory associated with the base memory handle of a virtual machine.

Parameters

EBX

Specifies the virtual machine handle.

ECX

Specifies the count of pages to manipulate.

EAX

Specifies the Linear or physical page number of first page to manipulate.

Return Value

If carry flag is set if the service could not manipulate the base handle.

Uses

Flags

V86MMGR_Set_EMS_XMS_Limits

```
include v86mmgr.inc

VxDcall V86MMGR_Set_EMS_XMS_Limits
```

The **V86MMGR_Set_EMS_XMS_Limits** service sets the EMS and XMS memory limits for a virtual machine. This service must be made during the Create_VM message for it to work properly. This service should not be called on the system virtual machine.

Parameters

EBX

Specifies the handle of the virtual machine to set limits for.

EAX

Specifies minimum EMS kilobytes.

EDX

Specifies the maximum EMS kilobytes.

ESI

Specifies the minimum XMS kilobytes.

EDI

Specifies the maximum XMS kilobytes.

ECX

Specifies the flag. See the V86MMGR.INC file for flag definitions.

Return Value

If carry flag is set, the service could not set limits or there was insufficient memory for the minimum allocation request. In this case, some of the limits may have been set. Use the **V86MMGR_Get_EMS_XMS_Limits** service to determine the new settings.

Comments

This service calls the **GetSetDetailedVMError** service to set error values.

To disable access to XMS or EMS memory, set maximum and minimum values to zero.

To set only one of the two limits, set the other maximum and minimum to -1.

The XMS limit does not include the HMA.

Uses

Flags

V86MMGR_Set_Mapping_Info

```
include v86mmgr.inc

VxDcall V86MMGR_Set_Mapping_Info
```

The **V86MMGR_Set_Mapping_Info** service notifies the V86MMGR mapper services of the amount of space a virtual device requires for calls to the mapper service calls. This service must be made during the Sys_Critical_Init or Device_Init message for devices with an init order less than V86MMGR_Init_Order. These settings are used by during the V86MMGR Device_Init message.

Parameters

AL

Specifies the minimum number of pages (4K) required for copy buffer.

AH

Specifies the maximum number of pages (4K) desired for copy buffer.

BL

Specifies the minimum number of pages required for private global mapping region.

BH

Specifies the minimum number of pages required for shared global mapping region.

CL

Specifies the maximum number of pages desired for global page mapping region.

Return Value

This service has no return value.

Uses

Flags

V86MMGR_Set_Xlat_Buff_State

```
include v86mmgr.inc

VxDcall V86MMGR_Set_Xlat_Buff_State
```

The **V86MMGR_Set_Xlat_Buff_State** service switches to an alternate mapping buffer. This feature is provided for protected-mode TSR programs which may need to switch to a private translation buffer before executing protected mode MS-DOS calls since the default buffer may be full.

A virtual device should get the current translation buffer state, set the new state, perform any MS-DOS call, and then set the state back to the original values.

Parameters

EBX

Specifies a virtual machine handle (any virtual machine handle valid).

EAX

Specifies the V86 segment of the translation buffer; high word is zero.

ECX

Specifies the number of bytes of the buffer not in use.

EDX

Specifies the total size of the buffer in bytes; maximum size is 10000h.

Return Value

This service has no return value.

Uses

Flags

V86MMGR_SetAvailMapPgs

```
include v86mmgr.inc

VxDcall V86MMGR_SetAvailMapPgs
```

The **V86MMGR_SetAvailMapPgs** service relinquishes regions above the last V86 page to the V86MMGR's mapper services for use as a mapper region.

This service is only available for Windows 3.1 and later.

Parameters

EAX

Specifies the starting page number of the region.

ECX

Specifies the size of the region in pages.

Return Value

The carry flag is clear if the service adds the region. Otherwise, the carry flag is set to indicate an error such as an invalid region.

Comments

Virtuals devices other than the V86MMGR (DOSMGR) can relinquish regions above the last V86 page to the V86MMGR's mapper services for use as a mapper region. These regions usually overlap with V86MMGR XMS UMB import pages, but this is not required. A virtual device can hand over a page that it has already marked as owned by the device in the Device_V86_Pages array. The V86MMGR marks the page as one it owns (even though it did not actually do the **_Assign_Device_V86_Pages** for it).

Once a region is relinquished, the virtual device must not attempt to access it. it. These regions may only be marked as in-use by the V86MMGR XMS driver. This happens when the region overlaps XMS UMB import pages.

This routine has a global effect, it does not take a virtual machine handle argument.

Uses

Flags

V86MMGR_SetLocalA20

```
include v86mmgr.inc

VxDcall V86MMGR_SetLocalA20
```

The **V86MMGR_SetLocalA20** service changes the default global behavior of A20 to local if the HMA is global. This service has no effect if the HMA is not global.

This service is only available for Windows 3.1 and later.

Parameters

This service has no parameters.

Return Value

This service has no return value.

Comments

When there is a global HMA user, the A20 state associated with the HMA is also global. Changing A20 in a virtual machine changes it in all virtual machines simultaneously. Some global A20 users (such as MS-DOS 5.0) desire that the A20 state be local even though the HMA is global.

The V86MMGR device does a V86 Interrupt 2Fh device broadcast which also can set this state. This service is effectively a duplicate of the broadcast service which can be called by a virtual device. It is not an error if the state is set using both methods.

Uses

Flags

V86MMGR_Xlat_API

```
include v86mmgr.inc

VxDcall V86MMGR_Xlat_API
```

The **V86MMGR_Xlat_API** service is a simple interpreter that executes scripts that are created using macros defined in the V86MMGR.INC file.

Parameters

EBX

Specifies the current virtual machine handle.

EBP

Points to a **Client_Reg_Struc** structure containing the register values for the virtual machine.

EDX

Points to the script to translate.

Return Value

The carry flag is clear if the script has executed successfully; the EDX register is destroyed.

If the carry flag is set, the service encountered an error while executing a script.

Uses

EDX, Flags

VCD API Reference

VCD_Get_Focus

```
include vcd.inc
VxDcall VCD_Get_Focus
```

The **VCD_Get_Focus** service returns the virtual machine handle of the current owner of a COM port. Focus can be set with a **Set_Device_Focus** control message sent using the **System_Control** service and specifying the VCD device.

Parameters

EAX

Specifies the hardware COM port number. It must be in the range 1 to 4.

Return Value

If the carry flag is clear, the EBX register contains virtual machine handle or zero if there is no owner.

The carry flag is set if the port is not available.

Uses

EBX, Flags

VCD_Get_Version

```
include vcd.inc
VxDcall VCD_Get_Version
```

The **VCD_Get_Version** service returns the VCD version number.

Parameters

This service has no parameters.

Return Value

If the carry flag is clear, the EAX register contains the version number. Otherwise, the VCD is not installed and VCD pages are not allocated.

Uses

EAX, Flags

VCD_Set_Port_Global

```
include vcd.inc
VxDcall VCD_Set_Port_Global
```

The **VCD_Set_Port_Global** service enables or disables the global handling of a COM port between multiple virtual machines. When a port is declared to be a global port, then no contention detection is performed, and no I/O ports are trapped.

This service is provided mainly for a COM port mouse, or other serial device, where a separate virtual device handles the arbitration of the port and its interrupts. A **Set_Device_Focus** control message sent using the **System_Control** service can specify which virtual machine should receive interrupt requests and **VCD_Get_Focus** returns the current owner of a port.

Parameters

EAX

Specifies the hardware COM port number. It must be in the range from 1 to 4.

EDX

Specifies whether the port is global (zero) or local (nonzero).

Return Value

The carry flag is clear if the service is successful. Otherwise, the carry flag is set if the port is not available.

Uses

Flags

VCD_Virtualize_Port

```
include vcd.inc
VxDcall VCD_Virtualize_Port
```

The **VCD_Virtualize_Port** service virtualizes a COM port. This service allows additional
virtual devices to provide enhanced capabilities to COM port virtualization. An example
virtual device is one which buffers high speed input data, and then simulates interrupts
into the owner virtual machine, at a slower rate, so that the virtual machine can keep up
with the data without losing input.

This service can only be called during processing of the **Sys_Critical_Init** message.

Parameters

EAX

Specifies the port number (1, 2, 3, or 4).

EBX

Specifies the operation flags. It is 00000001h if the IRQ is sharable. All other values
are reserved.

ECX

Specifies the number of extra bytes needed in the **VCD_COM_Struc** structure.

EDX

Specifies the number of extra bytes needed in the **VCD_CB_Struc** structure.

ESI

Points to the **VCD_ProcList_Struc** a structure which contains a list of callback
procedures. The VCD saves the pointer to this structure, so it must be placed in the
VxD_DATA_SEG segment.

Return Value

If the carry is clear, the port can be virtualized and the EAX register contains the COM
handle which points to the COM structure having the extra data allocated at its end.

Otherwise, the carry flag is set if the port is not available and the EAX register contains
one of the following values:

Value	Meaning
0	Port does not exist
1	Port already virtualized

Comments

Callback procedures are provided in the list pointed to by ESI.

The **VPS_Control_Proc** callback is called when the virtualization state changes for a COM port. Currently the only call is for ownership changes.

EAX   VCD_Control_Set_Owner

EBX   virtual machine handle of new owner or 0,if virtualization handled by a different device

EDX   virtual machine handle of previous owner or 0

ESI   points to a VCD_COM_Struc

On entry, when the EBX register specifies a new owner, port trapping will be enabled for all I/O ports of the COM adapter. The control procedure can disable any I/O trapping that it desires.

The IRQ virtualization procedures are the same as if the virtual device virtualized the IRQ directly using the VPICD, except that ESI points to the VCD_COM_Struc structure on entry. See the VPICD documentation for actual entry parameters and return values.

EAX   IRQ handle

EBX   virtual machine handle

ESI   points to a VCD_COM_Struc

The following callbacks have default actions, if the callback offset is set to 0:

Callback	Default Action
VPS_Hw_Int_Proc	Assign an owner to the current virtual machine if not owned, and request an interrupt in the owner's virtual machine.
VPS_Virt_Int_Proc	Not virtualized.
VPS_EOI_Proc	Physically EOI and clear interrupt request.
VPS_Mask_Change_Proc	Assign the owner to the current virtual machine if not owned.
VPS_IRET_Proc	Not virtualized.

The following callbacks deal with I/O for ports that have trapping enabled while the virtualizing virtual device owns a COM port.

- VPS_In_RxTxB

- VPS_Out_RxTxB

- VPS_In_IER

- VPS_Out_IER

- VPS_In_IIR

- VPS_Out_IIR

- VPS_In_LCR

- VPS_Out_LCR

- VPS_In_MCR

- VPS_Out_MCR

- VPS_In_LSR

- VPS_Out_LSR

- VPS_In_MSR

- VPS_Out_MSR

These callbacks have the following parameters:

EBX   virtual machine handle

ESI   points to a VCD_COM_Struc

EDX   port number

ECX   Byte_Input or Byte_Output value

AL   output data if ECX is Byte_Output

These procedures should return the AL register set to the input data if the ECX register is equal to the Byte_Input value.

Uses

EAX, Flags

VDD API Reference

VDD_Clear_Mod

```
include vdd.inc
VxDcall VDD_Clear_Mod
```

The **VDD_Clear_Mod** service clears the change state of a virtual machine.

Parameters

EDX

Specifies the system virtual machine handle.

EBX

Specifies the handle of the virtual machine to clear the change state for.

EDI

Specifies the VDD control block pointer.

EBP

Points to the **Client_Reg_Struc** structure for the virtual machine.

Client_EBX

Specifies the virtual machine handle.

Return Value

The carry flag is set if an invalid virtual machine handle is specified. Otherwise, this service has no return value.

Comments

This service allows proper text scrolling if an application runs between calls to the **VDD_Get_Mod** and **VDD_Clear_Mod** services.

This service assumes that **VDD_Clear_Mod** is called twice when the VDD sends a scroll event to 386 enhanced mode grabber; once in the **TextScroll** function and again in the **UpdateScreen** function.

If an application has accessed pages since the last call to the **VDD_Get_Mod** service and there is a scroll event generated in the previous **VDD_Get_Mod**, the service sets the *fVDD_UpdAll1Bit* value in *VDD_Flags* and transfers main memory to copy memory. The **VDD_Clear_Mod** service clears the *fVDD_UpdAll1Bit* value and sets *fVDD_UpdAll2Bit*. The **VDD_State_Query** service returns changes if *fVDD_UpdAll2Bit* is set. Since *fVDD_UpdAll2Bit* is set, the **VDD_Mod_Text** service returns the entire screen changed (no scrolls) and the **VDD_Clear_Mod** service clears the *fVDD_UpdAll2Bit* value and updates the copy memory.

If application accessed pages since the last **VDD_Get_Mod** and there was no scroll event in the previous **VDD_Get_Mod**, the copy memory is not updated.

Uses

Flags

VDD_Free_Grab

```
include vdd.inc
VxDcall VDD_Free_Grab
```

The **VDD_Free_Grab** service releases the copy of the video memory that was allocated when a screen grab was done.

Parameters

EDX

Specifies the system virtual machine handle.

EBX

Specifies the handle of the virtual machine to release the memory for.

EDI

Specifies the VDD control block pointer.

EBP

Points to the **Client_Reg_Struc** structure for the virtual machine.

Client_EBX

Specifies the virtual machine handle.

Return Value

This service has no return value.

Uses

Flags

VDD_Free_Mem

```
include vdd.inc
VxDcall VDD_Free_Mem
```

The **VDD_Free_Mem** service releases the scheduling freeze caused by a previous call to the **VDD_Get_Mem** service.

Parameters

EDX

Specifies the system virtual machine handle.

EBX

Specifies the handle of the virtual machine to release the freeze for.

EDI

Specifies the VDD control block pointer.

EBP

Points to the **Client_Reg_Struc** structure for the virtual machine.

Client_EBX

Specifies the virtual machine handle.

Return Value

The carry flag is set if an invalid virtual machine handle is specified. Otherwise, this service has no return value.

Uses

Flags

See Also

VDD_Get_Mem

VDD_Get_GrabRtn

```
include vdd.inc
VxDcall VDD_Get_GrabRtn
```

The **VDD_Get_GrabRtn** service returns address of video grab routine. The grab routine is called by the virtual shell device when the appropriate hot key is pressed by the user. It makes a copy of the visible screen and controller state of the current virtual machine. The copy is accessible using the **VDD_Get_GrbState** and **VDD_Get_GrbMem** services.

Parameters

This service has no parameters.

Return Value

The ESI register contains the address of the grab routine.

Uses

Flags, ESI

See Also

VDD_Get_GrbMem, **VDD_Get_GrbState**

VDD_Get_GrbMem

```
include vdd.inc
VxDcall VDD_Get_GrbMem
```

The **VDD_Get_GrbMem** service return the flat address and allocation bitmap for virtual machine's video memory. This service returns the address of the copy of the memory that was made by the grab routine.

Parameters

EDX

Specifies the system virtual machine handle.

EBX

Specifies the handle of the virtual machine to retrieve the memory for.

EDI

Specifies the VDD control block pointer.

EBP

Points to the **Client_Reg_Struc** structure for the virtual machine.

Client_EBX

Specifies the virtual machine handle.

Client_ES

> Specifies the selector identifying the segment containing the buffer to receive the **VDA_Mem_State**.

Client_EDI

> Specifies the address of the buffer to receive the **VDA_Mem_State**.

Client_CX

> Specifies the size of the buffer to hold the **VDA_Mem_State**. This is for debugging only.

Return Value

The **Client_CX** register contains the number of bytes copied to the buffer. Otherwise, it is zero to indicate an error such as the buffer is too small, an invalid selector, or a call to **VDD_Get_GrbMem** when no grab is active.

Comments

The allocation of memory to the bitmap is dynamic. The grabber must call this service each time it accesses the memory.

Uses

Flags

VDD_Get_GrbState

```
include vdd.inc
VxDcall VDD_Get_GrbState
```

The **VDD_Get_GrbState** service returns the state of the video adapter for the specified virtual machine at the point when the **VDD_GrabRtn** was called.

This service is called by the 386 enhanced mode grabber.

Parameters

EDX

> Specifies the system virtual machine handle.

EBX

> Specifies the handle of the virtual machine to retrieve the state for.

EDI

    Specifies the VDD control block pointer.

EBP

    Points to the **Client_Reg_Struc** structure for the virtual machine.

Client_EBX

    Specifies the virtual machine handle.

Client_ES

    Specifies the selector identifying the segment containing the buffer to receive the state.

Client_EDI

    Specifies the address of the buffer to receive the state.

Client_CX

    Specifies the size of the buffer to hold the state. This is for debugging only.

Return Value

The **Client_CX** register contains the size of the structure returned by the service (for debugging only). The service returns zero to indicate an error.

Comments

This service returns a video state structure. See the VDD.INC file for the structure definition.

Uses

Flags, Client_CX

VDD_Get_Mem

```
include vdd.inc
VxDcall VDD_Get_Mem
```

The **VDD_Get_Mem** service returns the flat address and allocation bitmap for the specified virtual machine's video memory. This service returns the main video-save memory and boosts the scheduling priority of the system virtual machine.

Parameters

EDX

    Specifies the system virtual machine handle.

EBX

Specifies the handle of the virtual machine to retrieve the memory for.

EDI

Specifies the VDD control block pointer.

EBP

Points to the **Client_Reg_Struc** structure for the virtual machine.

Client_EBX

Specifies the virtual machine handle.

Client_ES

Specifies the selector identifying the segment containing the buffer to receive the **VDA_Mem_State**.

Client_EDI

Specifies the address of the buffer to receive the **VDA_Mem_State**.

Client_CX

Specifies the size of the buffer to hold the **VDA_Mem_State**. This is for debugging only.

Return Value

The Client_CX register contains the number of bytes copied to the buffer. Otherwise, it is zero to indicate an error such as the buffer is too small or an invalid selector.

Comments

To prevent memory from changing between calls to the **VDD_Get_Mem** and **VDD_Free_Mem** services, this service boosts the system virtual machine's priority using the *Low_Priority_Device_Boost* value. This inhibits normal scheduling but does not hamper scheduling of virtual machine's to handle events such as interrupts.

The allocation of memory to the bitmap is dynamic. The grabber must call this service each time it accesses the memory.

A call to the **VDD_Get_Mem** service must be followed by a call to the **VDD_Free_Mem** service as soon as possible. No other virtual machine will be scheduled until the call to **VDD_Free_Mem** is made.

Uses

Flags

VDD_Get_Mod

```
include vdd.inc
VxDcall VDD_Get_Mod
```

The **VDD_Get_Mod** service returns changes in a virtual machine's video state. The changes are passed to the grabber in a buffer that includes a flag indicating what kind of changes occurred and what type of a memory change list follows. The flag is followed by a count of memory-change-list entries and the change list itself.

This service returns cumulative changes until the **VDD_Clear_Mod** service is called.

Parameters

EDX

Specifies the system virtual machine handle.

EBX

Specifies the handle of the virtual machine to retrieve the change list for.

EDI

Specifies the VDD control block pointer.

EBP

Points to the **Client_Reg_Struc** structure for the virtual machine.

Client_EBX

Specifies the virtual machine handle.

Client_ES

Specifies the selector identifying the segment containing the buffer to receive the change list.

Client_EDI

Specifies the address of the buffer to receive the change list.

Client_CX

Specifies the size of the buffer to receive the change list. This is for debugging only.

Return Value

The Client_CX register contains the size of structure returned by the service (for debugging only). The service returns zero to indicate an error.

Uses

Flags, Client_CX

VDD_Get_ModTime

```
include vdd.inc
VxDcall VDD_Get_ModTime
```

The **VDD_Get_ModTime** service specifies whether any video activity has occurred. The virtual poll device uses it to determine if the virtual machine is idle.

Parameters

EBX

Specifies the virtual machine handle.

Return Value

The EAX register contains the system time at last video modification.

Uses

Flags, EAX

VDD_Get_State

```
include vdd.inc
VxDcall VDD_Get_State
```

The **VDD_Get_State** service returns the current state of the virtual machine. This service should be called after a call to the **VDD_Get_Mem** service buts before calling the **VDD_Free_Mem** service.

This service is called by the grabber.

Parameters

EDX

Specifies the system virtual machine handle.

EBX

Specifies the handle of the virtual machine to retrieve the change list for.

EDI

Specifies the VDD control block pointer.

EBP

Points to the Client_Reg_Struc structure for the virtual machine.

Client_EBX

Specifies the virtual machine handle.

Client_ES

Specifies the selector identifying the segment containing the buffer to receive the state.

Client_EDI

Specifies the address of the buffer to receive the state.

Client_CX

Specifies the size of the buffer to receive the state. This is for debugging only.

Return Value

The Client_CX register contains the size of structure returned by the service (for debugging only). The service returns zero to indicate an error.

Comments

This service returns a video state structure. See the VDD.INC file for the structure definition.

Uses

Flags, Client_CX

VDD_Get_Version

```
include vdd.inc
VxDcall VDD_Get_Version
```

The **VDD_Get_Version** service returns the VDD version number and device identifier.

Parameters

This service has no parameters.

Return Value

The AH register contains the major version number.

The AL register contains the minor version number.

The ESI register contains the address of the 8-byte identifier string for the VDD.

Uses

Flags, AX, ESI

VDD_Hide_Cursor

```
include vdd.inc
VxDcall VDD_Hide_Cursor
```

The **VDD_Hide_Cursor** service sets or clears the hide-cursor flag. The virtual mouse device uses this service to turn on and off the hardware cursor such as when the virtual machine is windowed.

Parameters

EAX

Specifies whether the cursor should be hidden (nonzero) or displayed (zero).

EBX

Specifies a pointer to the control block.

Return Value

This service has no return value.

Uses

Flags

VDD_Msg_BakColor

```
include vdd.inc
VxDcall VDD_Msg_BakColor
```

The **VDD_Msg_BakColor** service sets up the background attribute for messages displayed when in message mode.

Parameters

EAX

Specifies the color. For EGA/VGA driver, this parameter is a text mode attribute.

EBX

Specifies the virtual machine handle.

Return Value

This service has no return value.

Comments

A virtual device that uses this service must issue a **Begin_Message_Mode** control message before calling this service.

Uses

Flags

VDD_Msg_ClrScrn

```
include vdd.inc
VxDcall VDD_Msg_ClrScrn
```

The **VDD_Msg_ClrScrn** service initializes the screen for messages displayed when in message mode. If the focus virtual machine is the current virtual machine, this service clears the screen immediately. Otherwise, it initializes the screen when the focus changes.

The virtual shell device uses this service.

Parameters

EBX

Specifies the virtual machine handle.

EAX

Specifies the background attribute.

Return Value

The EAX register contains the width in columns.

The EDX register contains the height in rows.

Comments

A virtual device that uses this service must issue a **Begin_Message_Mode** control message before calling this service.

Uses

Flags, EAX, EDX

VDD_Msg_ForColor

```
include vdd.inc
VxDcall VDD_Msg_ForColor
```

The **VDD_Msg_ForColor** service sets the foreground attribute for messages displayed when in message mode.

Parameters

EAX

Specifies the color. For EGA/VGA drivers, this parameter is a text mode attribute.

EBX

Specifies the virtual machine handle.

Return Value

This service has no return value.

Comments

A virtual device that uses this service must issue a **Begin_Message_Mode** control message before calling this service.

Uses

Flags

VDD_Msg_SetCursPos

```
include vdd.inc
VxDcall VDD_Msg_SetCursPos
```

The **VDD_Msg_SetCursPos** service sets the cursor position for messages displayed when in message mode.

Parameters

EAX

Specifies the row position.

EDX

Specifies the column position.

EBX

Specifies the virtual machine handle.

Return Value

This service has no return value.

Comments

A virtual device that uses this service must issue a **Begin_Message_Mode** control message before calling this service.

Uses

Flags

VDD_Msg_TextOut

```
include vdd.inc
VxDcall VDD_Msg_TextOut
```

The **VDD_Msg_TextOut** service writes the specified text to the screen using the foreground and background colors specified by the **VDD_Msg_BakColor** and **VDD_Msg_ForColor** services.

Parameters

ESI

Specifies the address of the string to display.

ECX

Specifies the length in bytes of the string.

EAX

Specifies the row position for the start of the displayed string.

EDX

> Specifies the column position for the start of the displayed string.

EBX

> Specifies the virtual machine handle

Return Value

This service has no return value.

Comments

A virtual device that uses this service must issue a **Begin_Message_Mode** control message before calling this service.

Uses

Flags

See Also

VDD_Msg_BakColor, **VDD_Msg_ForColor**

VDD_PIF_State

```
include vdd.inc
VxDcall VDD_PIF_State
```

The **VDD_PIF_State** service informs the VDD about PIF bits for virtual machine just created.

Parameters

EBX

> Specifies the virtual machine handle.

AX

> Specifies the PIF bits.

Return Value

This service has no return value.

Uses

Flags

VDD_Query_Access

```
include vdd.inc
VxDcall VDD_Query_Access
```

The **VDD_Query_Access** service specifies whether video memory can be accessed. Virtual devices that call software in the virtual machine use this service to determine whether a video display error will occur if the software attempts to access video memory.

Parameters

EBX

    Specifies the address of the control block.

Return Value

The carry flag is clear if a virtual device can access video memory.

Comments

The virtual device should call this service just before returning to the virtual machine such as while processing a virtual machine event. If the video memory cannot be accessed, the virtual device should avoid calling software that may attempt access even if not calling the software causes another error, such as leaving the mouse cursor on when the virtual machine runs in a window.

Uses

Flags

VDD_Set_HCurTrk

```
include vdd.inc
VxDcall VDD_Set_HCurTrk
```

The **VDD_Set_HCurTrk** service sets the flag passed to VMDOSAPP indicating that VMDOSAPP should maintain cursor position within display window for this application. The keyboard driver calls this service when a keyboard interrupt is simulated into a virtual machine.

Parameters

EBX

    Specifies the virtual machine handle.

Return Value

This service has no return value.

Uses

Flags

VDD_Set_VMType

```
include vdd.inc
VxDcall VDD_Set_VMType
```

The **VDD_Set_VMType** service informs the VDD of a virtual machine's type. The system calls this service prior to running the virtual machine and each time any of the virtual machine parameters are modified.

Parameters

EAX

Specifies the state flag. This parameter is nonzero if the virtual machine is running in a window.

EBX

Specifies the virtual machine handle. This handle can be used to examine the virtual machine status flags such as the exclusive and background flags.

Return Value

This service has no return value.

Comments

For a system critical Set_Focus this service may not be called before the Set_Focus. In that case, the VDD is responsible for doing an implied call to the **VDD_Set_VMType** service.

Uses

Flags

VDD_Unlock_APP

```
include vdd.inc

VxDcall VDD_Unlock_APP
```

The **VDD_Unlock_APP** service unlocks the Windowed OLDAPP from the grabber.

This service is also called from the **VDD_Free_Mem** service.

Parameters

EDX

Specifies the system virtual machine handle.

EBX

Specifies the handle of the virtual machine running the application to unlock.

EDI

Specifies the VDD control block pointer.

EBP

Points to the Client_Reg_Struc structure for the virtual machine.

Client_EBX

Specifies the virtual machine handle.

Return Value

This service has no return value.

Uses

EAX, Flags

VDMAD API Reference

VDMAD_Copy_From_Buffer

```
include vdmad.inc

VxDcall VDMAD_Copy_From_Buffer
```

The **VDMAD_Copy_From_Buffer** service allows another device to copy data from the VDMAD buffer to the actual DMA region associated with the buffer. This service is called after the **VDMAD_Request_Buffer** service, after a memory write transfer and before the **VDMAD_Release_Buffer** service.

Parameters

EBX

   Specifies the buffer identifier.

ESI

   Specifies the region linear.

EDI

   Specifies the offset within the buffer to the start of copying.

ECX

   Specifies the size of the buffer.

Return Value

The carry flag is clear if the data is copied from buffer into DMA region. Otherwise, the carry flag is set and the AL register contains one of the following error values:

Value	Meaning
0Ah	DMA_Invalid_Buffer: invalid buffer id supplied
0Bh	DMA_Copy_Out_Range: (ESI + ECX) is greater than buffer size

Uses

EAX, Flags

VDMAD_Copy_To_Buffer

```
include vdmad.inc

VxDcall VDMAD_Copy_To_Buffer
```

The **VDMAD_Copy_To_Buffer** service allows another device to copy data into the VDMAD buffer from the actual DMA region associated with the buffer. This service is called after the **VDMAD_Request_Buffer** service and before starting a memory read transfer.

Parameters

EBX

   Specifies the buffer identifier.

ESI

> Specifies the region linear.

EDI

> Specifies the offset within the buffer to the start of copying.

ECX

> Specifies the size of the buffer.

Return Value

The carry flag is clear if the data is copied from the DMA region into the buffer. Otherwise, the carry flag is set and the AL register contains one of the following error values:

Value	Meaning
0Ah	DMA_Invalid_Buffer: invalid buffer id supplied
0Bh	DMA_Copy_Out_Range: (ESI + ECX) is greater than buffer size

Uses

EAX, Flags

VDMAD_Default_Handler

```
include vdmad.inc

VxDcall VDMAD_Default_Handler
```

The **VDMAD_Default_Handler** service specifies the default DMA channel I/O callback procedure. This procedure receives notifications of virtual state changes and handles setting up the physical state to start DMA transfers.

Parameters

EAX

> Specifies the DMA handle.

EBX

> Specifies the virtual machine handle.

Return Value

This service has no return value.

Uses

All

VDMAD_Disable_Translation

```
include vdmad.inc

VxDcall VDMAD_Disable_Translation
```

The **VDMAD_Disable_Translation** service disables the automatic translation done for the standard DMA channels. It is necessary if a V86 application or driver or a PM application uses the DMA services through Interrupt 4Bh to determine actual physical addresses for DMA transfers. A disable count is maintained, so a matching call to **VDMAD_Enable_Translation** is required for each call to this service to re-enable translation.

Parameters

EAX

Specifies the DMA handle.

EBX

Specifies the virtual machine handle.

Return Value

The carry flag is clear is automatic translation is disabled for the channel. Otherwise, the carry flag is set if the disable count overflowed.

Uses

Flags

VDMAD_Enable_Translation

```
include vdmad.inc

VxDcall VDMAD_Enable_Translation
```

The **VDMAD_Enable_Translation** service decrements the disable count associated with a standard DMA channel. If the disable count goes to 0, the automatic translation is re-enabled.

Parameters

EAX

Specifies the DMA handle.

EBX

Specifies the virtual machine handle.

Return Value

The carry flag is clear if the service is successful. The zero flag is clear if automatic translation is re-enabled. Otherwise, the carry flag is set if the irtual device attempted to enable when translation was already enabled.

Uses

Flags

See Also

VDMAD_Disable_Translation

VDMAD_Get_EISA_Adr_Mode

```
include vdmad.inc

VxDcall VDMAD_Get_EISA_Adr_Mode
```

The **VDMAD_Get_EISA_Adr_Mode** service returns the EISA extended mode.

Parameters

EAX

Specifies the channel number. It must be in the range 0 to 7.

EBX

Specifies the DMA handle.

Return Value

The CL register contains one of the following values:

Value	Meaning
0	8-bit I/O, with count in bytes
1	16-bit I/O, with count in words and adr shifted
2	32-bit I/O, with count in bytes
3	16-bit I/O, with count in bytes

Comments

The hardware does not allow for reading the extended mode for a channel, so VDMAD defaults to the ISA defaults (channels 0-3 are byte channels and 5-7 are word channels with word addresses and counts). A SYSTEM.INI setting can specify an alternate setting.

Uses

ECX, Flags

VDMAD_Get_Region_Info

```
include vdmad.inc

VxDcall VDMAD_Get_Region_Info
```

The **VDMAD_Get_Region_Info** service returns information about the current region assigned to a DMA handle. This information can be used by a handler to call following services:

- VDMAD_Unlock_DMA_Region
- VDMAD_Release_Buffer
- VDMAD_Copy_To_Buffer
- VDMAD_Copy_From_Buffer

Parameters

EAX

Specifies the DMA handle.

Return Value

The BX, ESI, and ECX registers contain the following information:

Register	Description
BL	Specifies the buffer identifier.
BH	Specifies whether pages are locked (zero is not locked, nonzero is locked).
ESI	Specifies the region linear.
ECX	Specifies the size in bytes.

Uses

EBX, ECX, ESI

VDMAD_Get_Version

```
include vdmad.inc

VxDcall VDMAD_Get_Version
```

The **VDMAD_Get_Version** service returns the version number of the virtual DMA device.

Parameters

This service has no parameters.

Return Value

The AH register contains the major version number.

The AL register contains the minor version number.

The ECX register contains the buffer size in bytes. It is zero if the buffer is not allocated. A buffer is not available until the Init_Complete message.

The carry flag is clear.

Uses

EAX, ECX, Flags

VDMAD_Get_Virt_State

```
include vdmad.inc

VxDcall VDMAD_Get_Virt_State
```

The **VDMAD_Get_Virt_State** service allows a channel owner to determine the current virtual state of the channel. The virtual state consists of all the information necessary to physically program the DMA channel for a DMA transfer (linear address of target region, byte length of region, mode of transfer, and state of mask bit and software request bit)

Parameters

EAX

Specifies the DMA handle.

EBX

Specifies the virtual machine handle.

Return Value

If translation is enabled, the ESI register contains the high linear address of the user's DMA region. The high linear address is used so that the DMA can proceed even if a different virtual machine is actually running at the time of the transfer.

If translation is not enabled, the ESI register contains the physical byte address programmed (shifted left 1, for word ports).

The ECX register contains count in bytes.

The DL register contains the mode. This is the same as the 8237 mode byte with channel number removed and the following DMA_masked and DMA_requested values set as appropriate:

Value	Meaning
DMA_masked	Channel masked and not ready for a transfer
DMA_requested	Software request flag set

The DH register contains the extended mode (ignored on non-PS2 machines that do not have extended DMA capabilities).

Uses

ESI, ECX, EDX, Flags

VDMAD_Lock_DMA_Region

```
include vdmad.inc

VxDcall VDMAD_Lock_DMA_Region
```

The **VDMAD_Lock_DMA_Region** service attempts to lock a region of memory for a DMA transfer. It is called before a DMA transfer is started, that is, before the physical state is set for a channel and before it is unmasked.

Parameters

ESI

Specifies the linear address of the actual DMA region.

ECX

Specifies the numbers of bytes in the DMA region.

DL

Specifies the alignment. This parameter can be one of the following values:

Value	Meaning
1	region must be aligned on 64K page boundary
2	region must be aligned on 128K page boundary

Return Value

The carry flag is set if the lock failed. The ECX register contains the number of bytes that are lockable in the region (starting from ESI), and the AL registers contains one of the following error values:

Value	Meaning
1	DMA_Not_Contiguous: region not contiguous
2	DMA_Not_Aligned: region crossed physical alignment boundary
3	DMA_Lock_Failed: unable to lock pages

The carry flag is clear if the lock is successful. The EDX register contains the physical address of the DMA region the region has been locked.

Comments

The service first verifies that the region is mapped to contiguous pages of physical memory, then it determines whether the region results in a DMA bank (page) wrap.

On AT class machines each channel has a base address register and a page address register. The base address register is incremented after each byte or word transferred. If the increment of this 16-bit register results in the roll over from FFFFh to 0, then the transfer wraps to the start of the DMA bank because the page register is not updated. Normally MS-DOS watches for this condition and adjusts Interrupt 13h parameters to split transfers to avoid this wrap, but MS-DOS does not account for the difference between linear and physical addresses under Windows, so VDMAD checks again to prevent wrap from occurring.

If these checks pass, the service calls the memory manager to lock the physical pages.

This service does not check to see if the region is within some physical maximum constraint. If the region is lockable, then it locks the memory, and it is up to the caller to check to see if the physical region is acceptable. If the region is not acceptable, then the caller should unlock the region and perform a buffered DMA transfer.

Uses

EAX, ECX, EDX, Flags

VDMAD_Mask_Channel

```
include vdmad.inc

VxDcall VDMAD_Mask_Channel
```

The **VDMAD_Mask_Channel** service physically masks a channel so that it will not attempt any further DMA transfers.

Parameters

EAX

Specifies the DMA handle.

Return Value

This service has no return value.

Uses

Flags

VDMAD_Release_Buffer

```
include vdmad.inc

VxDcall VDMAD_Release_Buffer
```

The **VDMAD_Release_Buffer** service releases the VDMAD buffer assigned to a DMA channel from a previous call to the **VDMAD_Request_Buffer** service. This service exits from a critical section and the DMA buffer becomes available for other users. Any data in the buffer is not automatically copied, so the **VDMAD_Copy_From_Buffer** service must be called if the data is important.

Parameters

EBX

Specifies the buffer identifier.

Return Value

The carry flag is clear if the buffer is released. Otherwise, the carry flag is set to indicate an invalid buffer identifier.

Uses

Flags

VDMAD_Request_Buffer

```
include vdmad.inc

VxDcall VDMAD_Request_Buffer
```

The **VDMAD_Request_Buffer** service reserves the DMA buffer for a DMA transfer.

Parameters

ESI

Specifies the linear address of the actual DMA region.

ECX

Specifies the number of bytes in the DMA region.

Return Value

The carry flag is clear if the service is successful. The EBX register contains the buffer identifier and the EDX register contains the physical address of the buffer.

Otherwise, the carry flag is set and the AL register contains one of the following error values:

Value	Meaning
5	DMA_Buffer_Too_Small: region request is too large for buffer
6	DMA_Buffer_In_Use: buffer already in use

Uses

EAX, EBX, ESI, Flags

VDMAD_Reserve_Buffer_Space

```
include vdmad.inc

VxDcall VDMAD_Reserve_Buffer_Space
```

The **VDMAD_Reserve_Buffer_Space** service allows other devices that are going to handle DMA to make sure that VDMAD allocates a buffer large enough for any transfers that they might require. It also allows a device to specify a maximum physical address that would be valid for the device's DMA requests (such as 1Mb for an XT.) During the Init_Complete phase of initialization, VDMAD allocates the DMA buffer using all of the constraints specified by other devices. For example, the buffer is at least as big as the largest size specified by the calls to this service, and it allocates below the lowest maximum physical addresses specified.

This service is only available before the Init_Complete message.

Parameters

EAX

Specifies the number of pages requested.

ECX

Specifies the maximum physical address that can be included in a DMA transfer. If this parameter is zero, there is no limit.

Return Value

This service has no return value.

Uses

Flags

VDMAD_Scatter_Lock

```
include vdmad.inc

VxDcall VDMAD_Scatter_Lock
```

The **VDMAD_Scatter_Lock** service attempts to lock all pages mapped to a DMA region and return the actual physical addresses of the pages.

Parameters

EBX

Specifies the virtual machine handle.

AL

Specifies the operation flags. The parameter can be one of the following values:

Value	Meaning
0	Fills the DDS table with physical addresses and sizes of the physical regions that make up the DMA region.
1	Fills the DDS table with the actual page table entries.
2	Prevents not-present pages from being locked. This value is ignored if bit 0 is not set.

EDI

Points to the extended DDS (DMA Descriptor Structure) to receive the information.

Return Value

The carry flag is clear and the zero flag is set if the entire region is locked. The zero flag is clear if only a portion of the region is locked. If the carry flag is set, nothing is locked.

The EDX register contains the number of table entries needed to describe whole region, and the DDS_size field specifies the number of bytes locked.

If the request was for page table copy (AL set to 1 or 3), then The ESI register contains an offset into first page for start of the region.

Uses

EDX, ESI, Flags

VDMAD_Scatter_Unlock

```
include vdmad.inc

VxDcall VDMAD_Scatter_Unlock
```

The **VDMAD_Scatter_Unlock** service attempts to unlock all pages locked by a previous call to the **VDMAD_Scatter_Lock** service.

Parameters

EBX

Specifies the virtual machine handle.

AL

Specifies the operation flags. The parameter can be one of the following values:

Value	Meaning
0	Fills the DDS table with physical addresses and sizes of the physical regions that make up the DMA region.

1	Fills the DDS table with the actual page table entries.
2	Prevents not-present pages from being locked. This value is ignored if bit 0 is not set.
4	Prevents pages from being marked as dirty. If bits 0 and 1 are set but 2 is clear, then not-present pages are not marked.

EDI

Points to the extended DDS (DMA Descriptor Structure) to receive the information.

Return Value

The carry flag is clear if the lock counts have been decremented. If no other virtual devices had pages locked, the pages have been unlocked. The carry flag is set if the memory was not locked.

Comments

If Bits 0 and 1 in the AL register are set, the table at the end of the DDS is not required to unlock the previously locked pages; otherwise the table is not used and caller need not maintain the table after the lock call.

Uses

Flags

VDMAD_Set_EISA_Adr_Mode

```
include vdmad.inc

VxDcall VDMAD_Set_EISA_Adr_Mode
```

The **VDMAD_Set_EISA_Adr_Mode** service sets the EISA extended mode.

Parameters

EAX

Specifies the channel number. It must be in the range 0 to 7.

EBX

Specifies the DMA handle.

CL

Specifies one of the following mode values:

Value	Meaning
0	8-bit I/O, with count in bytes
1	16-bit I/O, with count in words and adr shifted
2	32-bit I/O, with count in bytes
3	16-bit I/O, with count in bytes

Return Value

This service has no return value.

Uses

Flags

VDMAD_Set_Phys_State

```
include vdmad.inc

VxDcall VDMAD_Set_Phys_State
```

The **VDMAD_Set_Phys_State** service programs the DMA controller state for a channel. The service takes the location and size of the buffer from the information passed in a previous call to the **VDMAD_Set_Region_Info** service.

Parameters

EAX

Specifies the DMA handle.

EBX

Specifies the virtual machine handle.

DL

Specifies the mode.

DH

Specifies the extended mode.

Return Value

This service has no return value.

Uses

Flags

See Also

VDMAD_Set_Region_Info

VDMAD_Set_Region_Info

```
include vdmad.inc

VxDcall VDMAD_Set_Region_Info
```

The **VDMAD_Set_Region_Info** service sets information about the current region assigned to a DMA handle. This service must be called before calling the **VDMAD_Set_Phys_State** service.

Parameters

EAX

Specifies the DMA handle.

BL

Specifies the buffer identifier.

BH

Specifies whether pages are locked (zero if not locked, nonzero if locked).

ESI

Specifies the region linear.

ECX

Specifies the size in bytes.

EDX

Specifies the physical address for the transfer.

Return Value

This service has no return value.

Uses

Flags

VDMAD_Set_Virt_State

```
include vdmad.inc

VxDcall VDMAD_Set_Virt_State
```

The **VDMAD_Set_Virt_State** service modifies the virtual state of a DMA channel. This service is used when a channel owner wants to change the virtual state of a channel from how the virtual machine programmed it. This might be used to split a DMA request into smaller pieces.

Parameters

EAX

Specifies the DMA handle.

EBX

Specifies the virtual machine handle

ESI

Specifies either a high linear address or a physical byte address. If translation is enabled, this parameter is the high linear address of the user's DMA region. A high linear address is used so that the DMA can proceed even if a different virtual machine is actually running at the time of the transfer. If translation is not enabled, this parameter specifies a physical byte address programmed (shifted left 1, for word ports).

ECX

Specifies the count in bytes.

DL

Specifies the mode. This is the same as the 8237 mode byte with channel number removed and the following DMA_masked and DMA_requested values set as appropriate:

Value	Meaning
DMA_masked	Channel masked and not ready for a transfer
DMA_requested	Software request flag set

DH

> Specifies the extended mode (ignored on non-PS2 machines that do not have extended DMA capabilities).

Return Value

This service has no return value.

Uses

Flags

VDMAD_Unlock_DMA_Region

```
include vdmad.inc

VxDcall VDMAD_Unlock_DMA_Region
```

The **VDMAD_Unlock_DMA_Region** service unlocks the DMA region previously locked to a channel. It is called after a DMA transfer is complete and the channel has been masked, preventing the controller from attempting any further transfers to the programmed address.

Parameters

ESI

> Specifies the linear address of the actual DMA region.

ECX

> Specifies the number of bytes in the DMA region.

Return Value

The carry flag is clear if the memory is unlocked. Otherwise, the carry flag is set to indicate an error.

Uses

Flags

VDMAD_UnMask_Channel

```
include vdmad.inc

VxDcall VDMAD_UnMask_Channel
```

The **VDMAD_UnMask_Channel** service physically unmasks a channel so that DMA transfers can proceed.

Parameters

EAX

Specifies the DMA handle.

EBX

Specifies the virtual machine handle.

Return Value

This service has no return value.

Uses

Flags

VDMAD_Virtualize_Channel

```
include vdmad.inc

VxDcall VDMAD_Virtualize_Channel
```

The **VDMAD_Virtualize_Channel** service allows another virtual device to claim ownership of a standard DMA channel. The new owner registers a callback procedure that is called whenever the virtual state of the channel is changed as a result of I/O done in a virtual machine.

Parameters

EAX

Specifies the channel number.

ESI

Specifies the callback procedure. If this parameter is zero, no callback procedure is called. See the "Comments" section for more information about the procedure.

Return Value

The carry flag is clear and the EAX register contains the DMA handle if the service is successful. Otherwise, the carry flag is set if channel is already owned.

Uses

EAX, EDX, Flags

Comments

The system calls the callback procedure by passing it the following input parameters:

```
EAX      ; DMA handle
EBX      ; virtual machine handle
```

The procedure can modify EAX, EBX, ECX, EDX, ESI, EDI, and Flags.

In some cases a virtual device does not allow a virtual machine to perform DMA to a channel. Instead, the virtual device handles programming based on a private API and not on virtualized hardware I/O. This means it is possible to pass a zero to specify no callback procedure. VDMAD continues to trap the I/O for the channel, but never changes the physical state of the channel as a result of any virtual machine I/O.

VHD API Reference

VHD_Allocate_Handle

```
include vhd.inc

VxDcall VHD_Allocate_Handle
```

The **VHD_Allocate_Handle** service allocates a handle for an operation.

Parameters

ESI

Specifies the address to call when the operation completes. If this parameter is zero, the address is not called.

Return Value

If the carry flag is clear, the EAX register contains the disk handle. Otherwise, the carry flag is set if the service could not allocate the handle.

Uses

EAX, Flags

VHD_Get_Version

```
include vhd.inc
VxDcall VHD_Get_Version
```

The **VHD_Get_Version** service returns the VHD version number.

Parameters

This service has no parameters.

Return Value

The AH register contains the major version number.

The AL register contains the minor version number.

The CL register contains the number of drives supported (0-based).

The EDX register can contain the following flag value:

Value	Meaning
1	Supports direct to hardware read and write operations.

The carry flag is clear.

Uses

EAX, Flags

VHD_Read

```
include vhd.inc
VxDcall VHD_Read
```

The **VHD_Read** service reads from the device.

Parameters

EAX

Specifies a disk handle previously created using the **VHD_Allocate_Handle** service.

EBX

Specifies the starting sector.

CL

Specifies the sector count. If this parameter is zero, 256 sectors are read.

CH

Specifies the drive number.

ESI

Points to the buffer to receive the sector data. This buffer must be locked.

Return Value

This service has no return value.

VHD_Write

```
include vhd.inc
VxDcall VHD_Write
```

The **VHD_Write** service writes to the device.

Parameters

EAX

Specifies a disk handle previously created using the **VHD_Allocate_Handle** service.

EBX

Specifies the starting sector.

CL

Specifies the sector count. If this parameter is zero, 256 sectors are written.

CH

Specifies the drive number.

ESI

Points to the buffer containing the sector data. This buffer must be locked.

Return Value

This service has no return value.

VKD API Reference

VKD_API_Force_Key

```
include vkd.inc

VxDcall VKD_API_Force_Key
```

The **VKD_API_Force_Key** service forces a key into a virtual machine as if it was typed on the keyboard. VKD will scan these forced keys for hot keys, so forcing VKD hot keys is allowed.

Parameters

EBX

Specifies the virtual machine handle or 0 for current focus.

CH

Specifies the scan code.

CL

Specifies the repeat count (1 or more).

EDX

Specifies the shift state (-1 means no change).

Return Value

The carry flag is set if an error occurs.

Comments

This service is currently limited to the focus virtual machine, so the service fails if the EBX register is not zero or not the focus virtual machine handle.

Uses

Flags

VKD_API_Get_Version

```
include vkd.inc

VxDcall VKD_API_Get_Version
```

The **VKD_API_Get_Version** service returns the version number of the VKD.

Parameters

This service has no parameters.

Return Value

The AH register contains the major version number.

The AL register contains the minor version number.

The carry flag is clear.

Uses

EAX, Flags

VKD_Cancel_Hot_Key_State

```
include vkd.inc

VxDcall VKD_Cancel_Hot_Key_State
```

The **VKD_Cancel_Hot_Key_State** service cancels the hot key state.

Parameters

This service has no parameters.

Return Value

This service has no return value.

VKD_Cancel_Paste

```
include vkd.inc

VxDcall VKD_Cancel_Paste
```

The **VKD_Cancel_Paste** service cancels the paste that was started in the virtual machine by the **VKD_Start_Paste** service.

Parameters

EBX

Specifies the virtual machine handle.

Return Value

This service has no return value.

VKD_Define_Hot_Key

```
include vkd.inc

VxDcall VKD_Define_Hot_Key
```

The **VKD_Define_Hot_Key** service defines a hot-key-notification callback procedure. Hot keys are detected by ANDing the shift state mask with the global shift state, then comparing the resulting state with the shift state compare value. If this matches and the key code matches, the callback procedure is called with the specified reference data in EDX.

Parameters

AL

Specifies scan code of the main key.

AH

Specifies the type of scan code. This parameter can be one of the following values:

Value	Meaning
0	Normal code
1	Extended code (ExtendedKey_B)
0FFh	Either normal or extended (AllowExtended_B)

EBX

Specifies shift state. The high word is a mask that is ANDed with the global shift state when checking for this hot key. The low word is the masked-shift-state-compare value.

CL

Specifies the operation flags. This parameter can be one of the following values:

Value	Meaning
CallOnPress	Calls callback when key press is detected.
CallOnRelease	Calls callback when key release is detected. Keyboard may still be in hot-key hold state.
CallOnRepeat	Calls callback when repeated press is detected.
CallOnComplete	Calls callback when the hot key state is ended (all shift modifier keys are released) or when a different hot key is entered. For example, assume that both ALT+1 and ALT+2 are hot keys. If the user holds the ALT key down, then presses and releases the 1 key and presses the 2 key, the callback for ALT+1 is called even though the ALT key has not been released.
CallOnUpDwn	Calls on both press and release.
CallOnAll	Calls on press, release and repeats.
PriorityNotify	Specifies that the callback can only be called when interrupts are enabled and the critical section is not owned. This value can be combined with any other value in this list.
Local_Key	Specifies that the key can be locally enabled or disabled.

ESI

Points to the callback procedure.

EDX

Points to the reference data to pass to the callback procedure.

EDI

Specifies maximum notification delay in milliseconds if the CL register specifies the PriorityNotify value. If this parameter is zero, the callback is always notified.

Return Value

If the carry flag is clear, the EAX register contains the definition handle. Otherwise, the carry flag is set to indicate an error.

Comments

The callback procedure is called when a hot key is detected, and detection meets mask requirements. The callback receives the following input parameters:

```
AL    ; scan code of key
AH    ; 0 if key just pressed (Hot_Key_Pressed)
      ; 1 if key just released (Hot_Key_Released)
      ; 2 if key is an auto-repeat press (Hot_Key_Repeated)
      ; 3 hot key state ended (Hot_Key_Completed)
EBX   ; hot key handle
ECX   ; global shift state
EDX   ; points to the reference data
EDI   ; elapsed time for delayed notification in milliseconds
```

The EDI register normally contains zero, but if the PriorityNotify value is specified this value could be larger.

The high bit of the AH register is set if the hot key is a priority hot key and the virtual machine which had the keyboard focus at the time the hot key was recognized was suspended or not executable. In this case, the priority event was scheduled for the system virtual machine rather than the keyboard owner. The Hot_Key_SysVM_Notify value can be used to check this bit.

The callback procedure can modify EAX, EBX, ECX, EDX, ESI, EDI, and Flags

Uses

Flags

VKD_Define_Paste_Mode

```
include vkd.inc

VxDcall VKD_Define_Paste_Mode
```

The **VKD_Define_Paste_Mode** service selects the virtual-machine paste mode and specifies whether Interrupt 16h pasting can be attempted or not. Some applications hook Interrupt 09h which often disallows pasting using Interrupt 16h. The VKD can detect this by setting a time-out to see if any Interrupt 16h handling is being done by the application. If not, the VKD switches to Interrupt 09h paste.

If an application does some Interrupt 16h handling, but cannot support the Interrupt 16h paste operation, a PIF bit can be set to indicate that only Interrupt 09h pasting should be used.

Parameters

AL

Specifies whether to use Interrupt 16h or Interrupt 09h paste. It can be one of the following values:

Value	Meaning
0	Allows Interrupt 16h paste attempts
1	Forces Interrupt 09h pasting

EBX

Specifies the virtual machine handle.

Return Value

This service has no return value.

Uses

Flags

VKD_Flush_Msg_Key_Queue

```
include vkd.inc

VxDcall VKD_Flush_Msg_Key_Queue
```

The **VKD_Flush_Msg_Key_Queue** service flushes any available keys from the special message mode input buffer.

Parameters

EBX

Specifies the virtual machine handle.

Return Value

This service has no return value.

Uses

Flags

VKD_Force_Keys

```
include vkd.inc

VxDcall VKD_Force_Keys
```

The **VKD_Force_Keys** service forces scan codes into the keyboard buffer just as if they had been typed on the physical keyboard. These keys are processed in the context of the focus virtual machine.

Parameters

ESI

Points to a buffer of scan codes.

ECX

Specifies the number of scan codes in the buffer.

Return Value

The carry flag is set if the keyboard buffer overflows. In this case, The ECX register contains the number of remaining scan codes that did not fit.

Uses

Flags

VKD_Get_Kbd_Owner

```
include vkd.inc

VxDcall VKD_Get_Kbd_Owner
```

The **VKD_Get_Kbd_Owner** service returns the virtual machine handle of the keyboard focus virtual machine.

Parameters

This service has no parameters.

Return Value

The EBX register contains the virtual machine handle of the keyboard owner.

Uses

Flags, EBX

VKD_Get_Msg_Key

```
include vkd.inc

VxDcall VKD_Get_Msg_Key
```

The **VKD_Get_Msg_Key** service returns the next available key from the special message mode input buffer and removes it from the buffer. If no key is available, then the zero flag is set.

This service does not block.

Parameters

EBX

Specifies the virtual machine handle.

Return Value

The zero flag is clear if a key is read. The AL register contains the scan code and the AH register contains a combination of the following modifier flag values:

Value	Meaning
MK_Shift	A shift key is down
MK_Ctrl	A control key is down
MK_Alt	An ALT key is down
MK_Extended	The key is an extended key

The zero flag is set if no key is available.

Uses

EAX, Flags

VKD_Get_Version

```
include vkd.inc

VxDcall VKD_Get_Version
```

The **VKD_Get_Version** service returns the VKD version number.

Parameters

This service has no parameters.

Return Value

The AH register contains the major version number.

The AL register contains the minor version number.

Uses

EAX, Flags

VKD_Local_Disable_Hot_Key

```
include vkd.inc

VxDcall VKD_Local_Disable_Hot_Key
```

The **VKD_Local_Disable_Hot_Key** service disables a hot key in the specified virtual machine.

Parameters

EAX

Specifies the hot key handle.

EBX

Specifies the virtual machine handle.

Return Value

This service has no return value.

Uses

Flags

VKD_Local_Enable_Hot_Key

```
include vkd.inc

VxDcall VKD_Local_Enable_Hot_Key
```

The **VKD_Local_Enable_Hot_Key** service enables a hot key in the specified virtual machine.

Parameters

EAX

Specifies the hot key handle.

EBX

Specifies the virtual machine handle.

Return Value

This service has no return value.

Uses

Flags

VKD_Peek_Msg_Key

```
include vkd.inc

VxDcall VKD_Peek_Msg_Key
```

The **VKD_Peek_Msg_Key** service returns the next available key from the special message mode input buffer without removing it from the buffer. If no key is available, the zero flag is set.

Parameters

EBX

Specifies virtual machine handle

Return Value

The zero flag is clear if a key is read. The AL register contains the scan code and the AH register contains a combination of the following modifier flag values:

Value	Meaning
MK_Shift	A shift key is down
MK_Ctrl	A control key is down
MK_Alt	An ALT key is down
MK_Extended	The key is an extended key

The zero flag is set if no key is available.

Uses

EAX, Flags

VKD_Reflect_Hot_Key

```
include vkd.inc

VxDcall VKD_Reflect_Hot_Key
```

The **VKD_Reflect_Hot_Key** service reflects a hot key into a specified virtual machine and cancels the hot key state. This service is normally called by a hot-key-notification callback procedure. It allows the callback to send the hot key into a virtual machine and without processing it as a hot key. VKD simulates the required key strokes to get the virtual machine into the specified shift state, then it simulates the key strokes for the hot key itself, and finally simulates key strokes to get the virtual machine to match the current global shift state.

Parameters

EAX

Specifies the hot key handle.

EBX

Specifies the virtual machine handle.

CX

Specifies the required shift state.

Return Value

This service has no return value.

Uses

Flags

VKD_Remove_Hot_Key

```
include vkd.inc

VxDcall VKD_Remove_Hot_Key
```

The **VKD_Remove_Hot_Key** service removes a defined hot key.

Parameters

EAX

Specifies the definition handle of the hot key to remove. This handle must have been previously created using the **VKD_Define_Hot_Key** service.

Return Value

This service has no return value.

Uses

Flags

VKD_Start_Paste

```
include vkd.inc

VxDcall VKD_Start_Paste
```

The **VKD_Start_Paste** service puts a virtual machine into paste mode by simulating keyboard activity with keystrokes taken from the specified paste buffer. Depending on the mode set with the **VKD_Define_Paste_Mode** service (default is to try Interrupt 16h pasting), VKD waits for the virtual machine to poll the keyboard BIOS through its Interrupt 16h interface. If the virtual machine does keyboard input through the BIOS, then VKD simulates the keyboard input at this high level (plugging in ASCII codes.) If the virtual machine fails to perform any Interrupt 16h within in a time-out period, or the mode has been set to avoid Interrupt 16h pasting, the VKD simulates the necessary hardware interrupts to perform the pasting. Hot keys are still processed while pasting is in progress.

Parameters

EAX

Points to the paste buffer containing an array of key structures having the following form:

```
OEM_ASCII_value       db    ?
scan_code             db    ?
shift_state           dw    ?
```

The shift_state field is 02h if a shift key is down and 04h is a ctrl key is down.

The scan_code is 0FFh and the shift_state 0FFFFh, if the VKD should convert the key to a ALT+numpad sequence. This information is identical to what is given by the Window's keyboard routine OEMKeyScan.

EBX

Specifies the virtual machine handle.

ECX

Specifies the number of paste entries in the paste buffer.

ESI

Points to callback procedure. This parameter can be 0. See the "Comments" section for more information about the procedure.

EDX

Points to reference data to pass to the callback procedure.

Return Value

The carry flag is clear if the paste is started. Otherwise, the carry flag is set to indicate an error such as insufficient memory to copy the buffer.

Comments

The callback procedure is called when the paste is complete or canceled. The callback receives the following input parameters:

```
EAX        ; Completion flags
           ; Paste_Complete - paste completed successfully
           ; Paste_Aborted  - paste canceled by user
           ; Paste_VM_Term  - paste aborted because virtual
           ;                  machine terminated
EBX        ; handle of virtual machine receiving the paste
EDX        ; reference data
```

The procedure can modify EAX, EBX, ECX, EDX, ESI, EDI, and Flags.

Uses

Flags

VMCPD API Reference

VMCPD_Get_Version

```
include vmcpd.inc

VxDcall VMCPD_Get_Version
```

The **VMCPD_Get_Version** service returns the VMCPD version number.

Parameters

This service has no parameters.

Return Value

The AH register contains the major version number.

The AL register contains the minor version number.

The ECX register contains one of the following flag values:

Value	Meaning
0	No coprocessor
2	80287
3	80387

Uses

EAX, ECX, Flags

VMCPD_Get_Virt_State

```
include vmcpd.inc

VxDcall VMCPD_Get_Virt_State
```

The **VMCPD_Get_Virt_State** service returns the virtual state of EM and MP bits for the given virtual machine.

Parameters

EBX

> Specifies the virtual machine handle.

Return Value

The AL register contains the virtual state of EM and MP bits. Bit 0 specifies the MPv bit; bit 1 the EMv bit.

Uses

EAX, Flags

VMCPD_Set_Virt_State

```
include vmcpd.inc

VxDcall VMCPD_Set_Virt_State
```

The **VMCPD_Set_Virt_State** service sets the virtual state of EM and MP bits for the given virtual machine.

Parameters

EBX

> Specifies the virtual machine handle.

AL

> Specifies the new virtual state of the EM and MP bits. Bit 0 sets the MPv bit; bit 1 the EMv bit.

Return Value

This service has no return value.

Uses

Flags

Virtual Mouse Device API Reference

Int33_API

```
include vmd.inc
VxDcall Int33_API
```

The **Int33_API** service is called by VMDOSAPP to inform the special mouse driver the new state of mouse buttons and position for the application being shown in a window. If the special mouse driver is not installed, then this call returns with carry flag set. If the API is not provided, then also it returns with carry flag set.

Parameters

EAX

Specifies the **Client_AX** register. The high word is always zero.

Value	Meaning	
1	Mouse API	

Register	Description
Client_EBX	Specifies Handle of virtual machine on whose behalf the call is made
Client_EDI	Specifies (X,Y) position of mouse in pixels
Client_ECX	Specifies (event flags,state) where state is the button state of the mouse and event flags convey the change in button state from previous call.

Value	Meaning
2	Special mouse API presence test.

EBX

Specifies the handle of virtual machine making call

Return Value

The carry flag is clear if the API is supported. Otherwise, carry flag is set to indicate the mouse driver is not special.

Uses

Flags

VMD_Get_Mouse_Owner

```
include vmd.inc

VxDcall VMD_Get_Mouse_Owner
```

The **VMD_Get_Mouse_Owner** service returns the handle of the virtual machine with the mouse focus.

Parameters

This service has no parameters.

Return Value

The EBX register contains the handle of virtual machine with mouse focus.

Uses

EBX, Flags

VMD_Get_Version

```
include vmd.inc

VxDcall VMD_Get_Version
```

The **VMD_Get_Version** service returns the version number.

Parameters

This service has no parameters.

Return Value

The AH register contains the major version number.

The AL register contains the minor version number.

The carry flag is clear.

Uses

EAX, Flags

VMD_Set_Mouse_Type

```
include vmd.inc

VxDcall VMD_Set_Mouse_Type
```

The **VMD_Set_Mouse_Type** service sets the mouse type.

Parameters

EAX

> Specifies an IRQ number (if positive or zero) or an interrupt number (if negative). If this parameter is negative, the absolute value is the interrupt vector.

ECX

> Specifies the mouse type. See VMD.INC for mouse definitions. If high bit of CL is set, then DL is equal to the COM port number (1-based).

Return Value

The carry flag is clear if the mouse is virtualized. Otherwise, The EAX register contains one of the following error values:

Value	Meaning
00	Mouse already virtualized
01	Could not virtualize interrupt

Uses

EAX, Flags

VMPoll API Reference

VMPoll_Enable_Disable

```
include vmpoll.inc

VxDcall VMPoll_Enable_Disable
```

The **VMPoll_Enable_Disable** service enables or disables polling of the specified virtual machine.

Parameters

AL

> Specifies whether to disable (zero) or enable (nonzero) polling.

EBX

Specifies the handle of the virtual machine to enable or disable polling for. If this parameter is zero, polling is globally enabled or disabled.

Return Value

This service has no return value.

VMPoll_Get_Version

```
include vmpoll.inc

VxDcall VMPoll_Get_Version
```

The **VMPoll_Get_Version** service returns the VMPOLL version number.

Parameters

This service has no parameters.

Return Value

The AH register contains the major version number.

The AL register contains the minor version number.

Uses

EAX, Flags

VMPoll_Reset_Detection

```
include vmpoll.inc

VxDcall VMPoll_Reset_Detection
```

The **VMPoll_Reset_Detection** service disables the virtual device's idle detection for the specified virtual machine.

Other virtual devices call this service to temporarily disable polling. For example, the virtual COM device uses the service to prevent terminal programs from being detected as idle while they transfer files.

Parameters

EBX

Specifies the handle of the virtual machine to disable idle detection for.

Return Value

This service has no return value.

Uses

Flags

VPICD API Reference

VPICD_API_Get_Ver

```
include bimodint.inc

mov     ax, VPICD_API_Get_Ver
call    [lpfnVPICD]              ; VPICD entry point address

jc      error                   ; carry set on error
mov     [Major], ah             ; major version number
mov     [Minor], al             ; minor version number
```

The **VPICD_API_Get_Ver** function returns the major and minor version numbers for the virtual PIC device.

Parameters

lpfnVPICD

Specifies the entry point address of the API handler for the virtual PIC device.

Return Value

The carry flag is clear and the AX register contains the major and minor version numbers, if the function is successful.

VPICD_Call_When_Hw_Int

```
include vpicd.inc

pushfd
cli                             ; disable interrupts
mov     esi, OFFSET32 Callback  ; points to callback
VxDcall VPICD_Call_When_Hw_Int
popfd
mov     [Next_Callback], esi    ; address of next callback
```

The **VPICD_Call_When_Hw_Int** service installs a callback procedure for hardware interrupts. The system calls the callback procedure whenever a hardware interrupt occurs.

The caller must disable interrupts before calling this service.

Parameters

Callback

Points to the callback procedure. When the system calls the procedure, the EBX register contains the handle of the current virtual machine.

Return Value

The ESI register contains the address of the next procedure in the callback chain.

Comments

Although any virtual device can use this service, the service is intended for use by the virtual DMA device to detect completion of DMA transfers. On systems with hardware devices that interrupt frequently, use of this service should be avoided. Installing a callback procedure to process every hardware interrupt can have a major impact on performance.

The callback procedure is responsible for chaining to the next handler in the interrupt chain. It also must preserve the EBX register for the next handler.

Uses

ESI, Flags

VPICD_Clear_Int_Request

```
include vpicd.inc

mov       eax, IRQHand     ; IRQ handle
mov       ebx, VM          ; current VM handle
VxDcall VPICD_Clear_Int_Request
```

The **VPICD_Clear_Int_Request** service resets an IRQ request that was previously set by a call to the **VPICD_Set_Int_Request** service.

Parameters

IRQHand

Specifies the handle of the IRQ to clear.

VM

Specifies the handle of the VM.

Return Value

This service has no return value.

Comments

If the IRQ is being shared and another device has also set the virtual IRQ, this service does not reset the virtual request immediately. Instead, the request is reset only after the other device calls **VPICD_Clear_Int_Request**.

Uses

Flags

See Also

VPICD_Set_Int_Request

VPICD_Convert_Handle_To_IRQ

```
include vpicd.inc

mov     eax, IRQHand       ; IRQ handle
VxDcall VPICD_Convert_Handle_To_IRQ

mov     [IRQNum], esi      ; IRQ number
```

The **VPICD_Convert_Handle_To_IRQ** service returns the number of the IRQ corresponding to the specified IRQ handle.

Parameters

IRQHand

Specifies the handle of a virtualized IRQ.

Return Value

The ESI register contains the IRQ number.

Uses

ESI, Flags

See Also

VPICD_Convert_Int_To_IRQ, **VPICD_Convert_IRQ_To_Int**

VPICD_Convert_Int_To_IRQ

```
include vpicd.inc

mov      eax, VecNum                    ; interrupt vector number
VxDcall VPICD_Convert_Int_To_IRQ

jc       not_mapped                     ; carry set if error

mov      [IRQNum], eax                  ; IRQ number
```

The **VPICD_Convert_Int_To_IRQ** service returns the IRQ number (if any) corresponding to the specified interrupt vector number.

Parameters

VecNum

Specifies an interrupt vector number.

Return Value

The carry flag is clear and the EAX register contains the IRQ number if the interrupt vector number is mapped to an IRQ. Otherwise, the carry flag is set.

Comments

Since virtual machines can map IRQ numbers of the virtual PIC to any interrupt vector numbers, virtual devices should always explicitly check which interrupt vector is mapped to a particular IRQ.

Uses

EAX, Flags

See Also

VPICD_Convert_Handle_To_IRQ, **VPICD_Convert_IRQ_To_Int**

VPICD_Convert_IRQ_To_Int

```
include vpicd.inc

mov      eax, IRQNum     ; IRQ number (not an IRQ handle!)
mov      ebx, VM         ; VM handle
VxDcall VPICD_Convert_IRQ_To_Int

jc       not_valid       ; carry set if IRQ number is not valid
mov      [VecNum], eax   ; interrupt vector number
```

The **VPICD_Convert_IRQ_To_Int** service returns the interrupt vector number that corresponds to the specified IRQ number for the specified virtual machine.

Parameters

IRQNum

Specifies an IRQ number.

VM

Specifies the handle identifying the virtual machine.

Return Value

The carry flag is clear and the EAX register contains an interrupt vector number if the IRQ number is valid. Otherwise, the carry flag is set.

Comments

Since virtual machines can map IRQ numbers of the virtual PIC to any interrupt vector numbers, virtual devices should always explicitly check which interrupt vector is mapped to a particular IRQ.

Uses

EAX, Flags

See Also

VPICD_Convert_Handle_To_IRQ, **VPICD_Convert_Int_To_IRQ**

VPICD_Force_Default_Behavior

```
include vpicd.inc

mov      eax, IRQHand        ; IRQ handle
VxDcall  VPICD_Force_Default_Behavior
```

The **VPICD_Force_Default_Behavior** service unvirtualizes an IRQ. This allows a virtual device to remove virtualization of an IRQ when it processes a **System_Exit** message.

Parameters

IRQHand

Specifies the handle of the IRQ to unvirtualize.

Return Value

This service has no return value.

Comments

This service invalidates the IRQ handle. After calling this service, a virtual device must not attempt to use the IRQ handle.

Uses

Flags

See Also

VPICD_Force_Default_Owner

VPICD_Force_Default_Owner

```
include vpicd.inc

mov       eax, IRQNum        ; IRQ number
mov       ebx, VM            ; owner VM handle or 0 for global
VxDcall VPICD_Force_Default_Owner

jc        error              ; carry set if can't set owner
```

The **VPICD_Force_Default_Owner** service forces VPICD's default interrupt handler to direct a specified IRQ to a particular virtual machine, or to make the IRQ global so that any virtual machine can receive the interrupt.

Parameters

IRQNum

Specifies the number of the IRQ for which ownership is set.

VM

Specifies the handle identifying the virtual machine to receive ownership. If this parameter is 0, the IRQ is given global ownership and any virtual machine can receive the interrupt.

Return Value

The carry flag is clear if the service set the owner to the specified virtual machine. If the service could not set the owner, such as if the IRQ has been virtualized or the IRQ number is not valid, the carry flag is set.

Uses

Flags

See Also

VPICD_Force_Default_Behavior

VPICD_Get_Complete_Status

```
include vpicd.inc

mov      eax, IRQHand        ; IRQ handle
mov      ebx, VM             ; VM handle
VxDcall VPICD_Get_Complete_Status

mov      [Status], ecx       ; IRQ status
```

The **VPICD_Get_Complete_Status** service returns the complete status for a virtual IRQ in a specified virtual machine.

Parameters

IRQHand

Specifies the handle identifying the IRQ for which to receive status.

VM

Specifies the handle identifying the virtual machine.

Return Value

The ECX register contains a combination of the following status flag values:

Value	Meaning
VPICD_Stat_IRET_Pending	A virtual iret is pending.
VPICD_Stat_In_Service	The IRQ is virtually in service.
VPICD_Stat_Phys_Mask	The IRQ is physically masked.
VPICD_Stat_Phys_In_Serv	The IRQ is physically in service.
VPICD_Stat_Virt_Mask	The virtual machine has masked the IRQ.
VPICD_Stat_Virt_Req	The virtual interrupt request for the virtual machine has been set (by a virtual device, not necessarily the caller).
VPICD_Stat_Phys_Req	The physical interrupt request has been set.
VPICD_Stat_Virt_Dev_Req	The virtual interrupt request has been set by the calling virtual device.

Uses

ECX, Flags

See Also

VPICD_Get_Status

VPICD_Get_IRQ_Complete_Status

```
include vpicd.inc

mov     eax, IRQNum              ; IRQ number
VxDcall VPICD_Get_IRQ_Complete_Status

jc      already_virtualized      ; carry set if error

mov     [Status], ecx            ; status
```

The **VPICD_Get_IRQ_Complete_Status** service returns the complete status for the specified IRQ. This service is similar to **VPICD_Get_Complete_Status** except that it takes an IRQ number as a parameter instead of an IRQ handle.

Parameters

IRQNum

Specifies the number of the IRQ for which to retrieve status.

Return Value

The carry flag is set if the IRQ has been virtualized. Otherwise, the carry flag is clear.

The ECX register contains a combination of the following status flag values:

Value	Meaning
VPICD_Stat_IRET_Pending	A virtual iret is pending.
VPICD_Stat_In_Service	The IRQ is virtually in service.
VPICD_Stat_Phys_Mask	The IRQ is physically masked.
VPICD_Stat_Phys_In_Serv	The IRQ is physically in service.
VPICD_Stat_Virt_Mask	The virtual machine has masked the IRQ.
VPICD_Stat_Virt_Req	The virtual interrupt request for the virtual machine has been set (by a virtual device, not necessarily the caller).
VPICD_Stat_Phys_Req	The physical interrupt request has been set.
VPICD_Stat_Virt_Dev_Req	The virtual interrupt request has been set by the calling virtual device.

Comments

Virtual devices typically use this service to inspect an IRQ before attempting to virtualize it, or to inspect the state of another virtual device's interrupt. Since the service indicates whether an IRQ has been virtualized, virtual devices use this service to avoid conflicts when more than one device may want to use an IRQ.

Uses

ECX, Flags

See Also

VPICD_Get_Complete_Status

VPICD_Get_Status

```
include vpicd.inc

mov      eax, IRQHand      ; IRQ handle
mov      ebx, VM           ; VM handle
VxDcall  VPICD_Get_Status

mov      [Status], ecx     ; IRQ status
```

The **VPICD_Get_Status** service returns the status for a virtual IRQ in a specified virtual machine. Although this service does not return the complete status, it returns the most commonly used information and is much faster than the **VPICD_Get_Complete_Status** service.

Parameters

IRQHand

Specifies the handle identifying the IRQ for which to receive status.

VM

Specifies the handle identifying the virtual machine.

Return Value

The ECX register contains a combination of the following status flag values:

Value	Meaning
VPICD_Stat_IRET_Pending	A virtual iret is pending.
VPICD_Stat_In_Service	The IRQ is virtually in service.

Uses

ECX, Flags

See Also

VPICD_Get_Complete_Status

VPICD_Get_Version

```
include vpicd.inc

VxDcall VPICD_Get_Version

mov      byte ptr [Major], ah      ; major version number
mov      byte ptr [Minor], al      ; minor version number
mov      [Flags], ebx              ; configuration flags
mov      [MaxIRQ], ecx             ; maximum IRQ supported
```

The **VPICD_Get_Version** service returns the VPICD major and minor version numbers.

Parameters

This service has no parameters.

Return Value

The carry flag is always clear, and the following registers contain the specified values:

Register	Value
AH	Specifies the major version number for the virtual PIC device.
AL	Specifies the minor version number for the virtual PIC device.
EBX	Specifies the configuration flag for the PIC. The flag can be the following value:

Value	Meaning
1	System has a master/slave (PC/AT-type) configuration. If this value is not given, the system has a single PIC (PC/XT-type) configuration.

All other values are reserved.

ECX	Specifies the maximum IRQ supported. It is either 07h or 0Fh.

Uses

EAX, EBX, ECX, Flags

VPICD_Install_Handler

```
include bimodint.inc

les     di, bis                ; points to Bimodal_Int_Struc
mov     ax, VPICD_Install_Handler
call    [lpfnVPICD]

jc      error                  ; carry set on error
```

The **VPICD_Install_Handler** function installs a bimodal interrupt handler for the IRQ specified by the BIS_IRQ_Number field in the **Bimodal_Int_Struc** structure.

Parameters

bis

Points to a **Bimodal_Int_Struc** structure containing information about the interrupt handler to install.

lpfnVPICD

Specifies the entry point address of the API handler for the virtual PIC device.

Return Value

If the carry flag is clear, the function is successful. Otherwise, the carry flag is set to indicate an error such as the IRQ has already been virtualized or the IRQ number is not valid.

Comments

This function virtualizes the specified IRQ and creates supervisor-mode selectors for the interrupt handler's code, data, and additional segments (if any). The function also sets the supervisor-mode API handler.

See Also

VPICD_Remove_Handler

VPICD_Phys_EOI

```
include vpicd.inc

mov     eax, IRQHand       ; IRQ handle
VxDcall VPICD_Phys_EOI
```

The **VPICD_Phys_EOI** service ends a physical interrupt, and allows further hardware interrupts from the specified IRQ.

Parameters

IRQHand

    Specifies the handle identifying the IRQ.

Return Value

This service has no return value.

Comments

An interrupt that is physically in service will not suppress interrupts to lower priority IRQs since VPICD does not prioritize hardware interrupts. Therefore, it is acceptable for an interrupt to be physically in service for any arbitrary length of time.

Uses

Flags

VPICD_Physically_Mask

```
include vpicd.inc

mov     eax, IRQHand       ; IRQ handle
VxDcall VPICD_Physically_Mask
```

The **VPICD_Physically_Mask** service masks the specified IRQ on the hardware PIC. This suppresses all hardware interrupts on the IRQ until the **VPICD_Physically_Unmask** or **VPICD_Set_Auto_Masking** service is called.

Parameters

IRQHand

    Specifies the handle identifying the IRQ.

Return Value

This service has no return value.

Uses

Flags

See Also

VPICD_Physically_Unmask, **VPICD_Set_Auto_Masking**

VPICD_Physically_Unmask

```
include vpicd.inc

mov     eax, IRQHand       ; IRQ handle
VxDcall VPICD_Physically_Unmask
```

The **VPICD_Physically_Unmask** service unmasks the specified IRQ on the hardware PIC.

Parameters

IRQHand

Specifies the handle identifying the IRQ.

Return Value

This service has no return value.

Comments

This service unmasks the physical IRQ without regard to mask state of the virtual machines. Even if every VM has masked the virtual IRQ, this service unmasks the physical IRQ.

Uses

Flags

See Also

VPICD_Physically_Mask, **VPICD_Set_Auto_Masking**

VPICD_Remove_Handler

```
include bimodint.inc

les     di, bis              ; points to Bimodal_Int_Struc
mov     ax, VPICD_Remove_Handler
```

```
call    [lpfnVPICD]
jc      error           ; carry set on error
```

The **VPICD_Remove_Handler** function removes a bimodal interrupt handler for the IRQ specified by the *BIS_IRQ_Number* field in the **Bimodal_Int_Struc** structure.

Parameters

bis

> Points to a **Bimodal_Int_Struc** structure containing information about the interrupt handler to remove.

lpfnVPICD

> Specifies the entry point address of the API handler for the virtual PIC device.

Return Value

The carry flag is clear if the function is successful and set if an error occurs. The function returns an error if the IRQ has not been virtualized or the IRQ number is not valid.

Comments

This function unvirtualizes the specified IRQ and frees the supervisor-mode selectors for the interrupt handler's code, data, and additional segments (if any).

See Also

VPICD_Install_Handler

VPICD_Set_Auto_Masking

```
include vpicd.inc

mov     eax, IRQHand        ; IRQ handle
VxDcall VPICD_Set_Auto_Masking
```

The **VPICD_Set_Auto_Masking** enables automatic masking for the specified IRQ. When automatic masking is enabled, the system automatically masks the physical IRQ if all virtual machines have masked the corresponding virtual IRQs. However, if at least one virtual machine has the IRQ unmasked, the physical IRQ remains unmasked.

Parameters

IRQHand

> Specifies the handle identifying the IRQ.

Return Value

This service has no return value.

Comments

Automatic masking is the default for every IRQ. It can be overridden by the **VPICD_Physically_Mask** and **VPICD_Physically_Unmask** services.

Uses

Flags

See Also

VPICD_Physically_Mask, **VPICD_Physically_Unmask**

VPICD_Set_Int_Request

```
include vpicd.inc

mov      eax, IRQHand    ; IRQ handle
mov      ebx, VM         ; current VM handle
VxDcall VPICD_Set_Int_Request
```

The **VPICD_Set_Int_Request** service sets a virtual interrupt request for the specified IRQ and virtual machine. Setting the request causes the system to simulate an interrupt. Although the simulation may occur immediately, in many cases it may not until a later point in time.

Parameters

IRQHand

Specifies the handle identifying the IRQ to set.

VM

Specifies the handle identifying the virtual machine.

Return Value

This service has no return value.

Comments

The interrupt is not simulated immediately if any of the following conditions are present:

- The virtual machine has interrupts disabled

- The virtual machine has masked the IRQ

- A higher priority virtual IRQ is in service

- The virtual machine is suspended, or not able to run

However, since the interrupt may be simulated immediately, a virtual device that has a virtual interrupt handler must be able to handle a call to the handler before this service returns.

Setting an interrupt request does not guarantee that the interrupt will be simulated. For example, if the VM has masked the interrupt and never unmasks it, the interrupt is never simulated. Also, a call to the **VPICD_Clear_Int_Request** service made before the virtual interrupt is simulated prevents the interrupt simulation.

The virtual VPIC device simulates a level-triggered PIC. This means that once a virtual EOI occurs, another interrupt will be simulated immediately unless the virtual interrupt request is cleared.

Uses

Flags

See Also

VPICD_Clear_Int_Request

VPICD_Test_Phys_Request

```
include vpicd.inc

mov     eax, IRQHand          ; IRQ handle
VxDcall VPICD_Test_Phys_Request

jc      irq_set               ; carry set if physical IRQ is set
```

The **VPICD_Test_Phys_Request** service returns with the carry flag set if the physical (hardware PIC) interrupt request is set for the specified IRQ.

Parameters

IRQHand

Specifies the handle identifying the IRQ.

Return Value

The carry flag is set if the physical interrupt request is set.

Uses

Flags

See Also

VPICD_Get_Complete_Status

VPICD_Virtualize_IRQ

```
include vpicd.inc

mov     edi, OFFSET32 vid       ; -> VPICD_IRQ_Descriptor
VxDcall VPICD_Virtualize_IRQ

jc      error                   ; carry set if error
mov     [IRQHand], eax          ; IRQ handle
```

The **VPICD_Virtualize_IRQ** service assigns a virtual interrupt request to the calling virtual device.

This is not an asynchronous service.

Parameters

vid

Points to a **VPICD_IRQ_Descriptor** structure containing information about the virtual IRQ. The *VID_IRQ_Number* and *VID_Hw_Int_Proc* fields in the **VPICD_IRQ_Descriptor** structure must be set before calling this service.

Return Value

If the carry flag is clear, the EAX register contains the handle for the virtual IRQ. This handle is used for all subsequent communication with the virtual PIC device.

The carry flag is set to indicate an error such as the IRQ has already been virtualized or the IRQ number is not valid.

Comments

The IRQ can be shared by up to 32 virtual devices if every virtual device specifies the VPICD_Opt_Can_Share value in the *VID_Options* field of the **VPICD_IRQ_Descriptor** structure.

Uses

EAX, Flags

See Also

VPICD_Force_Default_Behavior

VID_EOI_Proc

```
include vpicd.inc

mov     eax, IRQHand  ; IRQ handle
mov     ebx, VM       ; current VM handle
call    VID_EOI_Proc
```

The **VID_EOI_Proc** procedure handles the end of an interrupt. The system calls this procedure whenever a hardware interrupt handler in the virtual machine issues an EOI. The procedure typically calls the **VPICD_Clear_Int_Request** and **VPICD_Phys_EOI** services to clear the virtual interrupt and end the physical interrupt.

The system disables interrupts before calling this procedure. The procedure can re-enable interrupts if necessary.

Parameters

IRQHand

Specifies the handle for the interrupt request.

VM

Specifies the handle of the current virtual machine.

Return Value

This procedure has no return value.

Comments

This procedure is typically used by a virtual device, such as the virtual mouse device, that lets a corresponding MS-DOS driver process hardware interrupts. The virtual device reflects the interrupt to the virtual machine that owns the mouse. The MS-DOS driver services the interrupt and issues issues an EOI. At this point, the system calls the **VID_EOI_Proc** procedure.

This procedure may modify EAX, EBX, ECX, EDX, ESI, and Flags.

See Also

VPICD_Clear_Int_Request, **VPICD_Phys_EOI**

VID_Hw_Int_Proc

```
include vpicd.inc

mov     eax, IRQHand     ; IRQ handle
mov     ebx, VMId        ; current VM handle
call    VID_Hw_Int_Proc

jc      not_handled      ; carry set if interrupt not handled
```

The **VID_Hw_Int_Proc** procedure handles hardware interrupts for a virtual device. The system calls the procedure whenever a hardware interrupt occurs. Typically, **VID_Hw_Int_Proc** services the physical device, calls the **VPICD_Phys_EOI** service to end the physical interrupt, and sets the virtual IRQ request for a specific virtual machine.

The system disables interrupts before calling this procedure. The procedure can re-enable interrupts if necessary.

Parameters

IRQHand

Specifies the handle identifying the interrupt request.

VMId

Specifies the handle identifying the current virtual machine.

Return Value

The procedure clears the carry flag if it processed the interrupt. If the IRQ is sharable, the procedure can direct the system to pass the interrupt to the next handler by setting the carry flag. In this case, it must not process the interrupt.

Comments

The VMM services the procedure is allowed to call is limited. If processing the interrupt requires use of restricted services, this procedure should use the **Schedule_Call_Global_Event** service to schedule an event that performs the additional processing.

This procedure may modify EAX, EBX, ECX, EDX, ESI, and Flags.

This procedure must return using the ret instruction, not an iret instruction.

VID_IRET_Proc

```
include vpicd.inc

clc
cmp     [TimeOut],0
jz      no_timeout
stc                          ; carry set if interrupt timed-out

no_timeout:
mov     eax, IRQHand         ; IRQ handle
mov     ebx, VM              ; current VM handle
call    VID_IRET_Proc
```

The **VID_IRET_Proc** procedure handles attempts by a virtual machine to return from an interrupt. The system calls this procedure whenever a virtual machine executes an iret instruction or whenever a time-out occurs for a simulated interrupt.

The system disables interrupts before calling this procedure. The procedure can re-enable interrupts if necessary.

Parameters

IRQHand

Specifies the handle identifying the interrupt request.

VM

Specifies the handle identifying the current virtual machine.

Return Value

This procedure has no return value.

Comments

This procedure is useful for devices that must simulate large numbers of interrupts in a short period of time. For example, the virtual COM device simulates an interrupt, allows one character to be read from the COM port, and waits for the virtual machine to execute an iret instruction before putting more data into the virtual COM receive buffer.

This procedure may modify EAX, EBX, ECX, EDX, ESI, and Flags.

VID_Mask_Change_Proc

```
include vpicd.inc

mov     eax, IRGHand     ; IRQ handle
mov     ebx, VMId        ; current VM handle
mov     ecx, Mask        ; zero if unmasking IRQ,
                         ;      nonzero if masking
call    VID_Mask_Change_Proc
```

The **VID_Mask_Change_Proc** procedure processes attempts to mask or unmask the specified IRQ. The system calls this procedure whenever a virtual machine attempts to mask or unmask an interrupt.

The system disables interrupts before calling this procedure. The procedure can re-enable interrupts if necessary.

Parameters

IRQHand

Specifies the handle for the interrupt request.

VMId

Specifies the handle of the current virtual machine.

Mask

Specifies whether the IRQ is being masked or unmasked. This parameter is nonzero if the IRQ is being masked, and is zero if it is being masked.

Return Value

This procedure has no return value.

Comments

A virtual device typically uses this procedure to detect contention for a device. The default interrupt routines use this callback to detect conflicts with nonglobal interrupts.

This procedure may modify EAX, EBX, ECX, EDX, ESI, and Flags.

VID_Virt_Int_Proc

```
include vpicd.inc

mov     eax, IRQHand  ; IRQ handle
```

```
mov     ebx, VM        ; current VM handle
call    VID_Virt_Int_Proc
```

The **VID_Virt_Int_Proc** procedure handles virtual interrupts for a virtual device. The system calls the procedure whenever a simulated interrupt occurs. The procedure is useful for implementing critical sections around a simulated hardware interrupt.

The system disables interrupts before calling this procedure. The procedure can re-enable interrupts if necessary.

Parameters

IRQHand

Specifies the handle identifying the interrupt request.

VM

Specifies the handle identifying the current virtual machine.

Return Value

This procedure has no return value.

Comments

A virtual device requests a virtual interrupt by using the **VPICD_Set_Int_Request** service. Once set, the system simulates the interrupt at a convenient point in time. The call to this procedure signals that the simulated interrupt is underway and can no longer be canceled using the **VPICD_Clear_Int_Request** service.

A virtual device that uses this procedure usually also uses the **VID_Virt_IRET_Proc** procedure to detect the end of the simulated interrupt.

This procedure may modify EAX, EBX, ECX, EDX, ESI, and Flags.

See Also

VID_IRET_Proc

VPICD Structure Reference

Bimodal_Int_Struc

```
include bimodint.inc

Bimodal_Int_Struc        STRUC
  BIS_IRQ_Number         dw      ?
  BIS_VM_ID              dw      0
  BIS_Next               dd      ?
  BIS_Reserved1          dd      ?
  BIS_Reserved2          dd      ?
  BIS_Reserved3          dd      ?
  BIS_Reserved4          dd      ?
  BIS_Flags              dd      0
  BIS_Mode               dw      0
  BIS_Entry              dw      ?
  BIS_Control_Proc       dw      ?
                         dw      ?
  BIS_User_Mode_API      dd      ?
  BIS_Super_Mode_API     dd      ?
  BIS_User_Mode_CS       dw      ?
  BIS_User_Mode_DS       dw      ?
  BIS_Super_Mode_CS      dw      ?
  BIS_Super_Mode_DS      dw      ?
  BIS_Descriptor_Count   dw      ?
Bimodal_Int_Struc        ENDS
```

The **Bimodal_Int_Struc** structure contains information for a bimodal interrupt.

Members

BIS_IRQ_Number

Specifies the IRQ number.

BIS_VM_ID

Specifies the handle identifying the virtual machine; this field is used by the virtual PIC device.

BIS_Next

Points to the next **Bimodal_Int_Struc** structure in this chain.

BIS_Reserved1

Reserved for IRQ handle; this field is used by the virtual PIC device.

BIS_Reserved2

Reserved for BIS address; this field is used by the virtual PIC device.

BIS_Reserved3

Reserved.

BIS_Reserved4

Reserved.

BIS_Flags

Specifies the bimodal interrupt flags. It must be 0.

BIS_Mode

Specifies user or supervisor mode. It is 0 for user mode; 4 for supervisor mode.

BIS_Entry

Specifies the offset to the interrupt service routine for this interrupt.

BIS_Control_Proc

Specifies the offset to the control procedure for this interrupt.

BIS_User_Mode_API

Points to the user-mode API procedure for this interrupt. The procedure must check for and carry out the following functions:

Function	Description
BIH_API_EOI	End interrupt.
BIH_API_Mask	Mask the physical IRQ.
BIH_API_Unmask	Unmask the physical IRQ.
BIH_API_Get_Mask	Retrieve the mask state of the physical IRQ.
BIH_API_Get_IRR	Retrieve the set state of the physical IRQ.
BIH_API_Get_ISR	Retrieve service state of the physical IRQ.
BIH_API_Call_Back	Calls specified callback procedure when given virtual machine runs.

BIS_Super_Mode_API

Points to the supervisor-mode API procedure for this interrupt; this field is set by the virtual PIC device.

BIS_User_Mode_CS

Specifies the selector for the user-mode code segment for the interrupt handler.

Comments

Time-outs are very important to prevent 386 enhanced mode Windows from hanging while simulating a hardware interrupt.

VTD API Reference

VTD_Begin_Min_Int_Period

```
include vtd.inc

VxDcall VTD_Begin_Min_Int_Period
```

The **VTD_Begin_Min_Int_Period** service is used by virtual devices to ensure a minimum accuracy for system timing. When this service is called, if the interrupt period specified is lower than the current timer interrupt frequency, the interrupt period will be set to the new frequency.

Parameters

EAX

Specifies the desired interrupt period.

Return Value

If carry clear, the interrupt period is set. Otherwise, the specified interrupt period is not valid

Comments

Until a matching call to the **VTD_End_Min_Int_Period** service is made, the timer interrupt frequency is guaranteed to never be slower than the value specified.

A virtual device should call this service only once before calling **VTD_End_Min_Int_Period**.

Typically the **Begin_Min_Int_Period** and **End_Min_Int_Period** services are used by devices such as execution profilers that need extremely accurate timing. VMM system time out services rely on the VTD to keep time. Therefore, more frequent the timer interrupts, will allow the time-out services to be more accurate.

BIS_User_Mode_DS

Specifies the selector for the user-mode data segment for the interrupt handler.

BIS_Super_Mode_CS

Specifies the selector for the supervisor-mode code segment for the interrupt handler; this field is set by the virtual PIC device.

BIS_Super_Mode_DS

Specifies the selector for the supervisor-mode data segment for the interrupt handler; this field is set by the virtual PIC device.

BIS_Descriptor_Count

Specifies the number of additional EBIS_Sel_Struc structures immediately following this structure.

See Also

VPICD_Install_Handler, **VPICD_Remove_Handler**

EBIS_Sel_Struc

```
include bimodint.inc

EBIS_Sel_Struc STRUC
    EBIS_User_Mode_Sel  dw  ?
                        dw  ?
    EBIS_Super_Mode_Sel dw  ?
EBIS_Sel_Struc ENDS
```

The **EBIS_Sel_Struc** structure contains user- and supervisor-mode selectors for extra segments used by a bimodal interrupt handler.

Members

EBIS_User_Mode_Sel

Specifies an user-mode selector for an extra segment.

EBIS_Super_Mode_Sel

Specifies a supervisor-mode selector for an extra segment; this field is used by the virtual PIC device.

VPICD_IRQ_Descriptor

```
VPICD_IRQ_Descriptor   STRUC
     VID_IRQ_Number         dw    ?
     VID_Options            dw    0
     VID_Hw_Int_Proc        dd    ?
     VID_Virt_Int_Proc      dd    0
     VID_EOI_Proc           dd    0
     VID_Mask_Change_Proc   dd    0
     VID_IRET_Proc          dd    0
     VID_IRET_Time_Out      dd    500
VPICD_IRQ_Descriptor   ENDS
```

The **VPICD_IRQ_Descriptor** structure contains information about a virtualized IRQ.

Members

VID_IRQ_Number

Specifies the number of the IRQ to virtualize.

VID_Options

Specifies the options for virtualizing the IRQ. It can be a combination of the following values:

Value	Meaning
VPICD_Opt_Read_Hw_IRR	Reads the hardware interrupt register.
VPICD_Opt_Can_Share	Virtual IRQ can be shared.

VID_Hw_Int_Proc

Points to the callback procedure that handles hardware interrupts for this IRQ.

VID_Virt_Int_Proc

Points to the callback procedure that handles virtual interrupts for this IRQ.

VID_EOI_Proc

Points to the callback procedure that handles end-of-interrupt commands for this IRQ.

VID_Mask_Change_Proc

Points to the callback procedure that handles changes to the IRQ mask for this IRQ.

VID_IRET_Proc

Points to the callback procedure that handles iret instructions for this IRQ.

VID_IRET_Time_Out

Specifies the maximum amount of time in milliseconds that the virtual PIC device allows before the time-out occurs.

Appendix B

Int 2Fh Reference

This appendix contains a listing of the Microsoft Windows Interrupt 2Fh services and notifications.[1]

Windows Interrupt 2Fh Services and Notifications

The Microsoft Windows Interrupt 2Fh services and notifications help Windows device drivers and related MS-DOS device drivers and terminate-and-stay-resident (TSR) programs manage their operations in the multitasking environment of Windows. The services let drivers carry out actions such as relinquishing the CPU time slice. The notifications let drivers respond to events, such as starting up Windows, that Windows broadcasts using Interrupt 2Fh.

Although the Interrupt 2Fh services and notifications are primarily available under 386 enhanced-mode Windows version 3.x, some services are also available in standard-mode Windows.

About the Services and Notifications

The Interrupt 2Fh services are a set of functions that MS-DOS drivers and TSRs call to direct Windows to carry out specific actions. The notifications are a set of functions that Windows calls to notify drivers nd programs of Windows-related events. Although these functions were initially designed for use by MS-DOS drivers and TSRs, some Windows device drivers, such as display drivers and grabbers, also use them to manage the multitasking features of Windows.

---

[1]Reprinted with permission of Microsoft Corporation.

A driver can call the service functions using the MS-DOS multiplex interrupt, Interrupt 2Fh. The driver sets one or more registers to specified values, sets the AX register to the desired function number, and issues the interrupt using the int instruction.

A driver can receive notifications by installing its own interrupt-handling routine in the Interrupt 2Fh interrupt chain. Once the interrupt handler is installed, the driver checks the AX register on each interrupt for function numbers that match the notifications. When the driver matches a notification, it can carry out any related actions.

Service Functions

The service functions let drivers and TSRs obtain the Windows version number, obtain the current virtual-machine (VM) identifier, set critical sections, and retrieve the addresses of the entry points for virtual-device service functions. There are the following service functions:

- Get Enhanced-Mode Windows Installed State (Interrupt 2Fh Function 1600h)

- Get Enhanced-Mode Windows Entry-Point Address (Interrupt 2Fh Function 1602h)

- Release Current VM Time-Slice (Interrupt 2Fh Function 1680h)

- Begin Critical Section (Interrupt 2Fh Function 1681h)

- End Critical Section (Interrupt 2Fh Function 1682h)

- Get Current Virtual Machine ID (Interrupt 2Fh Function 1683h)

- Get Device Entry Point Address (Interrupt 2Fh Function 1684h)

- Switch VMs and CallBack (Interrupt 2Fh Function 1685h)

- Detect Interrupt 31h Services (Interrupt 2Fh Function 1686h)

The 386 enhanced-mode Windows display grabber uses the Get Device Entry Point Address (Interrupt 2Fh Function 1684h) to retrieve the entry point address for the virtual-display device (VDD). The grabber uses this address to call VDD service functions to carry out capturing display contexts and updating tasks.

Both standard- and 386 enhanced-mode Windows issues Windows Initialization Notification (Interrupt 2Fh Function 1605h) and Windows Termination Notification (Interrupt 2Fh Function 1606h). These notifications gives MS-DOS drivers and TSR programs in either Windows environment the opportunity to free extended memory before Windows starts, and reallocate the memory when Windows stops.

Standard- and 386 enhanced-mode Windows also support Detect Interrupt 31h Services. Supporting these services lets MS-DOS drivers and TSR programs check for and use these service functions.

If the user starts a TSR program after Windows starts, the TSR program can always use Get Enhanced-Mode Windows Installed State (Interrupt 2Fh Function 1600h) to determine whether Windows is running.

Notification Functions

Windows broadcasts the notification functions by setting registers and issuing Interrupt 2Fh. Drivers and TSRs use the notifications to load 386 enhanced-mode Windows installable devices, free extended memory, and enable or disable various device services or features. There are the following notification functions:

- Windows Initialization Notification (Interrupt 2Fh Function 1605)

- Windows Termination Notification (Interrupt 2Fh Function 1606h)

- Device Call Out (Interrupt 2Fh Function 1607h)

- Windows Initialization Complete Notification (Interrupt 2Fh Function   1608h)

- Windows Begin Exit (Interrupt 2Fh Function 1609h)

MS-DOS device drivers, such as network drivers, use Windows Initialization Notification to direct 386 enhanced-mode Windows to load a protected-mode installable device that provides 32-bit support for the real-mode driver while 386 enhanced-mode Windows runs. Other MS-DOS drivers (for example, disk-cache drivers) use the same notification to free any extended memory before Windows starts. The TSRs also use Windows Termination Notification to reclaim the extended memory when Windows stops.

If an MS-DOS driver or TSR programs installs a corresponding virtual device, that device can send notifications of its own to the driver or TSR using Device Call Out.

Critical Section Handling

Occasionally, an MS-DOS driver or TSR program may need to run for a period of time that may exceed its regular time slice. In such cases, the driver can create a critical section that prevents Windows from switching the CPU away from the driver or program.

A driver starts a critical section by using Begin Critical Section (Interrupt 2Fh Function 1681h). While the critical section is in effect, only device interrupts can divert execution from the driver. A driver ends the critical section by using End Critical Section (Interrupt 2Fh Function 1682h). In general, a driver should end the critical section as soon as possible to ensure that all drivers and programs in the system receive CPU time. If a driver starts a critical section n times, it must end the critical section n times before the critical section is actually released.

Ordinarily, Windows prevents rescheduling of the current virtual machine if the one-byte, MS-DOS InDOS flag is nonzero. One exception is when a driver or program issues the MS-DOS Idle interrupt (Interrupt 28h). In such cases, Windows may reschedule regardless of the value of the InDOS flag. The only way to prevent this rescheduling is to start a critical section using Begin Critical Section. While in a critical section, Windows disregards Interrupt 28h.

In previous versions of Windows (for example, Windows/386(TM) version 2.x), service functions to support critical sections were not supplied. Drivers and programs achieved a similar effect by incrementing and decrementing the MS-DOS InDOS flag. Although this method was acceptable for previous versions of Windows, drivers should not use this method in versions of Windows that supply Begin Critical Section and End Critical Section (Interrupt 2Fh Function 1682h).

Drivers and programs that use the InDOS flag method retrieve the address of the InDOS flag using Get InDOS Flag Address (Interrupt 21h Function 34h). The function returns the address in the ES:BX register pair. When using this method, drivers and programs check the flag value before decrementing because some error conditions (such as when the user types CTRL+C) set the InDOS flag to zero regardless of its current value. Decrementing the InDOS flag to a number less than zero is a serious error.

Releasing the Time Slice

MS-DOS applications can also use the Interrupt 2Fh service functions. In particular, applications can use Release Current VM Time Slice (Interrupt 2Fh Function 1680h) to release the current virtual machine's time slice. An MS-DOS application typically uses this function when waiting for user input. This function helps 386 enhanced-mode Windows multitask more efficiently by letting it reschedule the CPU for other work immediately, rather than waiting for the idle application to spend its entire time slice.

Virtual-Display Device Services and Notifications

The virtual display device for 386 enhanced-mode Windows also provides Interrupt 2Fh service and notification functions. Windows display drivers use these functions to check for and manage screen switching. There are the following functions:

- Enable VM-Assisted Save/Restore (Interrupt 2Fh Function 4000h)

- Notify Background Switch (Interrupt 2Fh Function 4001h)

- Notify Foreground Switch (Interrupt 2Fh Function 4002h)

- Enter Critical Section (Interrupt 2Fh Function 4003h)

- Exit Critical Section (Interrupt 2Fh Function 4004h)

- Save Video Register State (Interrupt 2Fh Function 4005h)

- Restore Video Register State (Interrupt 2Fh Function 4006h)

- Disable VM-Assisted Save/Restore (Interrupt 2Fh Function 4007h)

For more information about using these functions, see the Microsoft Windows Device Driver Development Kit, Display Drivers.

Service and Notification Function Reference

The following is an alphabetical listing of the Interrupt 2Fh service and notification functions.

Interrupt 2Fh Function 1600h

```
mov     ax, 1600h  ; Get Enhanced-Mode Windows Installed State
int     2Fh        ; multiplex interrupt

test    al, 7Fh
jz      No_EM_Win  ; 386 enhanced-mode Windows not running
```

Get Enhanced-Mode Windows Installed State (Interrupt 2Fh Function 1600h) etermines whether 386 enhanced-mode Windows is running. If a program intends to use a 386 enhanced-mode Windows function, it must first use this function to make sure that 386 enhanced-mode Windows is running.

This function is valid under all versions of 386 enhanced-mode Windows.

Parameters

This function has no parameters.

Return Value

The return value is 00h or 80h in the AL register if 386 enhanced-mode Windows is not running. If 386 enhanced-mode Windows is running, the return value depends on the version of Windows. Windows/386 version 2.x returns 01h or 0FFh. Windows version 3.x returns the major version number in the AL register, and the minor version number in the AH register.

Example

The following example determines whether 386 enhanced-mode Windows is running, then determines which version is running.

```
mov     ax, 1600h
int     2Fh
test    al, 7Fh
```

```
jz      No_EM_Win   ; 386 enhanced-mode Windows not running

cmp     al, 1
je      Ver_2x      ; Windows/386 version 2.x running
cmp     al, -1
je      Ver_2x      ; Windows/386 version 2.x running

mov     byte ptr [MajorVer], al
mov     byte ptr [MinorVer], ah
```

Interrupt 2Fh Function 1602h

```
mov  ax, 1602h        ; Get Enhanced-Mode Windows Entry Point
int  2Fh              ; multiplex interrupt
mov  word ptr [WinAddr], di
mov  word ptr [WinAddr+2], es ; es:di contains entry-point
```

Get Enhanced-Mode Windows Entry Point (Interrupt 2Fh Function 1602h) returns the address of the 386 enhanced-mode Windows entry-point procedure. Applications can call this procedure to direct Windows/386 version 2.x to carry out specific actions.

This function applies to Windows/386 version 2.x only. It is provided under Windows version 3.x for compatibility reasons.

Parameters

This function has no parameters.

Return Value

The return value contains the Windows entry-point address in the ES:DI registers.

Comments

Although the Windows entry-point address is the same for every virtual machine, an application can call this function any number of times.

To direct Windows to carry out a specific action, the application sets the AX register to 0000h. This function retrieves the current VM identifier and copies the identifier to the BX register.

Additionally, the application must place a return address in the ES:DI register pair and use the jmp instruction to transfer control to the Windows entry point.

Example

The following example shows how to obtain the current VM identifier:

```
mov     di, cs
mov     es, di
mov     di, OFFSET Win_Return
xor     ax, ax      ; Get Current VM Identifier
jmp     [WinAddr]
```

```
Win_Return:
    mov      [VM_Id], bx     bx contains the current VM identifier
```

See Also

Interrupt 2Fh Function 1683h Get Current Virtual Machine ID

Interrupt 2Fh Function 1605h

```
xor      bx, bx
mov      es, bx           ; es:bx contains 0000h:0000h
mov      cx, 0000h
mov      dx, [Flags]      ; bit 0 clear if 386 enhanced mode,
                          ; set if standard mode

mov      di, [Ver_Num]    ; major/minor version numbers
                          ; (in high/low bytes)

xor      si, si
mov      ds, si           ; ds:si contains 0000h:0000h

mov      ax, 1605h        ; Windows Initialization Notification
int      2fh              ; multiplex interrupt

cmp      cx, 0
jne      no_initialize    ; if nonzero, don't continue init
```

Windows Initialization Notification (Interrupt 2Fh Function 1605h) notifies MS-DOS device drivers and TSRs that standard- or 386 enhanced-mode Windows is starting. Windows calls this function as it starts allowing MS-DOS device drivers and TSRs that monitor Interrupt 2Fh the opportunity to prepare for running in the Windows environment.

Parameters

Flags

Specifies whether standard- or 386 enhanced-mode Windows is initializing. 386 enhanced-mode Windows sets bit 0 to 0; standard-mode Windows sets bit 0 to 1. Only bit 0 is used; all other bits reserved and undefined.

Ver_Num

Specifies the version number of Windows. The major version number is in the high-order byte, the minor version number in low-order byte.

Return Value

The return value is 0 in the CX register if all MS-DOS device drivers and TSRs monitoring Interrupt 2Fh can run in the Windows environment, and Windows can proceed with initialization. Otherwise, the CX register is nonzero and Windows must terminate.

Comments

Any MS-DOS device driver or TSR that either cannot run in the Windows environment, or must adapt its operation when in the Windows environment should add itself to the Interrupt 2Fh chain and watch for this function.

If the device driver or TSR cannot run in the Windows environment, it should set the CX register to a nonzero value, display a message informing the user of its incompatibility with Windows, and return. Windows does not print a message of its own. Instead, it calls Windows Termination Notification (Interrupt 2Fh Function 1606h) and returns to MS-DOS.

If the device driver or TSR can run in the Windows environment, it should do the following:

1. Call the next device driver or TSR in the Interrupt 2Fh chain to allow all device drivers and TSRs in the chain an opportunity to respond to this function.

2. Upon return from the interrupt chain, carry out the following actions:

    *   Free any extended memory. The device driver or TSR takes this action only if it has previously allocated extended memory using the Extended Memory Specification (XMS) interface.

    *   Switch the processor to real mode, or set the DS:SI register pair to the address of an Enable/Disable Virtual 8086 Mode callback function. The device driver or TSR takes this action only if it has previously switched the processor to virtual 8086 mode. If standard-mode Windows is starting, the device driver or TSR must switch the processor to real mode--the callback function is permitted for 386 enhanced-mode Windows only.

    *   Initialize a **Win386_Startup_Info_Struc** structure, and copy the address of the structure to the ES:BX register pair. The device driver or TSR carries out this action only if 386 enhanced-mode Windows is starting.

3. Return (using the iret instruction) but without changing the CX register.

For more information about these procedures, see the following Comments section.

The device driver or TSR must preserve all registers and restore the original values before returning. The only exceptions to this rule are changes made to the BX, CX, DS, ES, and SI registers as a result of following the previous procedure.

Enable/Disable Virtual 8086 Mode CallBack Function

Some device drivers and TSRs, such as expanded memory emulators, switch the processor to virtual 8086 mode. Because 386 enhanced-mode Windows cannot start successfully while the processor is in this mode, any device driver or TSR that switches to virtual 8086 mode must either switch back to real mode or supply the address of a callback function that can switch between real and virtual 8086 modes.

Windows uses the callback function to disable virtual 8086 mode before Windows itself enters protected mode. Windows calls the callback function again to enable virtual 8086 mode after Windows exits protected mode.

Windows calls the callback function using a far call instruction, and it specifies which action to take by setting the AX register to 0 or 1.

To disable virtual 8086 mode, Windows sets the AX register to 0, disables interrupts, and calls the callback function. The function should switch the processor to real mode, clear the carry flag to indicate success, and return. If an error occurs, the function sets the carry flag and returns. Windows checks the carry flag and terminates if it is set.

To enable virtual 8086 mode, Windows set the AX register to 1, disables interrupts, and calls the callback function. The function should switch the processor to virtual 8086 mode, clear the carry flag, and return. If an error occurs, the function sets the carry flag and returns. However, Windows ignores the carry flag, so if an error occurs no action is taken and the processor is left in real mode.

Whether an error occurs when enabling or disabling virtual 8086 mode, it is up to the callback function to display any error message to the user. Also, the callback function must not enable interrupts unless an error occurs, and the function sets the carry flag.

A device driver or TSR supplies a callback function by copying the address of the function to the DS:SI register pair when it processes the Windows Initialization Notification (Interrupt 2Fh Function 1605h). Windows permits only one callback function, so the device driver or TSR should first check to make sure that the DS and SI registers are both zero. If they are nonzero, the device driver or TSR should set the CX register to a nonzero value and return, directing Windows to terminate without starting.

Initializing a Win386_Startup_Info_Struc Structure

An MS-DOS device driver or TSR initializes a **Win386_Startup_Info_Struc** structure to direct 386 enhanced-mode Windows to load the virtual device and to reserve the instance data the device driver or TSR needs to operate in the Windows environment. The device driver or TSR is also responsible for establishing a chain of startup structures by copying the contents of the ES:BX register pair to the *Next_Dev_Ptr* member. It is assumed that any other device driver or TSR in the Interrupt 2Fh chain will have set the ES:BX register pair to the address of its own startup structure prior to returning.

Any device driver or TSR can use a Windows virtual device to help support its operation in the 386 enhanced-mode Windows environment. To specify a virtual device, the device driver or TSR sets the *SIS_Virt_Dev_File_Ptr* member to the address of the virtual device's filename. The device file is assumed to be in the Windows SYSTEM directory.

The device driver or TSR can also set the *SIS_Reference_Data* member to specify additional data to be passed to the virtual device when loaded.

Any device driver or TSR can reserve instance data for itself. Instance data is one or more blocks of memory used by the device or TSR, and managed by Windows. For device drivers or TSRs loaded before 386 enhanced-mode Windows starts, reserving instance data allows the device driver or TSR to keep separate data for each virtual machine. Whenever Windows switches virtual machines, it saves the previous VMs instance data and loads the current VMs instance data. If a device driver or TSR does not specify instance data, the same data is used for all virtual machines.

A device driver or TSR reserves instance data by appending an array of **Instance_Item_Struc** structures to the **Win386_Startup_Info_Struc** structure. The last structure in the array must be set to zero. Each **Instance_Item_Struc** structure specifies the starting address and size (in bytes) of an instance data block.

The device driver or TSR must copy the address of its startup structure to the ES:BX register pair before returning.

See Also

Interrupt 2Fh Function 1606h Windows Termination Notification

---

Interrupt 2Fh Function 1606h

```
mov     dx, [Flags]   ; bit 0 clear if 386 enhanced-mode,
                      ; set if standard-mode

mov     ax, 1606h     ; Windows Termination Notification
int     2fh           ; multiplex interrupt
```

Windows Termination Notification (Interrupt 2Fh Function 1606h) notifies MS-DOS device drivers and TSRs that standard- or 386 enhanced-mode Windows is terminating. Windows calls this function as it terminates allowing MS-DOS device drivers and TSRs that monitor Interrupt 2Fh the opportunity to prepare for leaving the Windows environment.

Parameters

Flags

Specifies whether standard- or 386 enhanced-mode Windows is terminating. 386 enhanced-mode Windows sets bit 0 to 0; standard-mode Windows sets bit 0 to 1. Only bit 0 is used; all other bits reserved and undefined.

Return Value

This function has no return value.

Comments

Windows calls this function when the processor is in real mode.

See Also

Interrupt 2Fh Function 1605h Windows Initialization Notification

Interrupt 2Fh Function 1607h

```
mov     bx, [DeviceID]  ; device identifier

mov     ax, 1607h       ; Device Call Out
int     2fh             ; Multiplex Interrupt
```

Device Call Out (Interrupt 2Fh Function 1607h) directs an MS-DOS device driver or TSR to provide information to the calling virtual device. Although the BX register specifies a device identifier, other registers may be used to specify the action to take.

Parameters

DeviceID

Specifies the device identifier for a virtual device.

Return Value

The return value depends on the specific action requested.

Comments

This function typically is used by a virtual device to communicate with the driver or TSR that explicitly loaded the virtual device. It is up to the virtual device to supply a correct device identifier and any other parameters that specify what action to take. It is up to the driver or TSR to monitor Interrupt 2Fh, and respond to the function appropriately.

A virtual device can call this function at any time, either in real mode or after 386 enhanced-mode Windows has started.

See Also

Interrupt 2Fh Function 1684h Get Device Entry Point Address

Interrupt 2Fh Function 1608h

```
mov     ax, 1608h       ; Windows Init Complete Notification
int     2Fh             ; multiplex interrupt
```

Windows Initialization Complete Notification (Interrupt 2Fh Function 1608h) notifies MS-DOS device drivers and TSRs that 386 enhanced-mode Windows has completed its initialization. Windows calls this function after it has installed and initialized all virtual devices allowing MS-DOS device drivers and TSRs that monitor Interrupt 2Fh the opportunity to identify instance data and perform other functions that are restricted to 386 enhanced-mode Windows initialization.

Parameters

This function has no parameters.

Return Value

This function has no return value.

Comments

When Windows calls this function, all virtual-device initialization is complete, so a device driver or TSR can call virtual-device entry points.

Windows does not necessarily call this function immediately after calling Windows Initialization Notification (Interrupt 2Fh Function 1605h). In particular, virtual devices may call Device Call Out (Interrupt 2Fh Function 1607h) or other functions prior to Windows calling this function. In such cases, any MS-DOS device driver or TSR responding to these calls is responsible for detecting and properly handling these calls.

See Also

Interrupt 2Fh Function 1605h Windows Initialization Notification

---

Interrupt 2Fh Function 1609h

```
mov     ax, 1609h   ; Windows Begin Exit
int     2fh         ; multiplex interrupt
```

Windows Begin Exit (Interrupt 2Fh Function 1609h) notifies MS-DOS device drivers and TSRs that Windows is about to terminate. Windows calls this function when it first begins termination to allow a device driver or TSR to prepare for a return to a non-Windows environment.

Parameters

This function has no parameters.

Return Value

This function has no return value.

Comments

Windows calls this function at the start of the Sys_VM_Terminate device control call. All virtual devices still exist, so a device driver or TSR can call a virtual device's entry point if necessary.

Windows does not call this function in the event of a fatal system crash.

Windows may execute real-mode code after this function has been called and before 386 enhanced-mode Windows returns to real mode. It is the responsibility of the device driver or TSR to detect and properly handle these situations.

Interrupt 2Fh Function 1680h

```
mov    ax, 1680h    ; Release Current VM Time-Slice
int    2Fh          ; multiplex interrupt
```

Release Current VM Time-Slice (Interrupt 2Fh Function 1680h) directs Windows to suspend the time slice of the current VM and start a new time slice for another VM. MS-DOS programs use this function when they are idle, such as when waiting for user input, to allow 386 enhanced-mode Windows to run other programs that are not idle.

Parameters

This function has no parameters.

Return Value

The return value is 00h in the AL register if the function is supported. Otherwise, AL is unchanged (contains 80h).

Comments

Only non-Windows programs should use Release Current VM Time-Slice; Windows applications should yield by calling the WaitMessage function. A program can call this function at any time, even when running in environments other than 386 enhanced-mode Windows environment. If the current environment does not support the function, the function returns and the program continues execution.

Windows suspends the current VM only if there is another VM scheduled to run. If no other VM is ready, the function returns to the program and execution continues. A program should call the function frequently (for example, once during each pass of the program's idle loop) to give Windows ample opportunity to check for other VMs that are ready for execution.

Before calling this function, a program should check that the Interrupt 2Fh address is not zero.

Example

The following example checks for for a valid Interrupt 2Fh address, then releases the current VM time slice:

```
    mov     ax, 352Fh       ; Get Interrupt Vector
    int     21h

    mov     ax, es
    or      ax, bx
    jz      Skip_Idle_Call  ; es:bx is equal to 0:0

    mov     ax, 1680h       ; Release Current VM Time-Slice
    int     2Fh
Skip_Idle_Call:
```

Interrupt 2Fh Function 1681h

```
    mov     ax, 1681h   ; Begin Critical Section
    int     2Fh         ; multiplex interrupt
```

Begin Critical Section (Interrupt 2Fh Function 1681h) prevents Windows from switching execution from the current VM to some other. MS-DOS device drivers and TSRs use this function to prevent a task-switch from occurring.

Parameters

This function has no parameters.

Return Value

This function has no return value.

Comments

When a virtual machine is in a critical section, no other task will be allowed to run except to service hardware interrupts. For this reason, the critical section should be released using End Critical Section (Interrupt 2Fh Function 1682h) as soon as possible.

See Also

Interrupt 2Fh Function 1682h End Critical Section

Interrupt 2Fh Function 1682h

```
    mov     ax, 1682h   ; End Critical Section
    int     2Fh         ; multiplex interrupt
```

End Critical Section (Interrupt 2Fh Function 1682h) releases the critical section previously started using Begin Critical Section (Interrupt 2Fh Function 1681h). Every call to Begin Critical Section must be followed by a matching call to End Critical Section.

Parameters

This function has no parameters.

Return Value

This function has no return value.

See Also

Interrupt 2Fh Function 1681h Begin Critical Section

Interrupt 2Fh Function 1683h

```
mov      ax, 1683h      ; Get Current Virtual Machine ID
int      2Fh            ; multiplex interrupt
```

Get Current Virtual Machine ID (Interrupt 2Fh Function 1683h) returns the identifier for the current virtual machine. MS-DOS device drivers, TSRs, and other programs use this function to determine which virtual machine is running. This is especially important for programs that independently manage separate data or execution contexts for separate virtual machines.

Parameters

This function has no parameters.

Return Value

The return value is the current virtual-machine identifier in the BX register.

Comments

Each virtual machine has a unique, nonzero identifier. Although Windows currently runs in virtual machine 1, programs should not rely on this. Windows assigns the identifier when it creates the virtual machine, and releases the identifier when it destroys the virtual machine. Since Windows may reuse identifiers from previous destroyed virtual machines, programs should monitor changes to virtual machines to ensure no mismatches.

Interrupt 2Fh Function 1684h

```
mov      bx, [DeviceID]  ; Device identifier

mov      ax, 1684h       ; Get Device Entry Point Address
```

```
int     2Fh                 ; multiplex interrupt

; es:di contains entry point address

mov     word ptr [DevAddr], di
mov     word ptr [DevAddr+2], es
```

Get Device Entry Point Address (Interrupt 2Fh Function 1684h) retrieves the entry point address for a virtual device's service functions. MS-DOS device drivers or TSRs typically use this function to communicate with virtual devices they have explicitly loaded.

Parameters

DeviceID

Identifies a virtual device.

Return Value

The return value is the entry-point address contained in the ES:DI register pair if the function is supported. Otherwise, ES:DI contain zero.

Comments

Any virtual device can provide service functions to be used by MS-DOS programs. For example, the virtual-display device provides services that the Windows old application program uses to display MS-DOS programs in a window. It is the responsibility of the MS-DOS program to provide the appropriate virtual-device identifier. The function returns a valid address if the virtual device supports the entry point.

MS-DOS programs call the entry point using a far call instruction. The services provided by the virtual device depend on the device. It is the responsibility of the MS-DOS program to set registers to values that are appropriate to the specific virtual device.

For versions of Windows prior to version 3.0, the program must set the ES:DI register pair to zero before calling this function.

Example

The following retrieves the entry point address for the virtual device identified by My_Device_ID:

```
xor     di, di              ; set es:di to zero for version 2.x
mov     es, di
mov     bx, My_Device_ID

mov     ax, 1684h
int     2Fh

mov     ax, es
or      ax, di
jz      API_Is_Not_Supported
```

Interrupt 2Fh Function 1685h

```
mov     bx, [VM_Id]              ; virtual-machine identifier
mov     cx, [Flags]              ; switch conditions

; dx:si contains 32-bit priority boost

mov     dx, word ptr [Priority+2]
mov     si, word ptr [Priority]

; es:di contains callback function address

mov     es, seg [CallBack]
mov     di, offset [CallBack]

mov     ax, 1685h    ; Switch VMs and CallBack
int     2Fh          ; multiplex interrupt
```

Switch VMs and CallBack (Interrupt 2Fh Function 1685h) directs Windows to switch to a specific virtual machine and begin execution. After Windows switches, it calls the specified callback function allowing a device driver or TSR to access the data associated with the specified virtual machine. This function is typically used by MS-DOS device drivers and TSRs that support networks, and that need to perform functions in a specific virtual machine.

Parameters

VM_Id

Identifies the virtual machine to switch to.

Flags

Specifies when to switch. This parameter is a combination of the following bit values.

Bit	Meaning
0	Set to 1 to wait until interrupts are enabled.
1	Set to 1 to wait until critical section is released.

All other bits are reserved and must be 0.

Priority

Specifies the priority boost for the virtual machine. It can be one of the following values.

Value	Meaning
Critical_Section_Boost	VM priority is boosted by this value when Begin_Critical_Section is called.

Cur_Run_VM_Boost	Time-slice scheduler boosts each VM in turn by this value to force them to run for their allotted time slice.
High_Pri_Device_Boost	Time critical operations that should not circumvent the critical section boost should use this boost.
Low_Pri_Device_Boost	Used by virtual devices that need an event to be processed in a timely fashion but that are not extremely time critical.
Reserved_High_Boost	Reserved; do not use.
Reserved_Low_Boost	Reserved; do not use.
Time_Critical_Boost	Events that must be processed even when another VM is in a critical section should use this boost. For example, VPICD uses this when simulating hardware interrupts.

The DX register contains the high-order word, the SI register the low-order word.

CallBack

Points to the callback function.

Return Value

The return value is a cleared carry flag if successful. Otherwise, the function sets the carry flag and sets the AX register to one of the following error values.

Value	Meaning
0001h	Invalid VM ID
0002h	Invalid priority boost
0003h	Invalid flags

Comments

Windows calls the callback function as soon as the conditions specified by the *Flags* parameter are met. This may be before or after Switch VMs and CallBack returns.

The callback function can carry out any action, but must save and restore all registers it modifies. The function must execute an iret instruction to return to Windows. The priority for the virtual machine remains at the level specified by *Priority* until the callback function executes the iret instruction.

See Also

Interrupt 2Fh Function 1605h Windows Initialization Notification

Interrupt 2Fh Function 1686h

```
mov     ax, 1686h    ; Detect Interrupt 31h Services
int     2Fh          ; multiplex interrupt

; ax is zero if interrupt 31h services available

or      ax,0
jz      int31_avail
```

Detect Interrupt 31h Services (Interrupt 2Fh Function 1686h) determines whether a set of protected-mode functions are available for use by protected-mode applications. Applications use the Interrupt 31h services to allocate and manage protected-mode memory.

Parameters

This function has no parameters.

Return Value

The return value is zero in the AX register if the Interrupt 31h services are available. Otherwise, the AX register contains a nonzero value.

Comments

Both standard- and 386 enhanced-mode Windows support the Interrupt 31h services. Interrupt 31h services are only supported for protected-mode programs.

Virtual-Display Device Function Reference

The following is an alphabetical listing of the Virtual-Display Device (VDD) service functions.

Interrupt 2Fh Function 4000h

```
mov ax, 4000h            ; Enable VM-Assisted Save/Restore
int 2fh

; al contains the video modes supported while in background

mov [ModesSupported], al
```

Enable VM-Assisted Save/Restore directs the virtual-display device (VDD) to notify the virtual machine (VM) application whenever the VDD needs to access the video hardware registers. The VDD returns a value specifying the number and type of video modes the VDD supports when the VM application is in the background.

A VM application calls this function during its initialization.

Parameters

This function has no parameters.

Return Value

The return value is one of the following values, if successful.

Value	Meaning
01h	No modes virtualized in background.
02h	Only text modes virtualized in background.
03h	Only text and single-plane graphics modes virtualized.
04h	Only text, single-plane, and VGA multiplane graphics modes virtualized.
0FFh	All supported video modes virtualized.

Otherwise, the function returns zero in the AL register if virtualization is not supported.

Comments

When a VM application calls this function, the VDD disables I/O trapping of unreadable registers. Thereafter, the VDD calls Save Video Register State and Restore Video Register State (Interrupt 2Fh Functions 4005h and 4006h) if it needs to access the video registers. The VM application must provide an appropriate interrupt handler to process these functions.

When an VM application calls this function, the VDD saves the current state of the video registers. The VDD uses this saved state later to restore video registers before it calls Notify Foreground Switch and Restore Video Register State (Interrupt 2Fh Functions 4002h and 4006h).

After a VM application calls Enable VM-Assisted Save/Restore, the VDD no longer saves video memory across screen switches; it becomes the application's responsibility to completely reinitialize video memory after a Notify Foreground Switch request.

See Also

Interrupt 2Fh Functions 4002h Notify Foreground Switch

Interrupt 2Fh Functions 4005h Save Video Register State

Interrupt 2Fh Functions 4006h Restore Video Register State

Interrupt 2Fh Function 4001h

```
mov ax, 4001h    ; Notify Background Switch
int 2fh
```

Notify Background Switch notifies a VM application that it is being switched to the background. The VM application can carry out any actions, but should do so within 1000ms. This is the amount of time the system waits before switching the application.

Parameters

This function has no parameters.

Return Value

This function has no return value.

Comments

After switching to the background, the application continues to run unless it attempts to access video memory. If the video adapter is in a video mode that the virtual display device (VDD) does not support in the background, the VDD freezes the application until the application can be switched back to the foreground.

VM applications that have called Enable VM-Assisted Save/Restore (Interrupt 2Fh Function 4000h) should avoid accessing video memory and registers to avoid being frozen. Applications that have not called Enable VM-Assisted Save/Restore, call access video memory and registers since the VDD saves theses after this function returns.

See Also

Interrupt 2Fh Function 4000h Enable VM-Assisted Save/Restore

Interrupt 2Fh Function 4002h Notify Foreground Switch

Interrupt 2Fh Function 4002h

```
mov ax, 4002h       ; Notify Foreground Switch
int 2fh
```

Notify Foreground Switch notifies a VM application that it has been switched to the foreground and can now access the video memory and registers without being frozen.

The virtual-display device (VDD) calls this function.

Parameters

This function has no parameters.

Return Value

This function has no return value.

Comments

If the VM application has called Enable VM-Assisted Save/Restore (Interrupt 2Fh Function 4000h), VDD restores the video registers to their state prior to the call to Enable VM-Assisted Save/Restore; the application is responsible for restoring video memory. If the VM application has not called Enable VM-Assisted Save/Restore (Interrupt 2Fh Function 4000h), the VDD automatically restores both video memory and registers.

Under certain error conditions, the VDD may call this function without calling a corresponding Notify Background Switch (Interrupt 2Fh Function 4001h).

See Also

Interrupt 2Fh Function 4000h Enable VM-Assisted Save/Restore

Interrupt 2Fh Function 4001h Notify Background Switch

Interrupt 2Fh Function 4003h

```
mov ax, 4003h        ; Enter Critical Section
int 2fh
```

Enter Critical Section notifies the virtual-display device that the VM application has entered a critical section and cannot respond to Save Video Register State (Interrupt 2Fh Function 4005h).

A VM application calls this function when it has started critical section processing.

Parameters

This function has no parameters.

Return Value

This function has no return value.

Comments

After the VM application enters the critical section, the virtual-display device postpones calling Save Video Register State for up to 1000ms or until the VM application calls Exit Critical Section (Interrupt 2Fh Function 4004h), whichever comes first.

If time elapses without the VM application calling Exit Critical Section, the virtual-display device reprograms the video hardware anyway and, when its operation is complete, calls Notify Foreground Switch (Interrupt 2Fh Function 4002h) in an attempt to reinitialize the application properly.

See Also

Interrupt 2Fh Function 4002h Notify Foreground Switch

Interrupt 2Fh Function 4004h Exit Critical Section

Interrupt 2Fh Function 4005h Save Video Register State

Interrupt 2Fh Function 4004h

```
mov ax, 4004h      ; Exit Critical Section
int 2fh
```

Exit Critical Section notifies the virtual-display device that a VM application has completed a critical section and can now respond to Save Video Register State (Interrupt 2Fh Function 4005h).

A VM application calls this function when it has completed critical section processing.

Parameters

This function has no parameters.

Return Value

This function has no return value.

Comments

Calls to Exit Critical Section not preceded by a corresponding call to Enter Critical Section (Interrupt 2Fh Function 4003h) are ignored.

See Also

Interrupt 2Fh Function 4003h Enter Critical Section

Interrupt 2Fh Function 4005h Save Video Register State

Interrupt 2Fh Function 4005h

```
mov ax, 4005h      ; Save Video Register State
int 2fh
```

The Save Video Register State function notifies VM applications that the virtual-display device (VDD) requires access to the video hardware registers. The VDD calls this function, for example, when preparing to copy the entire screen to the clipboard.

Parameters

This function has no parameters.

Return Value

This function has no return value.

Comments

The VDD calls this function only if the VM application has called Enable VM-Assisted Save/Restore (Interrupt 2Fh Function 4000h). VM applications that receive Save Video Register State must save any data necessary to restore the current video state and must return within 1000ms. If the application fails to return in time, the virtual-display device accesses the video hardware anyway. After accessing the video hardware registers, the VDD calls Restore Video Register State (Interrupt 2Fh Function 4006h) to notify the application that it can restore its video state.

The VDD calls Save Video Register State only at times when the hardware must be reprogrammed for what are essentially brief and nonvisible operations. For example, the VDD does not call this function prior to calling Notify Background Switch (Interrupt 2Fh Function 4001h).

See Also

Interrupt 2Fh Function 4000h Enable VM-Assisted Save/Restore

Interrupt 2Fh Function 4001h Notify Background Switch

Interrupt 2Fh Function 4006h Restore Video Register State

Interrupt 2Fh Function 4006h

```
mov ax, 4006h    ; Restore Video Register State
int 2fh
```

Restore Video Register State notifies a VM application that the virtual-display device (VDD) has relinquished its access to the video registers. The VM application should restore the video registers to any state necessary to continue uninterrupted foreground operation.

Parameters

This function has no parameters.

Return Value

This function has no return value.

Comments

The VDD calls this function only if the VM application has called Enable VM-Assisted Save/Restore (Interrupt 2Fh Function 4000h). Before calling this function, the VDD restores any registers it modified to the values they had when the VM application originally called Enable VM-Assisted Save/Restore. In other words, every register is guaranteed to be either unchanged or reset to a previous state; precisely which registers may be reset is undefined, but the set is restricted to those Sequencer and Graphics Controller registers that do not affect the display.

See Also

Interrupt 2Fh Function 4000h Enable VM-Assisted Save/Restore

Interrupt 2Fh Function 4007h

```
mov ax, 4007h       ; Disable VM-Assisted Save/Restore
int 2fh
```

Disable VM-Assisted Save/Restore directs the virtual-display device (VDD) to discontinue notifying the VM application when it needs access to video registers. VM applications call this function when they terminate.

Parameters

This function has no parameters.

Return Value

This function has no return value.

Comments

This function directs the VDD to restore I/O trapping of unreadable registers and to discontinue calling Save Video Register State and Restore Video Register State (Interrupt 2Fh Functions 4005h and 4006h) when it needs access to the registers. Furthermore, the VDD ignores any subsequent calls to Enter Critical Section and Exit Critical Section (Interrupt 2Fh Functions 4003h and 4004h).

This function does not disable Notify Background Switch and Notify Foreground Switch (Interrupt 2Fh Functions 4001h and 4002h).

See Also

Interrupt 2Fh Function 4001h Notify Background Switch

Interrupt 2Fh Function 4002h Notify Foreground Switch

Interrupt 2Fh Function 4003h Enter Critical Section

Interrupt 2Fh Function 4004h Exit Critical Section

Interrupt 2Fh Function 4005h Save Video Register State

Interrupt 2Fh Function 4006h Restore Video Register State

Structure Reference

The following is an alphabetical listing of the structures used with the Interrupt 2Fh service and notification functions.

Win386_Startup_Info_Struc

```
Win386_Startup_Info_Struc STRUC
SIS_Version                 db      3, 0
SIS_Next_Dev_Ptr            dd      ?
SIS_Virt_Dev_File_Ptr       dd      0
SIS_Reference_Data          dd      ?
SIS_Instance_Data_Ptr       dd      0
Win386_Startup_Info_Struc ENDS
```

The **Win386_Startup_Info_Struc** structure contains information that Windows uses to prepare an MS-DOS device driver or TSR program for operation with Windows.

Members

SIS_Version

Specifies the version number of the structure. 386 enhanced-mode Windows uses this member to determine the size of the structure. This member should contain 3 in the low-order byte and 10 in the high-order byte to indicate that it is version 3.1.

SIS_Next_Dev_Ptr

Points to the next structure in the list. The address of the next structure must be supplied by the next handler in the Interrupt 2Fh chain. A driver or TSR calls the next handler, then sets this member to the address returned by the handler in the ES:BX register pair.

SIS_Virt_Dev_File_Ptr

Points to a null-terminated string that contains the name of a 386 enhanced-mode Windows virtual device file. MS-DOS devices such as networks use this to force a special 386 enhanced-mode Windows virtual device to be loaded. If this member is zero, no device is loaded.

SIS_Reference_Data

Specifies reference data for the virtual device. This member, used only when SIS_Virt_Dev_File_Ptr is nonzero, is passed to the virtual device when it is initialized. The member can contain any value and often contains a pointer to some device-specific structure.

SIS_Instance_Data_Ptr

Points to a list of data to be instanced, that is, allocated uniquely for each new virtual machine. If the member is zero, then no data is instanced. Each entry in the list is an Instance_Item_Struc structure. The list is terminated with a 32-bit zero.

See Also

Interrupt 2Fh Function 1605h Windows Initialization Notification

---

Instance_Item_Struc

```
Instance_Item_Struc STRUC
    IIS_Ptr      dd  ?
    IIS_Size     dw  ?
Instance_Item_Struc ENDS
```

The **Instance_Item_Struc** structure specifies the starting address and size of a block of instance data.

Members

IIS_Ptr

Points to the starting address of a block of instance data.

IIS_Size

Specifies the size (in bytes) of the block of instance data pointed to by the IIS_Ptr member.

Index

How to Obtain the Samples File via FTP

The file 'samples.exe' contains the sample source code for the book *Writing Windows*™ *Virtual Device Drivers*.

Download the file via anonymous ftp from our server, ftp.aw.com. Login using 'anonymous' as your username and your complete email address as your password. Go to the directory \TCB\authors\thielen\wrtvxds, and download the file 'samples.exe' to your hard disk (make sure that your ftp program is set to 'binary').

The 'readme.txt' file is this set of instructions.

'samples.exe' is a self-extracting archive, so when you have placed the file in the directory where you want the files (for example 'c:\vxd'), type 'samples' at the command line and hit [enter]. The directory \samples and its subdirectories will be created and the files will be expanded (if the file has been placed in the root directory, the directory will be c:\samples). Afterwards, you may delete 'samples.exe.'

The sample code from this book can be obtained via anonymous ftp or by mailing in the coupon below.

If you'd like to receive the disk for *Writing Windows™ Virtual Device Drivers*:

1)   Fill out the coupon.
2)   Attach a check for $5 (shipping and handling). Make the check out to Addison-Wesley Publishing Company. (Make sure the check is in U.S. dollars, drawn on a U.S. or Canadian bank.)
3)   Send the check and coupon to:

Addison-Wesley Publishing Company
One Jacob Way
Reading, MA 01867
Attn.: Customer Service

Here's my $5 for the *Writing Windows™ Virtual Device Drivers* disk (ISBN: 0-201-85746-4). Mail the disk to:

Name:_____

Company:_____

Address:_____

City:_____State:_____Zip:_____

Please allow three weeks for delivery. This offer valid only in U.S. Customers outside the U.S. please contact your local Addison-Wesley distributor.